Praise for *Generation Me*

"Those vague hunches we have about this generation—Twenge does a huge, decidedly un-GenX amount of research and replaces them with actual data. Her writing is lucid and entertaining, and she's unafraid to draw bold conclusions when necessary. It's nothing new for a generation to be misunderstood by popular and commercial culture, but the one she describes has been misdrawn to the point of absurdity; refreshing, then, to have someone swap those persistent old myths for thoughtful, careful observations."

—Chris Colin, author of *What Really Happened to the Class of '93: Start-Ups, Dropouts, and Other Navigations through an Untidy Decade*

"Jean Twenge is not only dedicated as a researcher and social scientist, but she is clearly passionate about it. In this forward-thinking and clear-eyed book, she immediately stands out as a social critic of substance, in a world of dogmatic and chattering media pundits who are only guessing when they are "covering" major social trends and generational changes."

—Paula Kamen, author of *Feminist Fatale* and *Her Way: Young Women Remake the Sexual Revolution*

"Everyone knows that American society is changing, but no one until now has documented how the people themselves are changing. In this startling, witty, and refreshing book, a pioneering researcher explains how the very personality of the average American is different. An upbringing that featured forming rather than meeting high expectations, and feeling good before doing good, has resulted in a generation with the highest self-esteem on record—and the highest rates of depression. Based on careful, groundbreaking research but filled with touching and amusing stories, this book explains exactly how the American character is changing and evolving, sometimes for the better, sometimes not. Americans should read this book and ponder whether we should raise the next generation on unrealistic hopes, undisciplined self-assertion, and endless, baseless self-congratulation."

—Roy F. Baumeister, author of *The Cultural Animal: Human Nature, Meaning, and Social Life,* and Eppes Eminent Professor of Psychology, Florida State University

"Dr. Jean Twenge provides an insightful analysis of the young adults she labels 'GenMe'—their supreme self-confidence in their own worth, their concern with doing things 'their way,' and the benefits and costs that come from their focus on themselves. Twenge draws upon her outstanding research to describe generational differences and their sources, lending an authority to her analysis that few previous commentators on GenMe have enjoyed."

—Susan Nolen-Hoeksema, PhD, Yale University professor and author of *Women Who Think Too Much*

"Jean Twenge has the intelligence and courage to voice a concern that is in the minds of all today's parents. If you want your child to succeed in today's world, read this book."

—Mona Lisa Schulz, MD, PhD, author of *The New Feminine Brain*

"Twenge's book is comprehensive . . . filled with statistics and thoughtful observations about the group she's dubbed Generation Me . . . accessible and a must-read."

—*Booklist*

"[The] book is livened with analysis of films, magazines and TV shows, and with anecdotal stories from her life and others'. The real basis of her argument, however, lies in her 14 years of research comparing the results of personality tests given to boomers when they were under 30 and those given to GenMe'ers today. . . . Many of her findings are fascinating. And her call to "ditch the self-esteem movement" in favor of education programs that encourage empathy and real accomplishment could spare some Me'ers from the depression that often occurs when they hit the realities of today's increasingly competitive workplace."

—*Publishers Weekly*

"Twenge tells an engaging story, fueled and supported by a solid base of data, illustrative quotes from her and others' research, and barometric examples from TV shows, movies, comics, and advertisements. . . . Throughout the book, her analyses of myriad topics articulated a number of ideas on the tip of my mind's tongue."

—*AARP the Magazine*

"This book should be required reading for parents-to-be."

—*The Washington Post*

ALSO BY JEAN M. TWENGE

The Impatient Woman's Guide to Getting Pregnant

The Narcissism Epidemic (coauthor)

GENERATION ME

Why Today's Young Americans Are More Confident, Assertive, Entitled— and More Miserable Than Ever Before

REVISED AND UPDATED

Jean M. Twenge, PhD

ATRIA PAPERBACK
New York London Toronto Sydney New Delhi

ATRIA PAPERBACK
A Division of Simon & Schuster, Inc.
1230 Avenue of the Americas
New York, NY 10020

Note to readers: The names of some of the people quoted in this book have been changed. In some cases, persons described are composites.

First Atria Paperback edition September 2014

Cover photo illustration and design by Tony Mauro

Manufactured in the United States of America

10 9 8 7 6 5

Library of Congress Cataloging-in-Publication Data

Twenge, Jean M.
Generation me : why today's young Americans are more confident, assertive, entitled—and more miserable than ever before / Jean M. Twenge, Ph.D. —First Atria paperback edition.
pages cm
Revised and updated edition of the author's Generation me, originally published in 2006.
1. Young adults—United States. 2. Youth—United States. I. Title.
HQ799.7.T94 2014
305.2420973—dc23 2014008469

ISBN 978-1-4767-5556-4
ISBN 978-0-7432-8885-9 (ebook)

To Craig,
for my family

Contents

Preface to the Revised Edition

Young people are angry.

Told they could be anything they wanted to be, they face widespread unemployment. Raised on dreams of material wealth, more than a third live with their parents well into their 20s. No one told them it would be this hard, they say, and older generations don't understand how difficult it is to find a job, cover the rent, and pay off their huge student loans. Young people are told to "pull yourself up by your bootstraps," observed Tiffany Vang, 23, in the Twin Cities *Daily Planet*. "But we're not even wearing the same shoes anymore; we're given high heels to race in this catch-22 marathon. It's become a rite of passage for people my age to work for free even after college." It bothers her, she says, when someone tells a young person, "You will be fine." Because what if she's not?

"We are said to be entitled," writes cartoonist Matt Bors, 30, on cnn.com. "We think we deserve something, that the world should hand us something for being here. We do. Like jobs . . . because student loans can't be paid off with air." He concludes, "Stop hating on Millennials. We didn't create this mess. We came late to the banquet and were served up crumbs. Which we will Instagram before we eat. #YUM."

A lot has changed since the first edition of *Generation Me* was published in April 2006. At the time, the economy was doing well. Even so, I predicted that this generation would find the transition to adulthood difficult: After a childhood of optimism and high expectations, reality hit them like a smack in the face. That became even more true when the Great Recession hit in 2007.

Technology has also fundamentally changed our world and this generation in particular. Back in 2006, only college students could get a Facebook account. YouTube had premiered just a year before, Twitter went online a few months later, and the iPhone debuted soon after. The generational conversation is also very different. In 2006, the generation born after 1980—variously called GenY or Millennials—was rarely discussed, outside of a book declaring them "the next Greatest Generation," a few articles praising their high school community service, and—paradoxically—other articles describing them as "brash" and "entitled."

Things are different now. We take smartphones, social networking, and streaming video for granted. Gay marriage is legal and a black man has been elected president—twice. Millennials—the common label for the group I call Generation Me—are now endlessly dissected. At least 10 books advise managers on how to work with them. HBO's *Girls* depicts their struggles to reach independent adulthood, and *Glee* highlights their yearning for fame and tolerance for diversity. *Time* magazine, which featured Baby Boomers and Generation X on covers when their inaugural members were still in their 20s, finally published a cover article on Millennials in May 2013 when its oldest members were 31—seven years after *Generation Me* appeared. It was titled "The Me Me Me Generation."

The article spawned a huge reaction, from parody covers to opinion pieces. In the comments, the blog posts, and the videos, the emotion nearly leaps off the computer screen. One video featured a group of GenMe'ers mock-apologizing, saying, "You raised us to believe that we were special—so special we didn't have to do anything to earn it. . . . We're really sorry we suck so much." But, they say, it's the Boomers' fault, not theirs: "It's not like we jacked up college tuition prices, destroyed the manufacturing industry, started two quagmire wars, gutted the unions, destroyed the global economy, or left our offspring with an environmentally devastated planet. . . . It would be crazy if there were a generation that recklessly awful, huh?" GenMe's other responses to the article varied from "Yes, but we actually *are* awesome" to "But older generations have always said younger generations were more self-centered."

But *is* this generation more self-centered than previous generations were at the same age? And what other characteristics define them? We now know. The first edition of *Generation Me* featured 14 studies on generational differences, based on data from 1.2 million people. In the years since, my coauthors and I have published 19 additional studies based on the responses of 11 million people. Most of these new studies draw from large, nationally representative surveys (including of high school students), providing a view of the entire generation, not just one selected segment. These findings, along with those from other researchers, are featured here for the first time. This is the main difference you will notice in this revised edition: *much* more data. These data capture the opinions and self-views of young people—not what older generations are saying about them, but what they say about themselves. The trends demonstrate the impact of recent cultural change on a new generation of Americans.

These new studies confirm the conclusions of the first edition of *Generation Me*: this generation is more confident, assertive, entitled—and more miserable. They also add some new twists: exploring trends in religious belief, tolerance, trust in others, attitudes toward work, and even the names given to babies. Overall, the results suggest that GenMe's anger is somewhat justified: everyone told them they were special and didn't need anyone else, and then adulthood shows them, sometimes quite harshly, that these things just aren't true.

Because the studies described in this book survey people at the same age at different points in time, the differences cannot be due to age: they must reflect the changing times. This is a crucial point, as many people have argued that of course GenMe is self-focused—every generation is when young. But the studies show that GenMe is more self-focused than previous generations were when *they* were young.

But haven't older generations "always" criticized the younger generation? Perhaps, but the generational studies don't measure older people's criticisms—they measure how young people describe themselves. And if culture has become progressively more individualistic over the last century, each generation may actually *be* more self-focused than the last. Some, such as Elspeth Reeve in *Atlantic Wire*, have argued that "every generation" is the "me generation" because magazine articles have often described the next generation this way. However, that observation isn't particularly relevant to the research finding that GenMe—by their own description—is more self-focused than Boomers were at the same age. Perhaps Boomers were also more self-focused than the previous generation, but that has little to do with GenMe. At base, Reeve is arguing that because something has been said before, it must be wrong. That seems nonsensical at best.

But aren't this generation's characteristics the fault of their Boomer parents instead? Why blame GenMe for a world they didn't create? In my view, it is not necessary to assign fault or blame for generational differences. Cultures change, and generations reflect those changes. It's not a matter of blame. Focusing on whose "fault" it is also assumes that all cultural change is negative, yet of course it is not. For example, individualism—a now-prominent cultural influence—has advantages such as equality and tolerance, but disadvantages if it veers toward narcissism and overconfidence. GenMe reflects both trends.

All of these trends have had an impact in the workplace, and sure enough, generations at work has become a hot topic over the last decade. Many books, business-magazine articles, and consulting firms seek to explain GenMe to managers trying to figure out their young employees. Unfortunately, few of these sources rely on empirical data. Fewer still rely on data collected over time—the type necessary to conclude that generational differences have occurred. A few years ago, I coauthored the first paper on generational differences in work attitudes based on a nationally representative, over-time dataset. This edition of *Generation Me* thus features a completely new chapter ("Generation Me at Work," chapter 8) reviewing the evidence for generational differences in the workplace from this study and others. It also covers how managers can best recruit, retain, and motivate GenMe employees, and some tips for GenMe employees themselves.

Do these findings "stereotype" the generations? No, because these studies compare empirical data on generational differences, not the perceptions of others. However, these comparisons do rely on averages. Not everyone in a generation will fit the average. It's important to realize, though, that generational studies are far from unique in this respect: every scientific study looking at group differences uses averages. Sex differences are a good example. Some men cry more than some women, but those exceptions do not undermine the finding that, on average, women cry more often than men. Some in GenMe are extraordinarily humble, but that does not negate the finding that the average GenMe'er, compared to previous generations at the same age, is less humble.

These findings do not seek to "label" everyone in this generation; they instead aim to discover how, on average, cultural change has affected young people. People differ based on many factors; generation is just one of them. However, the generational trends are remarkably similar across race, gender, and class. The idea that generational trends only appear among the "rich, white kids," as some have asserted, is simply not true. However, almost all of the data on generational differences is based on US samples, so it is not clear whether the same trends appear in other cultures as well. Emerging research suggests that they do, but there's much more work to be done.

Along with the research results in this book, you'll find quotes from real young people, pop-culture examples, and anecdotes. These have been updated as well, to reflect the pop culture influencing GenMe now—including the new technology that shapes their lives. Generations are about culture, and about real people, so the book would not be complete without this material. It's also now possible to analyze pop culture more objectively. The Google Books Ngram Viewer can trace the use of any word or any phrase up to five words as far back as the 1800s. I've added many analyses from that database here. In the first edition of *Generation Me*, I guessed that the now-ubiquitous phrase *believe in yourself* was uncommon the 1950s. Now the Google Ngram Viewer can prove it.

Some have pointed out that pop culture examples and anecdotes are not data. I agree. The examples are meant to illustrate, *not* replace, the data. The data always come first in structuring a chapter and its conclusions. The data already paints a specific picture—the examples are the individual brushstrokes in that portrait. Yes, counterexamples could be found, but it would be confusing to include them when the examples are meant to illustrate the general trends in the data. So no, the examples are not data, but they are not meant to be.

Can the data be interpreted in different ways? Of course. To some people, a change from 47% to 52% sounds significant; to others, that might seem small. In most cases I will present the numbers so you can judge for yourself whether the change is small or big. Keep in mind, though, that a small change at the average can lead to larger changes at the extremes. A shift of a few points on the narcissism scale seems small, for example, until you realize that at least 50% more college students now score problematically high in narcissism. This is also a case where it's best to consider all of the data. Some may question a specific measure or a particular sample, but when similar results appear across many measures and samples, the overall picture becomes clear. In some cases, the data are contradictory, and I've included those too.

Along with the world's changing, I have also changed. When I began writing *Generation Me*, I was 32 years old and had just gotten married. I'm now 42 and have three children, all born after the book was published. So I'm not the representative of the young generation that I used to be. Thus I've taken out some of the examples from my own life and those of my friends and family born in the 1970s. Other examples, such as my experiences with self-focused projects in school, remain as illustrations of the nascent movement experienced full blown by those born after me.

I've also gained valuable perspective from others in the last decade, through talks at businesses, universities, nonprofit organizations, student-affairs groups, human-resource conferences, and military bases. During these visits, I was privileged to hear the perspectives of many people—both in GenMe and older—on how generational trends have affected them.

I owe a tremendous debt of gratitude to the readers who made the first edition of *Generation Me* a success. I was pleased when people told me it was a fun read, and even more pleased when young GenMe'ers told me they recognized the culture that shaped them. But we know so much more now about Generation Me, and I'm excited to be able to share it with you in this new edition. I hope you enjoy it.

Jean M. Twenge
San Diego, California
April 2014

Generation Me

Introduction

Linda was born in the 1950s in a small town in the Midwest. After she graduated from high school, she moved to the city and enrolled in secretarial school. It was a great time to be young: Free Love was in, and everybody smoked, drank, and had a good time. Linda and her friends joined a feminist consciousness-raising group, danced at the discos, and explored their inner lives at est seminars and through meditation. The new pursuit of self-fulfillment led Tom Wolfe to label the 1970s the Me Decade, and by extension the young people of the time the Me Generation.

Compared to today's young people, they were posers. Linda's Baby Boomer generation grew up in the 1950s and early 1960s, taught by stern, gray-suit-wearing teachers and raised by parents who didn't take any lip and thought that Father Knows Best. Most of the Boomers were well into adolescence or adulthood by the time the focus on the self became trendy in the 1970s. When Linda and her friends sought self-knowledge, they took the ironic step of doing so en masse—for all their railing against conformity, Boomers did just about everything in groups, from protests to seminars to yoga. Their youthful exploration also covered a brief period: the average first-time bride in the early 1970s had not yet celebrated her 21st birthday.

Today's under-35 young people are the real Me Generation, or, as I call them, Generation Me. Born after self-focus entered the cultural mainstream, this generation has never known a world that put duty before self. Linda's youngest child, Jessica, was born years after Whitney Houston's No. 1 hit song "Greatest Love of

All" declared that loving yourself was the greatest love. Jessica's elementary school teachers believed that they should help Jessica feel good about herself. Jessica scribbled in a coloring book called *We Are All Special*, got a sticker on her worksheet just for filling it out, and did a sixth-grade project called "All About Me." When she wondered how to act on her first date, her mother told her, "Just be yourself." Eventually, Jessica got her lower lip pierced and got a large tattoo on her lower back because, she said, she wanted to express herself. She dreams of being a model or a singer, takes numerous "selfies" a day, and recently reached her personal goal of acquiring 5,000 followers on Instagram. She does not expect to marry until she is in her late 20s, and neither she nor her older sisters have any children yet. "You have to love yourself before you can love someone else," she says. This generation is unapologetically focused on the individual, a true Generation Me.

If you're wondering what all of this means for the future, you are not alone. Reflecting on her role as a parent of this generation, *San Francisco Chronicle* columnist Joan Ryan wrote, "We're told we will produce a generation of coddled, center-of-the-universe adults who will expect the world to be as delighted with them as we are. And even as we laugh at the knock-knock jokes and exclaim over the refrigerator drawings, we secretly fear the same thing."

Everyone belongs to a generation. Some people embrace it like a warm, familiar blanket, while others prefer not to be lumped in with their age-mates. Yet like it or not, when you were born dictates the culture you will experience. This includes the highs and lows of pop culture, as well as world events, social trends, technology, the economy, behavioral norms, and values. The society that molds you when you are young stays with you the rest of your life. These kids didn't raise themselves: they are doing exactly what they have been taught. Generational differences are the clearest manifestation of cultural change.

Today's young people speak the language of the self as their native tongue. The individual has always come first, and feeling good about yourself has always been a primary virtue. Everything from music to phone calls to entertainment is highly personalized, enjoyed on a cell phone instead of with the whole family. Generation Me's expectations are highly optimistic: they expect to go to college, to make lots of money, and perhaps even to be famous. Yet this generation enters a world in which college admissions are increasingly competitive, good jobs are hard to find and harder to keep, and basic necessities such as housing and health care have skyrocketed in price. This is a time of soaring expectations and crushing realities. Joan Chiaramonte, head of the Roper Youth Report, says that for young people "the gap between what they have and what they want has never been greater." If you would like to start an argument, claim that young people today have it (a) easy or (b) tough. Be forewarned: you might need referees before it's all over.

I have researched generational differences for more than 20 years, since I was a 21-year-old undergraduate working on my BA thesis in the early 1990s. Back then, most of what had been written about generations was based on an amalgam of personal experience and educated guesses: it speculated about possible differences, but had little proof they actually existed. I read book after book that said such things as young people now are more likely to come from divorced homes, so they are more anxious and cynical (but were they really?). And, people born after 1982 entered a more child-centered society, so they would be more group-oriented (but was that really true?). It was all interesting, but vague and nonscientific. I kept thinking, "Where's your proof? Has anyone ever found the real differences among the generations, instead of just guessing?"

The next year, I entered a PhD program in personality psychology at the University of Michigan. I soon learned that academic psychologists measure personality traits and attitudes with carefully designed and validated questionnaires. Best of all, many of those questionnaires had been used thousands of times since they were first introduced (usually between the 1930s and the 1970s), and most people who filled them out were college students and schoolchildren. That meant I could compare scores on these measures and see exactly how young people's personalities and attitudes differed among the generations. To my surprise, no one had ever done this before.

As my colleagues and I continued with this work, we also drew from several large annual surveys of young people, such as the Monitoring the Future study of 500,000 US high school students, conducted since 1976; the American Freshman Survey of 9 million college students, conducted since 1966; and the General Social Survey of 50,000 US adults, conducted since 1972. All three are nationally representative, which means the results are more likely to apply to an entire US generation. We also started to consider how the culture was changing—for example, trends in baby names, song lyrics, written language, and TV shows, using new technology such as the Google Books database of 5 million books. These "cultural products" are a vitally important piece of the puzzle, as generational change is, at essence, cultural change. Young people do not raise themselves—they absorb the culture around them. As that culture shifts, so do the generations. Young people today may not have invented the culture they inhabit, but they absorb its messages from parents, teachers, and media until they begin to shape it themselves—and the cycle continues. When the Pew Research Center asked Americans in 2010 if they thought there was a large generation gap, 79% said yes—even more than had said so at the height of the Boomer youth wave of 1969.

This book presents the results of more than 30 studies on generational differences, based on data from 11 million young Americans. Many of the studies find that when you were born has more influence on your personality and attitudes than the family who raised you. Or, in the words of a prescient Arab proverb,

"Men resemble the times more than they resemble their fathers." When you finish this book, you'll be ready for an argument about which generation has it easy or tough and why—you might even want to start it.

I focus here on the current generation of young people, born in the 1980s and 1990s. Right now in the 2010s, GenMe ranges from high school kids to thirtysomething adults. They are sometimes called GenY or Millennials. I don't expect the Generation Me title to replace these other labels, but it does nicely capture the group of people who grew up in an era when focusing on yourself was not just tolerated but actively encouraged. This trend has been building for a long time—I was born in 1971, right in the middle of Generation X, yet was exposed to plenty of GenMe ideas, experiencing the first stirrings of the hyperindividualism GenMe would come to take for granted.

A neat twist on the Generation Me label is iGeneration. The first letter is nicely packed with meaning: it could stand for Internet (as it does in iMac, iPhone, and iPad) or for the first-person singular that stands for the individual. Its pronunciation also appropriately suggests vision, either the things inside young people's heads, which are usually glued to their cell phones, or the vision of young people in shaping a new world. It's an appropriate name for a generation raised with on-demand "iMedia," such as DVRs, the Internet, iPads, and iPhones. Maybe iGen will catch on as the label for the next group of youth, those born after 2000 (I have three kids in this group—maybe if I named their generation they would listen to me when I ask them to put on their shoes). The first edition of this book in 2006 marked the first appearance of the iGen label—we'll see if it endures.

Another issue: of course, any birth-year cutoffs for generations are necessarily arbitrary, drawing a sharp line where none actually exists. Someone born on December 31, 1981, was exposed to the same culture as someone born on January 1, 1982, yet the first is usually called a GenX'er and the second a Millennial/GenMe.

And who's to say the cutoff isn't 1980 instead? In general, the data back up this commonsense logic, showing gradual changes with time, not sudden shifts that cleave one generation from the next. It's also problematic to assume that someone born in 1982 was exposed to the same cultural influences as someone born in 1999. The data support this observation as well: because many trends are linear, those born later will express higher levels of the GenMe traits. Think of Generation Me as a broad description of cultural influences, not a rigid definition of a set of people, and remember that the year you were born—not necessarily your generational label—is a better indicator of the culture you've absorbed.

Just to make it easier, I employ the most common generational cutoffs and labels: Baby Boomers (roughly 1943–60), Generation X (1961–81), and Millennials (1982–99), whom I call Generation Me. But I do so under duress, and because no other easy solution has presented itself. These cutoffs are a switch from the first edition, when I defined GenMe as those born 1970 to 1999. The post-1982 cutoff conforms to that used in previous books and articles, many of which have a different perspective on this generation. Some wondered if the 1970 versus 1982 cutoffs were the cause of those different perspectives. I was fairly sure that was not the case, but this change removes that possibility. However, that decision was also made under duress, because in many cases those born in the 1970s and 1980s look fairly similar to each other. GenX and GenMe have a lot more in common than most people realize—the transition from Boomers to GenX'ers was the more profound shift, and GenMe has built on those trends. In some cases I present the studies showing the shift from Boomers to GenX and then describe further shifts with the transition to GenMe.

Many people comment that older generations have "always" described the next younger generation as too self-focused. There's no definitive proof that's true—the quote from Socrates often used to illustrate that belief ("Our youth now love luxury. They have bad manners, contempt for authority . . .") is apocryphal, penned by a British graduate student in 1907. But let's assume for the moment that older generations have "always" seen youth as more self-centered. If so, that doesn't undermine the Generation Me findings in the least. First, the research presented here is based on what young people say about themselves—not what older people think of them. Second, perhaps people have "always" observed more individualism among the young generation because younger generations have indeed "always" been more individualistic. Individualism has been increasing steadily for several decades now—perhaps even several centuries—so that observation may indeed "always" have been true.

Of course, generational differences are based on averages, so some people will be the exception. But those exceptions don't seem to occur systematically in certain groups: the generational trends are very similar across regions, racial and ethnic groups, social classes, and among men and women. In most cases, the changes have reached all segments of the generation, and we're even more certain of that now that we're drawing from nationally representative samples. Because the differences are based on data, they are not stereotypes. Yet they are generalizations, like any scientific study of groups. However, these shifts in averages are important. Marketing studies, for example, find that generational styles influence purchasing decisions as much or more than sex, income, and education.

Why the label Generation Me? Since GenMe'ers were born, they've been taught to put themselves first. Unlike the Baby Boomers, GenMe didn't have to march in a protest or attend a group session to realize that their own needs and desires were paramount. Reliable birth control, legalized abortion, and a cultural shift toward parenthood as a choice made them the most wanted generation of children in American history. Television, movies, and school programs have told them they were special from toddlerhood to high school, and they believe it with a self-confidence that approaches boredom: Why talk about it? It's just the way things are. This blasé attitude is very different from the Boomer focus on introspection and self-absorption: GenMe is not as much self-absorbed as self-important. They take it for granted that they're unique, special individuals, so they don't need to think about it.

This is not the same as saying that young people are spoiled, which would imply that they always got what they wanted. Although some parents are indeed too indulgent, young people today must overcome many difficult challenges that their elders never had to face. Once, families could achieve middle-class status on the earnings of one high-school-educated person, but it now takes two college-educated earners to achieve the same standard of living. The recession of the late 2000s only made that problem more acute, with unemployment hitting GenMe the hardest. But it started long before that. Many teens feel that the world demands perfection in everything, and some are cracking under the pressure. Many GenMe'ers in their 20s find that their jobs do not provide the fulfillment and excitement they had anticipated, and that their salary isn't enough to afford even a small house. An acronym describes how this growing self-reliance can be stressful: YO-YO (You're On Your Own).

GenMe believes that people should follow their dreams and not be held back by societal expectations—not necessarily a selfish viewpoint, but definitely an individualistic one. Taking a job in a new city far from one's family, for example, isn't selfish, but it does put the individual first. The same is true for a girl who wants to join a boys' sports team or a college student who wants to become an actor when his parents want him to be a doctor. Not only are these actions and desires not considered selfish today (although they may have been in past generations), but they're playing as inspirational movies at the local theater.

This is the good part of the trend—GenMe'ers enjoy unprecedented freedom to pursue what makes them happy and to look past traditional distinctions based on race, gender, and sexual orientation. But their high expectations, combined with an increasingly competitive world, have led to a darker flip side, in which they blame other people for their problems and sink into anxiety and depression. Perhaps because of the focus on the self, sexual behavior has also changed radically: these days, sex outside of marriage is not the main story—the focus is on hooking up, or sex without the benefit of a romantic relationship at all.

My perspective on today's young generation differs from that of Neil Howe and William Strauss, who argued in their 2000 book, *Millennials Rising*, that those born since 1982 will usher in a return to duty, civic responsibility, and teamwork. Their book is subtitled *The Next Great Generation* and contends that today's young people will resemble the generation who won World War II. I agree that in an all-encompassing crisis today's young people would likely rise to the occasion—people usually do what needs to be done. But there is little evidence that today's young people feel much attachment to duty or to group cohesion—high school students in the 2000s and 2010s are significantly less civically engaged and less trustful of government and other large institutions than Boomers were in the 1970s. Instead, young people have been consistently taught to put their own needs first and to focus on feeling good about themselves. This attitude is not conducive to following social rules or favoring the group's needs over the individual's. Fewer young people are interested in joining the military now than when the Boomers and GenX'ers were young; this generation is no more inclined than Boomers were to get killed in a war. Even the subtitle, *The Next Great Generation*, displays the hubris fed to the young by their adoring elders. When the World War II generation was growing up during the 1920s, no one was calling them the Greatest Generation and telling them they were the best kids ever. That label was not even applied to them until 2001, more than fifty years after their accomplishments during the 1940s.

Strauss and Howe also argue that today's young people are optimistic. This is true for children and adolescents, who have absorbed the cheerful aphorisms so common today (chapter 3 of this book, for example, is titled "You Can Be Anything You Want to Be"). Yet this optimism often fades—or even smashes to pieces—once Generation Me hits the reality of adulthood. If you are a Baby Boomer or older, you might remember the 1970 book *Future Shock*, which argued that the accelerating pace of cultural change left many people feeling overwhelmed. Today's young people take these changes for granted and thus do not face this problem. Instead, they face a different kind of collision: Adulthood Shock. Their childhoods of constant praise, self-esteem boosting, and unrealistic expectations did not prepare them for an increasingly competitive workplace and the economic squeeze created by underemployment and rising costs. After a childhood of buoyancy, GenMe is working harder to get less.

This book focuses on changes among young Americans—and on trends that have arrived at different times, or not at all, in many other cultures. However, many of the changes here can be generalized to other nations, particularly other Western nations such as Canada, Great Britain, Australia, and Germany. These cultures have also experienced the movement toward focusing on the needs of the self, as well as the dark flip side of increased depression and anxiety. Developing countries might well be next. Like McDonald's and Coca-Cola, American individualism is spreading to all corners of the globe. If current trends continue, Generation Me boomlets might soon be arriving around the world. The more exposure kids get to American culture, the more they will rebel against the family-first, group-oriented ethos of many cultures around the world.

The accelerated pace of recent technological and cultural change makes it more important than ever to keep up with generational trends. A profound shift in generational dynamics is occurring right now in the 2010s. Baby Boomers (born 1943–60) have dominated the culture since they were born because of their large numbers. But with many Boomers now in their 60s, they have already lost their grip on the marketers and advertisers of the world. As early as June 2000, *Time* magazine announced the "twilight of the Boomers." Marketers have already moved on to GenMe, which is now the entirety of the lucrative 18-to-35 age group. These are the young workers who will replace the Boomers, now retiring at a rapid clip. They are also the consumers everyone wants to reach, and it's time to understand them.

And I do mean understand, not change. I do not, for example, believe we should return to the supposedly ideal days of the 1950s (which were ideal only for some people). Nor am I suggesting that these trends are this generation's "fault." Instead, young people today are products of their culture—a culture that teaches them the primacy of the individual at virtually every step, and a culture that was firmly in place before they were born. Asking young people today to adopt the personality and attitudes of a previous time is like asking someone raised in the United States to instantly become Chinese. Morris Massey, for years a popular speaker on generations, put it this way: "The gut-level value systems are, in fact, dramatically different between the generations. . . . The focus should not be so much on how to change other people to conform to our standards, our values. Rather, we must learn how to accept and understand other people in their own right, acknowledging the validity of their values, their behavior." As Massey points out and research supports, our value systems are set in childhood and don't change much thereafter. Massey's favorite question is "Where were you when you were ten?" Put another way, you can't teach an old dog new tricks.

The empirical research on generational differences in personality and attitudes provides the backbone to this book: it shapes the chapter topics and provides the basis for how GenMe differs from previous generations. This makes the book unique among those that discuss generations because it summarizes a large amount of psychological and behavioral data collected at different times. We haven't surveyed the generations as they are now, with Boomers middle-aged and GenMe in youth and rising adulthood. Instead, we've found data on what Boomers were like when they were young in the 1960s and 1970s, and what GenX was like in the 1980s and 1990s, and compared it to data on young people in recent years. That means the differences aren't due to age or to people's misremembering what they were like when they were young (how many parents have fudged a detail or two about their own teenage years?). I've provided more details about this method in the next section and in the appendix.

I have also gathered a large amount of supplemental data from various sources. The *Statistical Abstract of the United States* is a gold mine of statistics going back decades (I often joke that it is my favorite book: what it lacks in plot it more than makes up for in information). Many other surveys, polls, research studies, and books reveal the feelings of today's young people. I have tried to bring to life a wide range of research on generational differences in personality, attitudes, and behavior—my own research and that of others, and from both academic and popular sources.

I have supplemented this numerical data with more qualitative opinions. Over 200 of my students at San Diego State University shared their stories through written essays. This diverse group included students of every ethnicity and background, ranging from first-generation college students to upper-middle-class kids. Another 100 young people from around the country contributed stories and thoughts through my websites, www.generationme.org and www.jeantwenge.com. In all cases, I have changed names and, in some instances, identifying details; stated ages reflect the person's age at the time of the quote.

I also include ample references to popular culture, including television, movies, music, and magazines, without which a book on young people today would not be complete. This is where the culture lives and breathes, especially for a generation that has always enjoyed cable TV with one hundred channels. American pop culture refers constantly to the self and individuality. I was astounded at how often I heard the word *self* from so many different sources. I had never noticed it before, as most of us haven't: like fish swimming in the ocean, we don't notice the water because it is all around us and has always been there.

These examples from pop culture are not meant to replace the hard data on generations, but instead to illustrate them. I present the results showing how the generations differ, then use examples to show how these trends appear both in real people's lives and in the media that shapes their worldviews. No, the characters on *Glee* aren't real, but their words both reflect and shape the views of Generation Me. (In the online survey, for example, several said they first learned about gays and lesbians from watching *Glee*). Since the last edition of this book, new technology has allowed researchers to more systematically examine popular culture. Now there's actual proof that phrases such as *you are special* and *I love me* were rarely used before the 1970s—but are much more common now.

Even the most innocuous TV comments now catch my attention. During an episode of her eponymous talk show, Ellen DeGeneres said that the most important thing is "how you feel and being happy." It's a statement most young people take for granted. Dan Atkins, 17, says in *Growing Up Digital*, "My basic philosophy toward life is, do whatever makes you happy." But when I asked my mother (born in 1943) about this, she said, "In the early 1960s, most people would have said the most important things were being honest, hardworking, industrious, loyal, and caring about others. I can't even remember thinking about whether I was 'happy.' That's not to say we weren't happy—we just didn't focus on it." We do now. Here's Mario, a recent college graduate quoted in the book *Quarterlife Crisis*: "I just try to do whatever will make me happier, and think of myself first." Welcome to Generation Me.

HOW IT ALL STARTED

The idea for this book began when I was a 21-year-old college student at the University of Chicago in 1992, working on my BA thesis. Unfortunately, and unknown to me at the time, my thesis was a rather undistinguished project that would ultimately be rejected by four journals and never published. However, an intriguing tangent of this work led to the 22 years of research and 33 scientific-journal articles that form the basis of this book.

One of the questionnaires I used in my ill-fated BA project was the Bem Sex-Role Inventory, which measures personality traits associated with one sex or the other. For example, "assertive" and "acts like a leader" are items on the "masculine" scale, and "compassionate" and "yielding" are items on the "feminine" scale. I had always been fascinated by how gender shapes our personalities and still had a copy of the scale I'd received nine years before at a Texas Tech University program designed to show middle school students what college was like (the program bore the clumsy name "Shake Hands with Your Future," and now that I've been to college, I think it would have been more accurate if it had included beer).

For my BA thesis, I gave this questionnaire and one about appearance choices to 150 college students, mostly by hijacking people everywhere I went. People filled out questionnaires at loud parties, during particularly boring classes, and between bites of barely edible food in the dining hall. Several questionnaires bore water stains from being penciled in at a swim meet. Most people were willing to help, although as word got around, the occasional potential victim would duck around a corner if I appeared carrying pencils.

I went about analyzing the data on my ultimately doomed project, looking for correlations between things such as hair length, earrings, and—yes—that test of gender-related personality traits. That's when I noticed something interesting: about 50% of the women in my sample scored as "masculine" on the gender-roles test, meaning that they had endorsed significantly more of the stereotypically masculine traits (such as "assertive") than the feminine items. When the test was written in 1973, only about 20% of women scored that way. This was completely tangential to the main question of my amateurish thesis, but interesting nevertheless.

I immediately thought that this might be a difference between generations—being a woman in 1973 was surely quite different from being one in 1992. On the other hand, my sample was far from random and consisted of students at the University of Chicago, a group not known for its normality: the school is intensely intellectual and proud of its asocial nerdiness. In his popular syndicated column, The Straight Dope, Cecil Adams once wrote that U of C undergraduates, like insects that eat book paste, developed their "intellectual predilections as the consequence of an unhappy sex life." So what if he was a biased Northwestern grad—he was basically right. So I didn't think much of it. Besides, I had a BA thesis to write, and it was going to change the world! (Insert ironic eye-rolling here.)

By the next fall, I was a graduate student at the University of Michigan, collecting more data on my gender-role project. This time, participants from an undergraduate class filled out questionnaires in a large classroom over a few evenings. The generational difference popped out again: more than half of the women in the sample had high scores on the scale of stereotypically masculine personality traits. I couldn't write it off to campus this time—the Michigan undergraduates were distressingly normal—and these differences were even more interesting than the main results of my thesis (did you know that college women, on average, own fifteen pairs of shoes, compared to five for men?).

But what did I have? Two recent samples to compare to the

original one in 1973. What had happened in between those years? Were my samples just a fluke? Fortunately, this scale had been used by a large number of people over twenty years, so the data had to be out there. One spring day in 1994, I decided I just had to find out if women did embrace more stereotypically masculine traits now, and I developed the method I ultimately used for many of the studies in this book. (As for the results of the "masculine" traits study, you'll find them in chapter 7.)

The method is fairly straightforward, though labor-intensive. I begin by searching computer databases for journal articles, master's theses, and dissertations that used a particular scale. I keep only those that used a normal population of a specific age—usually children or college students. Then I search to find them at the library or in full-text databases online, since only the entire article or thesis will have what I'm looking for: the average score of the sample on the questionnaire. Once I find all of the data, I can then graph those scores by the year the data were collected, showing how scores changed over a range of years—not just from one year to another, but across the entire period. Because the samples are roughly the same age, this shows how young people differ from one generation to the next. No one had ever done this type of analysis before, so I started from scratch, developing a way to find and analyze the data.

I did most of these searches in the labyrinthine stacks of the graduate library at the University of Michigan, a building so vast and confusing that red and yellow lines are painted on the floor to help people find the exits. The university had added on to the library in 1970, smushing two buildings of different styles and heights together with limited access between the two. The older building ended up with floors such as 4A, connected by narrow, apparently randomly placed staircases. The tall shelves filled with books created a nerdy form of a Halloween cornfield maze. I would often sit looking through journals only to see some poor soul walk past me, double back again, and then stand under the dim lights with a look of utter confusion on his or her face. During those years, I probably helped more people escape from the Michigan library than anyone else. I imagined these rescued students stumbling gratefully into the thin winter sunlight, relieved that they weren't going to wander around the library for hours until someone finally found them, weak and dehydrated, on floor 1A between HM and HQ.

During those years, I probably pulled half a million journals off the shelves. ("I hope you're not allergic to dust," my dissertation adviser quipped.) When I left one section of the library to move to another, I would leave behind several teetering stacks of colorfully bound journals, each about four feet tall. I felt sorry for the work-study students who had to reshelve my looming piles of discarded books, many of which were twenty or thirty years old. The workers must have thought someone left them as a joke, or that a book monster was loose in the library, pulling down old journals from the rusty shelves to create random stacks in scattered carrels. But there were perks as well. One of my favorite finds was an advertisement in a 1920s journal that announced a contest with a $20,000 prize, an enormous sum in those days. The money would go to anyone who proved he or she could perform telekinesis (moving an object with only the force of your mind). I was amused to see that one of the judges for the contest was Harry Houdini. A few issues later came the unsurprising conclusion: no one won the prize.

I also used the Interlibrary Loan Department to obtain endless dissertations and master's theses, another great source of data. I requested so many that the staff began to grimace when I walked up to the desk. I couldn't get every thesis that way, but I soon found out that the Library of Congress in Washington, DC, has a copy of every American doctoral dissertation on microfiche. I made many trips there, usually staying with friends in Baltimore, where I slept under a comforter that, despite my friends' best efforts, was their cat's favorite alternative litterbox. Fortunately, the data I got during the day and the great conversations with my friends in the evenings more than made up for it—what's a little cat pee when you're finding out how generations differ?

The dissertations were a study of change in themselves. The earliest, from the 1940s and 1950s, were on transparently thin, onionskin paper, with blurred typewriter print—there were no photocopiers, so documents had to be typed on carbon paper, with the copies made as the typing was done. Apparently, the library copy was never the original, and the type blurred as the typewriter keys struck through several layers of paper and carbon. Who knew? Certainly not a child of the computer age like me.

A little later, after copiers became more common, dissertations were still typewritten but clearer. In the 1950s and 1960s, almost every male student thanked his wife for typing his dissertation. I could just see those poor women, tired from a day in the secretarial pool, coming home to struggle through their husbands' scribbled sentences. By the late 1970s and 1980s, dissertations almost always appeared in the then-ubiquitous, straight-serif font of the IBM electric typewriter. Slowly, computer fonts began to appear; someone had bought one of the first Apple Macintoshes and would get overly creative using more than one font in a document. By the 1990s, almost every dissertation was in Times New Roman. No one thanked his wife for typing his dissertation anymore, and many of the dissertations were written by the wives themselves, who were now getting their own PhDs. The modern age had arrived.

After years of library searches, I overloaded on the tedium. Fortunately, by then I had wonderful and enthusiastic graduate students to help. In recent years I've also drawn from large databases I can wade through right on my computer. But I still feel a misty wave of nostalgia when I remember the library stacks I frequented in just about every place I lived and visited, including Iowa, Michigan, Texas, Ohio, Pennsylvania, Wisconsin, Washington, DC, and California. Every time I went to the library, it felt like a treasure hunt: somewhere amid those dusty books was the answer, and all I had to do was find it. I imagined the numbers I sought flying off the candlelight-yellow pages, swirling into the air between the metal shelves of the stacks, drawing a picture of change across the generations. (What can I say? I was an overeager graduate student.) Even as the years passed and I started new projects, I knew that those dusty books I mined contained a rich vein of information from which to reassemble the remarkable story of past and future generations. This book tells that story.

1

You Don't Need Their Approval: The Decline of Social Rules

Getting dressed in the morning is a fundamentally different experience today than it was fifty years ago. For all of Generation Me's lifetime, clothes have been a medium of self-expression, an individual choice in a range of alternatives and comfort. Contrast this to past decades, when men wore ties most of the time and women did not leave the house without crisp white gloves and a tight girdle. Pictures of crowds in the early 1960s show quaint sights such as men wearing three-piece suits at baseball games and ladies lined up in identical-length skirts. To GenMe, these images look like those of people on an alien planet—who wears a suit to a baseball game?

Even our shoes are different. Today's casual footwear are called tennis shoes because people once wore them only to play tennis or basketball. Not even kids wore these types of shoes on the street—their shoes were made of stiff leather, just like adults'.

Now that's all but forgotten. Except in the most formal of workplaces, few men wear suits to work, and virtually no one wears them to baseball games. Women have (thankfully) abandoned wearing tight girdles and white gloves everywhere they go (and many young women don't even know what a girdle is,

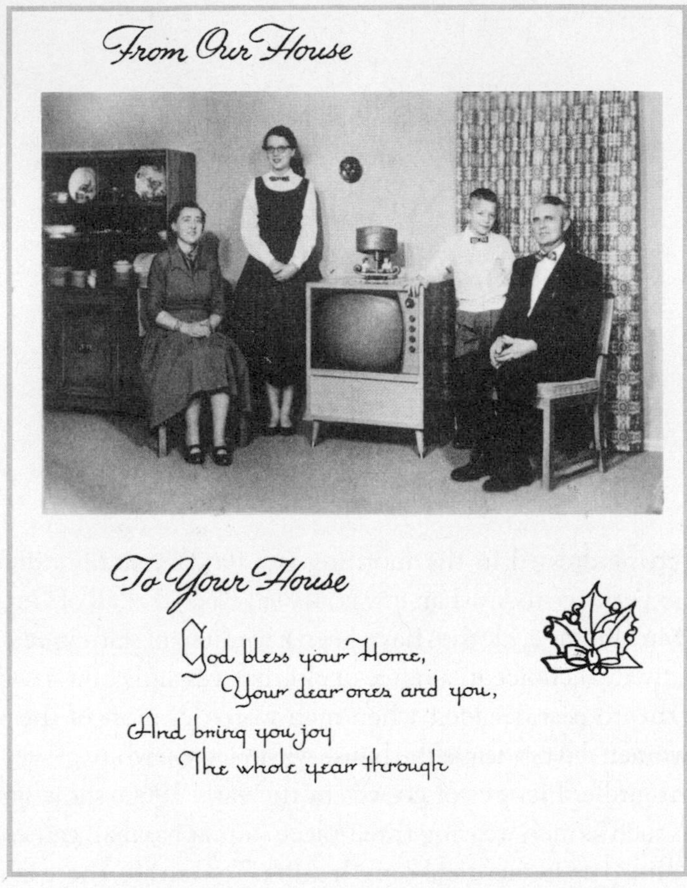

Holiday card, Minnesota, 1955. Not only are the clothes formal, but so is the posing and demeanor. The perfect family was proper and composed.

though some are devoted to Spanx, the GenMe version). The trend toward more informal dress has accelerated in the past ten years, with many companies opting for "business casual" and others going for just plain casual. The trend reached all the way to the top in July 2005, when about half the members of the Northwestern University women's lacrosse team wore flip-flops during their White House visit, resulting in a picture of the president of

Holiday card, Massachusetts, mid-2000s. Formal clothing is no longer necessary to make a good impression. It is now more important to dress for yourself or for your comfort; if you really wanted to do things "your way" and just for yourself, you'd wear jeans to work. Many of us already do.

the United States standing next to several young women wearing shoes that were once reserved for walking on sand or showering in scuzzy gymnasiums. Although most people still want to look good, we are a much more informal and accepting society than we once were. This is a perfect illustration of generational trends in attitudes, as the entire point in dressing up is to make a good impression on others and elicit their approval. You don't dress to be relaxed, natural, and happy.

The strict rules of previous decades went far beyond appearance. Beneath the wool suits and tailored hats, yesterday's men and women were bound by another type of conformity. Male or female, you were considered strange if you did not marry by age 25 and even stranger if you married outside your race or religion. It was expected that you would have children—it was not considered a choice. Your race and sex dictated your fate and behavior. When war came, you went to fight if you were male and able. Overall, duty and responsibility were held more important than individual needs and wants. You did certain things, you said certain things, and you didn't talk about certain things. End of story.

Today, few of these rules apply. We are driven instead by our individual needs and desires. We are told to follow our dreams, to pursue happiness above all else. It's okay to be different, and you should do what's right for you. The phrase *my needs* was four times as common in American books in the 2000s compared to those in the 1960s. Young people today are only half as likely as those in the late 1980s to believe that children should learn obedience above all else. Baby boys in the 2010s (versus the 1950s) were three times less likely to receive one of the ten most popular names. These changes are not clearly good or clearly bad, but they do indicate a strong shift toward individualism.

The choices of the individual are now held so paramount that the most common advice given to teenagers is "Just be yourself." (Not that long ago, it was more likely to be "Be polite.") This started with Generation X: Filmmaker Kevin Smith says, "My generation believes we can do almost anything. My characters are free: no social mores keep them in check." Or take Melissa, 20, who says, "I couldn't care less how I am viewed by society. I live my life according to the morals, views, and standards that I create."

This is the social trend—so strong it's a revolution—that ties all of the generational changes together in a neat, tight bundle: do what makes you happy, and don't worry about what other people think. It is enormously different from the cultural ethos of previous decades, and it is a philosophy that GenMe takes entirely for granted. "As long as I believe in myself, I really do not care what others think," says Rachel, 21.

GENERATIONS AT THE CINEMA

The ethos of self-belief appears frequently in popular movies; my favorite examples involve what I call "the apparent time traveler." The main character in these films is supposed to be a real person in the 1950s, but he or she actually represents the enlightened voice of the 21st century, which makes him (or her) the hero of the film. These movies were ubiquitous in the 2000s, when much of GenMe were forming their view of the world. In 2003's *Mona Lisa Smile*, Julia Roberts plays a professor at Wellesley College in 1953. Soon after arriving, she rallies her students against the restrictions of early marriage and training for motherhood. When she critiques sexist advertising during a class, the modern audience knows exactly what she is doing, but few people in the 1950s would have seen it before—or even thought to do it. Roberts's character has clearly taken the time-traveler shuttle to the future and absconded with a copy of the 1987 feminist antiadvertising film *Still Killing Us Softly*.

The Majestic, released in 2001, is an even worse movie. Jim Carrey's character, a Hollywood screenwriter, gets blacklisted and takes refuge in a small town. After he is asked to testify, he convinces the entire town that McCarthyism is bad and that free speech is our most treasured right. The whole town unites behind the accused writer, and the main female character says, "It doesn't really matter if you are a Communist or not—this is America and you can be one if you want to. It's nobody's business." Uh, not really. Had this actually been the 1950s, an accused Communist would have been everybody's business. This viewpoint was common even in the 1970s, when 48% of Americans believed Communists should not be allowed to give a speech, teach at a college, or have a book in a local library.

Movies that admit to time travel are somewhat more enjoyable. In *Pleasantville*, two modern teenagers help a 1950s town find passion and the freedom of ideas. Every character who discovers an individualistic freedom such as sex or intellectual questioning instantly turns from black and white into color. The film sinks into predictability once discrimination against the "colored" people begins. (Get it?)

Other movies travel across cultures rather than time, but they promote the same message. In 2002's *Bend It Like Beckham*, an

Indian girl living in London wants to play soccer. Her parents, already taken aback that their older daughter did not have an arranged marriage, want Jess to learn to cook and be a proper young lady. The plot comes to a head when Jess must shuttle back and forth between a game and her sister's wedding. By the end of the movie, Jess wants to join a professional women's soccer team and move to America. Her parents, finally convinced that it's right for Jess to follow her dreams, reluctantly agree. The overall message of all of these movies—whether they travel in time or cultures—is to rebel against restrictive social mores. Don't follow the rules; do whatever makes you happy.

And sometimes you don't even need to travel. The biggest box-office draw in late 2004 and early 2005 was *Meet the Fockers*, the sequel to the highly successful comedy *Meet the Parents*. The movie revolves around the culture clash between the conservative Byrnes family and the hippie Focker family. The Fockers provide most of the comedy in the film, with their sex-therapy business, their leather sandals, and their display of their son's ninth-place ribbons (because, they say, "It's not about winning—it's about what's in your heart"). But by the end of the movie, the Fockers are not the ones who have been convinced to change—it's the straitlaced Byrnes family who learns from them. Mr. Byrnes, played to crusty perfection by Robert De Niro, learns to loosen up and show emotion toward his daughter. He also decides that it might be good for him and his wife to enjoy more physical affection in their marriage, and he puts some of Mrs. Focker's sex tips to good use. Hippies may be laughable, but they teach us how to live. No need to walk around all uptight like that—which you must be if you're not a hippie. I'm exaggerating a bit, but the movie does make it clear which life philosophy is correct, and it's definitely Let It All Hang Out.

These movies dramatize two interlocking changes: the fall of social rules and the rise of the individual. As the individualistic viewpoint became prominent, concern with the opinions of others plummeted. This chapter discusses the decline in the need for social approval, and the following two chapters document the ascendance of the individual self. Over the last few decades, the entire nation has experienced the transformation parodied in an episode of *The Simpsons*, when Springfield's usual Do What We Say Festival (started, they say, in 1946 by German settlers) is replaced with the new Do What You Feel Festival.

DO YOUR OWN THING

Imagine you are seated at a table with six other people. Four lines are drawn on a chalkboard at the front of the room: a medium-length target line; along with line A, medium; line B, short; and line C, long. You're to say which of the lines is the same length as the target. You're all ready with the obvious answer of A, but the six others go first and say line C. What do you do?

When Solomon Asch first performed this experiment in 1951, 74% of people gave the group's incorrect answer on at least one trial, and 28% did on the majority of trials. People felt the need to conform to the group and not to stand out. The study became one of the most famous in social psychology, taught in every class as an example of the social nature of human beings. Yet some have pointed out that this was the essence of getting along in 1950s society, when no one wanted to be thought of as different. But when researchers tried to replicate the study in 1980, they got completely different results: few people conformed to the group anymore. Apparently, it was no longer fashionable to go along with the group even when they were wrong. The authors of the study concluded that the Asch study was "a child of its time." A similar thing happened when a psychologist tried to replicate the Milgram study, an early 1960s study finding that people would shock someone else at dangerous levels when told to do so by an authority figure. In 2009, nearly twice as many men refused to obey the experimenter's orders.

Throughout the 1970s, self-help books and therapists actively encouraged people to flout social rules, telling readers they should stop caring about what others think. A central chapter in the 1976 megabestseller *Your Erroneous Zones*, by Wayne Dyer, is called "You Don't Need Their Approval." The author argues that people can do anything they put their minds to, and that others' opinions only get in the way. (It's probably no coincidence that both the cover and back of the book feature oversize pictures of the author, complete with a 1970s, powder-blue, V-neck shirt and the resulting display of male chest hair.) Dyer rants on and on about how courteous acts such as giving a wedding gift or attending a funeral are "musterbation," his double-entendre term for unnecessary social rules. Dyer argues that seeking approval from parents, teachers, and bosses undermines self-reliance and truth. "Needing approval is tantamount to saying 'Your view of me is more important than my own opinion of myself,'" he writes. Another self-help book carries on the tradition with the title *What You Think of Me Is None of My Business*. Unlike the Baby Boomers, who learned these new standards as adults, GenMe takes these attitudes for granted and always has.

"Just be yourself" is the central ethos of modern parenting. In 1924, a group of sociologists did an extensive study of the citizens of a place they called Middletown (later revealed as Muncie, Indiana). When mothers were asked which traits they wanted their children to have, they named strict obedience, loyalty to church, and good manners. In 1988, when the first wave of GenMe were young children, few mothers named these traits; instead, they chose independence and tolerance. Modern mothers might be gratified to learn that these values sank in. In *Growing Up Digital*, an 11-year-old girl says, "I think the individual determines what is cool, and it is his or her opinion. What is cool to one person might not be to another. The days of conformity are over." Danielle, 29, agrees: "I refuse to do something because it's what everyone else is doing, or because it's the socially acceptable thing to do at the time." When I asked my undergraduate students to name the characteristics that best described their generation, the two most popular answers were "independent" and "open-minded."

GenMe has been taught these values since birth—beginning with the unique names bestowed upon them. Like just about everyone else, I'd noticed that baby names seemed to be getting stranger every year. When my husband and I were naming our first child in 2006, I discovered the Social Security Administration's database of 325 million Americans' names going back to the 1880s. So I had to see if there was a generational change. Sure enough, the parents of GenMe'ers, and GenMe'ers themselves, were more likely than those in previous eras to give their children unique names (so they could stand out) instead of common names (so they could fit in). In 1950, 1 out of 3 boys received one of the top 10 names. By 2012, less than 1 out of 10 did. Girls receiving a common name dropped from 1 out of 4 to less than 1 out of 10. (We also controlled the analyses for immigration and looked within states with low Latino populations, such as North Dakota and Mississippi, to make sure that ethnic changes didn't account for the effects, and they did not.) By 2012, new parents—the majority of whom were GenMe—took things a step further to proclaim their child's greatness. The boys' names that increased the most in popularity between 2011 and 2012 included Major, King, and Messiah. Somewhat high expectations to put on a newborn.

As Jaden, 25, puts it, "For my grandparents, questioning their religion, their country's system of government, or what they ate was not acceptable. The fear of standing out or being judged by others for their beliefs was strong. My generation is much more independent. I pride myself on being a free and independent thinker. My wish is to break down the walls that humans have socially constructed." A book on generations in the workplace notes that today's young people were instructed to "Never just do what an adult asks. Always ask, 'Why?'" Some people say this should be the label for the generation—not Generation Y, but Generation Why?

At times, this attitude can lead to the more questionable idea that there are no rules, so you might as well make up your own. In interviews of 18-to-23-year-olds conducted in 2008 for his books *Souls in Transition* and *Lost in Transition*, Christian Smith found that most young Americans espouse "moral individualism," believing that morality is a personal choice. "I have no other way of knowing what to do morally but how I internally feel. That's where my decisions come from. From me, from inside of me," said one. So should people follow rules for what the society says is right or wrong? the researchers asked. "I think it's your personal belief system," said another young person. "I don't think it's anything like social norms or like that. I think it's just . . . dependent on each person and their own beliefs and what they think is right or wrong."

Thus, it follows that everyone has his or her own individual moral views, and it's not right to question someone else's view. "I guess what makes something right is how I feel about it, but different people feel different ways, so I couldn't speak on behalf of anyone else as to what's right and what's wrong," said one young man.

This moral individualism can easily become, as Smith puts it, a "live and let die" philosophy. When asked if people have any moral responsibility or duty to help others, one young person replied, "No, not really." Would it be a problem if someone didn't want to help others? asked the interviewer. "No. . . . They can help themselves. . . . Do they really need anyone else?" he replied. "So if someone asks for help, we don't have an obligation to them?" prodded the interviewer. "Yeah, it's up to each individual, of course," the young adult asserted.

Smith concludes that most emerging adults seem unaware of any source of moral reasoning outside of themselves. "Instead . . . the world consists of so many individuals, and each individual decides for themselves what is and isn't moral and immoral," Smith writes. "Morality is ultimately a matter of personal opinion. Everyone should tolerate everyone else, take care of their own business, and hopefully get along." This is the razor's edge of modern individualism: tolerance is great, but perhaps not when each individual is free to decide for himself which rules to follow, and helping others is rarely one of those rules.

What about all of the GenMe'ers who are serving in the military, and who served in Afghanistan and Iraq when we were all sitting safe at home? Military service can certainly be an example of self-sacrifice, duty, and collectivism. However, the data suggest that GenMe service members are the exception, not the rule. According to the Pew Center, only 2% of GenMe has served in the military, compared to 6% of GenX and 13% of Boomers. Polls of 16-to-24-year-olds conducted by the Department of Defense show that fewer now say they are likely to join the military: 18% expressed interest in 2010, down from 26% in 1986. This is partially because many more young people automatically rule out military service. In a nationally representative sample of high school students, 2 out of 3 (67%) said they "definitely won't" join the military in 2012, up from 57% in 1976. This does not diminish the contributions of the GenMe'ers who do serve, but it contrasts them with the majority of their generation.

One upside to the individualistic attitude is lessened prejudice and discrimination. Amanda, 22, says that one of the main lessons in her Girl Scout troop was "being different is good." It's a mantra GenMe has heard over and over. They absorbed the lesson of tolerance with their baby food—not just for race and religion, but for sexual orientation. It also extends to beliefs, feelings, and all kinds of other intangibles. Just about the only difference that wasn't good? Someone who was prejudiced.

That's exactly what appears in our recent analysis of data from the nationally representative General Social Survey. Boomers set in motion strong trends toward tolerance of groups such as Communists, gays and lesbians, and those who oppose religion. Generation Me continued those trends throughout the 2000s and 2010s, but diverged from Boomers in one major way: they were less tolerant than Boomers toward someone who claimed that blacks are genetically inferior. GenMe is thus the most tolerant generation in American history—the only group they will not tolerate are those who are intolerant themselves.

WHO CARES WHAT YOU THINK?

Not caring what others think may also explain the apparent decline in manners and politeness. GenMe'ers do not believe there is one right way of doing things, and most were never taught the rules of etiquette. When that means wearing white shoes after Labor Day and using whatever fork you want, no problem. But most etiquette was developed to provide something often lacking in modern life: respect for other people's comfort. "Society has gotten increasingly callous and me-centered, and we're fed up with [the results]," says Corinne Gregory, founder of a class called the PoliteChild. A high school teacher told me that she noticed her students don't "clean up nice"—they find it difficult not to swear and to speak more formally when necessary. They talk to older people and authority figures the same way they talk to their friends. A business book relates the story of a company founder who visited one of his shops and asked a young employee how she was doing. "Well, a little hungover this morning, but okay," she replied.

A recent article related numerous stories of young job applicants' lack of perspective, from answering their cell phones during the interview to bringing their parents. Jaime Fall, vice president of the HR Policy Association, says GenMe's mind-set is "You're perfect just the way you are—do whatever you're comfortable doing"—an attitude that can backfire in interviews. "Life has gotten more casual," observes Mara Swan, executive vice president at Manpower. "They don't realize [the interview] is a sales event."

It goes beyond manners—people today are less likely to follow all kinds of social rules. Business professor John Trinkaus finds that fewer people now slow down in a school zone, and fewer observe the item limit in a supermarket express lane. More people cut across parking lots to bypass stoplights. In 1979, 29% of people failed to stop at a particular stop sign in a New York suburb, but by 1996 a stunning 97% of drivers did not stop at all. In Trinkaus's most ironic finding, the number of people who paid the suggested fee for lighting a candle at a Catholic church decreased from 92% to 25% between the late 1990s and 2006. In other words, 75% of people cheated the church out of money in the most recent observation.

Cheating is also rampant among students. A 2008 study found that 95% of high school students said they had cheated. That included 64% who have cheated on a test by copying from someone else or using crib notes. The rest merely told classmates what would be on a test, but, according to researcher Donald McCabe, most students don't even count that as cheating. Another survey found that 34% of high school students admitted to cheating on an exam in 1969, which rose to 61% in 1992 (GenX) and to an incredible 74% in 2002 (the first wave of GenMe). Fortunately, fewer in the second wave of GenMe, 51%, reported cheating on an exam in 2012. Of course, that's still the majority and may underestimate the actual number. High levels of cheating continue into college; a 2002 survey found that 80% of students at Texas A&M University admitted to cheating; a 2007 poll of students at 12 different colleges found that 67% admitted to cheating.

Although competition for grades may have fueled the increase, attitudes have shifted along with the behavior. In a 2012 study of 25,000 high school students, 57% agreed that "in the real world, successful people do what they have to do to win, even if others consider it cheating." In other words, the majority believed that the ends justified the means. McCabe has found this attitude especially prevalent in business schools, characterized by a "get-it-done, damn-the-torpedoes, succeed-at-all-costs mentality." "According to my research," McCabe wrote in *Harvard Business Review*, "the mind-set of most MBAs—bottom line—is to get the highest GPA possible, regardless of the means. After all, the students with the highest GPAs get the best shot at the six-figure jobs."

This breakdown in consideration and loyalty, and the increase in cheating, reaches all the way to the top. Business scandals, such as those at WorldCom and Enron, demonstrated that many people have little problem with breaking rules and telling lies in an attempt to make more money. The mortgage meltdown of the late 2000s was a quite spectacular example of this as well, with banks continuing to get rich as ordinary Americans lost jobs and had their homes foreclosed. In psychology and medicine, several researchers were recently shown to have published dozens of papers based on fraudulent data. Even honest businesses disregard other time-tested social rules, such as loyalty to employees. Companies are now more likely to raid pension funds and engage in mass layoffs to prop up a sinking stock price. Others ship jobs overseas if it will save money. "Downsizing" and "outsourcing" are the modern corporate equivalents of rudeness—and a lot more devastating. Because GenMe'ers grew up with this kind of ruthlessness, it should not surprise us that they think little of some occasional homework copying. It also suggests that the corporations of the future are going to need much stricter oversight to make sure that cheating and scams are kept to a minimum. Cheating on tests easily translates to cheating on the balance sheet. Expect to see more laws like Sarbanes-Oxley that ask corporations to prove that they are not cheating their stockholders. Even with these laws, more stock reports, research, and articles will have to be taken with a grain of salt—in an increasingly competitive world, the temptation to cheat will be ever stronger for GenMe.

CALL ME BETH

Boomers laid claim to the phrase *question authority* during the 1960s.

But GenMe doesn't just question authority—they disregard it entirely.

"Older generations trusted God, the church, government, and

elders," says Kevin, 22. "I have questioned things and people that earlier generations never would have thought to." This is the eventual outcome of increased informality and the loosening of social rules, and many people would rightly argue that questioning things is good. Sometimes "traditions" are outmoded and need challenging.

But sometimes GenMe takes the questioning of authority a little too far. Education professor Maureen Stout tells the story of a young man in her class who did not turn in his research paper. "After a lot of excuses and arguments he finally came out with it," Stout writes. "He believed he was entitled to do just as he pleased and refused to recognize my authority, as the instructor, to determine what the assignments in the class should be. It was as simple as that." Former journalist Peter Sacks related his frustration with the community college students he taught in his second career, observing that they seemed uncomfortable with "the idea that my knowledge and skills were important or even relevant." Student after student balked when he corrected their essays, several complaining that his comments were "just your opinion."

I recognized this phrase immediately, as I'd heard it over and over from my own students. I heard this complaint even when I corrected obvious errors such as run-on sentences and incorrect punctuation, things that were clearly not a matter of opinion. Even multiple-choice tests weren't free from this kind of challenge. In one class, I decided it might be a good idea to review the correct answers to exam questions—it would be a way to correct misconceptions and help the students learn, I thought. Almost immediately, several students began to argue with me about the questions, claiming that the answers they had chosen were right. Since there wasn't a grading mistake, I was forced to explain again why the answers were correct, but they continued to argue. It was the worst class I'd ever had. After it was over, an older student—who had not been one of the arguers—came up to me and said with disbelief, "Twenty years ago when I got my first degree, we never questioned teachers like that."

Apparently I was not alone. In a recent survey of college faculty, 61% reported that students had "verbally disrespected you or challenged your authority during class." Sixty-five percent said a student had "continuously rolled his/her eyes, frowned, or otherwise showed disdain while you were teaching." Many students have found their cell phones ringing during class—an honest mistake—but the new twist is to answer and conduct a conversation. Sixty-one percent of professors said they'd experienced this. They were the lucky ones: 24% said they had received "hostile or threatening communications (e-mails, letters, phone messages) from a student," and 29% said "a student yelled or screamed" at them.

New teaching philosophies sometimes explicitly acknowledge faculty's lack of authority. When Sacks, the community college professor, complained to a colleague about the lack of respect he experienced, she advised him to adopt the more informal approach that she used. In her first class, she always announced, "I have some expertise and you have some expertise. My job is to facilitate this process. And please call me Beth."

The message: We are all equals here. I might have more education and years of work experience, but that doesn't mean I know any more than you. This is a lot of the reason for the crumbling of authority and the new acceptance of questioning those in charge. This can have benefits for the free exchange of ideas and engaged student learning, but clearly has downsides as well. This new democracy in education and the workplace has been energized by the new informality in dress and names. While the boss was once "Mr. Smith" or "Mrs. Jones," bosses are now "Mike" or "Linda." Mr. and Mrs. sound too stiff and formal—and old-fashioned. When we're all on a first-name basis, the specter of authority takes yet another step back into the shadows of a previous era. That can bring us closer, but it can also set the stage for more disrespect and conflict.

The curriculum reflects this lack of a central authority as well.

It is no longer enough to teach only the "classics"; these are now known as DWMs (Dead White Males). Few academics still agree that there is a "canon" of Western literature that all students should learn. Instead, students must take classes teaching a variety of perspectives, in which the works of women and minorities are also covered. Whether you agree or disagree with this "multicultural" approach to education, it's clear that we no longer answer to one definite authority. There are many opinions, and each is considered valuable. Though this has many advantages, it does mean that people will be much less likely to conform to societal rules—after all, which rules would they follow? Which culture or society is "right"? GenMe is taught that none of them is, or all of them are.

Unless it's the Internet. Like most people old enough to remember a pre-Internet world, I marvel that we ever got along without it. (How did we find movie showtimes in the early 1990s? Oh, yeah, that weird recording where a teenager with acting aspirations would read off the movies and times.) As fantastic as the Internet is for research, it also democratizes the sources of information. Suddenly, you don't have to write a textbook or have a column in a major newspaper for thousands of people to read your words—just put up a Web page or a blog, and eventually someone, and maybe even lots of people, will stumble across it. In this environment, there is no authority: information is free, diffuse, and comes from everyone. (Whether it is correct is another matter.) In many Internet situations, you can abandon social roles entirely. Want to be a different age or sex? Go ahead. As a famous *New Yorker* cartoon showing two dogs in conversation puts it, "On the Internet, nobody knows you're a dog."

Parental authority also isn't what it used to be. "Parents are no longer eager to be 'parents.' They want to love and guide their children as a trusted friend," says family studies professor Robert Billingham. Chicago-area parent Richard Shields says that his 17-year-old son is his best friend. He prefers them to have fun together rather than impose strict rules or discipline. "It's better for them to see our values and decide to gain them for themselves," he says.

This also means that children play a much larger role in family decisions. The kids who chose their own outfits as preschoolers have grown into teenagers who help their parents choose which car to buy or even where to live. A *Chicago Sun-Times* article interviewed a large group of teens and their families, finding one where a teenage daughter helped her father decide on a new job, and another where the two teenage kids make all of the home-decorating and electronics-purchasing decisions. Forty percent of teens see their opinions as "very important" in making family decisions. In an earlier era of greater parental authority, that percentage would have been close to zero. One family's two daughters convinced their parents to buy a second car. "I always stress to my girls to be opinionated," said Christine Zapata, the girls' mother. "I guess that sort of backfires on me sometimes."

I wonder what will happen when this generation have their own children. Will they continue the move toward lesser parental authority or insist that they retain the authority they have grown accustomed to? If GenMe teaches our own children to be individualistic as well, we may have a full-scale battle of the wills once our kids become teenagers themselves.

BEING DIFFERENT IS GOOD, EVEN WHEN YOU'RE GETTING MARRIED

As one of society's most long-lived traditions, marriage and weddings illustrate the move away from social rules better than anything else. In 1957, 80% of people said that those who didn't marry were "sick, neurotic, or immoral." Now, when and whether you marry is considered a personal choice. Many do not: in 2012, 41% of babies in the United States were born to unmarried women—compared to 5% in 1960. Among women under 30 who gave birth in 2009, the majority were unmarried. The social rule that you should be married before you have a baby has all but fallen by the wayside. Many of these couples live together, but 39% of cohabitating couples break up within the first five years of a child's life (compared to 13% of those who are married). Art has imitated life, with single mothers portrayed more often on TV, with reactions shifting from outrage in the 1980s (*Murphy Brown*) to barely a peep in the 2000s (*Friends*). By 2013, the sitcom *The New Normal* portrayed a gay couple having a child using a surrogate—just as several gay celebrities (such as Elton John and Neil Patrick Harris) have done. Overall, this generation is much more likely to accept that there are many ways to make a family. When nearly half of babies are born to single parents, who has time to criticize them all?

Whom you marry is also much more up to the individual. My parents, a Catholic and a Lutheran (though both white and alike in every other way), had a "mixed marriage" when they wed in 1967. People in my mother's Minnesota hometown whispered about it behind cupped hands for weeks. Now this religious difference would be considered too minor to even be discussed.

Interracial marriage has become much more common, more than doubling since 1980 and accounting for more than 1 in 7 US marriages in 2010. Yet until the Supreme Court struck down miscegenation laws in 1967, whites and blacks could not legally marry each other in sixteen states. The last antimiscegenation law was not officially repealed until November 2000, in Alabama. Now these unions are everywhere, and between almost all ethnicities and races. My next-door neighbors for three years were a Mexican American man and his half-Jewish, half-Italian wife, and I've lost count of the number of Asian-white marriages among people I know. Almost half of Asian women will marry a white man. In 2012, 86% of Americans—including 93% of GenMe—agreed "I think it's all right for blacks and whites to date each other," up from 48% in 1987. Sixty percent of twentysomethings said they had dated someone from a different racial or ethnic background. In 2009, only 36% of Boomers said that more people of different races marrying one another has been a change for the better, compared to 60% of GenMe. Asked if they would be comfortable with someone in their family marrying someone of a different race, 55% of Boomers said yes, compared to 85% of GenMe.

Many young people I've talked to mention interracial dating as the biggest difference between them and their parents: many of their peers date across racial lines, but their parents don't agree with this. Several young women from Texas and North Carolina told me that if they dated a black man, their fathers would meet the poor guy at the door with a shotgun. Yet most of GenMe finds this perplexing: Who cares what race someone is? In one survey, only 10% of white young people said that marrying someone from their own ethnic group was important; however, 45% said it was important to their parents. Of young Asian Americans, 32% said same-ethnic-group marriage was important to them, but 68% said it was important to their parents. As YouTube star Kevin Wu, 19, said, "My parents like to constantly remind me that when I grow up I have to marry an Asian wife. Which is okay, I like Asian women, but I don't like narrowing my options. Girls are like a bag of M&Ms—they're all different colors on the outside, but on the inside, they're all the same, and they all taste good." He continues, "No one opens a bag of M&Ms and goes, hey, I'm only eating the yellow ones. You know why? Because that's racist. . . . I think the only way we can stop racism is to have more interracial babies." Interracial marriage is likely to become even more common in the future as more and more young people meet and date people from different backgrounds.

When we marry our other-race, other-religion, and possibly same-sex partners, we don't follow all of the wedding rules of previous generations. In the mid-1960s, *Brides* magazine insisted that "the only correct colors" for wedding invitations "are white, ivory, or cream, with absolutely no decorations such as borders, flower sprays, and so on." In other words, your invitation had to look just like everyone else's. Now people use wedding invitations in every possible theme and color—and wording. When my parents lived near Dallas, they received a wedding invitation with a picture of a cowboy and cowgirl inviting guests to "c'mon over for a big weddin' to-do." The reply-card choices were "Yes, we'll be there with our boots on" and "Shucks, we can't make it."

People are bending tradition in other ways. Some brides with male friends have a man of honor, and some grooms have best women. Another trend encourages brides to let each bridesmaid choose the style of her gown—it's no longer required that they all wear the same dress, a rule now seen as overly conformist. Many couples write their own vows, wanting a ceremony personalized to

Weddings, once governed by strict conventions for dress and behavior, now have few rules. It's your wedding, so you can wear shorts or a bikini if you want to.

speak for their individual love. The new trend in wedding photography is "journalistic" style: the photographers capture moments as they happen, putting less emphasis on formal posing. Weddings aren't about rules anymore, but about individual expression. Wedding gown designer Reem Acra says a bride should choose the look that encapsulates her personality. She says, "I always ask my brides, 'Who are you and what do you want to tell everybody?'"

THE CHURCH AND COMMUNITY OF THE INDIVIDUAL

What does the move away from social rules mean for religion? In *Millennials Rising*, Neil Howe and William Strauss predicted that those born in the 1980s and 1990s would be more committed to religion than previous generations, part of Millennials returning America to duty, communalism, and rule-following. They cited the growing popularity of high school prayer circles and quoted a youth minister who observed that this group liked "old-fashioned" religion. Others have argued that GenMe has moved away from religious institutions, but still maintains a private religiosity and spirituality.

I wanted to find out whether this was true, so my coauthors and I examined six nationally representative surveys of Americans collected over time. Our analysis included data on 8th- and 10th-graders—groups too young to be included in previous studies of trends in religion—and a sample of entering college students going back to 1966 (the American Freshman Survey) that at 10 million is the largest ongoing US survey with questions on religion. We also analyzed a survey of 12th-graders and two surveys of adults.

These massive datasets, with respondents aged 13 to 98, conveyed a clear conclusion: Americans' religious commitment has declined precipitously, especially since 2000. Most Americans still affiliate with a religion, but the number who do not is growing so quickly that they may soon be the majority. The number of entering college students who named "none" as their religious affiliation tripled between 1983 and 2012 (from 8% to 24%) and doubled among 12th-graders (from 10% in the late 1970s to 20% in the 2010s). The number who say they "never" attend religious services doubled between the 1970s and the 2010s. More young teens are also growing up without religion in their lives: 38% more 8th-graders in the 2010s (compared to the early 1990s) claim no religious affiliation and never attend religious services. Assuming that earlier generations were just as religious as those in the 1970s, Generation Me is the least religious generation in American history.

Two mechanisms seem to be at work. First, more teens are being raised by nonreligious parents. For example, four times as many college students in the 2010s (versus the early 1970s) said their mother did not affiliate with a religion. Second, young people are leaving religion as they grow into young adulthood, and this tendency grew stronger over the generations.

In *Soul Searching*, his extensive survey of teens, Christian Smith found that intellectual skepticism was the main reason teens moved away from religion: "It didn't make any sense anymore," said one. "Too many questions that can't be answered," said another. Others could not say exactly why they became less religious or said they simply lost interest: "It never seemed that interesting to me" or "It got kind of boring."

The flight from religion only accelerates during and after college. In 2012, 30% of Americans 18 to 29 claimed no religious affiliation—three times as many as in 1972. Only 14% of 18-to-29-year-olds attend religious services every week. Among high school seniors, most of whom still live with their parents, the figure is only 30%, down from 40% in 1976. GenMe'ers religious participation is still low even after they have their own children—nearly four times as many Americans in their 30s claimed no religious affiliation in 2012 compared to 1972.

Young people have also lost faith in religious institutions. In the late 1970s, 62% of Boomer 12th-graders thought that churches and religious organizations were "doing a good job." That slid to 53% in the 2010s. One out of three Boomer students in the late 1970s had already donated money to a religious organization; that number was nearly cut in half by 2012 (to 17%). GenMe'ers increasingly see religion negatively, so it makes sense that they are less willing to give their money to support it. In some cases, it's because GenMe's fundamental belief in equality (which we'll cover in chapter 7) and free sexuality (chapter 6) is at odds with the teachings of many religions. "Starting in middle school we got the lessons about why premarital sex was not okay, why active homosexuality was not okay, and growing up in American culture, kids automatically pushed back on those things," said Melissa Adelman, 30, in an interview with National Public Radio. "A large part of the reason I moved away from Catholicism was because without accepting a lot of these core beliefs, I just didn't think that I could still be part of that community." Even the pope has shown he understands this new reality; in 2013, Pope Francis said of issues such as gay marriage and birth control, "It is not necessary to talk about these issues all the time. We have to find new balance."

Some have argued that more Americans have moved away from religious institutions but are still privately religious or spiritual. That does not appear to be the case. The most stunning statistic comes from the nationally representative General Social Survey. Among those 18 to 29 years old in 1994 (GenX), only 2% never prayed. By 2012, 26% of 18-to-29-year-olds (GenMe) never prayed. Even when the question was asked as "prayer/meditation," recent numbers were lower: 37% of college students never prayed or meditated in 2005, compared to 33% just nine years earlier in 1996. The number of high school students who said that religion is "not important" in their lives increased 56% (from 14% in 1976 to 22% in 2012). Belief in God has also taken a hit. In 1994, 56% of 18-to-29-year-olds said they were sure that God exists; by 2012 that had shrunk to 44%. Between GenX and GenMe, belief in God went from winning the election to losing it. So it's not just that GenMe has moved away from religious institutions; they are also moving away from private religious belief and practice.

The idea that religion is being replaced by spirituality also doesn't hold up. The percentage of college students who described themselves as above average in spirituality declined from 59% in 1997 to 36% in 2012. When Christian Smith asked teens about spirituality in 2008, most did not even know what the term meant. ("What do you mean, 'spiritual seeking'?" many asked.) Smith concluded that few American teens are spiritual but not religious.

The decline in religious commitment and belief is one of the few generational trends that differs significantly by race and social class. At least among high school students, the decline has hardly touched black GenMe—only slightly fewer attend church and profess a religious affiliation now compared to the 1970s. So it's mostly the white kids who are singing "losing my religion." But—perhaps surprisingly—it's not the rich white kids. In the high school sample, religious participation declined the most among working-class youth whose fathers did not attend college.

Even among the majority of young people who affiliate with a religion, their beliefs are often rooted in what Christian Smith labels "therapeutic individualism." Within this system, "spirituality is re-narrated . . . as personal integration, subjective feeling, and self-improvement toward individual health and personal well-being—and no longer has anything to do with, for example, religious faith and self-discipline toward holiness or obedience." Even teens who identified as religious were, as Smith put it, "incredibly inarticulate about their faith, their religious beliefs and practices, and its meaning or place in their lives." Many could not say why they affiliated with a religion; if they did, they said that they prayed for things they wanted. For many GenMe teens, he observes, "God is treated as something like a cosmic therapist or counselor, a ready and competent helper who responds in times of trouble but who does not particularly ask for devotion or obedience." As a 14-year-old Catholic boy from Ohio put it, "Faith is very important, I pray to God to help me with sports and school and stuff and he hasn't let me down yet, so I think it helps you."

In *Emerging Adulthood*, Jeffrey Arnett describes the belief systems of young people as "highly individualized," which he calls "make-your-own religions." Many don't adhere to a specific belief system because, as one said, "I believe that whatever you feel, it's personal. . . . Everybody has their own idea of God and what God is. . . . You have your own personal beliefs of how you feel about it and what's acceptable for you and what's right for you personally." When Smith asked one young woman how she decided which interpretation of Scripture was correct, she simply said, "My own." A young man said he evaluated different religious claims with "pretty much just my authority." These beliefs seem to be growing: in a 2013 poll, 3 out of 4 American Catholics said they were more likely to "follow my own conscience" on difficult moral questions rather than follow "the teachings of the Pope."

Many young people abandon organized religion due to its restrictive rules. "Saturday nights I go out and hang out, and I don't have to necessarily worry about getting up to go to church in the morning. It's just a lot easier, I think, to leave certain things out," one teen said in *Souls in Transition*. Interviewed in *Emerging Adulthood*, Dana said she attended Jewish services growing up, but stopped going when she got older because "there was this pressure from the people at the synagogue to be, like, kosher, and I just didn't like having anyone telling me what my lifestyle should be." Beth was raised Catholic but by adulthood came to believe that humans all have natural, animalistic urges; she stopped believing because feeling guilty "made me unhappy." Charles grew up Episcopalian but stopped attending services because "I realized I was not being encouraged to think for myself. . . . It is, literally, 'This is black. This is white. Do this. Don't do that.' And I can't hang with that."

Many churches with growing memberships are fundamentalist Christian denominations that do require more strict adherence. However, these churches promote a personalized form of religion.

Many fundamentalist Christian faiths ask adherents to believe that "Jesus Christ is your personal savior" and that "He has a plan for your life." Many speak about having "a personal relationship with God." Rick Warren, author of the popular Christian book *The Purpose Driven Life*, writes, "Accept yourself. Don't chase after other people's approval. . . . God accepts us unconditionally, and in His view we are all precious and priceless." These denominations teach that one's personal faith guarantees acceptance into heaven, not the good works you perform and the way you treat others (which traditionally defined a proper spiritual outlook and its rewards). Even if you are a murderer, you will be saved if you accept Jesus as your personal savior. Most adherents strive to live good lives, but personal beliefs are considered more important.

Churches are not the only group hurting for members. As Robert Putnam documents in *Bowling Alone*, memberships in community groups have declined by more than one-fourth since the 1970s. Groups such as the Elks, the Jaycees, and the PTA have all seen memberships fall. Putnam labels the trend "civic disengagement" and concludes that it is linked to generational shifts. The title of his book comes from the observation that people used to bowl in organized leagues but now bowl alone or in informal groups. Young people would rather do their own thing than join a group. Across the board, youth are now less likely to approve of or be interested in large institutions such as government, mass media, and religious organizations. In 1976, 36% of high school seniors said they had already or would probably write to a public official, but by 2012 that had sunk to 19%. Twice as many (41% vs. 20%) said they probably won't. And this is in a time when it's easy to fill out an online form on a government website—yet fewer young people are interested in contacting public officials than in the days when that meant looking up an address at the library, typing a letter, addressing it, putting a stamp on it, and mailing it.

GenMe'ers are also less likely to trust their neighbors, and less likely to believe that the world is a welcoming place. In 1976, 46%

of high school students said that "most people can be trusted" (versus "you can't be too careful in dealing with people"). By 2012, just 16% of teens said they trusted others. In 2012, 47% of high school students said that most people are "just looking out for themselves" rather than "try[ing] to be helpful," and 49% said that most people "would try to take advantage of you if they got a chance." These were all-time or near-all-time lows in the 36-year history of the survey. GenMe trusts no one, suggesting a culture growing ever more toward disconnection and away from close communities. Trusting no one and relying on yourself is a self-fulfilling prophecy in an individualistic world where the prevailing sentiment is "Do unto others before they do it to you."

THE WORLDWIDE CONFESSIONAL

Maria, 20, says her mother's motto is "Other people don't have to know about the bad things that happen in the family." Few in GenMe share that belief. Many think that confession is good for the soul, and this no longer means whispering to a priest in a dark booth. It means telling everyone about your experiences and feelings, no matter how distasteful.

When I asked my students to relate true stories for an extra credit assignment, I assured them they could tell their own story in the third person if they didn't want me to know it was actually about them. Not one took me up on the offer; instead, I got myriad first-person stories, with names attached, about teenage sex, drug abuse, psychological disorders, ugly divorces, and family disagreements. One student wrote about losing her virginity at age 14 to a man who had only eight toes. So many students wrote candid essays about sex that I finally took it off the list of possible topics because I had more than enough stories. None of the students cared if I knew details of their personal lives that other generations would have kept as carefully guarded secrets.

This applies in spoken conversation as well. Jenny, 22, is an undergraduate at a small college in the South. When we met at a psychology conference, I asked about her career plans. Within two minutes, she was telling me about her broken engagement and how her former fiancé had been depressed. This was all done without pretense or embarrassment. In a mid-2000s survey of men, 62% of those 18 to 24 said they were comfortable discussing their personal problems with others, compared to only 37% of those age 65 and older. Many older people are amazed that young people will readily share their salary numbers with others, the disclosure of which once carried a strong taboo.

GenMe is also much more open about emotions. "In my generation, as opposed to my parents' or my grandparents', we are told to express our feelings and anger and sadness about our surroundings and not to hold them in," says Ashley, 24. She's not sure this is a good thing, however. "We are an emotionally spoiled generation. It can lead to more dramatic emotions when you are always discussing, sharing, analyzing them as our generation is led to feel they should do."

But that's not the message young people receive from most of the culture. Even sharing feelings that might muddle a situation is encouraged. In an episode of the teen show *Dawson's Creek*, one character does not want to confess her romantic feelings to her former boyfriend, who is now dating someone else. "If it broke my heart, I have no right to say so," she says. Her roommate can't believe what she's hearing. Clearly meant to be the show's Voice of Reason, she announces, "You have the right to say anything you want when it comes to how you feel."

TMI COMING UP!

Health issues are also the subject of much more honest and open discussion. Not that long ago, it was not acceptable to talk about health problems, particularly women's health problems. I once asked my grandfather why he and my grandmother had had only one child. "Too expensive," he said, though I knew he had made a good living. When I told my mother about this, she said my grandmother hadn't been able to have any more children. I asked why. "All she ever said was that she had 'female problems,'" my mother said. It was a term I'd heard before—for a certain generation, *female problems* was the closest anyone would ever come to uttering words such as *breast cancer*, *hysterectomy*, *endometriosis*, *uterus*, *infertility*, or even *menstrual period*.

These days, few people have qualms about using any of these terms, especially when talking with family or close friends—or even with total strangers. Women on Internet message boards discuss everything, and I mean everything: not just morning sickness, but miscarriages, PMS, the precise appearance of cervical fluid, the color of menstrual blood (brown or red today?), DTD (doing the deed), and BD (baby dancing) with their husbands. How often, and in what position, is also openly discussed, including any problems that might have arisen—or, sometimes, have not arisen (wink). Common phrases on these boards include *TMI coming up!* or *Sorry if TMI! TMI*, for those of you who are not GenMe, means "Too Much Information" (also called an overshare). I'm convinced the phrase was coined because there is so little that is now TMI, but we need a way to warn people before things become gross. After warning about the TMI, everyone goes ahead and posts the details anyway.

These boards are extremely helpful as they provide an enormous amount of information and support to women going through difficult life experiences. They're wonderful things—but an earlier generation of women would never have dreamed of discussing these topics in a public forum, and maybe not even with their closest friends. We live in a much more open age. Now we have not only tampon commercials, but ads for condoms, "personal lubricants" such as K-Y jelly, and erection drugs (my favorite: the one where the guy throws the football through the hole in the tire swing. So subtle).

Young celebrities seem to love the overshare just as much as GenMe's less famous members. "When I'm alone, I do masturbate a lot," notes James Franco. "We have sex like Kenyan marathon runners," boasts Olivia Wilde.

Oversharing is also the name of the game on Facebook and Twitter. Although people eventually learned that posting everything on Facebook was not the best idea (pictures of you drunk at a party = no job offer), social media still provides a much more public forum for our lives than previous generations had. A survey by babycenter.com found that half of new mothers sent text messages or updated their Facebook profiles while they were in labor—once among the most private of moments. Cell phones, with their ability to take pictures and instantly send them, provide another way to overshare: snap a nude picture of yourself to entice your crush. A recent survey found that 28% of 15- and 16-year-olds had sent a nude picture of themselves by e-mail or text—and 57% had been asked to. It's so common it even has a clever name: sexting.

GENERATION DIRECT

GenMe's openness extends to all kinds of communications at work and at home. Some older business managers complain that young people today are too blunt. These managers say that young employees ask for instant feedback that's straightforward and unapologetic, and give it in return. Some managers are surprised at young people's willingness to critique the performance of older people—it's a combination of the eroding respect for authority and the compulsive honesty of the younger generation. In a 2009 survey, GenMe'ers were much more likely than other generations to tell their manager they were looking for another job.

Young people see their directness as an asset. In one episode of the teen soap *The O.C.*, 16-year-old Seth makes a sarcastic comment, after which his father tells him, "Watch your mouth—I was trying to be polite. You might want to give it a try." Seth replies, "No, thanks, I'd rather be honest." So, to some GenMe'ers, if you're not true to yourself, and you conform to someone else's rules, you might be seen as dishonest or a victim of peer pressure—and avoiding that is more important than being polite. For GenMe "not being yourself" equates to being somehow unwhole and false. Kim, 21, says her mother worries too much about other people's opinions; her mother says Kim should be ashamed when she doesn't take care with her appearance. Kim disagrees: "She should be ashamed of herself for being fake."

One student of mine took this principle a little too far. Aaron, 22, was the kind of student a teacher dreads—well intentioned and even sweet, but unable to keep his unorthodox opinions to himself. By the end of the term, the other students were openly hostile toward him because he interrupted the class so many times. He didn't see things this way, however. "You might view me as a 'rebel without a cause,'" he wrote. "But I do have a cause. It is being true to me. When I am true to myself I feel confident and content. When I am untrue to myself I feel uneasy and fake. I have to be honest with myself as well as others." In other words, it's more important to be true to yourself than to be liked.

Overall, GenMe appreciates directness. "The older generations are so cautious and political in the way they phrase everything that half the time I don't know what they mean," said one young employee. The prevalence of texting might have something to do with this: when you're typing quickly, being blunt is easier. You also aren't there to see the immediate reaction on the other person's face. Smartphones are also one of the main offenders when bluntness gives way to rudeness—as you know if you've ever tried to have a conversation with someone who keeps looking down to text on his phone.

Even this pales in comparison to what's done anonymously online. There, comments sections are filled with statements that often cross the line from blunt to incredibly rude. Sitting in front of their computers, commenters seem to forget that they are communicating with other people, and about other people, treating others with a complete lack of respect. For example, the new term *fat-shaming* describes what happens when a celebrity is photographed showing even a little too much belly or thigh—the Internet promptly lights up with overly direct statements about how she might want to lose a few pounds.

Some don't even have to be anonymous to be cruel. Julia, 20, says, "I hate Facebook and other social networks. They have shaped my generation by making it easy to attack people and get away with it." Jimmy Kimmel now has celebrities read "mean tweets" users have posted about them, a sign of just how widespread the phenomenon has become. Others hide behind e-mail. When psychologist Bella DePaulo was publicizing her book *Singled Out*, someone e-mailed her, "I love your ideas, but with a mug like that I beg of you not to reproduce. Please remain single and consider a tubal ligation just to be safe." I don't know if this deplorable hater was GenMe—but I do think it's unlikely she would have said such a thing to DePaulo in person. Technology has in some ways made us meaner—or at least given us an anonymous venue for being so.

#$@%&*%$!

These days, saying anything you want often includes words you might not want to say in front of your grandmother. Whether you're for or against this trend, swearing is clearly just not the shocker it used to be. The relaxation of the rules against swearing mirrors the same social trend as all of the other examples here—we swear because we don't care as much about what other people think.

Sixties radicals threw around words like *motherfucker* because they knew it would shock the older generation. They were declaring their independence and showing that they didn't care if people disapproved of them. Some shock value still exists, but many young people swear now just because that's the way they talk. It proves the adage that *fuck* is the most versatile word in the English language, since it can be a noun, a verb, or an adjective. (Or even an adverb, as in Mr. Big's famous line in *Sex and the City*: "Absofuckinglutely.") The Google Books database proves the point: the word *fuck* was eight times more frequent in American books in 2008 (versus 1960), shit *three* times as frequent, and *ass* four times as frequent.

The number of four-letter words now heard regularly in movies and on television—or, actually, five- and three-letter words—has caused much public hand-wringing. Network TV began allowing *bitch* in the 1980s, and the 1990s brought the best gift late-night comedians ever got: the ability to say *ass* on TV. David Letterman liked this so much he started a segment called "big-ass ham" just so he could say *ass* over and over. Characters on HBO and in R-rated movies utter four-letter words as if they were being paid for each usage. In December 2013, the movie *The Wolf of Wall Street* set a new record for uses of f-bombs in a major motion picture: 544. People against this trend toward vulgar language often use an argument that should now sound familiar. American culture has become crude, rude, and socially unacceptable. Whatever happened to politeness and manners? Nobody cares what anyone thinks anymore. (I say @$#% them. Just kidding.)

CONFORMITY AND THE NEED FOR SOCIAL APPROVAL

Do you like to gossip sometimes? Have you ever pretended to be sick to get out of doing something? Have you ever insisted on having your own way? Before you vote, do you carefully check the qualifications of each candidate? Are you always polite? Are you always willing to admit it when you've made a mistake?

If you answered no to the first three questions and yes to the next three, you have a high need for social approval. You want other people to see you as a good person, and you place high value on conventional behavior. What other people think matters a lot to you.

You are also probably not a member of Generation Me. These questions are from a measure called the Marlowe-Crowne Social Desirability Scale. The scale measures a person's need for social approval, and people who score high on it, according to the scale authors, display "polite, acceptable behavior" and follow "conventional, even stereotyped, cultural norms." My student Charles Im and I analyzed 241 studies that gave this questionnaire to college students and children, 40,745 individuals in all.

Not surprisingly, scores on the need for social approval have slid downward since the 1950s. The average college student in 2001 scored lower than 62% of college students in 1958. Put another way, the 2001 student scored at the 38th percentile compared to his or her 1958 peers. These percentiles work just like those on standardized tests—imagine your child taking a test and scoring at the 50th percentile one time and the 38th percentile another time. You would consider her average the first time, but be fairly concerned about her slipping performance the next.

Similar results appeared on two other measures of social approval—the L and K scales of the Minnesota Multiphasic Personality Inventory. In a cross-temporal meta-analysis of 117 samples including 63,706 college students, GenMe scored lower on both scales, suggesting they were less concerned with the impression they were making and less defensive about how they would be seen. The average college student in 2007 scored lower than 79% of 1940s college students on the K scale (the 21st percentile), and 62% lower on the L scale (the 38th percentile).

I also wondered if children would show the same results—was it only college students who changed, or were kids also seeking social approval less? Sure enough, the results were similar. Children ages 9 to 12 showed rapidly decreasing needs for social approval. For example, the average 1999 GenMe fifth- or sixth-grader scored at the 24th percentile, or lower than 76% of kids in the 1960s. This is an even larger change than for the college students—you would be pretty upset if your child came home with a standardized-test score in the 24th percentile. These results suggested that the decline in social approval was pervasive: even children as young as nine showed the generational trend, with kids from GenMe scoring lower than kids from earlier generations.

The Baby Boomers began this trend. The data show that the need for social approval reached an all-time low in the late 1970s to the early 1980s. This is not that surprising—the Boomers practically invented youth rebellion in the 1960s. By the 1970s, the rebellion was mainstream, and the defiance of authority an accepted social value. Take the line yippie radical Jerry Rubin used in the late 1970s—if someone called him on the phone when he was, umm, otherwise occupied, he would say honestly, "Can't talk to you now—I'm masturbating."

The 1980s returned society to a somewhat more conventional existence. Slowly, men cut their hair (except for Ponch and Jon on *CHiPs*), pant legs went from flagrantly bell-bottom to normal (at least until bell-bottoms' resurgence around 1996), and pot smoking declined. It was not quite as necessary to rebel to fit in—which was always a rather ironic notion. GenMe turned this trend around to an extent, no longer thinking of social approval as something to be completely disdained. But the need for social approval did not even come close to the levels of the 1950s and 1960s—those days were gone forever.

A new movement dawned during the 1980s, however, a trend that GenMe would take to new heights, leaving Boomers in the dust. Generation Me believes, with a conviction that approaches boredom because it is so undisputed, that the individual comes first. It's the trend that gives the generation its name, and I explore it in the next two chapters.

2

An Army of One: *Me*

One day when my mother was driving me to school in 1986, Whitney Houston's hit song "Greatest Love of All" was warbling out of the weak speakers of our Buick station wagon with wood trim. I asked my mother what she thought the song was about. "The greatest love of all—it has to be about children," she said.

My mother was sweet, but wrong. The song does say that children are the future (always good to begin with a strikingly original thought) and that we should teach them well. About world peace, maybe? Or great literature? Nope. Children should be educated about the beauty "inside," the song declares. We all need heroes, Whitney sings, but she never found "anyone who fulfilled my needs," so she learned to depend on (wait for it) "me." The chorus then declares, "learning to love yourself is the greatest love of all."

This is a stunning reversal in attitude from previous generations. Back then, respect for others was more important than respect for yourself. The term *self-esteem* wasn't widely used until the late 1960s and didn't become talk-show and dinner-table conversation until the 1980s. By the 1990s, it was everywhere.

Take, for example, the band Offspring's rockingly irreverent 1994 riff "Self-Esteem." The song describes a guy whose girlfriend "says she wants only me . . . Then I wonder why she sleeps with my friends." (Hmmm.) But he's blasé about it—it's okay, really, since he's "just a sucker with no self-esteem."

By the mid-1990s—thus before most of today's college students were born—Offspring could take it for granted that most people knew the term *self-esteem* and knew they were supposed to have it. They also knew how to diagnose themselves when they didn't have it.

Offspring's ironic self-parody demonstrates a high level of understanding of the concept, the satire suggesting that this psychological self-examination is rote and can thus be performed with tongue planted firmly in cheek.

In the years since, attention to the topic of self-esteem has rapidly expanded. Researcher Sara Konrath found that the number of books mentioning self-esteem more than doubled between the 1940s and the 1990s. A search for *self-esteem* in the books section of amazon.com yielded 108,426 entries (sample titles: *Self-Esteem: A Proven Program of Cognitive Techniques for Assessing, Improving, and Maintaining Your Self-Esteem*, *The Self-Esteem Work Book for Teens*, *Breaking the Chain of Low Self-Esteem*, *Ten Days to Self-Esteem*, *200 Ways to Raise a Girl's Self-Esteem*). *O Magazine* published "Why Women Have Low Self-Esteem—How to Feel More Confident" in 2008, while *Parenting* offered "Proud to Be Me!" in April 2005, listing "5 simple ways to help your child love who he is." October 2011 saw the premier issue of a "self-esteem magazine for girls" called *BYOU* (Be Your Own You), telling readers of its purple and fuchsia cover to "be awesome!" and "discover your inner beauty" and find "fun ways to build self-esteem." TV and radio talk shows would immediately be shut down by the FCC if *self-esteem* were on the list of banned words. The 1998 edition of the American Academy of Pediatrics guide to caring for babies and young children used the word *self-esteem* ten times in seven pages in the first chapter, and that doesn't even count the numerous mentions of *self-respect*, *confidence*, and *belief in oneself*.

How did *self-esteem* transform from an obscure academic term to a familiar phrase that pops up in everything from women's magazines to song lyrics to celebrity interviews? The story begins centuries ago, when humans barely had a concept of a self at all: your marriage was arranged, your profession determined by your parents, your actions dictated by strict religious standards. Slowly over the centuries, social strictures began to loosen and people started to make more choices for themselves. Eventually, we arrived at the modern concept of the individual as an autonomous, free person.

Then came the 1970s, when the ascendance of the self exploded into the American consciousness. In contrast to previous ethics of honor and duty, Baby Boomer ideals focused instead on meaning and self-fulfillment. In his 1976 bestseller, *Your Erroneous Zones*, Wayne Dyer suggests that the popular song "You Are the Sunshine of My Life" be retitled "I Am the Sunshine of My Life." Your love for yourself, he says, should be your "first love." The 1970 allegory *Jonathan Livingston Seagull* describes a bird bored with going "from shore to food and back again." Instead, he wants to enjoy flying, swooping through the air to follow "a higher meaning, a higher purpose for life," even though his actions get him exiled from his flock. The book, originally rejected by nearly every major publishing house, became a runaway bestseller as Americans came to agree that life should be fulfilling and focused on the needs of the self. The seagulls in the animated movie *Finding Nemo* were still on message almost 35 years later: all that comes out of their beaks is the word *mine*.

BOOMERS AND THEIR "JOURNEY" INTO THE SELF

This book is not about Baby Boomers, and it's not about the 1970s. But because the Boomers pioneered the modern brand of self-focus, we have to understand them first so we can see how they differ from the younger Generation Me. Why aren't the Boomers—the Me Generation in the 1970s—the real Generation Me? It's about what you explore as a young adult versus what you're born to and take for granted.

For the Boomers, who grew up in the 1950s and 1960s, self-focus was a new concept, individualism an uncharted territory. In his 1981 book *New Rules: Searching for Self-Fulfillment in a World Turned Upside Down*, Daniel Yankelovich describes young Boomers struggling with new questions: How do you make decisions in a marriage with two equal partners? How do you focus on yourself when your parents don't even know what that means? The Boomers in the book sound like people driving around in circles in the dark, desperately searching for something. The world was so new that no road signs and no maps pointed the way to this new fulfillment and individuality.

That's probably why many Boomers talk about the self using abstract language full of introspection and "growth." New things call for this kind of meticulous thought and require time to process. Thus Boomers talk about "my journey," "my need to keep growing," or "my unfulfilled potentials." Sixties activist Todd Gitlin called the Boomer quest the "voyage to the interior." Icky as they are to today's young people, these phrases thrum with motion and time, portraying self-focus as a continuous project that keeps evolving as Boomers look around for true meaning. As P. J. O'Rourke puts it in *The Baby Boom*, "We're the generation that created the self, made the firmament of the self, divided the light of the self from the darkness of the self, and said let there be self. . . . Before us, self was without form and void, like our parents in their dumpy clothes and vague ideas." In a 1976 *New York* magazine article, Tom Wolfe described the "new dream" as "remaking, remodeling, elevating and polishing one's very self . . . and observing, studying, and doting on it." Sixties radical Jerry Rubin wrote that he tried just about every fad of the 1970s (Rolfing, est, yoga, sex therapy, finding his inner child); one of the chapters in his book *Growing (Up) at Thirty-Seven* is called "Searching for Myself."

Such introspection primarily surfaces today in the speech of New Agers, Rogerian therapists, and over-55 Boomers. When asked what's next in her life, Kim Basinger (born in 1953) replies, "Watching what the rest of my journey is going to be about." In answer to the same question, Sarah Ferguson, Duchess of York (born in 1959), says, "My coming to stay in America for a few months is like my blossoming into my true Sarah, into my true self. And I'm just coming to learn about her myself." Not all Boomers talk this way, but enough do that it's an immediately recognizable generational tic. It's also a guaranteed way to get a young person to roll her eyes.

In *Boomer Nation*, Steve Gillon argues that abstraction and spirituality are the primary hallmarks of the Boomer generation. Gillon describes Boomers as having a "moralistic style" and devotes a chapter to Boomers' "new fundamentalism." Whether joining traditional churches or exploring meditation or yoga, Boomers have been fascinated with the spiritual for four decades.

Even Boomers who don't adopt New Age language seek higher meaning in the new religion of consumer products—thus the yuppie revolution. In *Bobos in Paradise*, David Brooks demonstrates that upper-class Boomers have poured their wealth into such things as cooking equipment, which somehow feels more moral and meaningful than previous money sinks such as jewelry or furs. Even food becomes "a barometer of virtue," Brooks says, as 1960s values are "selectively updated . . . Gone are the sixties-era things that were fun and of interest to teenagers, like Free Love, and retained are all the things that might be of interest to middle-aged hypochondriacs, like whole grains."

The Boomers' interest in the abstract shows up in the American Freshman nationally representative survey of 9 million entering college students. In 1967, a whopping 86% of incoming college students said that "developing a meaningful philosophy of life" was an essential life goal. Only 46% of GenMe freshmen in 2012 agreed, cutting the Boomer number nearly in half. GenX started this move away from the abstract, and I'm definitely a member of my generation in this way. Despite being an academic,

I'm not sure I know what a "meaningful philosophy of life" even is. Jerry Rubin does—if you can understand him. "Instead of seeking with the expectation of finding, I experience my seeking as an end in itself," he writes. "I become one with my seeking, and merge with the moment." Okay, Jerry. Let us know when you've reentered the earth's atmosphere.

While up there, maybe Jerry met Aleta St. James, a 57-year-old woman who gave birth to twins in 2004. She explained her unusual actions by saying, "My whole world is about manifesting, so I decided to manifest children." It's not surprising that an enterprising GenMe'er put together a list of books on amazon.com titled "Tired of Baby Boomer Self-Righteousness?"

Boomers display another unique and somewhat ironic trait: a strong emphasis on group meetings. Boomers followed in the footsteps of their community-minded elders—they just joined the Weathermen instead of the Elks Lodge. This is one of the many reasons why Boomers are not the true Generation Me—almost everything they did happened in groups: Vietnam protests, marches for feminism, consciousness raising, assertiveness training, discos, and even seminars such as est. Maybe it felt safer to explore the self within a group—perhaps it felt less radical. No one seemed to catch the irony that it might be difficult to find your unique direction in a group of other people. Even Boomers' trends and sayings belied their reliance on groups: "Don't trust anyone over 30" groups people by age, as did the long hair many Boomer men adopted in the late 1960s and early 1970s to distinguish themselves from older folks. In a 1970 song, David Crosby says he decided not to cut his hair so he could "let my freak flag fly." If you've got a flag, you're probably a group. Boomers may believe they invented individualism, but like any inventor, they were followed by those who perfected the invention.

Boomers took only the first tentative steps in the direction of self-focus, rather than swallowing it whole at birth. Most Boomers never absorbed it at all and settled down early to marry and raise families. Those who adopted the ways of the self as young adults speak the language with an accent: the accent of abstraction and "journeys." They had to reinvent their way of thinking when already grown and thus see self-focus as a "process." In his book, Rubin quotes a friend who says, "We are the first generation to reincarnate ourselves in our own lifetime."

THE MATTER-OF-FACT SELF-FOCUS OF GENERATION ME

Generation Me had no need to reincarnate themselves; they were born into a world that already celebrated the individual. The self-focus that blossomed in the 1970s became mundane and commonplace over the next two decades, and GenMe accepts it like a fish accepts water. If Boomers were making their way in the uncharted world of the self, GenMe has its own GPS device—and most of the time they don't even need it, since the culture of the self is their hometown. They don't have to join groups or talk of journeys because they're already there. They don't need to "polish" the self, as Wolfe said, because they take for granted that it's already shiny. They don't need to look inward; they already know what they will find. Since they were small children, GenMe'ers were taught to put themselves first. That's just the way the world works—why dwell on it? Let's go to the mall.

GenMe's focus on the needs of the individual is not necessarily self-absorbed or isolationist; instead, it's a way of moving through the world beholden to few social rules and with the unshakable belief that you're important. It's also not the same as being spoiled, which implies that GenMe'ers always get what they want; though this does probably describe some kids, it's not the essence of the trend. (As I argue in chapter 4, GenMe's expectations are so great and reality so challenging that they will probably get less of what they want than any previous generation.) GenMe simply takes it for granted that we should all feel good about ourselves, we are all special, and we all deserve to follow our dreams. GenMe is straightforward and unapologetic about their self-focus. In *Conquering Your Quarterlife Crisis*, Jason, 25, relates how he went through some tough times and decided he needed to change things in his life. His new motto was "Do what's best for Jason. I had to make me happy; I had to do what was best for myself in every situation."

The matter-of-fact attitude of GenMe'ers appears in everyday language as well—a language that still includes the abstract concept of self, but uses it in a simple way, perhaps because they learned the language as children. They speak the language of the self as their native tongue. So much of the "commonsense" advice that's given these days includes some variation on "self":

- Worried about how to act in a social situation? "Just be yourself."
- What's the good thing about your alcoholism/drug addiction/murder conviction? "I learned a lot about myself."
- Concerned about your performance? "Believe in yourself." (Often followed by "and anything is possible.")
- Should you buy the new pair of shoes or get the nose ring? "Yes, express yourself."
- Why should you leave the unfulfilling relationship/quit the boring job/tell off your mother-in-law? "You have to respect yourself."
- Trying to get rid of a bad habit? "Be honest with yourself."
- Confused about the best time to date or get married? "You have to love yourself first before you can love someone else."
- Should you express your opinion? "Yes, stand up for yourself."

Or, as Lena Dunham's character on *Girls* puts it, managing to focus on herself without using the word *self*, "And then I am busy, trying to become who I am."

Even a brief frolic through the Google Books database shows

the incredible growth in such phrases. In American books between 1960 and 2008, *just be yourself* became 8 times more frequent, *learned about myself* 4.6 times, *believe in yourself* 6.5 times, *express yourself* 2 times, *respect yourself* 2.7 times, *be honest with yourself* 3 times, *love yourself* 5.7 times, *I love me* 6.7 times, and *stand up for yourself* 6 times. A recent study found that presidential State of the Union addresses have become more individualistic over time, with more mentions of the self (such as *I* and *me*) and fewer mentions of others and friends.

As you'll see later in chapter 7 on equality, individualism is a cultural system with many advantages. Yet recent culture seems to have crossed the line from individualism to hyperindividualism. For example, the self-focused phrases are not just individualistic—they're also, well, wrong. "Just be yourself" sounds like good advice at first, but what if you're a jerk? What if you're a serial killer? Maybe you should be someone else. "Believe in yourself" is fine, but "anything is possible"? No, it's not. Expressing yourself, respecting yourself, and being honest with yourself are somewhat tautological but not usually directly harmful. But "you have to love yourself first" has a crucial flaw: people who *really* love themselves are called narcissists, and they make horrible relationship partners.

Americans use these phrases so often that we don't even notice them anymore. Dr. Phil, the ultimate in plainspoken, no-nonsense advice, uttered both "respect yourself" and "stop lying to yourself" within seconds of each other on a *Today* show segment on New Year's resolutions. One of his bestselling books is entitled *Self Matters*. GenMe takes these phrases and ideas so much for granted that it's as if they learned them in their sleep as children, like the perfectly conditioned citizens in Aldous Huxley's *Brave New World*.

These aphorisms don't seem absurd even when, sometimes, they are. We talk about self-improvement as if the self could be given better drywall or a new coat of paint. We read self-help

THE SELF ACROSS THE GENERATIONS

Baby Boomers	Generation Me
Self-fulfillment	Fun
Journey, potentials, searching	Already there
Change the world	Follow your dreams
Protests and group sessions	Watching TV, surfing the Web, and texting
Interest in government	Interest in yourself and your friends
Spirituality	Things
Philosophy of life	Feeling good about yourself

books as if the self could receive tax-deductible donations. The *Self* even has its own magazine. Psychologist Martin Seligman says that the traditional self—responsible, hardworking, stern—has been replaced with the "California self," "a self that chooses, feels pleasure and pain, dictates action and even has things like esteem, efficacy, and confidence." Media outlets promote the self relentlessly; I was amazed at how often I heard the word *self* used in the popular media once I started looking for it.

Young people have learned these self-lessons well. Twenty-year-old Maria says her mother often reminds her to consider what other people will think. "It doesn't matter what other people think," Maria insists. "What really matters is how I perceive myself. The real person I need to please is myself."

Smart marketers have figured this out too. Ford tells us "Everything We Do Is Driven by You." Honda touts "The Power of Dreams." The Toyota Scion, marketed to young drivers, says it's "United by Individuality," promising it will help you "create a following by never following. Stand with us by standing out. Be the original, not the copy." The US Army, perhaps the last organization one might expect to focus on the individual instead of the group, followed suit. From 2001 to 2006, its standard recruiting slogan was "An Army of One."

In 2013, the *Oxford English Dictionary*'s word of the year was *selfie*, coined to describe the now-common practice of taking a picture of yourself and sharing it online with the world. By January 2014, people were competing to take the best picture of themselves in the Selfie Olympics.

Even the pronouns we use have changed: Between 1960 and 2008, American books used first-person singular pronouns (*I, me, mine, my, myself*) 42% more often, and first-person plural pronouns (we, us, our, ours, ourselves) 10% less often. The biggest change: the use of second person (you, your, yours, yourself, yourselves) quadrupled—most likely due to two interlocking, individualistic trends: authors speaking directly to readers (so you experience the book in a personal way) and the self-help genre emphasizing "*your* best life," "what *you* can do," and so on. This shows how the cultural change reaches beyond just one generation: even the language in the books we read has fundamentally changed.

CHANGES IN SELF-ESTEEM: WHAT THE DATA SAY

The data on changes in positive self-views over time mirror the social trends almost exactly. In an initial study, W. Keith Campbell and I examined the responses of 65,965 college students to the Rosenberg Self-Esteem Scale (RSE), the most popular measure of general self-esteem. I held my breath when I analyzed these data for the first time, but I needn't have worried: the change was enormous. By the mid-1990s, the average college man had higher self-esteem than 86% of college men in 1968. The average mid-1990s college woman had higher self-esteem than 71% of Boomer college women. Between the 1960s and the 1990s, college students were increasingly likely to agree that "I take a positive attitude toward myself" and "On the whole, I am satisfied with myself." That's especially interesting as GenX got a reputation for being depressed cynics;

however, they weren't depressed or cynical about their own self-confidence.

So what happened to self-esteem in the transition to GenMe in the 2000s? For her master's thesis with me, Brittany Gentile decided to find out. Among 28,918 college students, the average GenMe college student in 2008 had higher self-esteem than 63% of GenX students in 1988—and that's after the already large increase between the 1960s and the 1980s. By 2008, the most frequent self-esteem score for college students was 40—the highest possible score and thus "perfect" self-esteem.

We then turned to other data sources. The nationally representative high school survey doesn't show any change in the RSE items, probably because it mixed the self-esteem items together with those measuring hopelessness and risk-taking and changed the order of the questions several times over the years. However, it shows lots of other evidence of rising self-views. GenMe high school students anticipate being awesome employees in the future: 68% of high school students in 2012 said they would be "very good" as a worker (the highest rating), compared to only 57% of Boomer high school students in 1976. Fifty-eight percent of 2012 students believe they will be a "very good" spouse, up from 41% in 1976. Fifty-nine percent are sure they will be a "very good" parent, compared to only 38% who were that certain in 1976. And twice as many high school students in 2012 versus those in 1976 said they were "completely" satisfied with themselves (the highest possible response).

Both high school and college students are also more likely to believe they're superior to their peers. When asked to compare themselves to others their age, 61% of 2012 GenMe college students said they were above average in their leadership ability, compared to 41% of Boomer college students in 1966. Seventy-six percent thought they were superior in their drive to achieve, versus 60% in 1966. Fifty-eight percent thought they were above average in intellectual self-confidence, compared to only 39% in 1966—even though students in the 1960s earned higher SAT scores. The change wasn't due to college selectivity, either—more high school students enroll in college in the 2010s than in 1966, so the average GenMe college student is, objectively, less likely to be above average compared to others their age. GenMe high school students were also more likely to see themselves as above average: 65% of 2012 students believed they were above average in intelligence, compared to 57% in 1976. The number who described themselves as "far above average" in intelligence nearly doubled. Sixty-one percent believed they were above average in school ability, up from 56% in 1976. Yet on objective tests such as the National Assessment of Educational Progress, 12th-graders scored about the same in the 1970s and 2000s.

Children's self-esteem scores tell a different but even more intriguing story. We examined the responses of 39,353 children, most ages 9 to 13, on the Coopersmith Self-Esteem Inventory, a scale written specifically for children. During the 1970s—when the nation's children shifted from the late Baby Boom to the early years of GenX—kids' self-esteem declined, probably because of societal instability. Rampant divorce, a wobbly economy, soaring crime rates, and swinging-singles culture made the 1970s a difficult time to be a kid. The average child in 1979 scored lower than 81% of kids in the mid-1960s. Over this time, children were less likely to agree with statements like "I'm pretty sure of myself" and "I'm pretty happy" and more likely to agree that "things are all mixed up in my life." The individualism that was so enthralling for teenagers and adults in the 1970s didn't help kids—and, if their parents suddenly discovered self-fulfillment, it might even have hurt them.

But after 1980, with the later wave of GenX'ers, children's self-esteem took a sharp turn upward. More and more during the 1980s and 1990s, children were saying that they were happy with themselves. They agreed that "I'm easy to like" and "I always do the right thing." By the mid-1990s, children's self-esteem scores equaled, and often exceeded, children's scores in the markedly more stable Boomer years before 1970. The average kid in the mid-1990s—the first wave of GenMe—had higher self-esteem than 73% of kids in 1979. The rise in self-esteem only continued from there. In a later analysis of the self-esteem scores of 10,119 middle school students, 80% of GenMe in 2007 scored higher in self-esteem than their GenX counterparts in 1988.

This is a bit of a mystery, however. The United States of the 1980s to 2000s never approached the kid-friendly stability of the 1950s and early 1960s: violent crime rose, divorce was still at epidemic levels, and the economy went through several recessions. Such societal upheavals usually have a negative effect on self-esteem. So without the calm and prosperity of earlier decades, why did children's self-esteem increase so dramatically during the 1980s, 1990s, and 2000s?

THE SELF-ESTEEM CURRICULUM

The short answer is that they were taught it. The years after 1980 saw a pervasive, societywide effort to increase children's self-esteem.

The Boomers who now filled the ranks of parents apparently decided that children should always feel good about themselves, and GenX'er parents continued that trend. Research on programs to boost self-esteem first blossomed in the 1980s, and the number of psychology and education journal articles devoted to self-esteem doubled between the 1970s and the 1980s. Journal articles on self-esteem increased another 52% during the 1990s, and the number of books on self-esteem doubled over the same time. Generation Me is the first generation raised to believe that everyone should have high self-esteem.

Magazines, television talk shows, and books all emphasize the importance of high self-esteem for children, usually promoting feelings that are a lot closer to narcissism (a more negative trait usually defined as an inflated sense of self). One children's book, first published in 1991, is called *The Lovables in the Kingdom of Self-Esteem*. "I AM LOVABLE. Hi, lovable friend! My name is Mona Monkey. I live in the Kingdom of Self-Esteem along with my friends the Lovable Team," the book begins. On the next page, children learn that the gates of the kingdom will swing open if you "say these words three times with pride: I'm lovable! I'm lovable! I'm lovable!"

Another example is the *BE A WINNER Self-Esteem Coloring and Activity Book* pictured in this chapter. Inside, children find ac-

Parents are encouraged to raise their children's self-esteem even when kids are simply coloring. Even the cat has high self-esteem on this coloring book cover. However, the dog lacks a self-esteem-boosting ribbon. He probably has low self-esteem—after all, he drinks out of the toilet.

tivities and pictures designed to boost their self-esteem, including coloring a "poster for your room" that reads YOU ARE SPECIAL in yellow, orange, and red letters against a purple background. Another page asks kids to fill in the blanks: "Accept y_ur_e_f. You're a special person. Use p_si_iv_ thinking." A similar coloring book is called *We Are All Special* (though this title seems to suggest that being special isn't so special).

Remember, everyone is special. Maybe if you color the whole poster you can catch the irony.

Many school districts across the country have specific programs designed to increase children's self-esteem, most of which seem to promote self-importance and narcissism. One program is called "Self-Science: The Subject Is Me." (Why bother with biology? I'm so much more interesting!) Another program, called "Pumsy in Pursuit of Excellence," uses a dragon character to encourage children to escape the Mud Mind they experience when feeling bad about themselves. Instead, they should strive to be in the Sparkle Mind and feel good about themselves. The Magic Circle exercise designates one child a day to receive a badge saying I'M GREAT. The other children then say good things about the chosen child, who later receives a written list of all of the praise. At the end of the exercise, the child must then say something good about him- or herself. Boomer children in the 1950s and 1960s gained self-esteem naturally from a stable, child-friendly society; GenMe's self-esteem has been actively cultivated for its own sake.

One Austin, Texas, father was startled to see his 5-year-old daughter wearing a shirt that announced I'M LOVABLE AND CAPABLE. All of the kindergarteners, he learned, recited this phrase before class, and they all wore the shirt to school on Fridays. It seems the school started a bit too young, however, because the child then asked, "Daddy, all the kids are wondering, what does *capable* mean?"

After school, when kids play sports, the self-esteem emphasis continues. In most leagues, everyone gets a trophy just for playing—you sit on the bench, you get the trophy; you don't try, you get the trophy; you suck, you still get a trophy. My nephew has a large trophy engraved with EXCELLENCE IN PARTICIPATION. What does that mean—I'm good at showing up? In other leagues, everyone gets the same-size trophy no matter who wins or loses. In a widely read op-ed in the *New York Times*, Ashley Merryman reported that trophy and award sales are a $3-billion-a-year industry in the United States and Canada—even though, as she summarizes the research, "nonstop recognition does not inspire children to succeed. Instead, it can cause them to underachieve."

Some people have wondered if the self-esteem trend waned after schools began to put more emphasis on testing during the late 1990s. A quick Google search suggests that's not the case, with many schools mentioning self-esteem in their mission statements. And in 2012, my daughter Kate came home from kindergarten with a self-portrait worksheet proclaiming "I'm very happy to be me" and (worse) the same song I use in my talks to illustrate how we teach kids narcissism: "I am special / I am special / Look at me . . ." Kate now knows what (as she pronounces it) "narcissisms" is. (Her definition: "Narcissism is when you fart and then say, "I rule!")

Parenting books and magazines stress self-esteem as much as ever, and a large number of schools continue to use self-esteem programs. The mission statements of many schools explicitly announce that they aim to raise students' self-esteem. A Google search for *elementary school mission statement self-esteem* yielded 2.9 million Web pages in February 2014. These schools are located across the country, in cities, suburbs, small towns, and rural areas. "Building," "improving," "promoting," or "developing" self-esteem is a stated goal of (among many others) Monterrey Elementary School in Carlsbad, New Mexico; Memorial Elementary School in Milford, Massachusetts; James McHenry Elementary in Prince George's County, Maryland; Sechrist Elementary in Flagstaff, Arizona; Randolphville Elementary in Piscataway, New Jersey; Rockhill Elementary in Alliance, Ohio; Haynes Elementary in Lubbock, Texas; and Hume Elementary in Nelson, BC, Canada. Private religious schools are not immune: St. Francis of Assisi Catholic School in Louisville, Kentucky, aims to "help the student discover and develop a positive sense of self-esteem." Jahn World Language School in Chicago raises the bar, adding that students will "exhibit high self-esteem." So self-esteem must not just be promoted by teachers, but must actively be exhibited by students.

As John Hewitt points out in *The Myth of Self-Esteem*, the implicit message is that self-esteem can be taught and should be taught. When self-esteem programs are used, Hewitt notes, children are "encouraged to believe that it is acceptable and desirable to be preoccupied with oneself [and] praise oneself." In many cases, he says, it's not just encouraged but required. These exercises make self-importance mandatory, demanding of children that they love themselves. "The child must be taught to like himself or herself. . . . The child must take the teacher's attitude himself or herself—'I am somebody!' 'I am capable and loving!'—regardless of what the child thinks."

Most of these programs encourage children to feel good about themselves for no particular reason. In one program, teachers are told to discourage children from saying things like "I'm a good soccer player" or "I'm a good singer." This makes self-esteem contingent on performance, the program authors chide. Instead, "we want to anchor self-esteem firmly to the child . . . so that no matter what the performance might be, the self-esteem remains high." In other words, feeling good about yourself is more important than good performance. Children, the guide says, should be taught "that it is who they are, not what they do, that is important." Many programs encourage self-esteem even when things go wrong or the child does something bad. In one activity, children are asked to finish several sentences, including ones beginning "I love myself even though . . ." and "I forgive myself for . . ."

Teacher training courses often emphasize that a child's self-esteem must be preserved above all else. A sign on the wall of one university's education department says WE CHOOSE TO FEEL SPECIAL AND WORTHWHILE NO MATTER WHAT. Perhaps as a result, 60% of teachers and 69% of school counselors agree that self-esteem should be raised by "providing more unconditional validation of students based on who they are rather than how they perform or behave." Unconditional validation, to translate the educational mumbo jumbo, means feeling good about yourself no matter how you act or whether you learn anything or not. Although unconditional love from a parent has many benefits, unconditional validation of yourself may not be quite as positive. A veteran second-grade teacher in Tennessee disagrees with this practice but sees it everywhere. "We handle children much more delicately," she says. "They feel good about themselves for no reason. We've given them this cotton-candy sense of self with no basis in reality."

Although the self-esteem approach sounds as if it might be especially popular in liberal blue-state areas, it's common in red states as well, perhaps because it's similar to the ideas popularized by fundamentalist Christian churches. For example, the popular Christian children's book *You Are Special* promotes the same unconditional self-esteem emphasized in secular school programs. First published in 1997, the book notes, "The world tells kids, 'You're special if . . . you have the brains, the looks, the talent.' God tells them, 'You're special just because. No qualifications necessary.' Every child you know needs to hear this one, reassuring

Calvin knows exactly why the notion of unconditional self-esteem is so popular: it feels good and requires little work.

truth." Traditional religion, however, did have "qualifications" and rules for behavior. Adults hear this message of self-esteem as well. In an article in *Ladies' Home Journal*, Christian author Rick Warren writes, "You can believe what others say about you, or you can believe in yourself as does God, who says you are truly acceptable, lovable, valuable, and capable."

Even programs not specifically focused on self-esteem often place the utmost value on children's self-feelings. Children in some schools sing songs with lyrics like "Who I am makes a difference and all our dreams can come true" and "We are beautiful, magnificent, courageous, outrageous, and great!" Other students pen a "Me Poem" or write a mock TV commercial advertising themselves and their good qualities. The children's museum in Laramie, Wyoming, has a self-esteem exhibit where children are told to describe themselves using positive adjectives.

Parents often continue the self-esteem lessons their children have learned in school, perhaps because more children are planned and cherished. The debut of the birth control pill in the early 1960s began the trend toward wanted children, which continued in the early 1970s as abortion became legal and cultural values shifted toward children as a choice rather than a duty. In the 1950s, it was considered selfish not to have kids, but by the

1970s it was an individual decision. As a result, more and more children were born to people who really wanted to become parents. Parents were able to lavish more attention on each child as the average number of children per family shrank from four to two. This parental attention has many benefits, but it may also have resulted in a hothouse environment of specialness. Young people often say that their parents believed in building self-esteem. "My mom constantly told me how special I was," said Natalie, 19. "No matter how I did, she would tell me I was the best." Kristen, 22, said her parents had a "wonderful" way of "telling me what a great job I did and repeatedly telling me I was a very special person." The problem: "I think I am a special person" is one of the items on the Narcissistic Personality Inventory.

Popular media has also promoted this idea endlessly, offering up self-esteem as the cure for just about everything. In one episode of the family drama *7th Heaven*, one young character asks what can be done about war. The father on the show, a minister, says, "We can take a good look in the mirror, and when we see peace, that's when we'll have peace on earth." The rest of the episode features each character smiling broadly to himself or herself in the mirror. In other words, if we all just loved ourselves enough, it would put an end to war. (Not only is this tripe, but wars, if anything, are usually rooted in too much love of self, land, and nation—not too little.) But, as TV and movies have taught us, loving yourself is more important than anything else.

These efforts have had their intended impact. In *Souls in Transition*, Christian Smith concludes that the 18-to-23-year-olds he interviewed in 2008 "are as a group some of the most optimistic people we have ever encountered or listened to—at least when it comes to their own personal lives and futures." In a CBS News poll, the high school graduates of 2000 (the first wave of GenMe) were asked, "What makes you feel positive about yourself?" The most popular answer, at 33%, was the tautological "self-esteem." School performance was a distant second at 18%, with popularity third at 13%. Yet this is not surprising: saying that having self-esteem makes you feel positive about yourself—forget any actual reason—is exactly what the self-esteem programs have taught today's young generation since they were in kindergarten.

Yet when everyone wears a shirt that says I'M SPECIAL, as some of the programs encourage, it is a wide-open invitation to parody. The 1997 premier episode of MTV's animated show *Daria* features a character named Jane, who cracks, "I like having low self-esteem. It makes me feel special." Later in the episode, the teacher of a "self-esteem class" asks the students to "make a list of ten ways the world would be a sadder place if you weren't in it." "Is that if we'd never been born, or if we died suddenly and unexpectedly?" asks one of the students. Wanting to get out of the rest of the class, Daria and Jane recite the answers to the self-esteem "test": "The next time I start to feel bad about myself [I will] stand before the mirror, look myself in the eye, and say, 'You are special. No one else is like you.'"

By the time GenMe gets to college, these messages are rote. John Hewitt, who teaches at the University of Massachusetts, says his students are excited when they begin discussing self-esteem in his sociology class. But once he begins to question the validity of self-esteem, the students' faces become glum and interest wanes. Hewitt compares it to what might happen in church if a priest suddenly began questioning the existence of God. After all, we worship at the altar of self-esteem and self-focus. "When the importance of self-esteem is challenged, a major part of the contemporary American view of the world is challenged," Hewitt writes.

GIRLS ARE GREAT

It is no coincidence that the *Daria* episode parodying self-esteem programs features two girls. Feminist Gloria Steinem, who spent the 1970s and 1980s fighting for practical rights such as equal pay and maternity leave, spent the early 1990s promoting her book

Revolution from Within: A Book of Self-Esteem. In 1991, a study by the American Association of University Women (AAUW) announced that girls "lose their self-esteem on the way to adolescence." This study was covered in countless national news outlets and ignited a national conversation about teenage girls and how they feel about themselves. *Reviving Ophelia*, a bestselling book on adolescent girls, popularized this idea further, documenting the feelings of self-doubt girls experience as they move through junior high and high school. Apparently, girls' self-esteem was suffering a severe blow when they became teenagers, and we needed to do something about it.

Before long, programs such as the Girl Scouts began to focus on self-esteem through their "Girls Are Great" program. Girls could earn badges like "Being My Best" and "Understanding Yourself and Others." Amanda, 22, says that her Girl Scout troop spent a lot of time on self-esteem. "We did workshops and earned badges based around self-esteem-building projects," she says. "We learned that we could do anything we wanted, that it was good to express yourself, and being different is good." (I spent 10 years as a Girl Scout myself, but what I remember most is getting good and dirty on camping trips, which may have been more beneficial than any self-esteem program.)

In 2002, the Girl Scout Council paired with corporate sponsor Unilever to launch "Uniquely ME!"—a self-esteem program to "address the critical nationwide problem of low self-esteem among adolescent and preadolescent girls." The program includes three booklets for girls ages 8 to 14, each including exercises on "recognizing one's strengths and best attributes" and "identifying core values and personal interests."

However, there is little evidence that girls' self-esteem dives at adolescence. The AAUW study was seriously flawed, relying on unstandardized measures and exaggerating small differences. In 1999, a carefully researched, comprehensive study of sex differences in self-esteem was published in *Psychological Bulletin*, the most prestigious journal in the field. The study statistically summarized 216 previous studies on more than 97,000 people and concluded that the sex difference in self-esteem was fairly small—about 56% of men have higher self-esteem than the average woman. Exaggerating this difference might be unwise. "We may create a self-fulfilling prophecy for girls by telling them they'll have low self-esteem," said University of Wisconsin professor Janet Hyde, one of the study authors.

When Keith Campbell and I did a different analysis of 355 studies of 105,318 people, we also found that girls' self-esteem does not fall precipitously at adolescence; it just doesn't rise as fast as boys' self-esteem during the teen years. By college, the difference between men's and women's self-esteem was small. Another meta-analysis, by my former student Brenda Dolan-Pascoe, found that girls did have significantly lower appearance self-esteem, but that girls and boys scored about the same in academic self-esteem. Girls also scored higher than boys in behavior self-esteem and moral-ethical self-esteem. The achievements of adolescent girls also contradict the idea that they retreat into self-doubt: girls earn higher grades than boys at all school levels, and more earn college degrees.

In other words, adolescent girls don't have a self-esteem problem—there is no "critical nationwide problem of low self-esteem among adolescent and preadolescent girls" as the Girl Scouts claimed. But in a culture obsessed with feeling good about ourselves, even the hint of a self-esteem deficit is enough to prompt a nationwide outcry. The Girl Scout program premiered three years after the 1999 comprehensive study found a minuscule sex difference in self-esteem. Why let an overwhelming mass of data get in the way of a program that sounded good?

AN EDUCATION IN SELF-ESTEEM

There has also been a movement against "criticizing" children too much. Some schools and teachers don't correct children's mistakes, afraid that this will damage children's self-esteem. One popular method tells teachers not to correct students' spelling or grammar, arguing that kids should be "independent spellers" so they can be treated as "individuals." (Imagine reading a Web paj wyten useing that filosofy.) Teacher-education courses emphasize that creating a positive atmosphere is more important than correcting mistakes. A British teacher proposed eliminating the word *fail* from education; instead of hearing that they have failed, students should hear that they have "deferred success."

The emphasis on positive feedback to students has had another widespread effect: grade inflation. The number of "A students" has nearly doubled. Only 19% of high school graduates boasted an A average in 1976, compared to 37% of 2012 graduates. This wasn't due to improved performance, as standardized-test scores were unchanged or down. It also wasn't due to increased study time—21% of 2012 high school seniors said they studied 10 or more hours a week, compared to 23% in 1976. Entering college students show the same trend: 50% graduated high school with an A average, compared to only 19% in 1966. "Each year we think [the number with an A average] can't inflate any more. And then it does again. The C grade is almost a thing of the past," noted Alexander Astin, the former head of the American Freshman study. College students report studying for fewer hours in recent years: only 38% of American college freshmen in 2012 reported studying six or more hours a week during their last year of high school, compared to 47% in 1987. So why are they still getting better grades? "Teachers want to raise the self-esteem and feel-good attitudes of students," explains Howard Everson of the College Board. We have become a Lake Wobegon nation: all of our children are above average.

Many Generation Me students would instead believe that their substandard work deserved an A. Trudeau's comment on grade inflation in the service of self-esteem mirrors the views of many psychologists and education experts critical of the self-esteem movement.

The results of these policies have played out in schools around the country. Emily, 8, came home from school one day proud that she got half of the words right on her spelling test (in other words, a grade of 50). When her mother pointed out that this wasn't good, Emily replied that her teacher had said it was just fine. At 11-year-old Kayla's school near Dallas, Texas, she was invited to the math-class pizza party as a reward for making a good grade,

even though she had managed only a barely passing 71. The pizza parties used to be only for children who made A's, but in recent years the school has invited every child who simply passed.

As education professor Maureen Stout notes, many educational psychologists believe that schools should be "places in which children are insulated from the outside world and emotionally—not intellectually—nourished. . . . My colleagues always referred to the importance of making kids feel good about themselves but rarely, if ever, spoke of achievement, ideals, goals, character, or decency." The future teachers whom Stout was educating believed that "children shouldn't be challenged to try things that others in the class are not ready for, since that would promote competition, and competition is bad for self-esteem. Second, grading should be avoided if at all possible, but, if absolutely necessary, should be done in a way that avoids any indication that Johnny is anything less than a stellar pupil."

Grade inflation and lack of competition may be backfiring: in 2012, 38% of college freshmen reported that they were frequently bored in class during their last year of high school, up from 29% in 1985. This is not surprising: How interesting could school possibly be when there's little reward for stellar performance? If one-third of the students are getting A's, why put in the extra effort to be in the top 5 or 10%?

This emphasis on praise may be one reason why teachers and managers are noticing that GenMe has a difficult time with criticism. Employers, get ready for a group of easily hurt young workers. I've learned not to discuss test items that the majority of students missed, as this invariably leads to lots of whiny defensiveness and little actual learning. The two trends are definitely related: research shows that when people with high self-esteem are criticized, they became unfriendly, rude, and uncooperative, even toward people who had nothing to do with the criticism. Stephen Lippman quotes an e-mail from a college student who was upset that he couldn't take a class because he had not satisfied a prerequisite. "Do you really think it is absolutely necessary to require the completion of Soc151 to remain in this class? You're not teaching Finance 400, buddy. You teach Women's Studies. . . . But I guess if requiring the completion of a prereq makes you or the class you teach seem more important, then go ahead." The end of this e-mail is especially fascinating, as the student assumes the professor has the same motivation he apparently does: to "seem more important." This echoes a student I overheard recently on campus: "I think he makes the tests hard so he can feel smart."

Students also expect A's—or else. When I gave one student an A- on her class presentation, she immediately went to rate myprofessors.com and posted the comment "worst professor I've ever had!" Another, who received an A- in the class, wrote a long e-mail beginning, "I believe that I deserve an A in the course. I was marked down for things on both my paper and my presentation that I do not feel I should have been." She demanded that we meet in person to discuss changing her grade. After much back-and-forth about the university grade-change policy, I replied that I would not change the grade, but would be happy to provide further feedback on her paper. After writing back 12 previous times, she never replied to that offer. (And this was four years after the first edition of *Generation Me* was published—students clearly don't get the irony.)

I'm not alone. Lippman quotes an e-mail from an undergraduate unhappy with the B+ she received: "To me, if a student does/hands in all assignments, misses class no more than two times, participates during lecture, takes notes, attentively watches videos, and obviously observes/notes sociology in his/her life," she wrote, "it would make sense for that student to receive a respectable grade—an A." Notice that good performance is never mentioned—instead, the student is asking for an A for showing up. She has company—in a 2008 survey, 66% of college students agreed that "if I have explained to my professor that I am trying hard, I think he/she should give me some consideration with respect to my course grade." One-third agreed that "if I have attended most classes for a course, I deserve at least a grade of B." Thirty percent said "professors who won't let me take an exam at a different time because of my personal plans (e.g., a vacation or other trip that is important to me) are too strict," and 32% complained that "teachers often give me lower grades than I deserve on paper assignments." A LexisNexis search of print media shows a sixfold increase from 1996 to 2006 in the joint appearance of the terms *sense of entitlement* and *students*.

None of this should surprise us. Students "look and act like what the [self-esteem] theories say they should look and act like," notes Hewitt. "They tend to act as though they believe they have worthy and good inner essences, regardless of what people say or how they behave, that they deserve recognition and attention from others, and their unique individual needs should be considered first and foremost." This is exactly what has happened: GenMe'ers take for granted that the self comes first and often believe exactly what they were so carefully taught—that they're special.

When *Time* magazine labeled Millennials the "Me Me Me generation," one of the most common reactions was, in sum, "But we are awesome!" A *USA Today* article concluded, "Guess what? Twentysomethings aren't apologizing. They say it's a good thing." Matt Prince, 29, said, "I think it's true what they're saying—I just don't think it's as negative as it initially sounds. Our generation is so successful, there's a feeling of 'You know what? I do deserve this and should be able to do something to make me happy.'"

SELF-ESTEEM AND PERFORMANCE

But this must have an upside; surely kids who have high self-esteem go on to make better grades and achieve more in school. Actually, they don't. There is a small correlation between self-esteem and grades. However, self-esteem does not cause high grades—instead, high grades cause higher self-esteem. So self-esteem programs clearly put the cart before the horse in trying to increase self-esteem. Even much of the small link from high grades to high self-esteem can be explained by other factors such as income: rich kids, for example, have higher self-esteem and get better grades, but that's because coming from an affluent home causes both of these things, and not because they cause each other. This resembles the horse and the cart being towed on a flatbed truck—neither the cart nor the horse is causing the motion in the other even though they are moving together. As self-esteem programs aren't going to make all kids rich, they won't raise self-esteem this way either.

Here's an example that illustrates this finding. Which ethnic group in the United States has the lowest self-esteem? It's Asian Americans, and Asian American young people have the highest academic performance of any ethic group. Asian American adults have the lowest unemployment rate and the highest median income. Instead of focusing on self-esteem, Asian cultures tend to emphasize hard work—probably the reason their performance is better. This strongly suggests that the modern American idea that self-belief is crucial for success is not correct.

Yet try convincing GenMe of this. When I first began giving talks to undergraduates suggesting that their generation was more self-confident, even more narcissistic, than their predecessors, I was afraid they wouldn't buy it. Instead, their reaction was a collective shrug—yeah, we know, they would say. But when I told them that self-esteem does not cause success, suddenly they were skeptical. It was as if I'd told them the world was flat. In one classroom at Southern Connecticut State University, one young woman said, "At the end of the day I love me and I don't think that's wrong. I don't think it's a problem, having most people love themselves. I love me." Another said, "I am a narcissist—and that helps me succeed. I'm interviewing for jobs right now, and it helps me stand out."

Except it doesn't. Narcissists are not any more successful, beautiful, or intelligent than anyone else—they just think they are. Inflated self-belief, in the end, is a bust.

Nor does high self-esteem protect against teen pregnancy, juvenile delinquency, alcoholism, drug abuse, or chronic welfare dependency. Several comprehensive reviews of the research literature by different authors have all concluded that self-esteem doesn't cause much of anything. Even the book sponsored by the California Task Force to Promote Self-Esteem and Personal and Social Responsibility, which spent a quarter of a million dollars trying to raise Californians' self-esteem, found that self-esteem doesn't cause academic achievement, good behavior, or any other outcome the Task Force was formed to address.

Perhaps this emphasis on individualism and uniqueness has other benefits, though—say, in more creativity. However, Kyung Hee Kim of the College of William & Mary found that the opposite was the case—younger generations are actually significantly less creative. Drawing from 272,599 children, teens, and adults who completed the Torrance Tests of Creative Thinking, the standard objective measure of creativity, she found that creative-thinking scores declined between 1966 and 2008, and especially since 1990. She concluded, "Over the last 30 years, (1) people of all ages, kindergarteners through adults, have been steadily losing their ability to elaborate upon ideas and detailed and reflective thinking; (2) people are less motivated to be creative; and (3) creativity is less encouraged by home, school, and society overall." How can this be when uniqueness is emphasized so much? Perhaps people want to be unique, but cannot translate that desire into actual creative thinking. Kim points to the increased emphasis on standardized testing and the increased use of "electronic entertainment devices" as possible causes for the decline in creativity.

ARE SELF-ESTEEM PROGRAMS GOOD OR BAD?

Psychologist Martin Seligman has criticized self-esteem programs as empty and shortsighted. He argues that self-esteem based on nothing does not serve children well in the long run; it's better, he says, for children to develop skills and feel good about accomplishing something. Roy F. Baumeister, the lead author of an extensive review of the research on self-esteem, found that self-esteem does not lead to better grades, improved work performance, decreased violence, or less cheating. In fact, people with high self-esteem are often more violent and more likely to cheat. "It is very questionable whether [the few benefits] justify the effort and expense that schools, parents and therapists have put into raising self-esteem," Baumeister writes. "After all these years, I'm sorry to say, my recommendation is this: forget about self-esteem and concentrate more on self-control and self-discipline."

Self-esteem is an outcome, not a cause. It doesn't do much good to encourage a child to feel good about himself just to feel good; this doesn't mean anything. Children develop true self-esteem from behaving well and accomplishing things. "What the self-esteem movement really says to students is that their achievement is not important and their minds are not worth developing," writes Maureen Stout. It's clearly better for children to value learning rather than simply feeling good.

So should kids feel bad about themselves if they're not good at school or sports? No. They should feel bad if they didn't work hard and try. Even if they don't succeed, sometimes negative feelings can be a motivator. Trying something challenging and learning from the experience is better than feeling good about oneself for no reason. It's also important not to confuse self-esteem or overconfidence with self-efficacy, the belief that you can do something. That's very different from simply thinking you're great. Self-efficacy is more external—it's about trying something and seizing opportunities—and, unlike self-esteem, it is actually linked to success.

Also, everyone can do something well. Kids who are not athletic or who struggle with school might have another talent, such as music or art. Almost all children can take pride in being a good friend or helping someone. Kids can do many things to feel good about themselves, so self-esteem can be based on something. If a child feels great about himself even when he does nothing, why do anything? Self-esteem without basis encourages laziness rather than hard work. On the other hand, we shouldn't go too far and hinge our self-worth entirely on one external goal, such as getting good grades. As psychologist Jennifer Crocker documents, the seesaw of self-esteem this produces can lead to poor physical and mental health. A happy medium is what's called for here: don't feel that you are a complete failure because of one bad grade—just don't feel good about yourself if you didn't even study. Use your negative feelings as a motivator to do better next time. True self-confidence comes from honing your talents and learning things, not from being told you're great just because you exist.

Don Forsyth and his colleagues decided to directly test the effects of self-esteem boosting. College students who made low grades on their first exam in a psychology class were randomly assigned to receive study tips (the control group) or study tips plus a self-esteem boost such as "Hold your head—and your self-esteem—high" (the experimental group). So did the self-esteem boost help their performance on the final exam? No, it actually hurt their performance—the self-esteem-boosting group scored significantly lower on the final than the control group. They did excel in one area, however: they were more likely to say they felt "good about myself as a student in Psychology 101."

The practice of not correcting mistakes, avoiding letter grades, and discouraging competition is also misguided. Competition can help make learning fun; as Stout points out, look at how the disabled kids in the Special Olympics benefit from competing. Many schools now don't publish the honor roll of children who do well in school and generally downplay grades because, they falsely believe, competition isn't good for self-esteem (as some kids won't make the honor roll, and some kids will make C's). But can you imagine not publishing the scores of a basketball game because it might not be good for the losing team's self-esteem? Can you imagine not keeping score in the game? What fun would that be? The self-esteem movement, Stout argues, is popular because it is sweetly addictive: teachers don't have to criticize, kids don't have to be criticized, and everyone goes home feeling happy. The problem is they also go home with an unrealistically inflated sense of self.

Kids who don't excel in a certain area should still be encouraged to keep trying. This isn't self-esteem, however: it's self-control. Self-control, or the ability to persevere and keep going, is a much better predictor of life outcomes than self-esteem. Children high in self-control make better grades and finish more years of education, and they're less likely to use drugs or have a teenage pregnancy. Self-control predicts all of those things researchers had hoped self-esteem would, but hasn't.

Cross-cultural studies provide a good example of the benefits of self-control over self-esteem. When Asian students find out they did badly on something, they want to keep working on it so they can improve their performance. White American students, in contrast, prefer to give up and work on something else, preserving their self-esteem at the expense of doing better at a difficult task. This goes a long way toward explaining why Asian children perform better at math and at school in general.

Young people who have high self-esteem built on shaky foundations might run into trouble when they encounter the harsh realities of the real world. Kids who are given meaningless A's and promoted when they haven't learned the material will later find out in college or the working world that they don't know much at all. What will that do to their self-esteem, or, more important, their careers? Your boss isn't going to care much about preserving your high self-esteem. The self-esteem emphasis leaves kids ill prepared for the inevitable criticism and occasional failure that is real life. "There is no self-esteem movement in the work world," points out one father. "If you present a bad report at the office, your boss isn't going to say, 'Hey, I like the color paper you chose.' Setting kids up like this is doing them a tremendous disservice."

In any educational program, one has to consider the trade-off between benefit and risk. Valuing self-esteem over learning and accomplishment is clearly harmful, as children feel great about themselves but are cheated out of the education they need to succeed. Self-esteem programs might benefit the small minority of kids who really do feel worthless, but those kids are likely to have bigger problems that self-esteem boosting won't fix. The risk in these programs is in inflating the self-concept of children who already think the world revolves around them. Building up the self-esteem and importance of kids who are already egocentric can bring trouble, as it can lead to narcissism—and maybe it already has.

CHANGES IN NARCISSISM

Narcissism is the darker side of overly positive self-views. Narcissists are overconfident, not just confident, and are so focused on themselves they have a difficult time taking someone else's perspective. They also feel entitled to special privileges and believe that they are superior to other people. As a result, narcissists are bad relationship partners and can be difficult to work with. Narcissists are also more likely to be hostile, take too many risks, compromise their health, and fight with friends and family.

Unlike those merely high in self-esteem, narcissists admit that they don't feel close to other people. At its extreme, narcissism can become narcissistic personality disorder (NPD), but there's plenty of variation in narcissism in the normal population—it's usually referred to as narcissistic personality traits. (There's more on narcissism in my book coauthored with W. Keith Campbell, *The Narcissism Epidemic*.)

There were some early indications that narcissism might be on the rise. In the early 1950s, only 12% of teens aged 14 to 16 agreed that "I am an important person." By the late 1980s, an incredible 80%—almost seven times as many—claimed they were important. In another study, psychologist Harrison Gough found consistent increases on narcissism items among college students quizzed between the 1960s and the 1990s. The 1990s students were more likely to agree that "I would be willing to describe myself as a pretty 'strong' personality" and "I have often met people who were supposed to be experts who were no better than I." In other words, those other people don't know what they're talking about, so everyone should listen to me.

Narcissistic personality is usually measured with the Narcissistic Personality Inventory (NPI). The scale features statements such as: "I think I am a special person," "I can live my life any way I want to," and "If I ruled the world, it would be a better place." When I give this questionnaire in class, the discussion almost always begins the same way: the first person to raise his hand will say, "Well, I scored high, and I think . . ." (Clearly the scale does its job well.) The NPI is not a measure of clinically diagnosed narcissism—instead it measures narcissism among the normal population. It is by far the most commonly used measure of narcissistic personality, so almost everything researchers know about narcissism is based on the NPI.

My coauthors and I analyzed the responses of 49,818 American college students who completed the NPI between 1982 and 2009. The trend was clear: younger generations were significantly more narcissistic. The average college student in 2009 scored higher in narcissism than 65% of students in 1982. Only 19% of students (about 1 out of 5) answered the majority of the questions in the narcissistic direction in the early 1980s, compared to 30% (about 1 out of 3) in 2009. That last statistic is telling: the majority of college students are not highly narcissistic, but 58% more are. They're the ones who end up in your office.

College students' narcissism also increased in samples of 4,152 students from the University of South Alabama between 1994 and 2009, and among students from Frostburg State University between the 1980s and 2008. A 2009 study found that Americans in their 20s were three times more likely than those in their 60s to have suffered from NPD (a clinical level of narcissism) during their lifetime.

Soon after our initial study on increases in narcissism was released, a set of other researchers reported they found no increase in their dataset of students from University of California samples, a result that garnered widespread press. In the end, though, their samples showed the same increase we found in our nationwide study. Why? All of their 1980s and 1990s samples were from one campus (UC Berkeley), and all of their 2000s samples were from another (UC Davis, where students score particularly low on the NPI). That meant it was impossible to tell whether generation or campus was causing any difference or lack thereof. The UC campuses had also seen significant shifts in ethnic composition since the 1980s, with many more Latino and Asian American students (both groups tend to score low in narcissism). My coauthor Joshua Foster asked these researchers to send their data so we could look at NPI scores within campus and within ethnic group to eliminate the confounds. When I opened the Excel file, my jaw dropped: the UC Davis's students' scores rose steadily every year. The yearly increase among these students was twice as large as the yearly increase we found in our nationwide analysis.

Another paper by different authors noted that when our nationwide data were combined with the UC campus data, there was no change in narcissism. Of course—because the UC Davis samples score low in narcissism, and they were two-thirds of the recent data. When we added a simple control for campus (1 = UC Davis, 0 = not), narcissism increased at the same pace as always. Josh and I published this analysis the same month the other paper appeared, disproving its conclusions the moment it was published in January 2010. (Yet years later, some—such as Elspeth Reeve in *Atlantic Wire* in May 2013—still cited it as seeming proof that narcissism hasn't actually increased). Even more incredibly, this paper then went on to say that age was more important to narcissism than generation, but since all of the respondents in our study were the same age, this makes no sense. It also reported data from a one-time study showing that college students were more narcissistic than their parents and grandparents—but of course that could be due to either age or generation. It could actually be more evidence that narcissism is higher in GenMe.

High school students have not routinely been given the NPI, but we examined data on students' life goals, as these are reliably correlated with narcissism. Between 1976 and 2012, high school students in the nationally representative sample were more likely to focus on life goals centered on money, fame, and image—those correlated with narcissism such as "making lots of money." They became less likely to focus on goals around community feeling and deeper meaning, such as "finding meaning and purpose in life" and "working to correct social and economic inequalities." The same was true for college students. In 2013, 82% of college students said "being very well-off financially" was important, the highest percentage in the history of the survey since it began in 1966. In that year, only 42% of college students said being well-off financially was important.

Another item is more subtle. In the late 1970s, 22% of high school students said "being a leader in my community" was important, which rose to 48% in 2012. Aha, some have thought, that means GenMe/Millennials are focused on their communities. But it's not clear what this item means—are students interested in being leaders, helping the community, or both? The item needed to be validated against established questionnaires that could separate these two possible interpretations. So my coauthors and I had 181 college students complete the NPI and rate the life goals. "Being a leader in my community" had the highest correlation with narcissism of any item. The students who embraced this life goal were clearly focusing on the "leader" part of this statement, not the "community" part. It's not about helping others—it's about being a leader, something narcissists love unconditionally. Overall, life goals related to narcissism were valued more in recent years, while those related to more intrinsic values (such as affiliation and community feeling) were valued less.

Thus, the generation William Strauss and Neil Howe call the Millennials is not as other-focused and group-oriented as their theory predicts. Strauss and Howe define this group as those born in 1982 and afterward, so college-student samples were made up almost exclusively of Millennials by 2004. However, the 2004–9 college students are the most narcissistic group of all—the most likely to agree that "I find it easy to manipulate people," "I expect a great deal from other people," and "I insist upon getting the respect that is due me." Even after the recession of the late 2000s, the 2013 students were more focused on becoming rich than any group before them. By most indications, the Millennials are the most narcissistic generation in history. This may change with the effects of the late 2000s recession in the second wave of Millennials/GenMe, but the first wave produced all-time highs in narcissism and its correlates.

Even so, the rise in narcissism goes beyond just one generation to pervade the culture. Reality shows glamorize narcissistic people and behaviors. Regular people take numerous selfies a day or compete to have the most followers on Twitter. Nearly twice as many Americans got plastic surgery in 2012 compared to 1997.

Even song lyrics show the trend. My colleague Nathan DeWall was struck by the lyrics of a Weezer song: "I'm the greatest man that ever lived." "Who would actually sing that aloud?" Nathan wondered, and is that type of self-aggrandizement now more common in our culture? Nathan and his graduate student Richard Pond gathered the lyrics of the *Billboard* Top 10 hit songs from 1980 to 2007 and fed them into a word-analysis program. They found the same pattern we did for language use in books: More use of *I* and *me*, and less of *we* and *us*. The use of social words such as *love* and *sweet* decreased, and the use of antisocial words such as *kill* and *hate* increased. Even in a cursory read of the lyrics the trends stand out—most of the early 1980s songs are about love and togetherness, while the songs of the mid-2000s feature scenes such as Carrie Underwood smashing her ex-boyfriend's car so he'll think twice "Before He Cheats" and Justin Timberlake single-handedly bringing "Sexy Back." Nathan concluded that popular song lyrics indicate increased narcissism in American culture.

Almost every example of narcissistic song lyrics pales in comparison to Kanye West's 2013 declaration "I am a god," the title of a song he wrote after he was told he couldn't attend a Paris fashion show. "'Cause it's like, 'Yo! Nobody can tell me where I can and can't go. Man, I'm the number one living and breathing rock star,'" he said in an interview. "I am Axl Rose; I am Jim Morrison; I am Jimi Hendrix." Sample lyrics from the song: "I am a god / Hurry up with my damn massage / . . . Get the Porsche out the damn garage."

Narcissism is the darker side of the focus on the self and is often confused with self-esteem. Self-esteem is usually based on solid relationships with others, whereas narcissism comes from believing that you are special and more important than other people. Many of the school programs designed to raise self-esteem probably raise narcissism instead. Lilian Katz, a professor of early-childhood education at the University of Illinois, wrote an article titled "All About Me: Are We Developing Our Children's Self-Esteem or Their Narcissism?" She writes, "Many of the practices advocated in pursuit of [high self-esteem] may instead inadvertently develop narcissism in the form of excessive preoccupation with oneself." Because the school programs emphasize being "special" rather than encouraging friendships, we may be training an army of little narcissists instead of raising kids' self-esteem. The title of teen-advice columnist Josh Shipp's book is telling: *The Teen's Guide to World Domination: Advice on Life, Liberty, and the Pursuit of Awesomeness*. He clearly knows how to meet today's teens where they live, telling them how to avoid the "seven villains . . . keeping you from awesomeness."

The teenage years have always been a time of self-centeredness. But because the studies on narcissism compare different generations at the same age, the differences are due to change over time and not to just being a teen. Generation Me'ers might decrease in narcissism as they get older, but they're starting from a higher level than GenX'ers or Boomers did.

Many young people also display entitlement, a facet of narcissism—the belief that you deserve more than others. A scale that measures entitlement has items like "Things should go my way," "I demand the best because I'm worth it," and (my favorite) "If I were on the *Titanic*, I would deserve to be on the first lifeboat!" An

Associated Press article printed in hundreds of news outlets labeled GenMe "The Entitlement Generation." In the article, employers complained that young employees expected too much too soon and had high expectations for salary and promotions. In recent years, many in GenMe have expected their parents to pay their rent. Yes, times are tough and rents are high, but many see this expectation for support well into adulthood as a sign of entitlement—even some GenMe'ers themselves. It's no coincidence that Lena Dunham, 25 at the time, centered the first episode of her HBO series *Girls* around Hannah's parents cutting off their financial support. They are not rich, her parents explain, and after all, she's been out of college for two years and is 24 years old. Her response: "I could be a drug addict. Do you realize how lucky you are?" At the end of the episode, she takes the $20 tip her parents left for the hotel maid.

If narcissism has increased, how would young people behave? In short, they would be less giving (for example, to charity), have inflated expectations, display less empathy, have higher materialism, make more unique choices (such as for baby names), cheat more often, have less committed relationships, undergo more plastic surgery, and display more anger and aggression. As we'll explore elsewhere in the book, almost all of these have occurred. GenMe's higher narcissism is not simply a curiosity based on survey measurements. Scores on the NPI consistently predict many of the behaviors that are more common among this generation than among their predecessors.

But, some have wondered, if GenMe is so narcissistic, why are teen pregnancy, car accidents, and crime on the decline? The first two are easy: teen pregnancy and car accidents are not correlated with narcissism, so those trends are not particularly relevant. The decline in crime is caused by many factors, such as demographic shifts, better policing, the virtual disappearance of crack cocaine, the number of offenders in prison, economic shifts, and even the legalization of abortion in 1973 (economist Steven Levitt's theory).

Although the crime rate has declined, the number of mass,

attention-getting shootings has increased. The idea that someone can become famous by going to a public place and killing others is a recent notion. The shooter at Virginia Tech paused in his rampage to mail his media package to *NBC News*; in it, he compared himself to Jesus. Eric Harris, one of the Columbine shooters, said, "Isn't it fun to get the respect we're going to deserve?" (Chillingly similar to the narcissism item "I insist upon getting the respect that is due me.") The 22-year-old who killed six people near UC Santa Barbara in May 2014 talked about his vendetta on YouTube and left a 137-page manifesto describing how angry he was that the world—particularly women—did not pay him the attention he deserved. "This is the story of my entire life," he wrote. "In this magnificent story, I will disclose every single detail about my life, every single significant experience that I have pulled from my superior memory."

Less severe, though still hurtful, is the incredible amount of anger and cruelty displayed online. Singer Lorde casually mentioned that she didn't think the boys in the band One Direction were particularly attractive. The band's fans then took to Twitter to insult Lorde and her boyfriend, writing gems such as "how can lorde call one direction ugly, has she seen her boyfriend, hoe" and "Omg is it just me or does Lorde's boyfriend look like one of those awkward chinese people." Recent years have seen several well-publicized cases of teens who were relentlessly bullied online and then went on to kill themselves. Bullying is aggression too, as it hurts someone. Aggression can take many forms, and although this generation is thankfully less likely to commit serious crimes, other forms of aggression appear to be alive and well.

CARING AND CONCERN FOR OTHERS

High narcissism usually means less caring, so we analyzed 24 items that the Monitoring the Future high school study administrators identified as measuring concern for others. When the studies on increasing narcissism are covered in the press, someone will invariably respond that GenMe/Millennials are actually more committed to helping others than previous generations. "We are a socially conscious generation that cares about making an impact. Young people say they want to give back. Volunteer rates are up, and so are applications for service-oriented careers like Teach For America," said Hannah Seligson in *Forbes*. "So how does all of this square with the theory that we are all narcissists? It doesn't."

How does this square with the data from large, nationally representative surveys? GenMe'ers were *less* concerned for others than Boomers or GenX'ers were at the same age—fewer donated to charities, fewer were willing to change their actions to help others, fewer expressed empathy for other groups, and fewer wanted a job "directly helpful to others." For example, 22% of Boomers in the late 1970s said they had already contributed money to "charities to help fight diseases (cancer, heart disease, etc.)," compared to only 14% of GenMe in 2010–12. Forty percent of Boomers in 1976–78 said they would be "willing to eat less meat and more grains and vegetables, if it would help provide food for starving people," compared to 33% of GenMe in 2010–12. Eleven percent of Boomers took the easy way out in 1976–78 by agreeing that "maybe some minority groups do get unfair treatment, but that's no business of mine," which jumped to 17% in 2010–12. Even when compared to GenX in the 1990s, GenMe was lower in concern for others in the 2010s. These are not large declines, but they run directly counter to the narrative, such as that mentioned by Seligson, that GenMe/Millennials are instead more altruistic than previous generations.

Seligson is correct that volunteering and community service rose between GenX and GenMe. However, community service was increasingly required for high school graduation over this period. This, the only concern-for-others item that increased significantly, is also the only one with an outside explanation. The rise in volunteering is one reason that the popular perception of Millennials as socially conscious altruists has continued despite other evidence to the contrary. However, Boomer teachers and administrators required Millennials to perform community service—a kind of "involuntary volunteering." It was not their idea. They may have learned from it, and it may be a good experience, but the impulse did not originate with them.

Does this mean that no one in this generation wants to help others? Of course not. Many do—but slightly fewer than when Boomers and GenX'ers were the same age. And—another flaw in Seligson's argument—the studies do not find that "all" GenMe'ers are narcissists, simply that the average level is higher now than it once was.

What about the increase in Teach For America applications? It might not be a coincidence that applications increased just as the late 2000s recession hit and unemployment, especially for young college graduates, skyrocketed. Since the program has only been around for a decade, it's not possible to make a generational comparison with GenX or Boomers. The closest we can get is to compare the percentage of Boomers interested in the Peace Corps and GenMe interested in the Peace Corps or AmeriCorps in the college student survey, and GenMe's interest was lower. As we'll explore in chapter 8 on the workplace, GenMe's desire for jobs that are helpful to others or that contribute to society is no higher than Boomers' or GenX'ers' was at the same age.

Declining concern for others appears in the larger culture as well—specifically, in a large analysis of language from the Google Books database. Psychologists Pelin and Selin Kesebir found that the use of words describing moral virtues, such as *decency*, *honesty*, *patience*, and *compassion*, declined significantly in American books over time. UCLA psychologist Patricia Greenfield found that the use of individualistic words such as *choose*, *get*, *feel*, and *unique* increased, while communal words such as *obliged*, *give*, *act*, *obedience*, *authority*, and *belong* decreased. The increase in *get* and decline in *give* is a neat summary of the cultural changes of the last few decades.

Among the 18-to-23-year-olds interviewed by Christian Smith, few were interested in volunteering or giving to charity. "They are so focused on their own personal lives, especially on trying to stand on their own two feet, that they seem incapable of thinking more broadly about community involvement, good citizenship, or even very modest levels of charitable giving," Smith concludes. One of his young interviewees said, "Somebody needs to give money to *me*!" Another commented about volunteering, "I actually don't have the time for it. I feel like if I'm going to do something good for the community, I might as well do something good that I get paid for too. I mean like, uh-huh, but I don't have a lot of time."

The good news is that 72% of 2013 college students said that "helping others in difficulty" was important, about the same as the 70% of Boomers who thought this goal important in 1966 and more than the 62% who endorsed this goal in 2000. In addition, high school students expressed more concern for others during the recession years of 2008 to 2010, compared to those in 2004 to 2006. However, concern for others did not return to the higher levels of the 1970s. Compared to earlier generations, the overall GenMe profile is higher positive self-views and extrinsic goals and slightly lower communal and altruistic goals. With "becoming very well-off financially" and "helping others in difficulty" both ranked as highly important, some in GenMe may be following a "rich philanthropist" model.

Sara Konrath and her colleagues used the cross-temporal meta-analysis technique to examine another important aspect of concern for others: empathy, or the ability to identify with others' emotions and experiences. Among 13,737 college students who filled out the empathy questionnaire between 1979 and 2009, empathic concern and perspective-taking declined precipitously. By 2009, 75% of college students scored lower in empathy than the average 1979 student. In another over-time study, Lori Malahy and her colleagues examined scores on a scale measuring the belief in a just world, or that people get what they deserve (for example, agreeing that "people who meet with misfortune have often brought it on themselves"). They found that 75% of 2006 college students scored higher in belief in a just world than the average 1970s student.

Konrath's and Malahy's data strongly suggest that the idea of GenMe/Millennials as "the empathetic generation" or "Generation We" (promoted by Jeffrey Arnett, Eric Greenberg, and others) is not accurate. But what about GenMe's tolerance and belief in equality—doesn't that mean they understand others better? GenMe is indeed tolerant and accepting of equality based on gender, race, and sexual orientation—much more than Boomers and GenX'ers were when they were young. That's the focus of chapter 7. However, egalitarianism and empathy are two different things. Disregarding race, gender, or sexual orientation is not the same as feeling compassion for someone else's experience.

The case of two freshman roommates at Rutgers University illustrates this principle. Dharun Ravi thought it would be fun to use his webcam to live-stream his roommate Tyler Clementi's sexual encounter. When the opportunity presented itself a second time, he tweeted his friends, "It's happening again! Yay!"—so they could join him in watching Clementi make out with another man. Clementi, gay and struggling with his identity, was devastated. A few days later, he jumped off the George Washington Bridge to his death. Ravi was eventually convicted of 15 criminal counts including invasion of privacy and bias intimidation.

By all accounts, Ravi was not particularly homophobic; he sent Clementi a text saying, "I've known you were gay and I have no problem with it." But he did think that live-streaming Clementi's sexual encounter with another man was funny. Ravi was clearly not thinking about the effect this so-called prank would have on his roommate. Instead, he was focused on entertaining himself and his friends at Clementi's expense. The idea that everyone is equal didn't work out well: Ravi didn't seem to realize that Clementi's homosexuality made him more vulnerable. If he'd been truly empathetic and taken Clementi's perspective, things might have turned out very differently. Tolerance is not enough.

GenMe's belief in equality is one of this generation's greatest strengths, but it does not always mean GenMe'ers are good at empathizing. That's a different skill, and one that may not come easily in our self-focused culture.

LOOK AT ME! LOOK AT ME! I'M ON FACEBOOK!

When I describe the rise in narcissism, the most common question—actually more of a statement—I hear is "It's because of Facebook, right?"

Maybe, but maybe not. The rise in narcissism began long before Facebook, or even the Internet, existed. But some of the rise in recent years may be due to Facebook, Twitter, Instagram, and other social networking sites that allow users to share their pictures, witticisms, and breakfast choices with hundreds if not thousands of people. At least five studies have found a correlation between Narcissistic Personality Inventory scores and number of friends on Facebook—in other words, narcissists thrive on social networking sites. Larry Rosen and his colleagues found that people who spent more time on social networking sites were more likely to suffer from personality disorders such as narcissistic personality disorder or histrionic personality disorder (he calls the phenomenon iDisorders). Another study found that narcissists, especially those high in feelings of superiority or exhibitionism, posted to Twitter and Facebook more often.

But do social networking sites cause narcissism or self-esteem? That's a different question—perhaps people with positive self-views are drawn to social networking sites, instead of social networking sites causing positive self-views, or some third variable explains the correlation. My colleagues and I designed two experiments to get around this problem. Students who already had a social networking page were randomly assigned to either edit their social networking page or trace their route to campus on Google Maps. For the first experiment in 2007, we used MySpace, which was popular at the time. Students who edited their MySpace page subsequently scored higher on narcissism. Two years later we repeated the experiment using Facebook. Those who edited their Facebook page (versus using Google Maps) did not score any higher on narcissism, but they did score higher on self-esteem. This suggests that social networking sites do cause positive self-views, but that the results vary depending on the specific site.

Many more studies need to look carefully at the relationship between social networking and positive self-views before we can fully understand their relationship to each other. It seems clear that the two are connected, but which causes which and exactly what traits are affected needs much more study. It makes intuitive sense that social networking sites would increase self-focus: they give people a platform to express themselves to others, however and whenever they want. Some people take and post dozens of pictures of themselves (selfies) a day. The goal of Twitter is to amass *followers*, a term that smacks of narcissistic allusions to royalty or celebrity. Although many people use social networking sites to keep in touch with friends and family, others seem to see it as a platform for sharing every bit of themselves—or at least the alluring bits—with an adoring audience. Chloe, 18, writes of Instagram, "I have almost 10,000 followers and many of my friends are not even at 1,000. I take pride in my followers and try hard to gain them. I post glamorous pictures—I guess I enjoy portraying my life as fabulous."

Do social networking sites increase social connectedness—and thus increase community feeling and civic-mindedness? I reviewed the research literature on this topic for the *Journal of College and Character*. Although several studies have found that social networking sites improve the perception of social connectedness, they seem to do little to increase deeper involvement or engender actual help. For example, one study had students ask their Facebook friends to help them with a class project by rating a series of pictures. Only 21% helped. Another study examined whether college students' online engagement in a social issue (the 2011 Wisconsin public-employee union bill) translated to participation in off-line protests. Students who used Facebook to express their opinion were more likely to participate in off-line protests, but students who used Facebook to gather information were not any more likely to participate off-line. Thus students who were already interested in the issue used Facebook to tell others about their interest, but learning about the issue on Facebook did not produce off-line action. A third study, conducted just before the 2008 presidential election, found that those who spent the most time on Facebook were less likely to participate in politics outside of the site (such as watching the debates, signing a petition, or writing to a government official).

Another example is the "Kony 2012" video, which garnered tens of millions of views by the end of March 2012. The video depicted African warlord Joseph Kony's forced recruitment of child soldiers. Invisible Children, who produced the video, quickly sold out of "action kits" with posters and stickers, and the video made national news for weeks. However, when the April 20, 2012, "day of action" named in the video arrived, virtually no one appeared for the in-person protest.

The rise in narcissism has deep roots—technology is far from the only cause. The individualism in American culture also goes far beyond self-esteem and narcissism. It's not just that we feel better about ourselves, but that we even think to ask the question. We fixate on self-esteem, and unthinkingly build narcissism, because we believe that the needs of the individual are paramount. This will stay with us even if self-esteem programs end up in the dustbin of history, and it is the focus of the next chapter.

3

You Can Be Anything You Want to Be

In the animated children's movie *Planes*, Dusty wants to be a racing plane. "You are not built to race; you are built to dust crops," his friend Dottie warns him. But Dusty enters an international flying race—and wins. In another 2013 movie, Turbo is a snail who yearns to race. Close to the finish line in the Indianapolis 500, his once-skeptical brother urges him on: "It is in you! It's always been in you!" Turbo wins, "proving," as Luke Epplin observes in the *Atlantic*, "that one needn't be human nor drive a car to win the country's most prestigious auto race." Epplin notes, "The restless protagonists of these films never have to wake up to the reality that crop-dusters simply can't fly faster than sleek racing aircraft. Instead, it's the nay-saying authority figures who need to be enlightened about the importance of never giving up on your dreams, no matter how irrational, improbable, or disruptive to the larger community."

These movies are just the most recent example of the relentless cultural message to young people: you can be anything you want to be, as long as you believe in yourself. In the Google database of American books, the use of the phrase *you can be anything* increased 12 times between 1970 and 2008.

This got its start during the teen years of GenX. In his book *What Really Happened to the Class of '93*, Chris Colin notes that his classmates were constantly told, "You can be whatever you want to be" and "Nothing is impossible." His classmates mention this time and time again. Alexandra Robbins and Abby Wilner, authors of *Quarterlife Crisis*, agree: "For all of their lives, twentysomethings have been told that they can be whatever they want to be, do whatever they want to do." Lia Macko, the coauthor of a similar book (*Midlife Crisis at 30*), dedicates the work to her mother, "for truly instilling in me the belief that Anything Is Possible," which Macko describes as "the unqualified mantra of our youth."

These messages begin early. When the boy band 'N Sync appeared on the kids' show *Sesame Street*, they sang a song called "Believe in Yourself." Some people might tell you there are things you can't do, the song says. But you can be whatever you want to be, as long as you "believe in yourself." (What if they want to be brats?) One of the most popular Barney (the annoying purple dinosaur) videotapes for toddlers promoted a similar message: it's called *You Can Be Anything!*

And so it goes, into high school as well. On *Glee*, Brittany has always been portrayed as a poor student; she once said she had a 0.0 grade point average. But in her senior year, MIT suddenly discovers she's a math genius. How did that happen? "It wasn't until I joined this club that I really started believing in myself," Brittany explains. "And as soon as I did that, as soon as I started believing that maybe I was smart after all, I think the whole world did too." So the key to academic success is not hard work, involved parents, good teachers, or years of study, but believing in yourself.

As Epplin observes of the kids' movie characters, "It's enough for them simply to show up with no experience at the most competitive races, dig deep within themselves, and out-believe their opponents." When closely examined, these are ridiculous ideas, but they are routinely put forth as "inspirational" stories. Nor is this attitude surprising given other trends: The logical outcome of every kid's having high self-esteem is every kid's thinking that he can achieve anything.

In an episode of the family show *7th Heaven*, 21-year-old Lucy gives a sermon to the young women in the congregation: "God wants us to know and love ourselves. He also wants us to know our purpose, our passion. . . . So I ask you . . . 'What have you dreamt about doing?' . . . What you are waiting for is already inside of you. God has already equipped us with everything we need to live full and rich lives. It is our responsibility to make that life happen—to make our dreams happen." So if you want to do it, you can make it happen. But what if your dream is to be a movie star or an Olympic athlete? Or even a doctor? What if we're not actually equipped with absolutely everything we need—say, a one-in-a-million body, Hollywood connections, or the grades to make it into med school? Well, you should just believe in yourself more. Yes, some people will achieve these dreams, but it will likely be due to their talent and hard work, not their superior self-belief.

One professor encountered the GenMe faith in self-belief quite spectacularly in an undergraduate class at the University of Kansas. As she was introducing the idea that jobs and social class were based partially on background and unchangeable characteristics, her students became skeptical. That can't be right, they said, you can be anything you want to be. The professor, a larger woman with no illusions about her size, said, "So you're saying that I could be a ballerina?" "Sure, if you really wanted to," said one of the students.

GREAT EXPECTATIONS

This ethos is reflected in the lofty ambitions of modern adolescents. In 2012, 58% of high school students expected to go to graduate or professional school—nearly twice as many as in 1976. Yet the number who actually earn graduate degrees has remained unchanged at about 9%. High schoolers also predict they will have prestigious careers. Sixty-eight percent of 2012 high school students expected to work in professional or managerial jobs, compared to 40% in the 1970s. Unfortunately, these aspirations far outstrip the need for professionals in the future; about 20% of Americans work in professional jobs, about the same as in the 1970s. Short-term ambitions fare little better: In 2012, 84% of incoming college students in the United States expected to graduate in four years, but only 41% of students at their universities actually do so. In *The Ambitious Generation*, sociologists Barbara Schneider and David Stevenson label these "misaligned ambitions," and another set of sociologists titled their paper "Have Adolescents Become Too Ambitious?" Apparently the kids learned the lesson "you can be whatever you want to be" a little too well. This might benefit some, but many others will be disappointed.

Ambitions only grow stronger in college. In 2012, 3 out of 4 American college freshmen said they wanted to earn an advanced degree (such as a master's, PhD, MD, or law degree). For example, 42% say they will earn a master's degree, 19% a PhD, and 10% an MD. However, the number of PhDs granted each year is only 4% of the bachelor's degrees given, and MDs only 1%. Thus about 4 in 5 aspiring PhDs will be disappointed, and a whopping 9 in 10 would-be doctors will not reach their goals. And that's if students finish their bachelor's degree at all. A *Chronicle of Higher Education* study found that among the 4.3 million students who started college in fall 2004, less than 1 in 4 graduated. During the next decade, we are going to see a lot of young people who will be disappointed that they cannot reach their career goals.

Kate, 19, reflects, "As a child, I just didn't understand that even if you said 'I wanna be ____!' you couldn't necessarily do that. Adults made things seem easier than they were, and that made me grow up with unrealistic expectations of my future." Once they reach young adulthood, GenMe's overconfidence is often tempered by the dawning realization that reality may not live up to their fantasies. As aspiring writer Hannah says on *Girls*,

"I think that I may be the voice of my generation. Or, at least, *a* voice, of *a* generation."

Does this mean young people shouldn't be encouraged to aim high? Of course not. But they also need to get the message, contrary to those promoted in movies and on TV, that it takes more than self-belief to succeed. Young people need to know that it takes years of hard work to succeed in most professions; they are unlikely to start at the top. It might also be better for students to identify the best path for them, not just what parents and teachers think is the highest goal. That way they'll be less likely to waste their time pursuing a path that isn't a good fit for them. The world will probably be better off, too. If all of the PhDs suddenly disappeared one day, the world would keep ticking along fine for quite some time. But if all nurses, police officers, plumbers, trash collectors, and preschool teachers disappeared, things would get ugly quickly. If school is your thing, absolutely, get a graduate degree. But it is not the only path to success (or, take it from me, to a high salary).

There may be a silver lining to the trend of overly lofty ambitions. Perhaps some students who aim for graduate school will be more likely to make it through college. The best solution is to find the goals that will serve the student the best—whether that's a graduate degree or a trade certificate.

Young people also expect to make a lot of money. In a 2011 survey, 16-to-18-year-olds expected their starting salary to be $73,000, which they assumed would rise to $150,000 once they were established in their career. However, the median household income in 2009—for all adults—was $50,000, or around a third of the teens' aspirations. Overall, young people predicted a bright future for themselves, even during the years of the late 2000s recession and its aftermath. Fifty-seven percent of high school seniors in 2012 predicted that they would own more than their parents; only 10% thought they would own less. In the 2011 survey, 59% believed they would do better financially than their parents.

Expectations for advancement and promotion are also high. One young employee told a startled manager that he expected to be a vice president at the company within three years. When the manager told him this was not realistic (most vice presidents were in their sixties), the young man got angry with him and said, "You should encourage me and help me fulfill my expectations."

Related to "you can be anything" is "follow your dreams" or "never give up on your dreams"—like self-focus, a concept that

No wonder kids have such big dreams—even cheese is supposed to make them sports stars. The ad might be more accurate if the kid were standing on a hypodermic needle filled with steroids.

GenMe speaks as a native language. According to the Google Books Ngram Viewer, the phrase *follow your dreams* appeared 17 times more often in American books in 2008 versus 1990 and *never give up* appeared three times more often in 2008 compared to 1970. An amazing number of the young people interviewed in *Quarterlife Crisis* adhered fiercely to this belief. Derrick, struggling to be a comedy writer in Hollywood, says, "Never give up on your dreams. If you're lucky enough to actually have one, you owe it to yourself to hold on to it." Robin, a 23-year-old from Nebraska, says, "Never give up on your dreams. Why do something that won't bring about your dreams?" I was pretty well indoctrinated myself: the title of my high school valedictory speech was "Hold Fast to Dreams."

Some people might argue that this is just youthful hope—after all, hasn't every generation dreamed big during adolescence? Maybe, but GenMe's dreams are bigger. While our parents may have aimed simply to leave their small town or to go to college, we want to make lots of money at a career that is fulfilling and makes us famous.

"Following your dreams" sounds like a good principle, until you realize that every waiter in LA is following his or her dream of becoming an actor, and most of them won't succeed. Most people are not going to realize their dreams because most people do not dream of becoming accountants, social workers, or trash collectors—just to name three jobs that society can't do without but nevertheless factor into few childhood fantasies. And few dream of the white-collar jobs in business that many of us have or will have. "No one at my company is following his dream," says one of my friends who works in marketing. That doesn't have to be depressing—it's just the reality that the vast majority of jobs aren't particularly exciting or glamorous. With luck, you'll enjoy what you're doing and pay your bills, but dreams are called that for a reason: they are not real.

The most common dreams of young people are acting, sports, music, and screenwriting. In 2012, more college freshmen wanted to be an actor or entertainer than a college teacher, a foreign service worker, a school counselor, a member of the clergy, an architect, or a salesperson. Music was just as popular as acting, and even more said they wanted to be artists. Almost 1 out of 20 college students expects to become an actor, artist, or musician—more than want to be lawyers, accountants, business owners, scientific researchers, or high school teachers. "I just wanted to tell you not to give up on your dream," one student says to another on *Glee*. "If you can imagine it, it can come true."

GenMe also holds on to dreams more fiercely, and in a way that makes you wonder how they will react if they don't achieve their lofty goals. Morgan, 22, began her graduate school application essay by writing, "On my 70th birthday, I want to be able to reflect on my life and say 'I followed my dreams and lived for my passions.' In other words, I will not be discouraged by closed doors, and will not be denied the opportunity to live to my fullest potential." In *Quarterlife Crisis*, Emily, 22, says that if a young person "never gives up, then he or she will never have to admit to failure." Uh-huh. But you might have to live in your car.

Quarterlife Crisis does discuss one young person who "decided to change his dream rather than accept failure." Mark, 29, tried for years to make it as an actor in New York; he realizes now he should have moved to LA sooner, where "I bet I would have been cast on a soap opera." He finally decided to give up on acting and pursue another career. His new, and presumably more realistic, choice? To be a movie director. (I am not making this up, and the book's authors, both twentysomethings themselves, present this story without comment or irony.)

EXTENDING ADOLESCENCE BEYOND ALL PREVIOUS LIMITS

Mark's story illustrates another change from previous generations: the length of time GenMe has to pursue dreams. Because they expect to marry and have children later, GenMe thinks it's more acceptable to spend their entire 20s pursuing "dream" careers such as music, screenwriting, or comedy. Jeffrey Arnett calls that period emerging adulthood, a time when "no dreams have been permanently dashed, no doors have been firmly closed, every possibility for happiness is still alive." That period is getting longer and longer for people who spend years trying to make it in Hollywood or get their first novel published. Many twentysomethings struggle with the decision to keep pursuing their dream or to cut their losses and go home. Choosing something seems like giving up on endless possibilities. In her book *The Defining Decade*, therapist Meg Jay relates the stories of her twentysomething clients who are so afraid of "selling out" that they drift from one meaningless job to another. She told one client, Ian, "You need to claim something." Ian would reply, "But claiming something feels like I'm losing everything else. I don't want to settle for some ordinary thing."

Some of the forces behind these trends are economic, and I'll address those further in chapter 4. But many young people say that the reason they are postponing adult roles is, you guessed it, their desire to put themselves first. Jeffrey Arnett, author of *Emerging Adulthood*, says, "They're not just looking for a job. They want something that's more like a calling, that's going to be an expression of their identity." Overall, it's the pursuit of individual wants at its most undiluted. As *Time* magazine explains, young people are "making sure that when they do settle down, they do it the right way, their way." Their individual way.

Consider the characters on *Girls*. During the first season, 24-year-old Hannah's parents pay her rent as she tries to make a living from her writing; Marnie wants a career in art curatorship but doesn't get far; Jessa travels constantly and has numerous affairs; Charlie hopes his band will make it big; Ray is 33 and still works at a restaurant. If they had been born in the 1940s instead of the 1980s, they would probably be living very different lives—married, working at steady jobs, with a child or two. This means they have more time to explore their options, which has a lot of upsides, but Dr. Jay (among others) argues that your 20s are the best time to build your career and relationships. In her view, they are not for messing around. More and more young people are going to find themselves at 30 without a viable career, a house, or any semblance of stability.

"In the past, people got married and got a job and had kids, but now there's a new ten years that people are using to try and find out what kind of life they want to lead," said Zach Braff, the actor and screenwriter of the hit movie *Garden State*. The movie plays off these ideas: Braff's character works as a waiter in LA and is trying to break into acting. His friends back home in New Jersey live with their parents and work dead-end jobs, one quite literally as a gravedigger, and another as a knight-waiter, in full metal body armor, at the restaurant-cum-festival Medieval Times. The only guy with any money made it by inventing something ridiculous (silent Velcro) and spends his time getting laid, taking ecstasy, and riding around his giant house on a four-wheeler.

Extended adolescence also has a big impact on relationships. GenMe marries later than any previous generation, at 29 for men and 27 for women. In 1970, when the Boomers were young, these figures were 23 and 21—so much for Free Love. Only 20% of today's adults ages 18 to 29 are married, compared to 59% in 1960. In a Pew Center poll, 44% of GenMe'ers said they thought marriage was becoming obsolete. "I want to get married, but not soon," Jennie Jiang, 26, told *Time* magazine. "I'm enjoying myself. There's a lot I want to do by myself still." Marcus Jones, 28, says he won't marry for a long time: "I'm too self-involved. I don't want to bring that into a relationship now."

Delaying adulthood has psychological consequences as well as practical ones. A recent study found that in countries where young people take on adult roles more quickly (such as Mexico or Pakistan), people become more responsible, organized, and

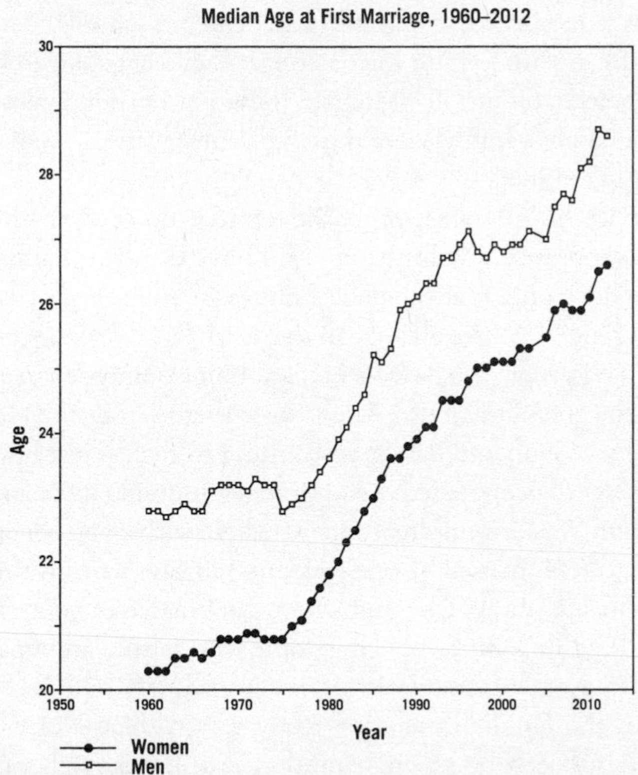

Generation Me'ers marry considerably later than their Boomer counterparts did in the 1960s and 1970s.

calm—basically, more mature—at younger ages than those in countries, such as the United States, that feature a long period of emerging adulthood.

Sometimes emerging-adulthood dreams are clearly thwarting more realistic goals. Arnett describes Albert, who works in an ice-cream store but says he wants to play professional baseball. Yet he did not play baseball in high school and does not play on a team right now either. So how will he make this happen? "I don't know," he says. "I'll see what happens." Adrianne, 16, dreamed of being on *American Idol*. But, her mother says, "Unfortunately she was so focused on it that she didn't care for school too much." Some dreams are not just big but huge. "My big goal is to have a shoe named after me, like Michael Jordan or LeBron James," says Corvin Lamb, 13, interviewed in *People* magazine. "I want to be something in life."

Movies have latched onto "never give up on your dreams" with a vengeance. My husband and I have decided that modern movies have only four themes: "Believe in yourself and you can do anything," "We are all alike underneath," "Love conquers all," and "Good people win." (Do try this at home; almost every recent movie fits one of the four.) All of these themes tout the focus on the self so common today; it is stunning to realize just how well movies have encapsulated the optimistic, individualistic message of modern Western culture. Romantic love with a partner of one's choice (often opposed by one's parents) always wins in the end; intolerance is always bad; and when you believe in yourself, you can do anything. Sure enough, people who pursue an impossible dream in a movie almost always succeed: Dusty and Turbo win races in the children's movies; Rudy gets to play Notre Dame football; formerly broke single mother Erin Brockovich wins her million-dollar lawsuit; and Will Smith's character in *The Pursuit of Happyness* goes from homeless to Wall Street tycoon. Former Hollywood producer Elisabeth Robinson tried to get the classic and sad story of Don Quixote made into a movie, but the studio insisted he win the duels he loses in the book and that "he dies in his bed because he's an old man—who lived his dream and now can die—not because his dreams have been crushed or 'reality' has killed him." It wouldn't be a movie if it wasn't an "inspirational" story of people never giving up—so what if it cuts the heart out of the world's first novel? No one wants to watch a movie more like real life, where people try hard but fail more often than they succeed.

At least GenMe doesn't want to watch this type of movie; pre-Boomer generations liked them just fine. Take the 1946 film *It's a Wonderful Life*, in which George Bailey gives up on his dreams of making it big to stay in his small town and run the local bank. After one particularly bad day, he decides to kill himself, but an angel stops him by showing him how all of his good deeds have benefited others. Many people love this movie for its message that self-sacrifice can lead to good outcomes. I saw *It's a Wonderful Life* for the first time when I was 18, and I hated it, probably because it violated the conventions of every other movie I had ever seen: Why should he have to give up his dreams? He should be able to pursue his ambitions, and—modern movies had taught me well—he could have won if he had tried hard enough.

THE BRIEF BUT HILARIOUS REIGN OF WILLIAM HUNG

Does anyone remember William Hung? Probably not, but his rise to fame in 2004 remains a sterling example of this system. A UC Berkeley engineering student, Hung stretched his fifteen minutes of fame to almost an hour with his spectacularly bad and uproariously funny rendition of Ricky Martin's "She Bangs." Hung's singing was tuneless, but it was his jerky, utterly uncoordinated dancing that caused the *American Idol* judges to hide behind their ratings sheets as they choked back their laughter. When judge Simon Cowell stopped him from finishing, Hung looked surprised and hurt. Cowell chided him, "You can't sing; you can't dance. What do you want me to say?" Hung replied, "I already gave my best. I have no regrets at all."

Judge Paula Abdul praised him, saying, "That's good, that's the best attitude yet." (Rule of the modern world: doing your best is good enough, even if you suck.) Hung then attempted to explain: "I have no professional training." "There's the surprise of the century," Cowell shot back.

In a later interview with *Star* magazine, Hung said he hoped to make a career as a singer. This was after the poor guy had become a national joke for not being able to sing. But he had done his best and had learned the lesson that "you can be anything." Sure enough, when asked if he had any advice for his fans, Hung said, "I want to say something to the public: Always try your best, and don't give up on your dreams." William, please, for the sake of all of us, give up on your dream of being a singer. (He apparently has; he is now working as an analyst for the California Department of Public Health.)

Simon Cowell, the British former *American Idol* judge who first gave Hung this advice, sees unflinching criticism as his personal mission. TV critic James Poniewozik noted that Cowell "has led a rebellion against the tyranny of self-esteem that is promoted on talk shows and in self-help books—the notion that everyone who tries deserves to win." Although Cowell admittedly takes things a little far, Americans think he's mean mostly because he bursts contestants' bubbles of unsubstantiated self-esteem. Even the nicer *American Idol* judges are surprised by the hubris of many of the hopefuls. "It's mind-boggling how horrific some of them are, [especially those] with unbelievably healthy egos [thinking] they are all that," said Paula Abdul. "Kenny [Loggins] said, 'Is it sick or healthy to walk around believing in yourself so much?' I said, 'Well, it's delusional.'" It sure is, but it's also young people doing precisely what they have been taught.

WE WILL ALL BE FAMOUS

Hung is not unusual: many GenMe'ers expect to be famous. Many kids today grow up thinking that they will eventually be movie stars, sports figures, or at least rich. These are the adults they see on television; hardly anybody on TV works in a white-collar job in an office as most kids will someday. A lot of young people also assume that success will come quickly. One of my students, who wasn't more than 22, noted during a class presentation, "There are lots of people our age who are CEOs of their own companies."

He probably read a profile or two of one of these rare beasts in a magazine and, fueled by the "you can be anything" mythos, decided that this was commonplace.

These attitudes are pervasive and have been for a while. When I was in high school, one of my friends decided to collect items from each of the talented people in our class—a tape of one student playing the piano, a mathematical proof from another, a set of handwritten poems from me. He was sure we would all become famous one day and these would then be worth money (and this was before eBay). The three of us have done fine, but none of us is famous. Somehow no one ever told us that this was unlikely to happen. In a 2007 survey, 51% of 18-to-25-year-olds said that the most important goal of their generation was "becoming famous"—which was trumped only by "getting rich," at 81%. Use of the phrase *want to be famous* was six times more common in 2008 than in 1960 in American books in the Google Books database. The phrase *famous for being famous* did not exist in American books until 1970, and its use has doubled since the late 1980s.

Many reality TV shows feed on this obsession with celebrity and fame. Flip channels for a few minutes during prime time, and you'll see *Survivor* contestants barely getting enough food, *Fear Factor* participants with bugs crawling all over them, and *Rebel Billionaire* CEO wannabes falling off cliffs. Why do people do these crazy things? Ostensibly, it's for the challenge and the money, but everyone knows the real attraction: you get on TV. For many people—particularly GenMe—instant fame is worth eating bugs. At least these contestants actually do something to gain fame—most recent reality TV shows instead feature those famous for being famous, such as *Keeping Up with the Kardashians*, the *Real Housewives*, *The Real World*, and *Jersey Shore*. As a *New York Times* article put it, "Reality television has spawned a generation of viewers who feel entitled to be on camera."

When musician Nellie McKay was 19, she said, "I've been telling [my friends] for years that I'm going to be famous. When I look at me in the mirror, I see someone on the front cover of *Us Weekly*." Even with a first album that sold moderately well, this is the quest for fame at its most bald and unrealistic. "Apparently everyone else sees a regular girl. I'm very disappointed in that," McKay continues. "I want them to see me as Frank Sinatra or Bill Clinton." Apparently, this fame is also supposed to happen overnight. "It tends to get on my nerves when people say, 'Wow, can you believe this is happening to you?'" says McKay. "I say, 'Yeah, I've worked hard for this.'" Perhaps, but how hard, for how many years, can you have possibly worked when you are nineteen years old?

In *What Really Happened to the Class of '93*, Chris Colin relates the story of his most accomplished classmate, Alo Basu, who went to Harvard and MIT and was a science prodigy in high school. Their senior year, she was voted most likely to appear on the cover of *Time* magazine. "Ten years after leaving high school, Alo has yet to grace *Time*," he notes, with no sarcasm that I could detect. Um, yes: most people—even most geniuses—won't ever be on the cover of *Time* magazine, much less before the age of 28. Basu has done well—she's now a professor of neuroscience. Her accomplishments led to a great career, just not to outsize fame and fortune.

Of course, the Internet has made fame seem as if it's just out of reach. And in a way it is—Justin Bieber parlayed his YouTube views into rock-star fame, and comedians such as Kevin Wu (KevJumba) and Ryan Higa (Nigahiga) built successful acting careers after the videos they made in their teenage bedrooms garnered millions of views. E L James became a bestselling author after her initially self-published book *Fifty Shades of Grey* became popular. This is the upside of the modern age: talent can be found by the masses instead of by record executives and casting directors. The downside: these success stories make it seem that fame is easy and common, when it is not.

In the Internet age, fame is also relative. Andy Warhol said that in the future everyone would be famous for 15 minutes, and some have quipped that on the Web everyone will be famous to 15 people. Or a lot more. Many people with Facebook pages and Twitter accounts have hundreds of "friends" to read their every thought. Teens are now more drawn to Instagram, where they can share the large numbers of pictures they take every day with their cell phones, and Snapchat, which lets them send pictures that disappear after a few seconds.

The quest for fame may explain the recent fascination with over-the-top weddings, and why, in general, Americans still have weddings when living together is so popular. Having a dress fit specifically for you, having someone else apply your makeup, having everyone admire your beauty—as author Carol Wallace points out, these experiences are usually shared by only two groups of women: celebrities and brides. Wedding vendors often emphasize that this is your one chance to be a "princess for a day," and we believe it. One bride said, "Finally, I got center stage in something." Finally. As Wallace writes, "Having 'center stage,' being the focus of all eyes, is so highly prized in today's culture that many of us, relegated to the background, feel diminished until we get our turn in the spotlight." Gwyneth Paltrow said that for many women "the whole wedding fantasy [is] their day at the Oscars."

Perhaps because of GenMe's comfort with the spotlight, today's young people are more confident in their social interactions. As part of my dissertation, I gathered data on 16,846 college students who completed a questionnaire measuring extroversion, or being outgoing and talkative. This trait rose markedly, with the average 1990s college student scoring as more extroverted than 83% of students in the 1960s. My former student Brittany Gentile found that this trend continued, with 2000s college students scoring still higher on extroversion. Compared to Boomers, GenMe is more comfortable talking to people at parties and social occasions, more confident when meeting new people, and accustomed to being surrounded by bustle and excitement. This makes sense: GenMe is more likely to have gone to day care, to have worked in a service job, or to meet new people regularly. High levels of extroversion have been GenMe's adaptation: they are a generation with few shrinking violets.

EXPRESS YOURSELF

Between 2005 and 2014, the SAT included an essay portion designed to measure students' writing ability. Instead of asking for a balanced treatment of a topic, however, the test instructed students to "develop your point of view on this issue. Support your position with reasoning and examples taken from your reading, studies, experience, and observations." This meant that to get a high score, it was necessary to argue only one side of the question: yours. As the test-prep book *Kaplan New SAT* advised, "What's important is that you take a position and state how you feel. It is not important what other people might think, just what you think."

Generation Me has always been taught that their thoughts and feelings are important. It's no surprise that students were tested on it. Even when schools, parents, and the media are not specifically targeting self-esteem, they promote the equally powerful concepts of socially sanctioned self-focus, the unquestioned importance of the individual, and an unfettered optimism about young people's prospects. High school senior Scot, a contestant on the reality show *The Scholar*, captured this notion when he said, "I feel it's very important to be your own hero." So forget presidents, community leaders, even sports figures—it's more important to look up to yourself.

Like self-esteem, self-focus and individuality have been actively promoted in schools. When I was in sixth grade in Irving, Texas, our fall assignment in Reading was the project "All About Me." We finished sentences like "I feel angry when . . ." and "Something special I want you to know about me is . . ." We were also asked to include pictures of ourselves. Many of my classmates spent hours on this project, mulling over their answers and making elaborate albums with their best photographic self-portraits. In effect, we were graded on how well we could present our opinions and images of ourselves. Later that year, our assignment was to make a personal "coat of arms" that illustrated our interests and hobbies. In the past, a coat of arms was the symbol of an entire extended family, so an individual coat of arms—particularly one created by an 11-year-old—is an interesting cultural construct.

A page from my "All About Me" project in sixth-grade Reading class, fetchingly illustrated with cutouts from magazine ads. The project promoted the idea that thinking about yourself is important—apparently more important than reading and writing, given the uncorrected spelling mistake.

My school was not the only one to value and promote children's individual feelings and thoughts. The popular school program called Quest has students keep track of their feelings for a day on an Emotion Clock or a Mood Continuum. Andrea, 22, told me that her junior high and high school English classes included weekly "free writing." She notes, "This not only encouraged writing but pushed expressing yourself." Even employers are getting in on the game: Xerox's recruiting slogan in the mid-2000s was "Express Yourself." *Glee* coach Mr. Schuester opines, "Glee club is not just about expressing yourself to anyone else. It's about expressing yourself to yourself." Or as Hannah puts it on *Girls*, "I'm an individual. And I feel how I feel when I feel it."

The growing primacy of the individual appears in data I gathered on 81,384 high school and college students. These young people completed questionnaires measuring what psychologists call agency—a personality trait involving assertiveness, dominance, independence, and self-promotion. Between the 1970s and the 1990s, both young men's and women's agency increased markedly, with the average 1990s college student scoring higher than 75% of college Boomers from the 1970s. I had expected women's agency to increase over this time, but men's feelings of agency also rose, suggesting that the trend went beyond gender roles. As the Boomers gave way to GenX, more and more young people were saying that they stood up for their individual rights, had a "strong personality," and were "self-sufficient" and "individualistic." This trend appears in more recent data as well. In the study of college students' beliefs about their abilities, the percentage who believed they were above average increased between 1966 and 2012 only for agentic traits such as leadership, drive to achieve, and intellectual self-confidence. However, GenMe college students were not any more likely than previous generations to believe they were above average in more communal traits such as cooperativeness or understanding others. So GenMe not only has high self-esteem, but they take pride in being independent actors who express their needs and wants.

The focus on the needs of the individual self begins when children are very young, sometimes before they are born or even conceived. Advertising convinces parents to spend lots of money on the perfect nursery, since the room should "reflect" the child's personality and individuality. (Yet, as *The Mommy Myth* by Susan Douglas and Meredith Michaels points out, "Remember, kid not born yet, personality unknown.") One of the most popular nursery decorations right now is 12-inch-tall letters spelling out the child's name, an obvious bow to individualism. Douglas and Michaels refer to the trends toward perfection and individuality in nurseries as our "narcissism around our kids . . . a hyperindividualized emphasis on how truly, exquisitely unique and precious our child is, the Hope diamond, more special than the others."

We also promote individuality and self-importance by giving our children choices. One of my psychology colleagues called me one day and said, "You know, I just realized how kids learn this self stuff so quickly. I just asked my one-year-old if she wanted apple juice or milk. Earlier today I asked her if she wanted to wear her red dress or her blue one. She can't even talk and I'm asking her what she wants!" My friend is not alone in asking his daughter such questions; most American parents begin asking their children their preferences before they can answer. When kids get a little older, many parents think it's important to let their children pick out the clothes they wear in the morning—the kid might end up wearing red polka dots with green and blue stripes, but it's okay because they are "expressing themselves" and learning to make their own choices.

Culture Shock! USA, a guidebook to American culture for foreigners, explains, "Often one sees an American engaged in a dialogue with a tiny child. 'Do you want to go home now?' says the parent. 'No,' says an obviously tired, crying child. And so parent and child continue to sit discontentedly in a chilly park. 'What is the matter with these people?' says the foreigner to himself, who can see the child is too young to make such decisions." It's just part of American culture, the book says: "The child is acquiring both a sense of responsibility for himself and a sense of his own importance." We expect our kids to have individual preferences and would never dream, as earlier generations did, of making every single decision for our children and asking them to be seen and not heard. Not coincidentally, this also teaches children that their wants are the most important.

This can sometimes cause problems when children get older. One mother says she treated her daughter "as if she had a mind of her own ever since she was a baby," asking her what she wanted to do next and what she wanted to wear. "But now that's she's four, sometimes I really want her to mind me. The other day I told her, 'Alexis, you're going to do this right now because I say so!' She looked up at me astounded, as if to say, 'What's going on here? You're changing the rules on me!'" And just wait until she's 14.

Some experts maintain that perhaps as a result more kids these days are behaving badly. Psychologist Bonnie Zucker, interviewed for the *People* magazine article "Kids out of Control," saw a 10-year-old whose parents let him decide whether to go to school—if he didn't want to go, he didn't go. Another mother didn't make her son do homework because it made him "unhappy."

Writer Martin Booe recently devoted an entire column to overindulgent parents who "let their kids run roughshod over themselves and other adults . . . they're rampant." Says educational psychologist Michele Borba, "Too many parents subscribe to the myth that if you discipline children, you're going to break their spirit. . . . The 'Me Generation' is raising the 'Me-Me-Me Generation.'" (By May 2013, *Time* magazine would agree, using "The Me Me Me Generation" as its headline for Joel Stein's cover story on the Millennials.)

Douglas and Michaels argue that because mothers are now expected to understand their child's inner feelings and wants, the child comes to believe "that he's the center of the universe, his thoughts and feelings the only ones worth considering, the ones that cut in line before everyone else's." Gone are the days, they say, when parents were told to "disabuse [their child] of the notion that he or she is the Sun King."

Paula Peterson's two kids, Abby and Joey, throw temper tantrums when they don't get the toys they want. And why does she put up with such behavior? Well, as the *People* article explains, "The same spark that sets off the kicking and screaming may also give Abby and Joey what they need to excel in a culture that rewards outspokenness and confidence." As *Culture Shock! USA* explains, "In most of the countries of the world, parents feel that their obligation is to raise an obedient child who will fit into society. The little ego must be molded into that of a well-behaved citizen. Not so here [in the United States] . . . the top priority is to raise an individual capable of taking advantage of opportunity."

YOU MUST LOVE YOURSELF BEFORE YOU CAN LOVE OTHERS

This is one of the most widely accepted of our cultural aphorisms. After *20/20* aired a segment on self-esteem programs in schools, anchor Hugh Downs asked, "Could it be that self-esteem, real self-esteem, comes from esteeming other people and not thinking so much about yourself, to begin with?" Barbara Walters clearly thought he was deluded. "Oh, Hugh!" she exclaimed, as if he had just said the silliest thing in the world. "First of all, you have to like yourself before you can like others."

The *7th Heaven* episode mentioned previously also promoted the "love yourself first" message. Lucy, 21 and just named associate pastor, uses the example of the woman from the Song of Solomon. "She loves who she is and she doesn't care what anybody thinks of her," she preaches. "She has self-love and self-esteem." So many of us, she goes on to say, make "loving ourselves dependent on something outside of ourselves. But it's not someone else's job to make us happy. It's your job to make yourself happy. And to know who you are. And if you don't know yourself, or love yourself, how can you expect someone else to?"

There are a number of problems with this. First, if you truly don't care what anybody thinks of you, you're probably not relationship material. And if we could all be happy alone, why be in a relationship at all? Also, plenty of people in earlier generations loved their spouses and children quite a bit, even though they never worried much about loving themselves. Lower rates of divorce in previous decades might even suggest that they were better at relationships than we are. Maybe we love ourselves a little too much.

But pop psych teaches us otherwise. "No person can be happy with others until they are happy with themselves," says Lindsay, 19. It is now commonly accepted that you should have your own life and develop your own identity first, before you settle down with someone. In *The Defining Decade*, one young man says, "I love my girlfriend. We've been together three years. But I'm not planning on factoring her in to where I go to graduate school. I'm just not supposed to be thinking about this in my mid-twenties. I imagined this would all come a lot later." GenMe believes you're supposed to date lots of people and find out who's right for you before you marry someone. As Jeffrey Arnett notes in *Emerging Adulthood*, "Finding a love partner in your teens and continuing in a relationship with that person through your early twenties, culminating in marriage, is now viewed as unhealthy, a mistake, a path likely to lead to disaster." Anyone who considers this will hear, "Why marry the first guy you date? You should have fun first," "Don't you want your own identity first?" and "How do you know he's the one if you've never dated anyone else?" This might be good advice, but these are new questions, rarely asked just two decades ago. Even compromises made later in one's 20s are scrutinized. One article describes Kathryn, 29, who, to the consternation of her friends, moved to England to be with her boyfriend. "We're not meant to say, 'I made this decision for this person.' Today, you're meant to do things for yourself," she says. "If you're willing to make sacrifices for others—especially if you're a woman—that's seen as a kind of weakness."

This is the dirty little secret of modern life: we are told that we need to know ourselves and love ourselves first, but being alone sucks. Human beings need other people to be happy—this is just the way we are built. Yet say this at a cocktail party, and someone will probably say, yes, sure, but it's better not to need someone. That's codependent, the resident psychotherapy expert will say and repeat the modern aphorism "You can't expect someone else to make you happy—you have to make yourself happy." Actually, you can expect this: having a stable marriage is one of the most robust predictors of happiness. And for single people, having good relationships with friends and family predicts happiness. We gain self-esteem from our relationships with others, not from focusing on ourselves. In other words, Hugh Downs was right. Study after study shows that people who have good relationships with friends and family are the happiest—these things consistently trump money or job satisfaction as predictors of happiness and life satisfaction. Even Abraham Maslow, the favorite psychologist of New Agers, says that belonging and love needs must be satisfied before esteem needs. We know this, which is why we continue to get married, have children, and make friends. Despite the idea that you can "be your own best friend," as the title of a popular self-help book claims, we know it's better to have real friends and real relationships.

Research by Sandra Murray and her colleagues does show that people with low self-esteem appreciate their partners less and feel less secure in their relationships. If you truly don't like yourself, you may feel insecure about the other person's affection. Insecurity doesn't mean you don't love your partner, however, and this same research finds no evidence that low-self-esteem people choose bad partners. In addition, talk of loving yourself, making yourself happy first, and being there for yourself can cross the line from self-esteem into narcissism. And narcissists—people who really love themselves—are not good at getting along with others. As Keith Campbell and I discuss in *The Narcissism Epidemic*, narcissists are spectacularly bad relationship partners: they cheat, they are unsupportive, they play games, and they derogate their partners to make themselves look better. They also tend to lie, manipulate other people, and exert control and power. A student in one of Keith's classes at the University of Georgia told this story: One evening, the student and her boyfriend went to his fraternity's spring formal dance, where several awards were announced. To the woman's surprise, her boyfriend of a year won the prize for "the most hookups during spring break." Instead of looking ashamed, he looked proud and commented on how hot the girls were. When his girlfriend got upset, he blamed her for "ruining his formal." Clearly, a man who loved himself, but maybe not someone good at loving another.

Despite their self-aggrandizing tendencies, narcissists freely admit that they are not as moral or as likable as other people. They think they are better than others at most things, but are also fully aware that they're not good at relationships. And, no, it's not because narcissists are actually insecure underneath—there's no evidence for that. They act this way because they put themselves first. As Keith points out matter-of-factly, "If I were to name the top ten things that are important for a good relationship, loving yourself wouldn't make the list." When asked what traits they value in a partner, most people name things like kindness or consideration—in other words, loving and caring for other people, not yourself.

Apparently, a deeply rooted psychological trend lies behind these relationship difficulties. Psychologists have found that many relationship issues can be traced to insecurity in attachments to others. These issues begin in childhood, shaped by our relationships with our parents, and resonate throughout our adult relationships, for good or for ill. One way to understand attachment is through our views of ourselves and others. In a cross-temporal meta-analysis of 25,243 college students between 1988 and 2011, Sara Konrath and her colleagues found that three times as many 2011 students (32%) had a negative view of others compared to GenX'ers in 1988 (10%). GenMe is not GenWe.

One young woman, interviewed in the book *Flux*, broke up with her boyfriend not because she was unhappy, but because she thought she might be happier with someone else. "I'm not inspired by you. Don't you think I deserve to be inspired?" she said to the hapless young man. Even if you haven't faced this kind of narcissism (and count yourself lucky if you haven't), we all face little tugs-of-war in our relationships on occasion: Should we go to his favorite restaurant or hers? Who does the dishes tonight? Who gets the rights to the TV? And who has to watch the children this evening?

This last question brings the focus on the self crashing down to earth. In an analysis of data from 47,692 respondents, Keith Campbell, Craig Foster, and I found that couples with children were less satisfied with their marriages than childless couples were. This effect has rapidly accelerated in recent decades. Compared to previous generations, younger generations experience a 42% greater drop in marital satisfaction after having children. Researchers at the National Marriage Project found similar results and concluded that "children seem to be a growing impediment for the happiness of marriages."

Although economic pressures may partially explain this change, it is likely rooted in the radical shift away from the self that parenthood requires. Having a baby suddenly means that you have little control over your life—the freedom to which you were accustomed vanishes, and your individual accomplishments are not as valued anymore. Parenthood has always been a difficult transition, but it's even more difficult for GenMe. When you're used to calling the shots, and then the baby dictates everything, it's hard to keep your sanity, much less get along with your spouse. The idea of individual choice also makes things more difficult; in previous generations, having children was a duty rather than a choice. Now that we "choose" parenthood, we presumably have no one to blame but ourselves when the baby has kept us up for two months in a row.

OUTCOMES OF THE FOCUS ON THE SELF

The Appearance Obsession

More and more people every year get nose jobs, breast implants, face-lifts, and a long list of less invasive procedures such as Botox injections and lip plumping. Invasive plastic surgeries have doubled since 1997. Eyebrow waxing has become a near requirement for women, and today's body-hugging fashions are enough to make women long for the big-shirt-and-leggings days of the early 1990s. With the rise of the metrosexual, more men are focusing on their physical appearance as well.

We have come to equate looking good with feeling good, and to say that we should do whatever makes us feel good or makes us happy. FOX's controversial show *The Swan* justified the expensive, painful surgeries of its contestants by claiming that the women now felt better about themselves. MTV has a show called *I Want a Famous Face*, in which young people undergo plastic surgery so they can look like their favorite celebrity. Crystal, 23, underwent a breast enlargement and liposuction, ostensibly to resemble actress Brooke Burke. Immediately after the surgery, Crystal was in so much pain she said, "I just want to die right now." A few months later, however, she's confident that her surgically enlarged breasts will help her reach her goal of becoming a bikini model. She says that the surgery "definitely built up my self-esteem." Her boyfriend, who thought she looked great before, says he's fine with it as long as "you're happy with yourself."

When *People* magazine interviewed several celebrities about

An ad clearly aimed at Generation Me: the product is "unique," "individual," and "yours alone." Plus, it makes you look hot.

their views on plastic surgery, all of those who supported it said almost exactly the same thing. "If it makes you happy, if it makes you feel good, you should do whatever that is," said Julia Roberts. "Anything that makes you feel better, go for it," said Jennifer Aniston. But it was the youngest interviewee—Hilary Duff, then 17—who summed it up the best: "If it's going to boost their self-esteem and make them feel better about themselves, then I don't see a problem with it." This is pure GenMe: do whatever it takes to feel better about yourself, because that's the most important thing in the world. More important, apparently, than keeping a scalpel off your face.

Tattoos, Nose Piercings, and God-Knows-Where Piercings

Unless you've been in a cave for the past fifteen years, you've probably noticed that young people today are much more likely to adorn themselves in unconventional ways. Tattoos are no longer the sole province of bikers and sailors, but a trendy self-decoration employed by large numbers of young people, including the rich and famous. Young people pierce regions that older generations won't even mention in polite—or any—conversation. Lips, tongues, belly buttons, and eyebrows are adorned with metal rings and studs. A recent exchange on a pregnancy message board addressed the best way to remove your belly-button ring before your swelling abdomen made it pop out. Thirty-eight percent of GenMe has at least one tattoo, compared to 32% of GenX and 15% of Boomers.

I didn't think piercings and tattoos had anything to do with psychological changes over the generations until Jay, 20, told me a story about his tattoos and his reasons for getting them. Jay went to his grandparents' house one day and took off his shirt before jumping in the pool. His grandmother, shocked to see his heavily tattooed upper back, gasped audibly and expressed her disappointment in him, since he'd always been "the good grandkid." Jay tried to enlighten his grandmother: "I explained to her that to me my tattoos are an expression of who I am and how I view myself. My tattoos show the different sides of who I am," he wrote. Jay's motivations are representative. In a survey of 766 college students with tattoos or body piercings, the most common reason given for their choices was "self-expression." Eighty-one percent of tattooed college students named self-expression, independence, or uniqueness as a motivation. Sixty-nine percent of students with body piercings named self-expression or "to be different" as their reasons. Natasha, 25, has several tattoos and piercings, including several studs at the nape of her neck. During a class presentation on the topic, another student asked Natasha why people get unusual piercings when they so often elicit negative comments and appalled looks from other people. "They do it to express themselves and be different," Natasha said. "Most people who get piercings don't care what other people think. They do it to make themselves happy, and that's what's most important to them."

So tattoos and nose rings might not be just random fashion trends after all. Instead, they are a medium for self-expression and the communication of individuality. They fit the generational trend perfectly: they are outward expressions of the inner self. They allow you to be different and unique. It's so important to be an individual, and to communicate that to others, that young people routinely tattoo it onto their skin.

Materialism

GenMe's brand of self-importance also shows up as materialism. In 1967, when the Boomers were in college, 42% of freshmen said it was important to be well-off financially. By 2013, a stunning 82% embraced this life goal—an all-time high. More now say their reason for going to college is "to make more money"—75% in 2012 compared to 45% in 1971. It's not just college students—high school students are now more likely to say that it's important to have a new car every two to three years, a vacation home, and lots of money.

Some of this is probably due to necessities such as housing being more expensive—it takes more money to get by now. But notice the question says "*very* well-off financially"—not merely comfortable. And no one needs a vacation house or a new car every two to three years.

GenMe has always lived in a time when possessions were valued. Boomers were exposed to the nascent beginnings of marketing to children in the 1950s, but advertising aimed specifically at children has increased exponentially within the last few decades. If it's plastic and advertised on TV, kids want it. As Juliet Schor documents in her book *Born to Buy*, kids have much more spending power these days, and parents include them in many more consumer decisions. Advertising is common in many schools, and children can identify brands when they are 18 months old. College students have fully ingrained these attitudes—the new trend is designer dorm rooms with coordinated bedding and new couches. College kids spend $50 billion a year on decorating their spaces, about $900 each on average.

Materialism is prominently displayed on reality shows, especially the "famous for being famous" shows such as the *Real Housewives* (none of whom do much housework in their mansions) and *Keeping Up with the Kardashians* (a play on the materialistic desire to "keep up with the Joneses"). Many people don't just watch displays of materialism but flaunt it themselves: YouTube features an entire genre of posts called haul videos, in which people display their "haul" from their latest shopping trip. Some of these videos have been viewed tens of millions of times.

Materialism is the most obvious outcome of a straightforward, practical focus on the self: you want more things for yourself. You feel entitled to get the best in life: the best clothes, the best house, the best car. You're special; you deserve special things. Seventeen-year-old Jocelyn Bower's uncle, Kevin Arnett, bought her a $8,275 Versace gown to wear to her high school prom. Arnett explains, "She's a very good girl, one of a kind, and she should have it." Next year, Jocelyn says, "We'll hopefully go back to Versace and get an even more expensive dress!" This might be unusually extravagant, but the days of a $100 dress and a dance in the gym are clearly over. A recent survey found that the average family spends $1,078 on prom; in the early 2000s, the average was instead $300.

In his survey of 18-to-23-year-olds, Christian Smith found

that 65% said that shopping and buying things gave them a lot of pleasure. The vast majority—91%—saw no problems or only minor problems with mass consumerism. Going into their in-depth interviews, Smith and his colleagues expected they would hear "a variety of perspectives" on consumerism—perhaps focusing on the effects on the environment, the political implications of consumerism, or the importance of personal or spiritual growth instead of possessions. "But," he writes, "we heard almost none of that. We actually started off in these discussions very cautiously, determined not to be leading in these directions with our questions, since we assumed that many emerging adults would be primed to criticize mass consumerism. But when we heard no such critiques, we began to press harder. Soon we were nearly pushing the emerging adults we interviewed to consider any plausible problematic side to mass consumerism, if they could. They could not." As to why they liked buying things, most said it was because it made them happy, or because "consuming is good for the economy." And why did they not criticize people who own too much? "To each his own" was a common theme—consistent with the rise in individualism.

A Sears ad for girls' clothing ties it all together: "You gotta believe in your dreams. You gotta stand up for yourself. You gotta be there for your friends. But, hey, first you gotta have something to wear. You gotta have the clothes." And the clothes the model is wearing? The outfit costs $267. A young woman in Smith's survey put it this way: "When I'm having a bad day, a bad week, whatever, there is nothing that makes me feel better about myself than going and buying myself a whole new wardrobe." When another was asked if mass consumption might be at all destructive to society, she answered, "I love to shop."

The virtue of expensive things is comfort, enjoyment, and getting what you want. In the past, many people wanted a big house to impress people. GenMe wants a big house so each family member can have as much personal space as possible, consistent with the needs of the individual. Kids don't want to share rooms anymore, and parents like to have "retreats" off the master bedroom where they can relax away from the kids. Plus we need places to put all of the stuff we buy, such as our computers and our game systems. And everyone wants to move out of the apartment where he can smell his neighbor's food and hear his neighbor's music. SUVs serve much the same purpose, building an impenetrable fortress around the individual even when driving to the grocery store. We also shun used things and hand-me-downs; in the pursuit of individualism, we want something made just for us that's shiny and new. "Why go on your honeymoon with the same old luggage?" asks an ad. (I dunno—because your old luggage is just fine?) It's a long way from my father's and grandfather's favorite phrase: "Use it up, wear it out, make it do, or do without."

So many products now cater to the tastes of the individual. Instead of listening to the radio and hearing what everyone else does, we program our own special mix on our iPhone, put in our headphones, and enter an individually created world. We even choose unique ringtones for our cell phones. Instead of three or four network stations, we can watch cable channels dedicated to our own interests. Instead of watching TV live with everyone else in our time zone, we record it and watch it when we want to. "I want to do things that conform to my time frame, not someone else's," said UCLA senior Matthew Khalil on why he rarely goes to the movie theater anymore but instead watches DVDs at home.

Individualism has driven the increasingly large universe of consumer choice in other things as well. Within a few decades, cream and sugar became decaf skim cappuccino grande to go. The coffee choices at Starbucks amount to 19,000 combinations—what better way to feel like an individual? From clothing to cars to jewelry, consumer products are designed to exhibit the wants of the unique self. "Shopping, like everything else, has become a means of self-exploration and self-expression," writes David Brooks.

The individualistic ethos of America also explains a lot of negative trends that we see around us every day. A trip to the grocery store, as just one example, often involves aggressive drivers, sullen clerks, and screaming children. Then there's that ultimate modern annoyance: the people who talk loudly on their cell phones, oblivious of their effect on others. GenMe didn't pioneer this trend—it's popular among middle-aged people as well—but young people are certainly continuing it. It's not the technology that causes the problem, but the attitude that comes with it, an attitude that captures the trend toward self-importance better than almost anything else. "Years ago, cell phones were the province of the powerful, but now that they are mass-market items, everyone has delusions of grandeur," says Eric Cohen, editor of the *New Atlantis*. "Now there are 280 million masters of the universe in America."

4

The Age of Anxiety (and Depression, and Loneliness): Generation Stressed

In most ways, Kim looks like a well-adjusted college student. She dates her high school sweetheart and is studying psychology at a university in the Midwest. For the past five years, however, Kim has struggled with severe depression. When it was at its worst, she could not force herself to get out of bed to go to class. After hours of therapy and courses of antidepressant drugs, Kim was stable and ready to graduate; then she had a relapse. Now it will take her another year to finish college as she tries to manage her depression.

Jason, 22, appeared from the outside to have everything: he had just graduated with honors from an Ivy League university and was starting his first job at a leading investment-banking firm. But he soon found that his job was not what he had imagined—the bosses doled out constant criticism and expected sixteen-hour days. The work was boring. Jason hated it, so after three months, he quit. Suddenly uncertain about what he wanted to do with his life, he sank into depression. He was devastated that a lifetime of achieving his goals had not brought him happiness.

Beth, 19, became severely depressed in high school and seriously considered suicide. "My parents thought I was just a grumpy teenager," she says. "They didn't realize there were demons inside my head that screamed at me and ripped my life apart." Although her parents were opposed to the idea, she eventually saw a therapist and began to take antidepressant medication. "I have so many more opportunities now that I can control the depression and the crippling panic attacks," she says.

Being young has not always carried such a high risk of being anxious, depressed, suicidal, or medicated. Only 1% to 2% of Americans born before 1915 experienced a major depressive episode during their lifetimes, even though they lived through the Great Depression and two world wars. Today, the lifetime rate of major depression is ten times higher—between 15% and 20%. Some studies put the figure closer to 50%. Although some of this trend might be due to more frequent reporting of mental illness, researchers have concluded that the change is too large and too consistent across studies to be explained solely by a reporting bias. In addition, these studies use a fairly strict definition, counting only depression severe enough to warrant medication or long-term therapy. If more mild depression were included, the vast majority of young people would raise their hands in recognition.

Depression is oddly commonplace. In a mid-2000s TV commercial, a frowning, oval-shaped blob becomes happy and smiling after taking the antidepressant medication Zoloft. Panic attacks and OCD are the subject of cocktail-party conversation and TV episodes. Almost every high school and college student knows someone who committed suicide or tried. In past generations, suicide and depression were considered afflictions of middle age, as it was unusual for a young person to be depressed, but for Generation Me, these problems are a rite of passage through adolescence and young adulthood. Karen, 23, became depressed during college, as did her brother. One thing that helped, she said, was realizing that for young people "going through a time of depression is normal."

It wasn't always "normal," but it is certainly heading in that direction. One out of 10 Americans took an antidepressant in 2008, twice as many as in 1996. At the Kansas State University

The ubiquitous sad blob of Zoloft. Correct your chemical imbalances and you might become a happy blob.

counseling center, the number of students treated for depression doubled between 1988 and 2001, and the number who were suicidal tripled. A 2010 study found that college counseling centers increasingly saw students with more severe mental-health issues, and twice as many used psychiatric medications as compared to

1997. In a nationwide survey of teens in 2011, 29% said they had felt sad or helpless almost every day for two or more weeks in a row—a common definition of depression.

I wanted to find out if this trend extended to feelings of anxiety, which often lead to depression as well as to intestinal problems, relationship dysfunction, and low life satisfaction. If anxiety had increased, this would truly be bad news for young people. As part of my doctoral dissertation, I gathered data on 40,192 college students and 12,056 children aged 9 to 17 who completed measures of anxiety between the 1950s and the 1990s. I was stunned by the size of the changes. Anxiety increased so much that the average college student in the 1990s was more anxious than 85% of students in the 1950s and 71% of students in the 1970s. The trend for children was even more striking: children as young as 9 years old were markedly more anxious than kids had been in the 1950s. The change was so large that "normal" schoolchildren in the 1980s reported higher levels of anxiety than child psychiatric patients in the 1950s.

This study had another surprising finding: when you were born has more influence on your anxiety level than your individual family environment. Previous research found that family environment explains only about 5% of variations in anxiety (much of the rest is a combination of genetics, peer influence, and unknown factors). Generational differences explained about 20% of the variation in anxiety—thus four times more than family environment. So even if you come from a stable, loving family, growing up in the late 20th century might be enough to make you anxious.

So did this trend continue into the 2000s, and thus into GenMe? My coauthors and I analyzed data from 63,706 college students and 13,870 high school students who completed the Minnesota Multiphasic Personality Inventory (MMPI) between 1938 and 2007. Recent students were much more likely to score at a problematic level on the MMPI's scales of psychopathology. Seven times more scored high on hypomania, five times more on psychopathic deviation, and seven times more on depression. Thirty-one percent of the recent students scored above the cutoff for hypomania, characterized by an unrealistically positive self-appraisal, overactivity, and low self-control. Samples of high school students showed similar increases in psychopathology. Anxiety also increased: Thirty percent of college freshmen reported feeling "overwhelmed by all I have to do" in 2012, nearly twice as many as in the 1980s. More also described themselves as below average in mental health.

The picture is not completely bleak: teen suicides are down 22% since the 1990s, and self-reports of anxiety and depression have leveled off—though, admittedly, at levels that are still markedly higher than those of the 1960s and 1970s. With 1 out of 10 Americans taking an anti-depressant, we may have medicated away any continued rise in anxiety, depression, and suicide.

Stress is also showing up in physical symptoms—complaints most people don't even connect to mental health (which get around the possibility that GenMe is simply more willing to admit to mental health issues). More high school students in 2012 (versus 1982) reported common psychosomatic symptoms of depression and anxiety. Three times as many high school students in 2012 (versus 1982) said they had trouble sleeping most nights. Twice as many students in 2012 (versus 1982) reported being seen by a doctor or other professional for mental health issues. Yet slightly fewer said they suffered from a cold, suggesting that GenMe wasn't simply more likely to complain about everything.

Adults also seem to be suffering more. Drawing from the nationwide DDB Needham Life Style Survey, Chris Herbst found that 2005 (versus 1985) adults were much more likely to report psychosomatic symptoms. More said they suffered from headaches, more had trouble sleeping, fewer agreed they were in good physical condition, and more said they were "under a great deal of pressure most of the time."

Many young people shared their stories of depression and anxiety with me through my website. In answer to the question "Have you experienced anxiety, stress, or depression?" Josie, 19, wrote, "Duh. The first time depression really showed up in me was probably age 11. Anxiety has been a thing in my life for as long as I can remember." Emma sounds like many high school students these days: "I face anxiety and stress on a daily basis due to the pressure of school. Parents are pushing their kids much harder so they can get into a prestigious college and be successful. Everyone around me seems to be better than me—there's a lot more pressure to do well in everything."

Several young people confessed to being suicidal in their early teens. Clarissa, now 20, became depressed when she was 11. At 13, she locked herself in her room for a week and refused to speak to anyone. She took apart a plastic razor, thinking "about slicing my wrist open and watching the life drain away, taking the pain and loneliness with it." Fortunately, she realized what she was doing and soon began counseling. Matt, 28, stood at the top of a rock quarry when he was 13 and thought of "ending it all by jumping." He didn't, but only because he wondered what the future would bring: "Even though that day and the preceding days basically sucked, tomorrow may suck in a novel way." Debbie, 20, says that when she was 13, "I became unable to see that people around me cared. I was confused and unsure of how to get through the transition of child to young adult. I contemplated suicide, but when it came to it, I couldn't actually cut my flesh because I thought about my family and how awful they would feel if they buried me."

Someone commits suicide every eighteen minutes in the United States. While the suicide rate for middle-aged people has declined steeply since 1950, the suicide rate for young people is now twice as high (even though it's lower now than in the early 1990s). The suicide rate for children under age 14 has doubled just since 1980. Suicide is the fourth leading cause of death for people aged 15 to 24. In 2011, 16% of high school students admitted that they had seriously considered attempting suicide during the past year, and most of those said they had made a plan for exactly how they would kill themselves. These suicidal thoughts are often brought on by depression. Miranda, an 18-year-old from the Midwest, tried to commit suicide by overdosing on drugs. "Depression tends to grab people and suck them in," she says.

Headline after headline in the past few years has announced the suicide of a teen who was bullied. Years of bullying led 15-year-old Bart Palosz to kill himself with a shotgun after the first day of his sophomore year at Greenwich High School in Connecticut. That June, he had written to a friend, "I have chosen to go with 3 peoples advice and kill myself, I just wish it was faster." After a dispute over a boy, girls sent 12-year-old Rebecca Ann Sedwick texts such as "can u die please?" "why are you still alive?" and "go kill yourself." She did, stepping off a platform at an abandoned cement plant.

BUT SHOULDN'T WE BE HAPPIER NOW?

At first, it seems paradoxical that GenMe feels so much anxiety and pain. After all, the lives of people born in the 1980s and 1990s have been remarkably free of traumatic historical events. There have been no world wars, and fewer worries of nuclear war. The threat of terrorism to Americans did not emerge until after the rise in depression was well established. GenMe has never been drafted. Advances in health care and safety mean that more kids live longer and better lives. More students graduate from high school, and fewer are involved in crime than in the early 1990s. Teen pregnancy rates have also markedly declined since the early 1990s. These improving youth trends are one place where Howe and Strauss's *Millennials Rising* got it right.

In many ways, there's no better time to be alive than right now. Think of all of the advantages we have that earlier generations did not: television, cell phones, better medical care, computers and the Internet, more education, less physical labor, the freedom to make our own choices, the ability to move to a more desirable city. These last two, however, begin to hint at the underlying problem. The growing tendency to put the self first leads to unparalleled freedom, but it also creates enormous pressure to stand alone. This is the downside of the focus on the self—when we are fiercely independent and self-sufficient, our disappointments loom large because we have nothing else to focus on. Generation Me has been taught to expect more out of life at the very time when good jobs and nice houses are increasingly difficult to obtain. All too often, the result is crippling anxiety and crushing depression.

Or just plain unhappiness. In a well-publicized 2009 report, two economists found that women's self-reported happiness had slid in national surveys between the 1970s and 2006. Chris Herbst analyzed another national survey of adults (average age 47) and found that both men and women decreased in happiness between 1985 and 2005. More agreed that "I wish I could leave my present life and do something entirely different" and "If I had my life to live over, I would sure do things differently." Interestingly, fewer in 2005 agreed that "I have more self-confidence than most people," suggesting that by adulthood, the generational increase in self-esteem may have begun to falter, replaced by unhappiness and regret.

Why has this generation, and this cultural moment, seemingly so full of promise, also resulted in more stress, anxiety, and depression? We'll explore a number of possible reasons.

LONELINESS AND ISOLATION

My friend Peter moved to an apartment on the North Side of Chicago after graduating from college. He did not seem happy when I visited him that fall. He had several hellish stories about going out on dates through personal ads, including with one woman who told him outright that he was not good-looking enough. His friends from college were either still living near campus or had scattered to graduate schools around the country. In his apartment, he showed me the feature on his cable TV that allowed him to buy movies. "This is what I do most weekends," he said, a sad smile on his face.

He's not the only one. More than four times as many Americans describe themselves as lonely now than in 1957. In *Bowling Alone*, Robert Putnam documents the steep decline in all kinds of social connections: we're less likely to belong to clubs and community organizations, less likely to have friends over for dinner, and less likely to visit our neighbors. Across many studies, people who do these things are more likely to be happy and satisfied with their lives. Putnam found that regular participation in clubs and other social activities increased happiness as much as obtaining a college degree or doubling your income. Yet close social connections may be harder to come by. One study found that in 1985, the average American had three people with whom he or she could "discuss important matters"; by 2004, that had shrunk to zero. Our social contacts are slight compared to those enjoyed by earlier generations.

It's almost as if GenMe is starving for affection. "There is a kind of famine of warm interpersonal relations, of easy-to-reach neighbors, of encircling, inclusive memberships, and of solid family life," argues political scientist Robert Lane. To take the analogy a little further, we're malnourished from eating a junk-food diet of instant messages, Facebook posts, e-mail, and phone calls, rather than the healthy food of live, in-person interaction. One of the few exceptions: with more in GenMe living with their parents, they do get more family interaction in their 20s than previous generations did.

But that can't take the place of an adult romantic relationship. It helps explain a new kind of get-together that's popping up in cities around the country: cuddle parties. It's a deliberately non-sexual (though usually coed) gathering where pajama-clad people can enjoy the hugs and touch of others, overseen by a "cuddle lifeguard on duty," who keeps things friendly and nonthreatening. One 26-year-old participant called it "rehab for lonely people." As the official website (www.cuddleparty.com) explains, "In today's world, many of us aren't getting our Recommended Daily Allowance of Welcomed Touch." Most cuddle party participants are young and single. As the website notes, "It's okay to touch the one you're dating or married to . . . but what about the single people? . . . We are touch-and-snuggle deprived."

For many in GenMe, the instability in close relationships began at an early age with their parents' divorce. In *Prozac Nation*, her memoir of adolescent depression, Elizabeth Wurtzel describes her father's departure from her life and her mother's subsequent struggle to raise her. When Wurtzel told her therapists about her background, they would say, "No wonder you're so depressed." She was not as sure. "They react as if my family situation was particularly alarming and troublesome," she writes, "as opposed to what it actually is in this day and age: perfectly normal." And she's right: almost half of GenMe has seen their parents divorce or have never known their father at all. This has a clear link to the rise in depression, as children of divorce are more likely to be anxious and depressed. Beyond the statistics, the personal stories of children of divorce—painted in such books as *The Unexpected Legacy of Divorce*—vividly illustrate the lifetime of pain, cynicism, and uncertainty that divorce can create among young people. Ashley, now 24, attended a group counseling session at her elementary school, unofficially known as the "divorce club," where she and the other kids would "share our feelings of anger, sadness and confusion and listen to our peers who were sharing the same."

GenMe's own romantic relationships often don't go much better. Although a little extreme, the situations faced by the four characters on *Sex and the City* (or, more recently, HBO's *Girls*) are right on the mark; the young women I know describe similar dating pitfalls of strange behavior and dashed hopes. Even when the date goes well and becomes a relationship, there is no guarantee it will last. The cycle of meeting someone, falling in love, and breaking up is a formula for anxiety and depression. Although previous generations also went through these relationship ups and downs, they did so for a much shorter time. GenMe's lengthened adolescence has led to a lengthened time for heartbreak. As Emma Koenig puts it in her 2012 book *F*ck! I'm in My Twenties*, "There should be some kind of loyalty rewards program for getting hurt over and over again."

Some young people think there has to be a better way. One day in a graduate class on cultural differences, I was surprised when the students—almost all Americans from the Midwest and West—expressed their approval of arranged marriage. Two women in their mid-20s were particularly adamant: they hated dating, living alone sucked, and they wanted to settle down. The men in the class agreed. Arranged marriage is probably not the solution, but the students' attraction to the idea is telling—young people clearly feel that something is missing in the current dating scene. The Broadway musical *Avenue Q* includes a song that sums up dating in the modern era pretty well: "There's a fine, fine line between love—and a waste of time." The book *Motherhood, Rescheduled* tells of the ups and downs of the romantic lives of four women who choose to freeze their eggs. Although all want to have children, none was able to settle into a stable romantic relationship before 40.

A record 28% of US households are headed by a single person. Though later marriage has some advantages, it also means that many in GenMe spend their 20s (and sometimes 30s) in pointless dating, uncertain relationships, and painful breakups. Many relationships last several years and/or include living together, so the breakups resemble divorces rather than run-of-the-mill heartbreak (as if there were such a thing). By the age of 24, my friend June had been in five serious relationships. All had lasted more than a year, and all resulted in a wrenching breakup (often because she or her boyfriend was moving to a new city for college, graduate school, or a career). Other friends dated or lived with someone for seven years or more before breaking up. Divorce after only a few years of marriage has become so common that Pamela Paul wrote a book called *The Starter Marriage*. Only the rare member of GenMe has not experienced the breakup of a serious romantic relationship (or two or five or ten).

The deadline for having children— generally somewhere between 35 and 40—makes life extremely anxious for many single women. They constantly perform the calculation I call "woman math": "If we get married next year, I'll be thirty-four; we'll want a year or two to be married without kids, so I'll be thirty-six or thirty-seven before I'm pregnant and probably thirty-eight when the child is born. Then if we wait until the first kid is two years old before we try for another one, I'll be trying to get pregnant at forty. Crap."

Even—or especially—women who are living with their boyfriend hear the loud ticking of the biological clock as years go by and no proposal is imminent. The new equation of premarital sex and living together before marriage might be liberating, but it has major downsides. Waiting for a guy to pop the question can be almost as anxiety-producing as being alone. Laurie, interviewed in *Emerging Adulthood*, says that during the five years she lived with the man she eventually married, "I was really stressed because I didn't know exactly whether or not I was going to be with him or if I was wasting that much time in my life." Another couple described in the book has been living together for eighteen months. Jean, 26, wants to be engaged by Christmas. When the author interviews her boyfriend Trey, 28, however, "it becomes clear that Jean can forget about getting engaged by Christmas. . . . Trey says he might get married—'possibly someday . . . I'm not ready to settle down yet.'" Men have the advantage of a biological clock set at a later time. As Jake puts it, "I could be thirty-five and marry someone who's twenty-three. I mean, I've got all the time in the world." (Women have a word for guys like this, and it ends with *hole*.)

But plenty of lonely guys are out there too. Thousands more young men than women are single—between the ages of 25 and 39, for every unmarried woman there are 1.2 unmarried men. Even when you look only between the ages of 35 and 39, thousands more men are unmarried. I can hear women immediately yelling that all of the good ones are taken, but single men should be the ones anxious and complaining. Men get lonely too, though we rarely see that addressed on TV or in the movies. (For a noteworthy exception, check out the great movie *Swingers*, which features a fairly realistic look at young men talking about loneliness and their anxiety around dating.) For GenMe, loneliness is an equal-opportunity experience.

As a result of modern dating, later marriage, and the higher divorce rate, a lot of people spend a great deal of time living alone. In 1950, only 9% of Americans lived alone. By 2010, 28% did. Almost half of all households in Washington, DC, and Manhattan consist of one person. A recent in-depth study found that Chicago residents, on average, spend half of their adult lives single. Being single does not have to be lonely, but for many people it often is, especially if they have been moving around and don't have friends who live close to them.

That's the other sad reality: not only is GenMe single for longer, but they often don't stay in one place long enough to make friends. More than 1 out of 4 people aged 25 to 29 moved in the last year. It is shocking to consider the number of professions that require frequent moves for advancement. This is definitely true in academia: I have lived in six states, my friend Kathleen has lived in all four North American time zones, and few of my friends live within 500 miles of where they grew up. Doctors must move to medical school and to a residency before looking for a city in which to practice. Even professions that don't require an advanced degree often involve frequent moves. I recently met a group of people who work in sales for a hotel chain. All had worked at more than four locations, requiring them to move every few years. Author Chris Colin summed it up this way when he was in his late 20s: "Since high school I've had five lines of work . . . eight street addresses, two bad trips, and one cat. I had a lousy breakup with doors slamming—house doors, car doors. I lived in New York and California and Chile. . . . I worry, but really I'm happy, though I worry."

Even if you stay in the same place, just having time to date and make friends is difficult. With the workweek expanding from relatively sane nine-to-five hours into countless evenings and weekends, it's often impossible to find the time and energy to be with other people. "A decade after high school, that which most impacts my classmates' love lives might be busyness," says Colin. Seventy-five percent of women aged 25 to 35 say that their work lives interfere with their personal lives, and 35% say that the conflict is extreme. This goes for men as well—in the first years of his career, my brother worked so many hours that when I visited him, his refrigerator contained nothing but a bottle of water ("I bought that for you," he said helpfully). I started to make a grocery list and then stopped short, wondering if I needed to buy more than food. "Do you even have any bowls?" I asked. "I have bowl," he quipped, opening the cabinet to reveal his lone dish.

Friends of mine who are lawyers and accountants often find it difficult to spare the time for a movie, a phone call to a long-distance friend, or a casual chat with a neighbor. In *The Costs of Living*, Barry Schwartz describes a former student who says his friendships "were not that close. Everyone was too busy. He thought twice about burdening friends with his life and his problems because he knew how consumed they were with their own, and what a sacrifice it would entail for them to spend the time required to listen to him and to help him out." I put a Post-it note on that page and wrote, "This is a very familiar story."

Is this better in the age of Facebook? That's unclear. Some studies suggest that using Facebook leads to more happiness; others suggest it leads to less. It may depend on whether social networking takes the place of in-person interaction or enhances it. It remains to be seen whether social networking helps build true and healthy social connections or whether these online interactions are too shallow to be helpful.

Isolation and loneliness readily lead to anxiety and depression. A mountain of scientific evidence links loneliness (and being alone) with negative mental health outcomes. Single and divorced people are significantly more likely to become depressed or suffer other mental health problems. Even people in unhappy marriages are happier than those who divorce. In many situations divorce is necessary and best in the long run, but even then it is painful and can lead to depression. When you consider the loneliness felt by many young people today, it's surprising that a larger number aren't depressed. Many in GenMe are one breakup or one move away from depression—their roots are not deep enough, their support systems too shallow.

The sadness of being alone is often the flip side of freedom and putting ourselves first. When we pursue our own dreams and make our own choices, that pursuit often takes us away from friends and family. An independence-minded society such as ours would never accept rules that encouraged arranged marriage or multigenerational households. Even marriage before a certain age—these days, around 25—is viewed as unwise and overly restricting. There is nothing wrong with individual freedom; this is the advantage of the social change of the last few decades. But there are consequences, and loneliness is often one of them. Janis Joplin presciently captured the GenMe dilemma when she sang in 1971, "Freedom's just another word for nothing left to lose."

One of the strangest things about modern life is the expectation that we will stand alone, negotiating breakups, moves, divorces, and all manner of heartbreak that previous generations were careful to avoid. This may be the key to the low rate of depression among older generations: despite all the deprivation and war they experienced, they could always count on one another. People had strong feelings of community; they knew the same people all their lives; and they married young and stayed married. It may not have been exciting, and it stymied the dreams of many, but this stable lifestyle avoided the melancholy that is so common now.

STRESS IN COLLEGE ADMISSIONS AND JOBS

We live in an increasingly competitive world, and nowhere is this more evident than in college admissions. Many high school students determined to attend an Ivy League university strive for perfect grades, perfect SAT scores, and a long list of extracurricular activities. But even perfection is not enough these days: most Ivy League schools admit less than 10% of applicants overall. Each year, Harvard rejects between 25% and 50% of applicants with perfect SAT scores. This stringent selectivity extends beyond the Ivy League: Duke University rejected 60% of high school valedictorians who applied. Public universities have become more discerning as well. In recent classes, the majority of freshmen at the University of Wisconsin graduated in the top 10% of their high school class. San Diego State University, where I teach, used to be a party school almost anyone could get into, but these days the average undergraduate earned a 3.8 GPA in high school and scored around the 70th percentile on her SATs.

At the same time, young people and their parents are increasingly aware that a college education—sometimes the right college education—is a virtual necessity for securing a good job. Erica, 18, felt this pressure during high school: "I have gotten down on myself for not trying as hard or doing as well as I should have. I put all the pressure on myself. I knew I needed to do well to get into a good college. It seems to be very difficult to get a decent-paying job nowadays without a college education." And although the local state university might be fine for most jobs, for others only the right school will do. Many New York investment banks, for example, focus their recruiting on Ivy League universities, and many graduate schools favor applicants from prestigious schools.

The new level of competition means that more and more high school students are going to great lengths to stand out. Two million high school students took Advanced Placement (AP) exams in 2012, four times as many as in 1994. *Time* magazine interviewed Marielle Woods, 17, who participates in twelve extracurricular activities and keeps up a 4.0 average. This can lead to a lot of stress. Jill, 23, describes her overachieving family as "a recipe for quiet terror." Although she's done well in school, "always, *always* before those grades come out, I struggle under the weight of a cloud of fear and depression," she says. "Every year I'm silently convinced that this will be the one—this time I'll actually screw it all up. It's a scary way to live."

The battle is not over after college, either. Medical schools and law schools, especially the prestigious ones, admit only a small fraction of applicants. Yale Law School lets in only 8% of applicants; the University of Virginia law school, 9%. Medical schools are even more competitive—Harvard Medical School admitted only 4% of applicants in 2010; UCLA, 4%; and the University of Wisconsin, 10%. Most years, more than half of medical school applicants are not admitted to any program. Other fields are fiercely competitive as well: graduate schools in clinical psychology often admit less than 10% of hopefuls. For example, the SDSU/UCSD joint doctoral program in clinical psychology at my school lets in only 4% of those who apply. One of my brightest, hardest-working master's students applied to six PhD programs in counseling psychology, which are usually easier to get into than clinical programs. Nevertheless, she wasn't admitted to a single program. MBA acceptance rates are a little higher, though at the best schools they hover around 10% to 15%. And these decisions are crucial: many economists say that a graduate degree is now the key to "making it," in the same way a college degree used to be.

Young college graduates often find the job market difficult even during boom times, particularly if they majored in the liberal arts. "I spent four months crashing on a friend's couch and looking for a job—every job from technical writer to bellhop," writes Kevin, 25, who graduated from college with a degree in English. "Flash forward a year later and I'm working in a warehouse. Then the boss cut our hours. Eventually I quit and moved into my grandfather's basement at the age of 24." Even business graduates can have a hard time. "When I graduated from college, I thought getting a job would be a snap, because that's the impression we got from the career counselors and everyone around us. Boy, was I wrong," says Kristina, interviewed in *Quarterlife Crisis*. "For the first six months after school, I couldn't even get an administrative position."

Academia is also not a guaranteed career path anymore. The majority of people who earn PhDs in English and history cannot find a university teaching job and consequently drop out of the field. Those in scientific fields must often complete several two- or three-year-long postdocs (temporary research jobs) after obtaining their PhDs—and then might still not find a job. A recent *New York Times* article described a Harvard physics PhD who had four postdocs in ten years and could still not find a faculty position. At 43, he finally left the field. He's not unusual; many young scientists are 35 or 40 by the time they've finished enough postdocs to get a job. One friend of mine was a postdoc for six years before he had a nervous breakdown that landed him in the university medical center. He did eventually find a faculty job, but it was a long road.

There is also a pervasive uncertainty about finding the right profession. It's great to have the freedom to be whatever you want, but what exactly is that? I remember making a list of all the possible college majors and crossing them off one by one, as if the process of elimination would help me figure out what to do with my life. Settling on a career goal is even more challenging, and many people continue to struggle with this question throughout their 20s. It's particularly difficult because good information about professions is hard to come by—it's hard to know what being a lawyer, an accountant, or an engineer is like day-to-day. So you might go through four or seven years of school only to find out you hate your profession. Or you might settle on a lucrative one but then wonder if you're doing the world any good by practicing it. GenMe'ers worry about making the right choice and have no one but themselves to blame when their choices go wrong. Personal freedom, the hallmark of our times, is glorious, but too often GenMe'ers stand alone with their self-doubts about their choices.

It's often difficult for young people to make the transition from the more certain world of college to the working world—or even graduate school—where "doing your best" isn't always enough and choices aren't always clear. Drew Lichtenberger, whom I met on a generations chat board when he was 28, called the pervasive malaise of his generation "the twenties beatdown"—and that was before the late 2000s recession. When he was starting his first job in business and his then girlfriend was in law school, they talked frequently about how their 20s were turning out to be much more challenging than they'd expected. Even his friends who were successful wondered about fulfillment, asking, "Is this what I want to do with my life? Is it meaningful enough?" His summary of his friends' 20s experiences was "they used to be supersuccessful people and now they're just freshmen in life."

THE NEW ECONOMICS

This is the scenario for young people today: To get a decent job, you must have a college degree, preferably from a good school. It is harder to get into a good college, and it's more expensive. Once you get in and graduate, it is difficult to get into graduate school and sometimes even more difficult to find a job. Once you find a job, corporate downsizing and restructuring create the constant threat of layoffs. By the time you're in your 30s, career pressures are compounded by the demands of raising children when both of you have to work to pay the bills.

It is easy to say that this is just GenMe whining; things have always been tough—stop complaining and deal with it. Looked at objectively, however, things *are* harder now for young people. The age distribution of wealth has changed markedly in this country: between 1984 and 2011, the wealth of older adults in the United States increased 37% when adjusted for inflation, while younger adults' wealth fell by 44%. As the Pew Center's Paul Taylor puts it, "Millennials and Xers are not only in far worse financial shape than Boomers and Silents now, they are also in worse shape than these older generations were back when they were at the age that Millennials and Xers are now."

In addition, income inequality has raised the stakes for getting by, creating a bigger divide between the haves and have-nots. It's not just that the rich are getting richer, it's that the rest of us are getting poorer. It was once possible to support a family on one middle-class or even working-class income. No longer. Many blue-collar jobs with good wages have been shipped overseas, and many white-collar jobs don't pay that well either. "You need a college degree now just to be where blue-collar people the same age were twenty or thirty years ago," says sociologist James Côté.

Anne, 20, has experienced this firsthand. "When my parents were growing up, all they really needed was a high school degree to get by, but now things are so much harder, and the pressure is put on you to go to college and get a degree," she says. "It seems more people in today's generation are depressed because they can't achieve their dream of owning their own house because the world has become so much more competitive." The link to mental health issues is more than theoretical: women living in states with greater income inequality—where the rich are richer and the poor are poorer—are more likely to be depressed. The effect held even when the researchers controlled for other factors such as age, unemployment, and education.

Feeling surrounded by wealth when you're struggling to get by is depressing. That's exactly the change of the past decades: since 1970, the share of the wealth held by the top 1% has more than doubled, from 9% to 23%. The top 10% once held about 33% of the wealth; they now hold a full 50%. A shocking 96% of the growth in incomes between 1981 and 2008 went to the top 10%. The median wage of American men declined 28% between 1968 and 2010. Even before the late 2000s recession, incomes for the middle class were declining. Then they plunged another 12%.

These days, the essentials are astronomically expensive: education, housing, day-care, and health-care costs have all far outstripped inflation—so much so that more young people than ever live with their parents well into adulthood.

Most GenMe'ers begin their foray into adulthood by starting college—and soon learn just how expensive that can be. Americans now owe more in student debt than they do on credit cards. In 2010, 40% of all American families headed by someone under 35 had student loan debt, more than double the 17% who carried student loan debt in 1989. College students in the 1960s or even the 1980s could work their way through school with part-time jobs; that's virtually impossible now that yearly tuition, books, and room and board total $44,750 at the average private university and $22,826 at the average public university. Total cost for four years: over $179,000 for a private college and $91,304 for public.

Today's young people are the most highly educated generation ever—more than 30% of people between the ages of 25 and 39 have a college degree. But all of that education comes at a price. Student loan debt has doubled just since 2007; the average member of the class of 2013 owed about $27,000. And that's just undergrad; add graduate or professional school loans and things get even worse. Sarah, 29, wrote, "I have a TON of debt from my law school loan. Think six digits." Casey, 25, describes his English degree as a "framable bill" for $33,000.

After writing the check to pay the installment on the student loan, it's time to write the hefty check for the rent or mortgage. That check is a much larger chunk of the budget than it once was. In 1960, only 12% of renters paid more than 50% of their pretax income for rent, but by 2009 the figure had doubled to 25%. Casey, the college graduate, finally found a job paying about $1,200 a month; rent on his one-bedroom apartment was $700 a month. This is a relative bargain. The median rent in San Francisco was $3,475 in 2013 (and not because places were huge: the average for a one-bedroom was $2,800). Rent in New York City averages over $3,000 a month. The median rent for a one-bedroom in Chicago's Lincoln Park neighborhood will run you $1,550. The median rent in LA County is $1,435. Yes, these are the big cities, but they are also where most of the jobs are, especially for young people. In San Francisco, even the middle to upper-middle class finds rent unaffordable. Former mayor Art Agnos says that the main struggle is "to keep people who make between $60,000 and $150,000 a year." When those making six-figure incomes are struggling to pay the rent, there's clearly a problem. And what about the truly low income? As Agnos says, "Frankly, it's all but over for the poor in this city."

Buying a house is little better. In 1970, the median home price was about three times the median household income. In the mid-2000s, at the height of the housing boom, when many older GenMe'ers and young GenX'ers bought their houses, the median housing price was six times the median income. Even after the crash, the median home price (around $200,000) is still four times the median income. Even after millions of foreclosures, housing still eats up a larger portion of young people's paychecks than it did in the 1970s. And that's just for an average home, presumably in an average school district and an average neighborhood (which often means not very good on either count).

Those who bought at the peak are even less fortunate, with many losing all of their savings and good credit in a foreclosure or paying the mortgage on a house worth 30% less than what they paid for it. Before the crash, the conservative advice was to buy a house if you thought you would stay for at least seven years, because based on historical trends that was more than enough to protect against the ups and downs of the housing market. In 2013, seven years after the housing crash of 2006, most people who bought that year were still living in a house worth less than what they paid—or, worse, they foreclosed or sold at a loss.

Jennifer, 29, is a teacher near Boston. Scanning the newspaper for houses, she would read the ad if the price was under $250,000. "Usually, I would get only a few syllables into it and would ultimately hit one of the following words: *condo*, *duplex*, *mobile home*, *fixer-upper*, or *handyman special*," she says. When she and her husband went to see the few homes in their price range, she says that the ads should have read, "This pile of rotted wood offers 4 rooms and resembles a double-wide trailer. You can store all kinds of crap that you don't care about in the musty, damp cellar that looks like something out of a horror movie" or "Very small house just a few miles into the ghetto. You'll be the envy of your neighbors as they push their shopping-cart homes by your overpriced dump."

Some people have asked me if young people's complaining about the cost of housing was just another sign of entitlement. I didn't think so, given how housing costs had outpaced inflation in most places. Now, fewer people make that comment, perhaps because even people making six-figure incomes struggle to pay the rent in some large cities. There's also much more awareness of income inequality now, after the Occupy protests and the bailouts that protected the rich while the rest of the population saw shrinking incomes. True, GenMe's valuing becoming "very well-off financially" may indicate some entitlement. But wanting to afford the rent on a one-bedroom apartment, not so much. (And, yes, it's possible that high expenses are the reason why GenMe values money so much. However, 90% of the 2010–12 high school senior sample expected to own as much or more than their parents, suggesting not all of their overly optimistic materialism is based on practical considerations.)

Another counterargument: some have pointed out that homes are larger now on average than they were in the 1950s and 1960s. However, this has been driven by McMansions at the high end of the market, not the ridiculously expensive—and often small—houses GenMe is buying. Even though houses are larger on average, even one-bedroom condos and apartments are out of reach for many people in many cities.

A tale of two housing markets.
Top: A young couple poses outside their newly purchased house in Minneapolis, Minnesota, about 1,450 square feet and built in the 1930s. Price tag: $300,000.

Below: A housing development in San Diego, California. Despite their proximity, each of these three houses of 1,300 to 1,700 square feet is worth at least $400,000.

Affordable housing is increasingly scarce even as wages for service workers remain low. In *Nickel and Dimed*, Barbara Ehrenreich reports that the service industry workers she met often lived in their cars because they couldn't afford even a small apartment. Even borderline-affordable apartments were difficult to find, so during much of her yearlong experiment as a service worker, Ehrenreich lived in fleabag motels. "Something is wrong, seriously wrong, when a single person in good health . . . can barely support herself by the sweat of her brow," writes Ehrenreich. "You don't need a degree in economics to see that wages are too low and rents too high."

Many in GenMe don't even try to afford rent. A stunning 1 out of 3—36%—of GenMe'ers (ages 18 to 31) live with their parents. That includes 56% of those between the ages of 18 and 24, and 40% of men under 31. Many young people simply cannot find a job. Unemployment for Americans ages 20 to 24 was 13.4% in the first half of 2013, twice as high as the rate for those ages 25 to 54 (6.5%). Even for those who find jobs, expenses such as rent and student loans often overwhelm their meager resources. This was true even before the late-2000s recession. "I graduated from college with honors in three years but could not find a job that allowed me to become financially independent," wrote Tricia Engelhardt in a letter to *Time* in 2004. "So I moved back in with my parents. I was surprised to find that the majority of my high school class had done the same thing." By 2013, things were even worse. "When my parents were my age, they had their own place already, and they came from Mexico," Patricia Guerra, 24, told the *Los Angeles Times*. "I'm a US citizen with a college degree—and it's really hard for me to achieve that for myself at this point."

The *LA Times* profiled Andrew Post, an academic superstar who began college at 13 and earned a law degree by 22. At 24, he was living with his parents. In 2010, the year he graduated from the University of Southern California's law school, he says, "I competed with three hundred people in my year for the attention of only seven private employers and a handful of government agencies." Unable to find a job, he freelanced as a lawyer for small-business clients. "There were times when I had to decide on whether to buy enough gas to get back to court or buy lunch. The last time I went to court, I was wearing something I got at Goodwill. The two lawyers on the other side were each wearing suits worth more than my car." Post did finally find full-time employment as a programmer for a website operator, but will continue to live at home, primarily because his student loans total $215,000, with a minimum monthly payment of $2,756.

For those who do manage to pay the rent or the mortgage, where does the extra money for housing come from? Primarily from women's salaries. Many families have been able to stay afloat mostly because both adults are in the workforce. Summarizing data from several large studies, political scientist Robert Putnam concludes, "Virtually all of the increase in full-time employment of American women over the last twenty years is attributable to financial pressures, not personal fulfillment."

The dual-income formula works—until the woman (or the man) wants to take some time off to care for a child. With shrinking incomes and higher basic expenses, this is becoming a virtual impossibility for many families. Several couples I know live in apartments or commute two hours to their jobs because that's all they can afford on one income. My childless friends wonder how they will be able to stay in their homes (or buy one) after they have children, given that they both have to work to afford the mortgage payment and the prohibitive cost of full-time day care for an infant (usually $1,200 a month or more—for each kid). The cost varies from state to state, but as of 2010 full-time yearly care for an infant was $11,823 in California, $14,980 in Massachusetts, and a stunning $20,178 in Washington, DC (perhaps because big cities have the highest costs). For the average single mother, day care costs for an infant will eat up 38% of her income. For a family making twice the poverty level (about $37,060), child care for two children would require almost half of their income. When I told my undergraduate class the price of day care, they were stunned; most guessed it cost about $500 a month. I heard a woman in the back row exhale audibly. "I'm not having kids," she said ruefully.

In 35 states and DC, child care for an infant costs more than in-state tuition at a public university; even for 4-year-olds, child care costs more than tuition in 19 states and DC. Child care center fees for two children (an infant and a 4-year-old) cost more than rent in all 50 states and DC. It's difficult to overestimate just how stressful looking for—and paying for—day care is on young families. It is a frequent topic of discussion among pregnant women on message boards. Over and over, women expressed surprise and shock at the outrageous price of day care; most had no idea how expensive it was before they made a few calls. Words such as *nightmare*, *insane*, *freaked-out*, and *scary* were frequent. Describing a day care facility that charged $845 a month, Lauren, 23, wrote, "I nearly choked." Alexandra, 27, responded, "I want to live where you live," explaining that day care was at least $1,000 a month in her city. Many also found long waiting lists and numerous day cares that didn't take infants under six months, or even two years old. With most paid maternity leaves lasting only six weeks (and that's if you even get paid maternity leave), this is a big problem.

Health care costs are also astoundingly high. Even people with good jobs often find themselves paying $500 a month or more for their family's health care premiums—if they have health care at all. The self-employed can lay out over $1,000 a month for just a basic health care plan. And the cost keeps going up: health care premiums have nearly doubled since 2001. Even people who have coverage can run into serious financial trouble if they or their family members develop major health problems. *People* profiled several families, even some with health insurance, who went bankrupt after unexpected medical crises. It remains to be seen whether the implementation of Obamacare will improve these issues.

Many older people seem to have only a faint grasp of how much it costs to raise a family these days, which can subject many young parents to guilt-inducing advice. The current trend is toward attachment parenting, in which you "wear" your baby in a sling, breast-feed for at least a year, and sleep in the same bed with your child. Some of this is still possible if you're working, but William and Martha Sears, the high priest and priestess of attachment parenting, make it clear that this is not desirable. In *The Baby Book*'s 2003 edition, the Searses recommend that couples get used to living on one income before the baby arrives so they don't get too accustomed to having two salaries. (Are they kidding? Most of GenMe is "accustomed" to the mortgage payment eating up one entire salary.) Mothers should stay at home if at all possible, they say, and children under a year should not go to day care centers because of the risk of infectious diseases. Their subheading "I Have to Work—We Need the Income" is placed in quotes as if to question its veracity, and it's followed by advice on how this might not be true—you probably only need that second income for "desired luxuries," they say.

When I read this, I wondered how the authors could be so clueless about housing costs. I turned to the back of the book to scan the "About the Authors" blurb, thinking perhaps the Searses lived in Dallas, Indianapolis, or another undervalued housing market. Nope. They live and practice in San Clemente, California, where (as of October 2013) the least expensive two-bedroom condo was going for $300,000, and the least expensive single-family house cost $449,000 (and this winner had power lines running through the backyard, was 954 square feet, and had just two bedrooms). Three-bedroom houses in San Clemente usually sell for well over $500,000. Yes, this is an especially expensive place to live, but many large cities—the places where most of the jobs are—are not far behind. Unless you've married someone making over $100,000 a year when you're ready to have kids, learning to live on one income is going to mean learning to raise a family in a small apartment (and even that will set you back $2,000 a month in their town). So when the Searses talk about doing without "desired luxuries," do they mean a place to live? What a great idea for the new century—let's all quit work, wear our babies, and live in a cardboard box on the street. (C'mon, kids, it'll be fun!) At least we'd be "attached" to our children, though I bet they'd get a few more infectious diseases than they would have caught at day care.

The Two-Income Trap, by former Harvard professor and US senator Elizabeth Warren, provides a summary of the balance sheet. Fixed costs such as housing, health insurance, and child care have doubled for the average family since the early 1970s, while discretionary income has gone down. (The gap has been filled by more women working.) Families with children are significantly more likely to go bankrupt than childless couples, probably because living in a safe neighborhood with good schools is expensive. Bankruptcy is more common now, Warren argues, because fixed costs such as housing are higher, so there is no way to cut back when things get tough.

To sum up: One parent should stay at home, but to afford a house—and sometimes even the rent—both parents have to work. You "choose" between expensive, difficult-to-find day care and renting an apartment where your child has no space to run around. Even if you don't have children, you face huge bills just for the necessities of life: housing, health care, and paying for those student loans. More and more people are filing for bankruptcy or are on the verge of it. Young people feel screwed no matter what they do—no wonder they're anxious.

WHY GENME YUPPIES ARE UNHAPPY: EXPECTATIONS VERSUS REALITY

So in this world where the essentials are so astronomically expensive, what messages has GenMe been fed? Save your money? Feel lucky to have a house even if it's not a mansion? Of course not. In the world of individualism and consumer longing, GenMe'ers have been taught to expect more. Perhaps because of media exposure, they want to be millionaires, to be famous, to live in a large house and drive fancy cars. It's all they've seen on TV and in movies since they were babies. In the movie *Fight Club*, the character Tyler Durden captures this perspective with searing accuracy: "Our generation has had no Great Depression, no Great War. Our depression is our lives. . . . We were raised on television to believe that we'd all be millionaires, movie gods, rock stars, but we won't. And we're starting to figure that out. And we're very, very pissed off."

These movie lines are ironic; after all, they are delivered by Brad Pitt, a "movie god" if there ever was one. But that's the point: not everyone can grow up to be Brad Pitt or Kobe Bryant or Bill Gates or Jennifer Lopez. It has always been normal for kids to have big dreams, but the dreams of kids today are bigger than ever. By the time kids figure out that they're not going to be celebrities or sports figures, they're well into adolescence or even their 20s. Brian, a character in *Avenue Q*, says that as a kid he thought he'd "grow up to be a comedian on late-night TV." Ten years out of college, he's broke and unemployed. Before long the entire cast is singing a song called "It Sucks to Be Me."

As you might remember from chapter 3, twice as many in GenMe (compared to Boomers in the 1970s) expect to earn graduate degrees and have professional jobs, even though actual attainment of these goals has not changed. Some have even bigger dreams: in 2005, 31% of American high school students said they expected to become famous someday. A 2010 survey raised the bar: 26% of teens expected to become famous by age 25. That survey also found that 93% of teens said they expected to get a college degree, and 81% expected to have a "great-paying job" by 25. On the "Teen Advice" section of about.com, a teen writes, "I want to be famous. I'm not sure what my talent is but I really want to give it a try. Any tips for getting things started?" The answer from the website begins, "OK, first I need to state the obvious . . . who doesn't want to be famous?"

High expectations can be the stuff of inspiration, but more often they set GenMe up for bitter disappointment. *Quarterlife Crisis* concludes that twentysomethings often take a while to realize that the "be whatever you want to be, do whatever you want to do" mantra of their childhoods is not attainable. When they do come to this harsh realization, they say, the feeling resembles that of Charlie Brown falling flat on his back after Lucy pulls away the ball. "I remember hearing things like never give up on your dreams often," writes James, 18. "Learning how meaningless these words truly are reminds me of a kid learning the truth about Santa Claus." Georgia, 19, observes, "My generation thinks they should be doing something great with their lives but don't really try to do anything about it. I've seen several friends drop out of college because they felt they were not doing what they were meant to do. But after they drop out, they don't get a job or anything to try and FIND what they are meant to do. It's like they think a brick is going to come flying in through their window with a note attached telling them their life's purpose and career."

Tim Urban recently published an article in the *Huffington Post* titled "Why Generation Y Yuppies Are Unhappy." This generation, he observes, is "wildly ambitious" and has continually been told they're special. Urban likens Boomers' career expectations to a nice green lawn. But GenMe, he says, is "delusional" as well as ambitious. Each GenMe'er thinks, "I am unusually wonderful and as such, my career and life path will stand out amongst the crowd." So every GenMe'er expects not just the "flowery lawn" but "a shiny unicorn on top." Urban illustrates this with a steeply rising career trajectory with the words "because just wait till the world sees how amazing I am."

The problem, Urban notes, is that the world is not an easy place and building a career takes years of hard work—but GenMe struggles to accept that reality. GenMe's "arrogance" and "huge expectations," he says, mean that reality can't possibly satisfy them—which is why they are unhappy. Urban's piece struck a nerve: before long, the article had 1 million likes on Facebook, had generated almost 4,000 comments, and was e-mailed more than 14,000 times.

Some of these high expectations may have been fostered by a childhood of media consumption. Teens spend a lot more time with media than they used to. A Kaiser Family Foundation study found that teens spent almost eight hours a day with media in 2009, two hours more than they had just five years before; if multitasking with multiple media platforms is included, teens in 2009 spent a jaw-dropping 10 hours and 45 minutes a day with media. This is enough to shape a worldview, and the worldview of media is almost relentlessly exciting and glamorous. Characters on TV shows and in movies rarely have boring jobs working for corporations, building houses, or working a cash register. And even those who work at professions often featured on TV—such as doctors and police officers—will tell you that the day-to-day reality is far less exciting than what you see. In between the shows, advertising constantly asks us if we are good enough, thin enough, rich enough. Writer Cathi Hanauer sums this up as "the ideas and belief—courtesy of a culture ever more mired in materialism, consumerism, and false advertising—that we should have it all, do it all, and be it all, and be Happy. And if we're not, by God, something is wrong." Lynn, 19, agrees that television has inspired many of these unrealistic expectations. "I think there is so much anxiety and depression because of the pressure the media is putting on the world to be perfect. On television, stars are portrayed as beautiful and worry-free. People are spending more and more time trying to make themselves a replica of what they see on TV." That is even more true now that many of the most popular shows are "reality" TV—not a scripted fantasy, but someone's real life. Of course, it's almost always someone whose life is more glamorous, exciting, and dramatic than most people's. This is where "you can be anything" and reality collide—right at the intersection of anxiety and depression.

GenMe'ers are also often woefully unprepared for what they encounter in the "real world" of the workplace. Years of self-esteem instruction, of being told they are special and can do anything, leave them confused and hurt by the harsh realities of many jobs. In *Quarterlife Crisis*, Joanna says, "College doesn't prepare you for the real world emotionally, which definitely brought on depression." The environment in her first job, she says, was "sterile, not nurturing, and full of people who didn't care about my welfare or happiness or well-being."

Young women in particular often feel that they have to "have it all," balancing primary responsibility for a family with lofty career aspirations. In her book on eating disorders, Joan Jacobs Brumberg lists the goals of young women as "to be brainy and beautiful; to have an exciting $75,000-a-year job; to nurture two wonderful children in consort with a supportive but equally high-powered husband." To achieve such a perfect life, "young women must be extremely demanding of themselves. . . . The kind of personal control required to become the new Superwoman . . . parallels the single-mindedness that characterizes the anorexic." It's a tall order to do this and still maintain your sanity. As *Midlife Crisis at 30* puts it, "The 'you can do anything' promise has a tendency to transform into an unrealistic 'you should be everything' brand of guilt."

Even if they reach many of their goals, GenMe'ers are likely to remain unsatisfied unless they earn heaps of money. The average person is now much more aware of all of the things she can't have. Author Gregg Easterbrook calls this "catalog-induced anxiety" after the glossy pages of expensive things that land in our mailboxes. But it goes beyond that; we constantly see expensive things through TV, the Internet, movies, and magazines. Reality shows such as *Rich Kids of Beverly Hills* portray the careless wealth of those born into privilege. The show got its start when its protagonists started posting pictures of their expensive jewelry, cars, private jets, and purebred dogs on an account called Rich Kids of Instagram. Its tagline: "They have more money than you and this is what they do." One post is a hotel bill for $10,000 with the caption "You stay a week, we stay a night." Shows such as VH1's *The Fabulous Life of . . .* display the expensive trappings of the famous; the details of indulgence are then followed by the cost, usually delivered in a riveting accelerating cadence: "The tile in the kitchen alone cost over two *million dollars*!" The Travel Channel regularly runs shows like *Millionaires' Hawaii*, which demonstrate how nice a place would be—if only you had a huge pile of money. Sure enough, research shows that the more television you watch, the more materialistic you are.

The Internet contributes to the problem as well. For example, the site realtor.com makes it possible to view pictures—and sometimes 360-degree video—of houses listed for sale. No matter how I try to look only at the houses I might conceivably buy, they just keep going up in price until suddenly I am drooling over a $2 million house I'll never be able to afford. I often feel anxious after looking at this site, trying to figure out how I can possibly make enough money to buy one of these houses. Mostly, though, the experience is just abjectly depressing.

Our perceptions are also skewed by modern life. Television wasn't always a world devoid of working-class people. Witness 1970s shows such as *Sanford and Son* (father and son run a junkyard and live in a house apparently furnished from it), *All in the Family* (Archie Bunker's working-class family lives in a duplex in Queens), and *Good Times* (family of five lives in a Chicago housing project). Because fewer of us ride buses and subways, send our children to public schools, and live in mixed-income neighborhoods, middle-class people rarely rub shoulders with poor people in real life either, which prompted a *New York Times Magazine* article titled "The Invisible Poor." We're constantly exposed to people who have more than we do and rarely see those who have less—a lack of perspective that's a formula for dissatisfaction.

People whose primary motivations are financial are much more likely to be anxious and depressed than people who value strong relationships with others. Psychologist Ed Diener got many of the hundred wealthiest Americans (from a *Forbes* list) to fill out a happiness questionnaire, and they turned out to be only marginally happier than people with average incomes. This is probably due to the adjustment of expectations; you think you'll be happier when you get that raise, but a few months later you've adjusted to your new standard of living and want yet more. People who win the lottery are ecstatic at first but, a year after their win, are no happier than other people.

GenMe also has high expectations for romantic partners. Marriage was once seen as a practical partnership for raising children, but is now expected to fulfill the most romantic ideals. In a Gallup poll, 94% of single women in their 20s agreed that "when you marry, you want your spouse to be your soulmate, first and foremost." Norval Glenn, an expert on marital satisfaction, states bluntly, "People now believe that a relationship with one person should meet all of their emotional needs. In most cases, that isn't going to happen." The authors of *Midlife Crisis at 30* call this the "romantic expectation gap." They note, "Most of the women we interviewed insisted that they were not looking for a Prince Charming—then, without missing a beat, they described an equally unattainable ideal. It's ironic that we've developed such lofty expectations of our potential husbands at a time when nearly 50 percent of marriages still end in divorce."

Few people can reach the goal of the perfect life, so more are anxious and depressed. "It's as if some idiot raised the ante on what it takes to be a normal human being," Martin Seligman writes. In many ways, the higher expectations of GenMe are rooted in our focus on the self. We've been told all our lives that we're special, so we think we deserve to be famous and rich. We also have higher expectations for jobs and romantic partners, expecting fulfillment in all realms of life. It would be wonderful if these appetites could always be sated, but they can't. Not everyone can live in a huge house, and most people's jobs, by economic necessity, are not going to be fulfilling, at least not all of the time. You might be married to a great guy, but he's not going to be your perfect soul mate all the time. We focus so much on our individual wants, feeling empty inside, that depression is often the result.

But our dissatisfaction can't solely be blamed on individualism. It's not just that we expect more, it's that the necessities of life are so much more expensive. GenMe anticipates more at a time when it's more difficult to attain even the bare minimum. Movies are filled with people who have glamorous jobs, but it's harder and harder just to get into a good college. TV shows are set in mansions, yet even a small house is outside the reach of most people. It's like a cruel joke—GenMe has been raised to expect riches and can barely afford a condo and a crappy health care plan.

DANGERS AND THREATS

Even before the threat of terrorism made the world such a frightening place, many other modern dangers terrorized us and still do, from crime to school shootings to kidnappings. The role of the media is important here. The evening news (particularly the local broadcast) portrays a world filled with dangers. The mantra in local news is "If it bleeds, it leads," which is why murders are often the top story. Sure enough, people who watch many hours of news coverage are more afraid of crime than people who do not watch much TV news. In the quest for ratings, many news programs focus on the terrible things that can happen to children, knowing that this is a natural source of anxiety for parents. (I often joke that the teaser for every TV news story is "And how will it affect your children?")

Most people, fortunately, will never be the victim of a violent crime. But the atmosphere created by crime is pervasive and painful. Living in a dangerous society can make people enormously anxious: Is it safe to walk down that street? What if I get raped? Will I get carjacked if I take a wrong turn? What if my child is abducted? Crime affects you even if you are never a victim. Even though the crime rate wasn't much different from now, I often walked home alone from elementary school in the early 1980s and rode my bike for miles around our suburb (without a helmet!). Now parents are afraid to let their children walk to school alone, and many don't allow their children to ride their bikes around their neighborhood for fear of kidnappers and child molesters. Magda, 24, has two little sisters. "Because of all the bad things that happen to children that are shown in the media," she says, her mother "feels worried that something is going to happen to my sisters. She feels the world is a much more unsafe place now than twenty years ago."

Parents' fears of child abduction have led many to tell their kids they should never, ever talk to strangers. Sometimes children absorb this lesson a little too well. Boy Scout Brennan Hawkins, 11, got lost in the Utah mountains. Rescuers finally found him four days later, alive but weak and dehydrated. Why did it take so long to find him, considering he was alive and walking around all of this time? Because he got off the trail and hid every time he saw someone. After all, never talk to strangers. "His biggest fear, he told me, was someone would steal him," said his mother. In other words, Brennan was so concerned about being abducted by the people who were trying to rescue him that he almost starved to death.

As Barry Glassner writes in *The Culture of Fear*, media reports often make us afraid of things that are unlikely to occur, as small scares are turned into seemingly large dangers. Few children are abducted by nonrelatives. Other scares are considerably sillier. A few years ago, forty people in San Diego got food poisoning from the salad lettuce at a restaurant chain. The local media covered this story endlessly. Kristina, 25, commented on this sarcastically in one of my classes: "Now we're supposed to be scared of lettuce?" And this was before the threat of terrorism scared us all out of our wits.

Dangers and threats are nothing new. Previous generations faced world wars without suffering from high rates of depression. Perhaps uniting against a common enemy inoculated that generation against depression; people knew who the enemy was and set about saving scrap metal and planting victory gardens to stop it. Now the violence is much more random, the enemy unseen: children are shot because they went to school; adults die because they went to work on a Tuesday morning in September. The random violence of crime and terrorism is somehow more frightening.

CONCLUSION

In some ways, the shift toward melancholy in young people seems paradoxical: Generation Me has so much more than previous generations—they have been better protected, enjoy countless modern conveniences, and are better educated. But Generation Me often lacks other basic human requirements: stable close relationships, a sense of community, a feeling of safety, a simple path to adulthood and the workplace. Our grandparents may have done without television and used an outhouse, but they were usually not lonely, scared by threats of terrorism, or obsessing about the best way to get into Princeton. As David Myers argues in his book *The American Paradox*, the United States has become a place where we have more but feel worse. Technology and material things may make life easier, but they do not seem to lead to happiness. Instead, we long for the social connections of past years, we enter a confusing world of too many choices, and we become depressed at younger and younger ages.

5

Yeah, Right: The Belief That There's No Point in Trying

Seventeen-year-old Caitlin begins her day early, with a quick check of her e-mail to see if there's any news from the ten colleges she applied to. She hopes to be admitted to an Ivy League school, but with acceptance rates at less than 10%, it's a long shot even with her stellar grades and numerous extracurricular activities. After a long day at school and soccer practice, she makes it home in time to watch some TV with her family. Flipping between CNN and FOX News, she watches coverage of the most recent shooting at a mall interspersed with news of the latest government shutdown. Her parents get online to file their protest with their congressman. "Why would you do that?" Caitlin asks. "It's not going to do any good." Her parents try to convince her otherwise, but Caitlin replies with the universal teenage expression of cool cynicism: "Yeah, right."

Most of Generation Me's days are like this: filled with events and circumstances they can't control. So why should they try? Perhaps as a result, older people complain that the idea of personal responsibility has faded, that young people blame others for their problems, and that apathy is rampant. They're not just Generation Me; they're Generation Whatever. The young are the new cynics.

The days when young Americans marched in the streets to change the world are, for the most part, gone. Although some protests (such as 2011's Occupy) still draw crowds and collective action, the young person who believes that she can make a difference in world events, national politics, and sometimes even her own life is more and more rare. Despite the recent talk about young people getting involved in political campaigns through the Internet, the vast majority of young people couldn't care less about politics. Based on his extensive 2008 survey, Christian Smith concluded that 94% of 18-to-24-year-olds were politically and civically disengaged.

THE DATA ON CYNICISM AND FEELINGS OF CONTROL

I became interested in youthful cynicism after I had been doing research on generational differences for several years. I had concentrated on personality traits, such as anxiety or self-esteem. But I suspected that generations also differed in how they saw the world and what they believed. I came across a popular psychological scale that measures a fundamental belief: Are you in control of what happens to you, or do other people, luck, and larger forces control your fate? People who believe they are in control are "internal" (and possess "internality"); those who don't are "external" (and have "externality"). When I read the internal items of the scale, I had a strong feeling that there would be big generational differences. Some of the items:

- By taking an active part in political and social affairs, the people can control world events.
- With enough effort we can wipe out political corruption.
- The average citizen can have an influence in government decisions.

Even though I was in my late 20s at the time, I reacted to these items the way a teenager would: I snorted sarcastically and said, "Yeah, right!" I thought, "Who believes that pie-in-the-sky crap anymore?" It sounded like the kind of stuff Boomers believed in when they thought they could change the world, and not at all like my generation or anyone younger.

Then I read some of the items on the external side, which measure the opposite beliefs:

- The world is run by the few people in power, and there is not much the little guy can do about it.
- Getting a good job depends mainly on being in the right place at the right time.
- Who gets to be boss often depends upon who was lucky enough to be in the right place first.

"No kidding," I thought. These items sounded a lot more truthful to me than the idealistic statements measuring internality.

But this was just my own opinion. I wanted to know if college students' responses to these questions actually changed over the generations. Liqing Zhang, Charles Im, and I found 97 studies reporting data from 18,310 college students who filled out the control questionnaire between 1960 and 2002.

The results showed a remarkably clear change: college students increasingly believed that their lives were controlled by outside forces. The average GenX/GenMe college student in 2002 had more external control beliefs than 80% of college students in the early 1960s. External control beliefs increased about 50% between the 1960s and the 2000s.

What's happened since 2002 and the full transition to GenMe/Millennials, supposedly a much less cynical and more engaged group? The nationally representative high school survey includes several locus-of-control items, and they suggest that GenMe has continued the trends toward disengagement begun by GenX. In the late 1970s, when Boomers were in high school, 33% agreed that "people who accept their condition in life are happier than those who try to change things," but by 2012, 42% of GenMe'ers agreed. Agreement with items such as "planning only makes a person unhappy since plans hardly ever work out anyway" also increased. Most of this increase took place after 2000—when GenMe'ers born in the 1980s entered the samples—with an especially large upswing during the late-2000s recession years.

These results also gel with polling data collected by other researchers. From the 1950s to the 1990s, adult Americans were increasingly likely to agree with cynical statements such as "the people running the country don't care what happens to people like me," "the rich get richer and the poor get poorer," and "what you think doesn't count very much anymore." In contrast, they were less likely to agree that "hard work always pays off." More recently, a Pew survey of adults found that agreement with "hard work offers little guarantee of success" rose from 29% in 1999 to 35% in 2012. The percentage of who agreed there are few "limits to growth in this country" sank from 67% in 1987 to 51% in 2012. The perception that "the rich just get richer while the poor get poorer" jumped from 65% in 2002 to 76% in 2012.

What's even more disturbing is how early in development these changes begin. After finding the large change for college students, I wondered if children would show the same results. Maybe only adolescents had become more cynical. As it turned out, kids were just as jaded—41 samples of 6,554 children aged 9 to 14 showed that kids in the 2000s were more likely to believe that things are out of their control. The magnitude of the change was about the same as it was in college students, with the average GenMe child scoring more externally than 80% of his or her counterparts in the early 1970s. Kids as young as 9 caught the rising wave of apathy and cynicism.

The items on the children's form of the control scale are particularly telling. Many speak in general terms about trying hard, or studying. But others hint at the kind of bad behavior I mentioned in chapter 3, exemplified by the *People* magazine article "Kids out of Control." The scale asks:

- Are you often blamed for things that just aren't your fault?
- Most of the time, do you feel that you have little to say about what your family decides to do?
- When you get punished, does it usually seem it's for no good reason at all?

More kids now agree with these statements, suggesting that they are more likely to blame their parents or teachers when things go wrong. I can just hear millions of kids yelling, "But it's not my fault!"

POLITICS ARE BORING, CONGRESS SUCKS, AND WE MIGHT AS WELL LET THE EARTH ROT

The trend in control has two parts: First, there's the declining belief in personal responsibility and the efficacy of hard work and sacrifice—I'll talk about that later in this chapter. Then there's the fading idea that collective action will have an effect on politics, society, and the world.

Some commentators—particularly those who label GenMe "Millennials"—argue that those born after 1980 are "the most civic-minded since the generation of the 1930s and 1940s," as Morley Winograd and Michael Hais, the authors of 2008's *Millennial Makeover*, opine. William Strauss and Neil Howe, authors of 2000's *Millennials Rising*, introduced this notion, predicting that this generation would be civically engaged, highly interested in politics, and focused on helping others. The 2008 book *Genera-*

tion We—perhaps intended as a counterpoint to this book's first edition—made a similar argument.

Most of these books relied on a few select survey items and some one-time interviews with young people to make their points. I wondered what would happen if we analyzed all the items on life goals, concern for others, and civic orientation from the two largest over-time surveys of young people. That's what Keith Campbell, Elise Freeman, and I set out to do, using the nationally representative high school and college surveys of 9 million people. Going in, I wasn't sure what we would find. Perhaps part of the generation was more civically oriented and the other part narcissistic, or perhaps the narcissists were trying to seek attention through public activism.

But that's not what the data showed. Out of 30 items measuring civic orientation, not a single one was higher among GenMe than it had been among the Boomers when they were young. Twenty-eight were lower among GenMe than among the supposedly more disengaged GenX; only two were higher. GenMe/Millennial high school students were less likely to "think about the social problems of the nation and the world," were less likely to say they trusted government, were less likely to be "interested in government affairs," and were less likely to participate in political affairs such as "writing to a public official." GenMe/Millennial college students were less likely to say it was important "to keep up to date with political affairs" and less likely to vote in a student election, though they were slightly more likely than GenX'ers (though not Boomers) to discuss politics.

In later analyses, we found that some of these trends had turned around with the late 2000s recession—for example, more said they thought about social problems. But GenMe/Millennials' responses were still less civically engaged than Boomers' were at the same age. Three times as many GenMe'ers in 2010–12 than Boomers in 1976–78 said they "never" thought about social problems. Sixty percent of college student Boomers said it was important to keep "up to date with political affairs" in 1966, compared to 35% of GenMe in 2012. And many of the other civic activities, such as being interested in government affairs or writing to a public official, continued to decline through the recession years. Another study comparing generations of young workers found that GenMe was, contrary to popular wisdom, *less* interested than Boomers were in working for socially conscious companies. "These young adults are not the revolutionary environmentally and socially conscious beacons of light we had hoped they would be," Rena Rasch and Brenda Kowske concluded.

In *Lost in Transition*, sociologist Christian Smith summarizes the results of his large survey and in-depth interviews of young adults. He found that only 4% were civically or politically engaged—even though his survey was conducted in the summer of 2008, when youth enthusiasm for Barack Obama's campaign was supposedly at its height. The vast majority of young adults, 69%, said they were not at all interested in politics. Twenty-seven percent expressed only a weak interest. Many described politics as "boring." Even among the minority who said they paid some attention, that usually meant occasionally watching TV news. When the interviewer asked, "Do you pay attention to politics and world and national events?" one young man said simply, "No." "What would you say your own political position is?" "I don't have one," he replied. One young woman summed up her apathy this way: "I'm really bad at having invested forethought to things that aren't happening around me."

Smith concludes, "The idea that today's emerging adults are as a generation leading a new wave of renewed civic-mindedness and political involvement is sheer fiction. The fact that anyone ever believed that idea simply tells us how flimsy the empirical evidence that so many journalistic media stories are based upon is and how unaccountable to empirical reality high-profile journalism can be." And why is GenMe this way? Smith found that young adults have "extremely low estimations of anyone's ability to make a positive impact on the world." Just as we found in our analyses, Smith's respondents believe things are beyond their control.

But what about concern for the environment? Surely that's one place where today's young people are interested in taking action. But are they more interested in environmental issues than Boomers and GenX'ers were at the same age?

The high school survey has a long list of questions on taking action to help the environment and save energy. These, I guessed, would be the exception to the trend toward disengagement. However, I was wrong. GenMe'ers were significantly less likely to say they did anything to help the environment than Boomers and GenX'ers, across a wide variety of questions, even those asking about specific behaviors. Three times as many Gen Me'ers (compared to Boomers) answered "none" to the question "In your own actions—the things you buy and the things you do—how much of an effort do you make to conserve energy and protect the environment?" Sixty-eight percent of high school age Boomers in the 1970s said they made an effort to cut down on electricity use to save energy, but only 51% of GenMe did. Seventy-eight percent of Boomers said they tried to reduce heat use in their house in the winter, but only 56% of GenMe did. In a later analysis, we found that environmental action rose during the recession years of 2008–10. Once again, though, it was not enough to bring environmental interest back to the levels of the 1970s or 1990s, and interest in the environment went back down when the economy began to improve in 2012. So even on concern for the environment—the issue purported to be of special concern to this generation—GenMe expresses little interest in getting involved.

Although at first this conclusion seems unbelievable, it has consistently been confirmed by other polls. In a Pew Center poll, 43% of Americans agreed that "people should be willing to pay higher prices in order to protect the environment" in 2012, down from 67% in 1992. In 1992, 90% of American adults agreed that "there need to be stricter laws and regulations to protect the environment," but that sank to 74% by 2012. Between 2000 and 2013, twice as many Americans described themselves as "unsympathetic" to the environmental movement, and fewer described themselves as "sympathetic but not active." (The number who say they are "active" has stayed steady at about 17%, suggesting the number of die-hard supporters has stayed the same while the opposition grew and the number of those mildly supportive shrank.) More say the government is doing "too much" to protect the environment.

The return of the youth vote has also gotten a lot of press in recent years. Barack Obama's campaigns in 2008 and 2012 presumably brought large numbers of excited, engaged young voters to the polls. That's partially true—youth voter turnout was higher in 2008 than in the three previous elections, though at 49% it did not exceed the high-water marks for previous generations (52% among 18-to-29-year-old Boomers in 1972, and 49% for GenX in 1992). However, young people's voter turnout went right back down again in 2012, to 45%. The most comprehensive and fair comparison might be to combine the turnout data for the presidential election years for each generation when they were young (so 1972–80 for Boomers, 1984–2000 for GenX, and 2004–12 for Millennials/GenMe). In this analysis, 51% of Boomers voted when they were 18-to-29-year-olds, 46% of GenX'ers, and 48% of GenMe/Millennials. A 2-percentage-point increase in youth voter turnout is certainly a good thing, but not quite the "Millennial Makeover" some predicted. So voting—arguably the civic activity that requires the least effort—has a slightly more encouraging trend. Instead of declining precipitously, it has stayed about the same from one generation to the next.

With the disinterest in politics comes a deep distrust in government and other large institutions such as the national news media, religious organizations, medicine, and schools. In the high school survey, confidence in institutions reached an all-time low in 2012—lower than in the late 1970s after the Watergate scandal, lower than during the 1980s government and religious scandals, and lower than in the mid-2000s during the failed search for weapons of mass destruction in Iraq. In the late 1970s, 31% said Congress was doing a good job, which sank to 20% in 2012. "I have been lied to all my life," says Ana, 17. "My government is corrupt and evil."

But the distrust goes far beyond government. Sixty-two percent of high school students thought the news media were doing a good job in the late 1970s, compared to only 37% in 2012. Students also had a more negative view of churches and religious institutions, large corporations, colleges and universities, public schools, the Supreme Court, and the president and his administration. Adults are not far behind—in the General Social Survey, confidence in virtually every large American institution has declined since the 1970s. Confidence in the press and in medicine show some of the largest decreases. Apparently nobody else knows what they are doing anymore—we only trust ourselves.

Another reason young people are disengaged is that they don't pay much attention to the news. Less than 20% of young people read newspapers, and the average age of people watching CNN or the network evening news is around 60. (Have you noticed all the commercials for dentures and arthritis medications during these programs?) Young people may be getting some news from the Internet, but most use the Web for specific interests instead (what media expert Nicolas Negroponte calls "The Daily Me"). Only 32% of people aged 18 to 24 agree that they "need to get the news every day," compared to 62% of those ages 55 to 64.

As a result, young people know little about news and politics. David Mindich, author of *Tuned Out: Why Americans Under 40*

Rock the Vote and MTV's Choose or Lose spend a great deal of money and time encouraging voter registration among young people. Despite these efforts, even the 2008 youth voter turnout that got so much attention was lower than young Boomers' turnout in 1972 and GenX's in 1992.

Don't Follow the News, found that 60% of American young people could not name a single Supreme Court justice, 48% did not know what *Roe v. Wade* was, and 62% could not name any of the three countries President George W. Bush had identified as the "axis of evil" (Iraq, Iran, and North Korea). In another poll, high school seniors were asked to say, in their opinion, the most important problem facing the country. One in three could not name a single issue. Christian Smith's survey of 18-to-23-year-olds yielded similar results in 2008, with most young adults unable to name a political issue they cared about.

NO CONTROL ON THE BIG-SCREEN TV

Media exposure probably explains a large part of the increase in externality. News broadcasts in the early 1960s were confined to a fifteen-minute evening segment. Can you imagine—only fifteen minutes of TV news? Now, four national cable channels cover the news twenty-four hours a day, and the networks have not only the daily thirty-minute broadcast but three-hour morning shows and several hours of local news every day.

A lot of news coverage has turned to fluff about celebrities, television shows (starring celebrities), and movies (sometimes starring celebrities playing celebrities). Yet the "big" news stories—the ones to which CNN, FOX News, and MSNBC will devote twenty-four hours a day—are almost always bad news, and they're almost always events that the average viewer cannot control.

It's not just large disasters; media outlets' other favorite stories include plane crashes, mall shootings, school shootings, murders of pregnant women, child abductions, stock market crashes. Sitting in their living rooms, modern citizens may increasingly feel that they belong to a huge, complex, confusing, and terrible world that is utterly beyond their control to change.

Media saturation has had an impact on GenMe. Not that long ago, many older folks thought that young people were idealistic and willing to believe the best of people. But that was before 6-year-olds wanted to know if they were safe at school, or asked why a congressman would send a young woman pictures of himself in his underwear. It's not just that these events happened—sex scandals and mass deaths have occurred in every generation—but that their every detail is exposed on television. As author Neil Postman notes, "From the child's point of view, what is mostly shown on television is the plain fact that the adult world is filled with ineptitude, strife, and worry."

It's just one part in the larger trend of "kids growing up too fast." Along with adult information and adult themes, they've also managed to absorb the cynicism that once came only with age. Some of this is simple self-protection brought on by information overload—much of it false and not to be believed. When GenMe is not watching TV, they're on the Internet, sometimes on traditional-news offshoots such as cnn.com, but other times trolling through places where they have to wear their skepticism cap at every moment. Even people who are older than GenMe have learned not to forward the e-mail that says doing so will contribute money to help a child dying of cancer (it's a hoax). We know that e-mails with the subjects "I love you" or "Your prescription has expired" are a computer virus and spam for Viagra, respectively, and can be deleted without being opened. We know that your friend's aunt's hairdresser did not put her poodle in the microwave to dry it off (and if we believed it for a second, we confirmed it wasn't true on the Urban Legends reference pages on snopes.com). We are suspicious of anyone who calls on the phone and wants to sell us something. We don't believe for a second that the "tests" in laundry-detergent ads are true.

Prime example: the "fake news" outlets such as Jon Stewart's *Daily Show*, *The Colbert Report*, or the satirical newspaper the *Onion* that are so popular among young people. GenMe enjoys knowing that it's false—at least it's funny and entertaining. Then there's the other trend in journalism, the *TMZ* beat, or what's generally known as infotainment. GenX grew up on the "tabloid" shows of the 1990s such as *Hard Copy* and *A Current Affair* (complete with the triangle making that *whump!* noise), and now even regular news outlets have taken up the cause of celebrity watching. Both trends expose the cynical attitude of GenMe. If they're not laughing about the news, they're laughing at the celebrities—a little schadenfreude directed toward the rich and famous people they'd like to be.

SELF-ESTEEM VERSUS REALITY

Generation Me has also lost hope in their ability to make choices in their own lives. In some ways, these changed attitudes seem at odds with the focus on the self. If GenMe'ers see themselves as independent individuals, why are they increasingly blaming others when things go wrong? It comes back again to the idea of self-esteem and feeling good about yourself. Suppose that you're a student and you fail a test. If you acknowledge that you were lazy about studying—or just plain stupid—your self-esteem will suffer. If you can blame the teacher's unfair test, however, you can slide though the experience still feeling good about yourself. We say that bad things aren't our fault in an effort to preserve our self-confidence. "When there are few winners and many losers, it may be easier to protect one's sense of self-worth by not trying than to try and still not succeed," notes an education book that argues against competition. What's the point in trying something difficult? If we do, we might learn something—even if it's just our own limitations. But the popular GenMe belief is to protect the self at all costs. John, 23, says, "It makes more sense psychologically to believe in fate. If you don't, your self-esteem will plummet each time you fail."

GenMe'ers high self-esteem also doesn't lead them to believe they're in control because, as one of the self-esteem programs puts it, they were taught to value "who we are and not what we do." You're unique and special even if you don't work hard, so why do it? Educational psychologist Maureen Stout argues that the self-esteem movement disconnects reward from achievement, producing cynical kids. She points out that 5- and 6-year-olds start school eager to learn, but that "when they encounter teachers who give them an A just for turning up in class . . . they have no choice but to become cynical about the educative process."

And if they don't become cynical then, Stout says, they will once they reach adulthood and discover that they have not been prepared for the real world. This cynicism comes from the mismatch between self-esteem and reality. GenMe'ers are faced with an unusual set of circumstances. From infancy, they were taught to express themselves, to believe in themselves, to follow their dreams. Then they enter a world where getting into an Ivy League university depends just as much on luck and circumstance as on work and talent, and where even the local public university might not admit them if they got B's in high school. The good job or the desirable promotion might go to the person who works the hardest, or it might go to the person who catches a lucky break. Your entire romantic life might turn on the luck of meeting the right person at the right time. Even when you decide to give it up for the day and relax, you read *People* and watch *TMZ* or ESPN to worship movie stars and athletes—the modern-day gods and goddesses who, for the most part, gained their ascendance through genes and circumstance. GenMe'ers parents and teachers told them how special they were but skimped on the lesson that life isn't fair.

LIFE DETERMINATION BY LOTTERY

Generation Me'ers external beliefs are somewhat ironic considering the better health and safety they enjoy. Neither GenX nor GenMe has ever been drafted to fight in a war. Life expectancy is at an all-time high, and advances in medical technology and pharmaceuticals make countless lives better. Safety measures have radically improved in the last thirty years, on everything from cars to playground equipment. Can you believe that babies used to ride in cars without car seats, and that kids rode bikes without wearing helmets? Even considering the threat of terrorism, fewer negative random events occur now than in previous eras.

It's easy to take those things for granted, however, especially since this relatively safe world is the only one GenMe'ers have ever known. Instead they focus on the things they've seen change, such as the economy and the volatile job market. In an increasingly complex, competitive world, jobs and investments seem to depend more on luck than achievement. When only 5% of people are admitted to a graduate program—and most of the applicants are highly qualified—GenMe quickly learns that luck plays a big role in their lives. Or as Gaby, 20, puts it, "A typical saying in my generation is 'I was in the right/wrong place at the right/wrong time.'"

Recent college graduates find it difficult to summon up enthusiasm for the job market. "Putting in effort does not seem to be related to getting the appropriate reward," says Andrea, 22. "Getting a degree does not guarantee a stable job." Eric, 23, has the same beliefs even though he has been successful. He described being "handed" a management job in a time-share company, making $45,000 a year when he was only 18. When the company was restructured and 75% of the employees lost their jobs, Eric says he "got lucky" and wasn't let go. Even though most of the breaks went his way, Eric says, "In truth I had nothing to do with it."

Though some of this attitude is based in realism, other members of GenMe have developed a skewed view of how success works. Perhaps because many role models on TV are actresses and athletes, becoming rich looks like a matter of luck. Apparently, some young people also believe that success in business usually happens overnight. *Generation X Goes to College* quotes Kelly, 18, who says, "Kids see people like Bill Gates who get rich out of nowhere. . . . It seems a lot of people get it that way, by not having to work. They just come into it real quick, like the lottery." Bill Gates is many things, but he's not a lottery winner; he founded a company and worked hard to make it grow. He may have been lucky, and he may have been opportunistic, but it's astonishing that anyone thinks he got rich without working.

THE VICTIM MENTALITY

Some GenMe'ers take things too far and make excuses when things don't go their way. Susan Peterson, who teaches at a community college in Arizona, has noticed this trend toward a lack of personal responsibility in her students: "Parents have always done [everything] for them, including choosing all their teachers in the public school system and arguing about every grade they received. As a society, we've created a new generation of young adults who blame everyone else for their failures."

In his book *A Nation of Victims*, social critic Charles Sykes argues, "The impulse to flee personal responsibility and blame others [is] deeply embedded within the American culture." It's gotten so bad, he says, that "the National Anthem has become the Whine." Other people blame a "disease" for their ineptitude—such as the man who sued after getting fired for never showing up on time. It wasn't his fault, he said, because he had "chronic lateness syndrome." *The Myth of Laziness* author Mel Levine says there is no such thing as laziness—instead, people who can't get things done have "output failure." Defense attorneys will sometimes say that their clients were abused as children and are thus not responsible for their actions. And there's always the famous Twinkies defense, that junk food and sugar are the real cause for murder. As Sykes puts it, "The plaintive cry is always the same: I am not at fault. [Fill in the Blank] made me do it."

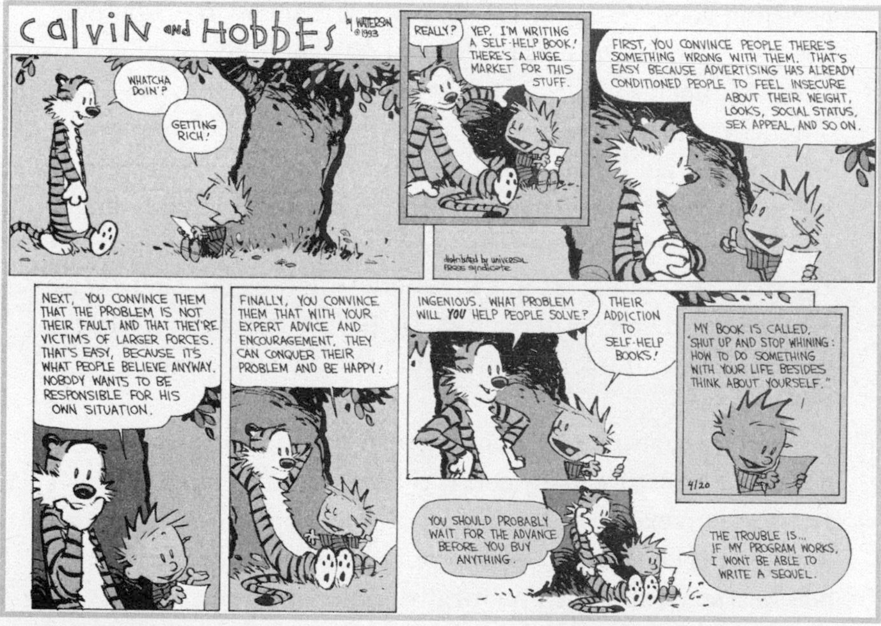

Watterson's satire of self-help books illustrates the growing popularity of blaming others for your problems and codifies the somewhat paradoxical link between externalizing blame and focusing on yourself.

Before the 1970s, lawyers considered product-liability cases no-wins; they were matters of personal responsibility, and no jury would convict a corporation for the choices of an individual. In 1940, about 20,000 civil lawsuits were heard; by 2012, this had increased more than tenfold—or 1,000%—to around 275,000. In contrast, the number of criminal cases merely doubled over this same period, suggesting that civil lawsuits increased five times faster than they should have. You don't even have to make a faulty product to get sued. One young man sued the Wake Forest University Law School because his professors used the Socratic method to question him and his classmates, which, he says, caused him fatigue and weight loss.

Many other lawsuits have become the butt of numerous jokes: the woman who sued because her coffee was too hot, or the teens who sued McDonald's for making them fat. It seems that when anything goes wrong, many people just want to sue whatever company is in reach. This is a foreign concept to the older generation. My uncle Charles, who owned an avocado farm, was using a trencher one weekend when he reached down too quickly and the machine cut off his thumb. Fortunately, doctors were able to reattach the digit. When he got back to work, one of his younger coworkers asked him if he was going to sue the company that made the trencher. "No!" exclaimed Charles. "It was my fault. Why would I sue them?" Although many people still share Charles's attitude, others think that it's natural to blame the product when things go wrong.

Of course, at times excuses are real. "Personal responsibility," a favorite mantra of many conservatives, can't extend to cases of true racism, sexism, or lack of opportunity. Some true hardships and true explanations exist that deserve to be heard. Chris Colin was heartened when his politically conservative classmate John Doyle readily acknowledged that the playing field isn't always level. "Hard work is still the fundamental element of success, but some people, based on their situation, their circumstances, can work as hard as they want, but unless somebody steps in and gives them that boost . . . they're not gonna get to that level. And to say that they can . . . is foolish."

AN EDUCATION IN EXCUSES

The victim mentality arises full force in schools, where teachers often bear the brunt of these attitudes. Many public school teachers have told me that parents blame them when their children don't do well in school. Arguing over grades has become commonplace, perhaps because of the self-esteem curriculum and the "you can do anything" mentality. "Kids today have extremely high expectations," one student said. "And if they receive a D or an F, it always winds up being the teacher's fault somehow."

Community college professor Peter Sacks describes students who wouldn't show up for class or do the required assignments and would then complain when their grades suffered. One student who turned in abysmally written papers complained to the administration about Sacks's "tough grading." Another student asked if she still had to do a restaurant review assignment because "I've had a cold all week, and so I don't have any taste buds." From what I have heard from faculty across the country, Sacks was observing only the first modest wave of such excuses.

Sacks reports with irony that he had to throw out his "traditional approach to higher education whereby teachers assume students take responsibility for their decisions." He is not alone. "Students who receive a C, D, or F on a test or paper tend to hold the teacher personally responsible," said Daniel Kazez, a professor of music, in a letter to the editor in *Newsweek*. In his book *I'm the Teacher, You're the Student*, Emory University professor Patrick Allitt describes dealing with "those who didn't fulfill their assignments, or who plagiarized, and are now casting about angrily for someone to blame." Even "I meant to do that" has apparently become a worthwhile excuse. After Sacks pointed out some awkward passages in a student's writing, the student claimed, "Sometimes I like to write awkwardly. It livens up the material and doesn't make it boring."

Misbehavior is also explained away with excuses. In her book *Not Much Just Chillin': The Hidden Lives of Middle Schoolers*, Linda Perlstein reports that the most commonly uttered sentence at Wilde Lake Middle School is "But I didn't do anything!" When students are asked why they were sent to the office, they say things like "Because Mrs. Wright blamed me for talking and I wasn't even talking." Youthful excuse making was probably common in other generations as well, but back then, parents took the teacher's side. Now, Perlstein reports, more than half the time parents don't back up the teachers. One veteran seventh-grade social studies teacher says, "I'm tired of the kids talking back, the parents talking back, the lack of interest in learning."

This is the new wrinkle: it's not just the kids who are defiant and argumentative—it's also the parents. *Time* magazine ran a cover story called "What Teachers Hate About Parents." Teachers described parents who specified that their children were not to be corrected or "emotionally upset," who argued incessantly about grades, and even one father who, after his daughter was reprimanded, challenged a teacher to a fistfight. In a study conducted by MetLife, new teachers ranked handling parents as their most challenging task. Parents can also take the victim mentality to new heights. One set of parents sued a school that expelled their kids for cheating, saying that a teacher had left the exam on a desk, making it easy to steal it (thus, it's the teacher's fault that my kid cheated and was expelled). Teachers will see this attitude more and more as GenMe'ers have their own kids and believe that they couldn't possibly do anything wrong either.

Scott McLeod, the headmaster at a private school in New Orleans, has witnessed this trend firsthand. "The parents' willingness to intercede on the kids' behalf, to take the kids' side, to protect the kid, in a not healthy way—there's much more of that each year," he said in a *New York Times Magazine* article. Outside of school, some runaway parents apply these principles to sports as well; thus the increasingly common image of the soccer mom or dad yelling at the coach to let the parent's kid play. And if the kid isn't any good? It's the coach's fault. McLeod sees it at his school; if parents "see their kid fail—if he's only on the JV, or the coach is yelling at him—somehow the school is responsible for that." The rest of the article goes on to describe the parents' dissatisfaction with a coach who told it straight and didn't let kids get off by making excuses. Alums say that the coach made them men and want to name the gym after him; current parents think he's too hard on the kids because he "yelled" at them when they didn't do what they promised to do. With the older generation of gruff coaches rapidly retiring, parents will soon have less to complain about, but their kids will be cheated out of a character-building experience they would never have forgotten.

CONSEQUENCES OF EXTERNALITY AND CYNICISM

These externalizing and cynical beliefs can be adaptive; they help protect the self-esteem of GenMe in an increasingly difficult world. But too much cynicism and alienation can be self-defeating: Why study for a test if it's going to be unfair? Why vote or learn about politics if it's not going to do any good? The startling growth of these attitudes goes a long way toward explaining the apathy and inaction so common today. With college and work getting more competitive, the trend toward believing things are out of your control is likely to continue. Teens who have been told their whole lives that they are special will desperately try to protect their self-esteem, and many will choose cynicism as their armor of choice.

Unfortunately, psychologists are virtually unanimous in their condemnation of external-control beliefs. This is somewhat stunning, as psychologists consider most traits and beliefs to be normal variations, with no "right" or "wrong" answers. But the research on externality is definitive. People who believe that outside forces determine their fate are more likely to be depressed, anxious, and cope poorly with stress. As we saw in the last chapter, GenMe displays record high levels of anxiety and depression. Believing that you don't have control might be part of the reason. If nothing you do matters, it's easy to give in to lethargy and despair. Psychologists call it learned helplessness.

Externality also doesn't bode well for meeting important goals. Perhaps because they don't think their actions will have consequences, externals have weakened self-control and an inability to delay gratification. They are less likely to work hard today to get a reward tomorrow—an especially important skill these days, when many good jobs require graduate degrees.

Another overwhelming stack of research finds that externals consistently achieve less in school, which makes sense, as externals believe that there's no point in studying. Having an internal feeling of control—believing that you can change your fate—is especially important for underprivileged children. A definitive report concluded that feelings of control were a better predictor of school achievement in minority children than any other variable.

The consequences for society as a whole are alarming. If everyone believes that nothing can be changed, that prophecy is likely to be self-fulfilling. And if we blame others for our problems, we might never make the changes we need to improve as people (sorry to sound like a Baby Boomer). As Robert Putnam argues in *Bowling Alone*, we are rapidly heading for a society low in the critical social capital it needs to grow. GenMe's concerns will be ignored if we do not get involved in politics and social change.

Julian Rotter, the author of the control scale I studied, began to realize in the 1970s that people were increasingly feeling that things were out of their control. The trend was in its infancy then, but Rotter knew what to look for, and he wasn't happy. "Our society has so many critical problems that it desperately needs as many active, participating, internal-minded members as possible," he wrote in *Psychology Today*. "If feelings of external control, alienation and powerlessness continue to grow, we may be heading for a society of dropouts—each person sitting back, watching the world go by." Dr. Rotter, welcome to GenMe's world. Whatever.

6

Sex: Generation Prude Meets Generation Crude

In Valerie Frankel's novel *The Not-So-Perfect Man*, 40-year-old Peter asks out a 23-year-old woman. She replies:

> "I can't go out with you, Peter . . . you seem like the kind of guy who wants a relationship. I don't do that. I hook up."
>
> "Hooking up?" he asked. It sounded painful.
>
> "Going out in groups of girls, and picking up groups of guys, taking them back to someone's apartment and having safe-yet-casual sex," she said. "I think I'm leaning toward lesbianism anyway. And even if I were attracted to you, I couldn't do much about it until my labial piercings heal."
>
> "Labial piercings," he said.
>
> "Four of them. Two on each side. Very tasteful. Refined," she said. Peter checked his watch, straightened his tie, cleared his throat.
>
> He said, "I'll be going now."

In case you haven't heard, "hooking up" has replaced dating among many young people, even among those without "tasteful" labial piercings. *The Hookup Handbook* notes that hookups can range from "making out to full-on sex" but are most distinguished by being "between two people who don't necessarily have any foreseeable future or even a hint of commitment." A recent article in the *Atlantic* quotes a business school student from Argentina who experienced sexual culture shock in coming to the United States. "Here in America, the girls, they give up [everything] before they even know the guy. It's like, 'Hello.' 'Hello.' 'You wanna hook up.' 'Sure.' They are so aggressive! Do they have hearts of steel or something? In my country, a girl like this would be desperate. Or a prostitute."

"Friends with benefits" is defined as a friend you do sexual things with—no romantic relationship or commitment implied. "I think you can compare friends with benefits to the driving range," says Sam, 16, interviewed for an NBC special on teens and sex. "There's no commitment to playing a round of golf—you just go there to work on your game, figure out what shots are working for you." (Casual golf, anyone?)

Or take Kristen, 21, who says, "I lost my virginity at the age of thirteen. But I would like to mention how mature I was about sex in general. I should be applauded, not shunned."

This is not your father's sex life—and it's definitely not your mother's. Hooking up is increasingly common, and even sex within boyfriend-girlfriend relationships begins at younger and younger ages. Waiting for marriage is, to put it mildly, quaint. The vast majority of Generation Me does not wait until they are married to have sex. Most do not even wait to graduate from high school. Emma, now 24, lost her virginity at 17 "to a boy I could just barely call my boyfriend." She explains, "No one I knew believed in waiting for marriage." Some of this is simple demographics: 80% of people age 18 to 29 are not married (compared to 41% in 1960).

Even religious teenagers with strict parents soon find themselves sexually active. Patrick, 31, grew up in a strict Catholic family and attended a Catholic high school, but, he says, "I lost my virginity at the age of seventeen to a girl I had known only a week." Things changed even more once he lived in a college dorm: "I found myself having more sexual partners and not feeling guilty about a one-night stand." Is this trend good or bad? Your opinion may depend on your generation. Many young people see these trends as the long-overdue shedding of arbitrary restrictions on sexuality, while some older people are often shocked by the sexual behavior of the young.

Whether you see the new sexuality as freeing or wanton, the tie to individualism is obvious: do what feels good for you and ignore the rules of society. On the other hand, the changes in sexual behavior are so dramatic that it's not clear that any universally agreed-upon rules about sex exist anymore. Why not do something pleasurable? It's your body—express yourself. Or as an ad for the birth control method Mirena puts it, "All you'll remember is the freedom" when you "put yourself in control." In one survey, college students' primary motivations for having casual sex were exploration or experimentation, satisfying their sexual desire, and "spontaneous urge." Sonia, 21, believes, "Different sexual behaviors bring more awareness and more confidence about yourself." Sometimes self-esteem comes in handy for appraising things later. CBS interviewed one young woman who slept with three boys by the time she was 15. However, she says, "I don't regard myself as a slut because I have more self-respect than that."

When I asked my students to write about differences among the generations, most chose changes in sexual behavior. It's one of the most noticeable changes in the lives of young people over the last few decades. Perhaps because of the trend toward openness, my students had no problem writing at length about when, where, and how they had sex and how comfortable they were with it. And how uncomfortable their parents were—even though most of their parents are Boomers.

GIVING IT UP

The 1960s might have been called the time of the Sexual Revolution, but apparently they were just the beginning. For her master's thesis with me, Brooke Wells gathered data on sexual behavior and attitudes from research reports on 269,649 young people collected over four decades—at the time, the most comprehensive study ever done of change over time in sexual behavior. Both men's and women's sexual behavior shifted with time, but the changes for women were the most striking. In the late 1960s, the average young woman lost her virginity at age 18; by the late 1990s, the average was 15. The change slowed down after the 1990s. The Centers for Disease Control's Youth Risk Behavior Survey found that the majority of high school students had lost their virginity by the spring of 11th grade in 2011, about the same as in 1991. The percentage of 9th-to-12th-graders who'd ever had intercourse declined slightly, from 54% in 1991 to 47% in 2011. By 12th grade, 63% of the 2011 teens had lost their virginity (compared to 67% in 1991). So in recent years about 6% fewer high school students were having sex by spring of their senior year than in the early 1990s. Overall, Boomers started having sex in college, while GenX and GenMe started having sex in high school. "Most people had the 'everybody's doing it' mentality in high school," says Miranda, 20.

Boomers also had less time to rack up a long list of conquests: in 1970, the average woman was 20.8 years old when she married for the first time. So even at the height of the hippie years, almost half of Boomer women getting married for the first time were teenagers! The average age at first marriage for men was 23.2 in 1970, which is now considered shockingly young for a man to marry. Clearly, even college-age Free Love was experienced by only a minority of Boomers, while for GenMe sex in high school is common. An Oregon high school sophomore interviewed by CBS puts it this way: "Sex is something that everyone does except for, like, the pope and Mother Teresa." Another sophomore added, "I don't think it's wrong to have sex when you're fourteen or so. Your body's ready, so why isn't it right?"

This has created a noticeable generation gap. Many students told me that sex was not even discussed in their household. "All of our parents would have heart attacks if we told them we had sex," says Bill, 19. "My mom won't even let a boy and girl share the same bed if they aren't married." Allissa, 22, agrees: "My parents found my diary a few years back and freaked out. It is hard to live in a generation where sexuality is acceptable and have parents from a generation where it's not. All you can do is live life according to your generation, because it is all you know." Andy, 20, says, "From frat houses to the White House, there's no denying that sex is present everywhere. Everywhere but my parents' house, that is!" In a 2013 Gallup poll, twice as many GenMe'ers (48%) as Boomers (22%) said that sex between teenagers was morally acceptable.

All of my students who wrote about sex confessed to losing their virginity in high school—15 and 16 were the usual ages mentioned, though 12 and 14 also came up. And the same was true among their friends. Jose, 21, said his parents were upset when he confessed that he'd had sex: "The majority of my friends had already lost their virginity after freshman year of high school. This was my sophomore year. I just assumed they knew."

Attitudes toward teen sex have become more permissive in the last few years. The General Social Survey (GSS) asks adults if sex among young teens—those age 14 to 16—is "always wrong," "almost always wrong," "wrong only sometimes," or "not wrong at all." In just the four years between 2008 and 2012, the percentage of those 18 to 29 who said teen sex was "always wrong" dropped 15 percentage points (from 63% to 48%). Nearly twice as many young people in 2012 said that teen sex was "not wrong at all" compared to those in 2004 (9% versus 5%). As more GenMe'ers born in the late 1980s and early 1990s enter the survey, a "Why not?" attitude toward early sexual activity becomes more prominent. Slightly fewer in GenMe have sex during high school than GenX'ers did in the early 1990s, but they are less likely to believe it is wrong. They may have personal reasons for waiting to have sex, but their highly individualistic ethos makes them more reluctant to judge others' choices. It's not quite "anything goes"—but it's close.

WAITING UNTIL MARRIAGE? ARE YOU KIDDING?

Brooke's comprehensive study also showed a radical shift in attitudes toward premarital sex. In the late 1950s, only 30% of young people approved of sex before marriage; by the late 1990s, 75% approved. The change in attitudes was even more striking among young women: only 12% approved of premarital sex in the 1950s, compared with 80% more recently. Just as earlier generations found it somewhat shocking to hear about premarital sex, GenMe is shocked by the lack of it. Many ask how you'd know if you were sexually compatible with someone if you didn't have sex before you got married. "You wouldn't buy a car you haven't test-driven, would you?" asks Emily, 25. Angela, 23, uses a similar analogy: "Not having sex with your future husband is like not trying on clothes before you buy them."

Similar to the trends for teen sex, approval for premarital sex in the GSS has spiked in recent years. As recently as 2004, only 47% of 18-to-29-year-olds said sex before marriage was "not wrong at all," about the same that said so in the early 1970s (48%). But by 2012, 64% said it was not wrong at all. The number who said sex before marriage was "always wrong" was nearly cut in half between 2004 and 2012 (from 22% to 12%). Once again, the second wave of GenMe'ers is shifting attitudes toward more sexual permissiveness. In the 2013 Gallup poll, 72% of GenMe said that sex between an unmarried man and woman was morally acceptable, compared to only 56% of Boomers.

"Premarital sex is a must for me," explains Elaine, 24. "Sex is like anything else—it takes practice. The more practice, the more we feel at ease with the act and with ourselves." Felicita, 19, says, "I strongly disagree with people who say it is not morally correct to have sex before marriage. Marriage is a promise, but all promises can be broken. Marriage should not be the reason why someone chooses to have sex—love should be."

Christina, 23, has been married for a year. "I don't see having premarital sex as a problem," she says. "As a married woman, I am actually happier knowing that I have experienced other people and I won't spend the rest of my life wondering what someone other than my husband might have been like." Christina's attitude is typical for GenMe women, who approach sex similarly to the way men do. Today's young women are not afraid to pursue sexual pleasure and are assertive in going after what they want.

Author Paula Kamen studied magazines for young women (such as *Cosmopolitan* and *Glamour*) and concluded that they were "unabashedly prosex for women. Their lack of shame in speaking candidly about a wide array of fears, experiences, and pleasures delivers a strong message to readers. The effect of such confident articles is ultimately to fight the age-old double standard for women." Many young women scour these magazines for sex advice, and the general message is, it's your body, have fun, and do whatever you want to do.

What about those abstinence pledges you hear so much about? They don't work. A whopping 88% of teens who take abstinence pledges have sexual intercourse before marriage. These teens do tend to wait about a year and a half longer to have sex and have fewer partners. However, participants in abstinence programs were less likely to use condoms and thus more likely to acquire sexually transmitted diseases such as chlamydia or HIV infection.

High school students who make these pledges often forget them completely once they get to college. "My freshman year in college, only two of the fifteen girls I knew were still virgins. Now in our junior year neither of those girls is," says Lindsay, 20. Just about every aspect of college culture encourages sex: fraternity parties with abundant booze, the exhilaration of being free from prying parental eyes, the easy availability of partners in a coed dorm. The University of Texas at Austin has a fountain with a stone sculpture of three leaping horses. Students joke that the horses will take off and fly when a virgin graduates.

"My only friend who always claimed he was going to wait until marriage lost his virginity about a month ago," says Lisa, 21. "The guy had talked and talked about how special it was going to be, and then he just decided to do it! And not even with a girlfriend but with a friend." Afterward, he described it as "not that big a deal." Lisa concludes, "And that's what sex is today to so many teenagers, not that big a deal."

THE NEW THIRD BASE

Many other sexual behaviors are also now more common. Oral sex is now sometimes called "the new third base." In the mid-2000s, numerous newspaper stories covered a supposed epidemic of oral sex among 12- and 13-year-olds in middle schools. Many kids say that oral sex is common by eighth or ninth grade. In a mid-2000s NBC special, 13-to-17-year-olds agreed that oral sex was "casual" and "not a big deal—it's not sex." If that phrase sounds familiar, recall that these kids were in elementary school when President Clinton was impeached: they learned a lot more in third grade than just their multiplication tables. In the 2010s, they're now in their 20s.

The results from Brooke's comprehensive study confirm that oral sex has become more popular, a trend that began long before anyone had ever heard of Monica Lewinsky. In the late 1960s, only 42% of high school and college-age women had engaged in oral sex. By the 1990s, 71% had. These trends have continued: In a 2010 study conducted by Indiana University, 77% of men in their late 20s reported receiving oral sex from a woman in the past year. These numbers drop among GenX'ers and Boomers in their 40s and 50s, to 56% for men and 43% for women.

Of course, oral sex in college seems quaint now that 12-year-olds are doing it in junior high school bathrooms. Actually, most teens aren't having oral sex; in the Indiana University 2010 survey, 31% of 16-to-17-year-olds had engaged in oral sex in the past year, along with 12% of 14-to-15-year-olds. But even 12% is a large number when you're talking about kids who are in eighth and ninth grade. Kids who aren't doing it still know what it is. Linda Perlstein, the author of *Not Much Just Chillin'*, relates seeing a note passed in a seventh-grade class that said, "I want to give you oral sex. I really want to suck on your head." The mid-2000s teen novel *Rainbow Party* describes a gathering at which high school girls put on different shades of lipstick and provide oral sex to several guys, thus forming a rainbow at the base of the boy's penis. Because the book was aimed at the teenage market, adults were in an uproar about whether this was appropriate for teens to read, and whether "rainbow parties" were actually common among teens. That's hard to say, but clearly oral sex is popular among teens because it can't get you pregnant and it's seen as less serious than sexual intercourse. That trend is likely to continue.

Yet you do have to wonder what's in it for the young women (as oral sex is more often female-on-male instead of the other way around). When Katie Couric posed this question to the girls gathered for the NBC special, several answered "self-esteem." Giving oral sex to guys, they said, helped them become popular and feel good about themselves. So not only does sex satisfy the needs of the self, but oral sex performed on someone else does too. I'm not sure I believe it, though—this sounds like self-esteem being used as an excuse. It's tough to see how something so one-sided could truly make you feel better about yourself.

However, more women are also receiving oral sex. Few women of earlier generations asked for this from men, and many didn't even know what it was. In Alfred Kinsey's studies in the 1950s, only 3% of the young women had received oral sex from a man. By the mid-1990s, however, 75% of women aged 18 to 24 had experienced cunnilingus. In the 2010 survey, 72% of women in their late 20s had received oral sex from a man in the last year.

And then . . . there's the new fourth base. The 2010 survey found that 46% of women had tried anal sex at least once, up from 33% in 1992. And many have done it recently: 27%—more than 1 in 4—of men in their late 20s had had anal sex in the past year, and 21% of late-20s women had had a partner use the back door. In 2010, members of the Delta Kappa Epsilon fraternity at Yale University stood outside the freshman dorms chanting, "No means yes! Yes means anal!" Their misogynistic chant demonstrates how once-taboo sexual behaviors are now seen as commonplace.

Why has anal sex surged in popularity? Hugo Schwyzer, a gender studies professor, theorizes that anal sex has become mainstream due to its frequent portrayal in pornography. And porn has, it seems, also become ubiquitous.

CHOOSING THE RIGHT STRIPPER POLE FOR YOUR HOME

Watching porn has moved from being a dirty secret to an openly acknowledged, even celebrated, experience. Porn stars such as Jenna Jameson publish bestsellers. Porn star Traci Lords, whose memoir also hit the bestseller list, observed, "When I was in porn, it was like a back-alley thing. Now it's everywhere."

Sex tapes, once a source of shame, are now the key to fame: Paris Hilton and Kim Kardashian both became household names because of sex tapes. Kardashian's even has its own website: kimkrayjsextape.com, which also advertises a long list of sex tapes featuring other reality TV stars. "Soft" porn has also become more acceptable—as Ariel Levy documents in *Female Chauvinist Pigs*, college women are apparently willing participants in videos such as *Girls Gone Wild* (which, if you have not had the pleasure, features young women baring their breasts). "Spectacles of naked ladies have moved from seedy side streets to center stage, where everyone—men and women—can watch them in broad daylight," Levy writes. In her 2013 book, *Masterminds and Wingmen*, Rosalind Wiseman found several high school boys who taped themselves having sex with girls and showed the videos to classmates. "For the selfie generation, raised in an era when celebrity sex tapes are commonplace, public sexuality doesn't always seem particularly taboo," Wiseman observes. In a 2013 Gallup poll, half (49%) of GenMe'ers said that pornography was morally acceptable, compared to only 28% of GenX and 19% of Boomers. It was the largest generation gap of all of the items in the poll.

And what self-respecting woman, before the last ten years, even thought to take a pole-dancing class? Pole dancing was once the sole province of strippers, not exactly the highest rung in society. Now middle-class, middle-aged women take classes to learn now to dance like a stripper. A quick Google search led me to the pole-dance studio in San Diego, called Fun Pole Fitness. Its website describes the classes as "a group fitness experience where you will have fun while you get stronger dancing and moving with a pole. Pole dancing is the most fun you can have while building your confidence, strength, flexibility and self-esteem." The website features pictures of women wearing platform heels, fishnet stockings, and feather boas, posing on stripper poles. And once you've learned your moves, several companies will install a stripper pole right in your bedroom. One website even offers "4 tips for choosing the right stripper pole for your home."

The influence of porn and strippers is indirect as well. Three times as many women got breast implants in 2012 compared to 1997. Twice as many got a procedure known as a buttock lift. Thong underwear, virtually unheard of before the 1990s, is now common—thongs accounted for 1 in 4 women's underwear sales in 2012. Spray tanning is featured on reality TV shows.

And how did I get this far in a chapter about sex without mentioning Miley Cyrus? The video for her song "Wrecking Ball" was porn without the nipples. She showed virtually everything else, saved from complete full frontal only by clever camera angles. Her performance at the 2013 MTV Video Music Awards popularized the dance style known as twerking, or dancing with thrusting hips and a low, squatting stance. Her performance was both widely watched and viciously panned. Cyrus maintained her popularity based on our cultural inability to look away from a train wreck, giving us whiplash in her seemingly instant transformation from Disney-show star to all-but porn star.

HOOKING UP

The most striking shift in teenage and twentysomething sexual behavior in the last decade is the disconnect between sex and emotional involvement. An article in the *New York Times Magazine* by Benoit Denizet-Lewis detailed the new pastime of "hooking up," or casual, unattached sex or fooling around. Dating and boyfriend-girlfriend relationships, it noted, were out. "Most of the teenagers I spoke to could think of only a handful of serious couples at their school," Denizet-Lewis noted. One guy with a girlfriend said that his friends made him feel like a "loser" for being in a relationship. Teens believe that "high school is no place for romantic relationships. They're complicated, messy, and invariably painful. Hooking up, when done 'right,' is exciting, sexually validating and efficient." An article in the *Atlantic* by Hanna Rosin came to a similar conclusion about the hookup culture during college. Heather, 24, neatly summarizes the generational change: "Once, sex was something you did with your husband, then it was what you did with the person you love, and now it is more for recreational purposes."

Older adults may be surprised by the idea of sex as "recreation," as if it were tennis or jogging. But many young people see relationships as too emotionally fraught, a dangerous world of feelings and closeness. "Guys can get so annoying when you start dating them," says Caity, 14, in the *New York Times Magazine* article. Young people's behavior and beliefs reinforce the shift toward casual, or at least nonrelationship, sex. In an NBC/*People* poll, almost half of young teens said their sexual contact was outside of a relationship. A survey conducted between 2005 and 2012 found that the average college student hooks up with eight people over four years.

Boys seem especially thrilled with this state of affairs. "Being in a real relationship just complicates everything. You feel obligated to be all, like, couply. And that gets really boring after a while," says Brian, 16, in the *New York Times Magazine* article. "When you're friends with benefits, you go over, hook up, then play video games or something. It rocks." If the girl wants to date you, some guys say, you simply stop hooking up. Says high school student Haris, "Now that it's easy to get sex outside of relationships, guys don't need relationships." The trend has now reached adults: 38% of US adults in 2010–12 said they'd had sex with "a casual date or pickup" in the last year, up from 28% in 1988.

That often means more sex partners—a lot more sex partners. In 1988, the average American adult reported having 7 sex partners; by 2010–12 this had risen to 11.Jack, now 20, wrote that he was popular in high school and had sex with sixteen girls before he turned 18. Denizet-Lewis found that this was one of the reasons boys disdained steady relationships: it kept them from sleeping with many different girls. Boys would only date if they weren't hot enough to get lots of girls. Or, as a character on *Law & Order: SVU* put it, "Only ugly people date." When Hanna Rosin asked a 19-year-old Yale University student in 2011 what she wanted instead of a hookup, she said, "Some guy to ask me out on a date to the frozen-yogurt place." As Rosin puts it, "That's it. A $3 date."

Yet many young women are willing participants. Sociologist Elizabeth Armstrong observes, "The ambitious women calculate that having a relationship would be like a four-credit class, and they don't always have time for it, so instead they opt for a lighter hookup." One young woman Rosin interviewed said she wanted to be "one hundred percent selfish." Another was stringing along a guy she didn't want to marry: "He fits my needs now because I don't want to get married now. I don't want anyone else to influence what I do after I graduate."

The Hookup Handbook provides a more lighthearted look at the sexual mores of the new millennium. Young authors Andrea Lavinthal and Jessica Rozler say that hooking up has definitely replaced dating, which, they say, "has gone the way of the dinosaurs, eight-track players, and stirrup pants. Extinct. Vanished. Kaput." Features of the hookup, they say, often include "drunk dialing" (what used to be known as a booty call) and "the walk of shame," which is what happens when you have to walk home from his place the next morning still wearing your attire from the night before: "a boobalicious top, a skintight pair of jeans (or an ass-cheek-exposing miniskirt), open-toed shoes, and a teeny-tiny purse that barely fits a tampon." Types of hookups include "The Fall-Down-Drunk Hookup," "Oops, I Did It Again (The Ex-Boyfriend)," and "The Snuffleupagus" ("the hookup you deny but everyone else knows really exists"). Occasionally, a series of hookups with the same guy leads to a relationship and skips the dating stage entirely. One woman says she knew she and her hookup were finally in a relationship when "they just hung out at his apartment and watched TV instead of going out, getting drunk, and hooking up."

Hooking up has been facilitated by technology, especially cell phones. It's pretty simple—you can text your potential hookup even if he's blocks away at another bar. As *The Hookup Handbook* puts it, "If we didn't have these instant forms of communication (like text messaging and IM), hooking up would be dating because you'd actually have to put more than just minimal effort into making something happen." The Internet helps too, with its myriad hookup sites; phone apps such as Tinder and Grindr can even tell hookup seekers who's available in proximity. Interviewed on NPR, Clinton Fein says he uses Grindr because it's "quicker and more efficient. The whole premise of going to a bar is to drink. And you don't have to necessarily drink to have sex now, because there's technology."

All of this means a whole lot of fun. Think about it: you can make out with that cute guy in the bar or the guy from your psych class, and nobody has to worry about who's going to call whom the next day. It's acceptable to hook up with someone you'd never actually date, so you can satisfy your urges with younger guys (what *The Hookup Handbook* calls "pass the sippy cup"), cute but dumb guys, older guys, whatever. There's no turning down dates for Saturday if they're not made by Wednesday; no rules say how many dates you have to go on before you're "allowed" to kiss him or have sex with him. Just do what you want to do—how many other generations of women (or men) have had that privilege? As *The Hookup Handbook* notes in its last line, "Your mother never had this much fun." Whether you think this sounds like fun probably depends on your generation.

ART IMITATES LIFE, OR VICE VERSA?

Sex outside of marriage is common on TV and in movies. "It was no big deal to me or my friends that we had sex before we were married," said David, 19. "We see it on TV and in the movies all the time." Monica, 16, said on the *Today* show, "If you just turn on MTV one day, you're going to see sex everywhere."

Portrayals of teen sex have become more common and accepted in the two decades since GenX'ers were teens. Most 1980s movies showed teenagers talking about sex, but not actually doing it. In 1985's *The Breakfast Club*, one character claims she slept with her therapist, but then later admits she made that up. Another says that he slept with a girl, but "you don't know her—she lives in Canada." But this is just a lame lie—he's actually a virgin.

Nearly all of the characters on *Glee* lost their virginity during high school. *The O.C.* portrayed teen sex as commonplace and relatively casual. Ryan talked about hookups at parties. Seth and Summer, both 16, had sex even though they had never been on a date together. Summer confesses to Seth afterward that she was a virgin, explaining that she didn't tell him before because "I had this reputation to uphold, and I figured you'd think less of me or something." Not so long ago, a high school girl with a "reputation" was a bad thing—now it's a good thing. This is art imitating life; according to Tunesia, 16, interviewed on the *Today* show, "Any publicity is good publicity when it comes to girls and sex."

But life also imitates art quite a bit. A study of almost 2,000 teens found that those who watch TV with a lot of sexual content are twice as likely to engage in intercourse as those who watch less. "The impact of television viewing is so large that even a moderate shift in the sexual content of adolescent TV watching could have a substantial effect on their sexual behavior," said study author Rebecca Collins. Watching sexually explicit TV led to teens having sex two to three years earlier, with media-savvy 13-year-olds acting the same as more sheltered 15- or 16-year-olds. Another study found that young black women who watch many rap-music videos are more likely to have multiple sex partners and to acquire a sexually transmitted disease.

Fashion reflects the shift toward freer sexuality. Although it makes me feel old to say it, girls did not wear belly-exposing shirts when I was in high school in the late 1980s. Well into the mid-1990s, the fashion was to wear big, blousy shirts (gather round, children, and let me tell you about the wonderful days of stirrup pants). This look covered your body pretty well, which is perhaps why it's now so out of fashion. Now the style is the more skin, the better, and bonus if your T-shirt says something provocative. Thirteen-year-old Maya, interviewed for a mid-2000s *People* magazine story, said she's going to "wait until I'm twenty" to have sex. In the picture accompanying the article, however, she's wearing a T-shirt ripped into a V-neckline that declares in large letters HOT N' NAUGHTY.

Some of the worst offenders are in advertising and music. Sex sells, and "barely legal" is a theme. Pediatrician Meg Meeker calls it the "very aggressive marketing of sex to our kids. Everywhere they go they are saturated with visual and auditory messages about sex." Linda Perlstein, the author of the book on middle schoolers, says that at teen dance clubs many kids imitated "freaking," something they'd seen in music videos, where a boy rubs himself against a girl's butt. "Children as young as eleven simulate sex on the dance floor as rappers bleat about oral gratification," Perlstein reports. The lyrics, she notes, "made great use of the fact that 'motherfucker' and 'dick sucker' rhyme."

In *The Disappearance of Childhood*, Neil Postman argues that television and movies have removed the usual barriers to young people's learning about sex. Any casual flip through the channels confirms this argument. Perlstein saw the effects of this in middle school, where sexual terms and talk are "part of their vocabulary and psyche in a way that it didn't used to be."

The Internet has brought this situation to a whole new level. So much porn is out there that the hit musical *Avenue Q* claims, in its funniest song, that "The Internet Is for Porn." When 12-year-olds are looking at it, though, it's not funny anymore. In the *New York Times Magazine* article on hooking up, many boys said they'd begun looking at porn on the Internet pretty regularly by 12 or 13. "Who needs the hassle of dating when I've got online porn?" asked one Boston teenager. A Kaiser Family Foundation study found that 70% of 15-to-17-year-old teens have seen Internet porn. In case you're behind on your Web surfing, this is not just ordinary erotica we're talking about; a lot of it is hard-core bondage and lots of other stuff I don't even want to think about. If that weren't scary enough, young girls who post to Internet message boards sometimes find themselves pursued by older men. It's no wonder that parents are concerned about these issues—sex just seems so much more available, and so much more dangerous, than it was when they were young.

About a third of teens over 15 have sexted—sent nude or nearly nude pictures of themselves. Not only are they titillating, but receiving such a picture accomplishes another important goal among GenMe: "It's a big ego boost," explained Ethan Anderson, 17, in a *Time* magazine story. Teens can also send explicit pictures using Snapchat, which deletes the picture within a few minutes. This is useful in a world in which explicit pictures can be used as weapons if they don't automatically disappear. "If the girl . . . goes around saying she doesn't like me . . . I'll have that picture of her," says Dre Gambrell, 18. With teens communicating primarily by text, cues to sexual availability are now different—but still given. "There's some that have the 'Heyyy' with the extra y's and the [emoticon], and that means this conversation could possibly go somewhere," says Dre. "They're probably the hooking-up type."

THE DOWNSIDES: STDS AND UNWANTED PREGNANCY

Possibly because of all of this hooking up, rates of sexually transmitted diseases (STDs) have increased over the last decade: the rate of syphilis cases doubled between 2001 and 2012, and chlamydia cases increased 82% (the exception: gonorrhea cases declined 16%). In an interview in *Emerging Adulthood*, one young man said he found out that a woman he slept with had been with a male stripper. After "doing the math," he says he thought, "'Holy cow! I had sex with California just now!' And that made me nervous."

One study examined the sexual geography of a small-town high school in the Midwest over eighteen months. About half of the students were sexually active, and these teens began having sex, on average, at age 15. Of the 832 students surveyed, 288 were linked in an elaborate chain of sexual contacts that, the authors say, is "the worst-case scenario" for the spread of STDs. This occurred because many students had several partners, who themselves had several partners, thus creating an elaborate web of connections. This map differed quite a bit from previous studies on adult sex, which usually find that only a few people provide most of the links in the chain; the chain ends with less promiscuous people. Not so here, where 61% of the sexually active adolescents had had more than one sexual partner in the eighteen-month span. The recent prevalence of hooking up suggests that STDs may increase in the coming years.

The spread of STDs may be exacerbated by young people's seeing sex portrayed on television without any reference to safe-sex practices. A Kaiser Family Foundation study found that 75% of TV shows contain sexual content, but only 15% of those mention safe sex. Movies are similar—sexual encounters rarely feature condoms. Presumably, this is because sex sells but protection doesn't. When watching TV, says college freshman Joyce Bryn, "No one wants to see anyone say, 'Hold on, let me put on a condom.'"

But maybe they should, because sex can now kill you. Just as the early wave of GenX was heading into our teenage years in the mid-1980s, the threat of AIDS broke onto the national media scene after Rock Hudson's death from the disease. We were welcomed into sexuality by the scary equation that sex = death. GenMe'ers have never known a world without AIDS. If you want to capture the purest form of terror and anxiety in a bottle, talk to someone who has just taken an HIV blood test and is waiting for the results.

The threat of AIDS has become somewhat less terrifying in the years since the drug cocktail was invented, and being HIV-positive is not such an immediate death sentence. But even though AIDS doesn't get the press it used to, it's still out there. The rate of HIV infection among gay men increased between 2008 and 2010, with the largest increase (22%) among the youngest in GenMe (ages 13 to 24). In the United States in 2007, 11,295 people died of HIV. Many Boomer gay men, who came of age in the 1980s when AIDS first entered the scene, are frustrated to see young gay men with a complacent or even cavalier attitude about getting HIV.

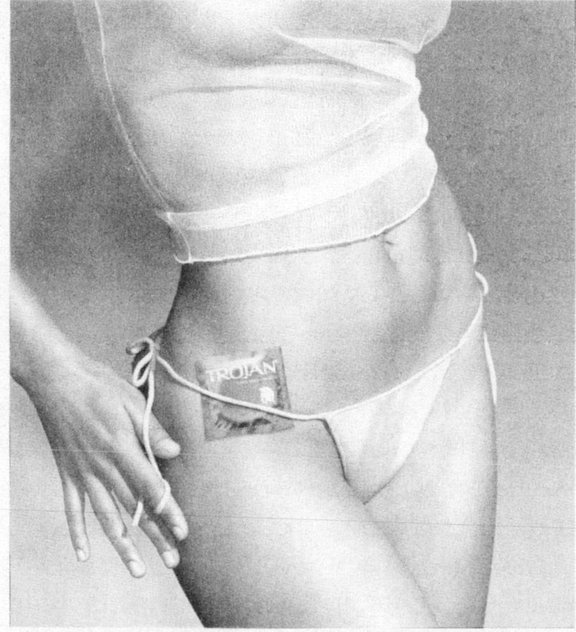

The sexual life of GenMe has always included AIDS. With the new prevalence of hookups, condoms are pretty close to becoming the fashion statement this Trojan ad suggests they are.

Unfortunately, they may be right: 20% more gay men had unprotected sex in 2011 compared to 2005.

On the other hand, GenMe has turned around the statistics on teen pregnancy. Births to teens aged 15 to 19 hit a record low in 2011, with the rate cut fully in half since 1990. The pregnancy rate (which includes abortion and miscarriages as well as births) has declined 42% since 1990. Fifty-nine percent fewer teens had an abortion in 2008 compared to 1988.

Clearly, more teens are using birth control responsibly. These two might even go together: teenagers who assume they will soon have sex might be more likely to carry condoms or go on the pill. Their permissive attitudes may make them more prepared for the reality of their sexual activity.

I'M SINGLE

During the late 2000s, 48% of women ages 15 to 44 were living with someone while unmarried, up from 35% in 1995. Of those, 40% got married, 32% were still cohabitating after three years, and 27% broke up. In a 2001 poll, 62% of young people said that living together is the best way to predict if a relationship will last, and 43% say they wouldn't marry someone unless they had lived with him or her first.

Being single is not what it used to be. Someone who is technically "single" (as in not married) may have been in a live-in relationship for many years. Although most middle-class couples still get married eventually, it is seen as a later step in a process that begins with dating (or hooking up), moves on to seeing each other almost every night, and makes an intermediate stop at living together. Many people, especially the younger half of GenMe, have begun to use "single" to mean "not dating anyone." Author Linda Perlstein saw a girl's website that said, "Hi, I'm Adrienne. I am 11 and single."

Living together has radically changed the landscape of "single" people. Previous generations would have been shocked if couples lived together before marriage—and they are shocked when young people do so today. Tyler, 20, moved in with his girlfriend after they had dated for about six months. When his grandmother found out, she yelled at him, saying that she was "so disappointed." Tyler's sister Michelle, 22, also lives with her boyfriend; she describes her grandmother's comments as "rude." The authors of *Midlife Crisis at 30* relate one of their mother's comments about living together in her day: "My mother would have absolutely killed me. Actually, scratch that. I wouldn't have ever thought about doing something so unrespectable. . . . It would have been like saying, 'Hmmm, should I take that express shuttle to the moon?'"

As of 2010, 77% of US married couples lived together first, up from 61% in 1995. Unmarried cohabitation also lasts longer now—an average of almost two years, compared to about a year in 1995.

Brian, 23, said that living with his girlfriend happened naturally. They had been spending a lot of time together, and he cleared some space for her things at his apartment. "Oh my gosh, I have a shelf!" she said. Before long, they were living together. Brian understands just how different his situation is from in previous generations. "My girlfriend's grandmother would say, 'If you give out the milk for free, nobody will buy the cow.' Now, living together is a normal step in a relationship."

There are also large financial incentives to live together. Sharing the rent with someone—even if you need a bigger place—is a huge savings these days with rents and mortgages so high. And if you're making a middle-class income, you'll pay less tax to Uncle Sam if you stay single. This "marriage tax penalty," once several thousand dollars on average, has been rolled back considerably in the last few years. However, people with taxable incomes of $73,200 or more in 2013 still paid more tax when married—thousands of dollars more if they were high income. Then there's the cost of a wedding—the latest estimate puts the average at a whopping $28,487. In major cities such as New York, it's over $50,000. Living together sounds pretty good when you think about it this way.

ARE THESE CHANGES GOOD OR BAD?

Well, that depends on whom you ask. Some young women believe their greater sexual freedom is an unmitigated good. This fits the trends discussed earlier in the book—if we're going to have more freedoms, why not sexual freedom? "I definitely think our generation is lucky because we didn't have the same constraints our parents did," says Priya, 18. The authors of *The Hookup Handbook* dedicate their book to "every girl who lives life by her own rules—not The Rules."

When one of my students, then 23, wrote a paper on changes in sexuality, she did not describe younger people as more sexually active; instead, she wrote that they were "less sexually repressed." Older people may think that the younger generation is disturbingly promiscuous, but the younger generation flings it right back—sure, we're a little loose, but you're just uptight. Sometimes neither characterization is complimentary. Lynda, 25, suggested the title for this chapter, and although it's a great title, neither *prude* nor *crude* is flattering.

In other words, how you perceive the generational trend depends on your generation. No matter what your opinion, it's clear that individual freedom has once again won out against restrictive social rules. Don't forget the condoms.

7

The Equality Revolution: Minorities, Women, and Gays and Lesbians

On March 7, 1965, five hundred people began to walk in Selma, Alabama. The crowd of protesters, black and white, planned to march to the state capital, Montgomery, to demand equal voting rights for black people.

They made it only to a bridge on the outskirts of town. There, state troopers pelted them with tear gas and beat them with billy clubs so brutally that many were left bleeding or unconscious. Some of the troopers' horses stepped on protesters and broke their ribs. The violence was so great that this became known as Bloody Sunday.

Reflecting on the events forty years later, Congressman John Lewis noted that in 1965 all of the troopers were white men. When they re-created the Selma march in 2005, however, he said, "The group of troopers were men and women, white, black, and Hispanic. And when we reached the bridge, they cheered."

Lewis's comment is striking for a number of reasons. First, the principles of the civil rights movement have been fully accepted by most Americans—they are ideas to be cheered and celebrated rather than beaten out of people. Not only that, but state troopers are now every race and both male and female. So are engineers, lawyers, doctors, and many other professions that were once almost exclusively white and male—such as president of the United States. The same country that had to pass a law in 1964 to make sure blacks could vote elected a black president just 44 years later—and then did it again in 2012.

In just a few decades, the United States underwent a transformation of attitudes about women, minorities, and gays and lesbians. The revolution of equality was, without question, the largest social change in America in the last half of the 20th century. No other trend has had such a colossal impact on every aspect of our lives. We might debate the particulars of affirmative action, same-sex marriage, and sex differences in intellectual ability, but even conservatives now accept the general principle that race, gender, and sexual orientation should not preclude people from pursuing the profession they desire.

It is difficult to overestimate the enormity of this change, and the relatively short amount of time it took. Segregation was still rampant in the 1960s, and Hispanics were still referred to as Spanish. In 1970, just 5% of graduating law students were women. By 2009 it was 46%, a ninefold increase. In the 1970s, police still raided gay bars and arrested people, and no one on TV was gay—not even Liberace, and especially not the dad on *The Brady Bunch*. When the first edition of this book was published in 2006, gays and lesbians could not openly serve in the US military, and same-sex marriage was outlawed at the federal level. Now neither is true.

This is one of the last chapters in the book precisely because these changes are so pervasive and strong. These are not the trends that surprise people. Yet you may not realize just how much things have changed until you consider the details. We take so many things for granted now that it is easy to forget what things used to be like, especially if you are a GenMe'er and never saw it with your own eyes. GenX and especially GenMe have been taught equality since we were babies, if not by our parents, then by TV. This tolerance goes hand in hand with the decline in social rules in chapter 1; GenMe may have left behind some of the good social rules about politeness, but following in the footsteps of the Boomers, they also left behind some of the bad social rules about everyone's living life in the same way, minorities and women staying in their "place," and gays and lesbians facing systematic discrimination. GenMe'ers are less likely to believe in moral absolutes and are thus tolerant and accepting of diversity in all its forms.

This is the good-news portion of the book. Most people would agree that equality is the upside of the focus on the self. In valuing the individual, our society looks beyond race, sex, and sexual orientation to the talents of each person. In practice, it doesn't always happen—the most powerful among us are still white men—but a staggering amount of progress has been made. Whether it reflects reality or not, the American ideal in the 21st century is for each person to realize his or her potential. We no longer believe, as many people once did, that people of color should limit themselves to menial jobs or that a college education is wasted on a woman (because she will "just" have children and stay home).

These changes in beliefs have been accompanied by large changes in behavior, life paths, and personalities. GenMe lives these differences every day. And that goes for white men too. Compared to your father or grandfather, you're much more likely to have a female boss, a friend of another race, or a wife who works outside the home. And even if you don't, you will see those things all around you.

CHANGES FOR MINORITIES

As the example of the Selma march illustrates, race relations in the United States have undergone a sea change. Racism and even segregation still exist, but they are not the systematic, institutionalized practice they once were. Monique, 21 and African

American, notes that her grandmother went to segregated schools and wasn't even allowed to play with white children. Although Monique says she has seen racism in her life, her grandmother's experiences "seem like another world. I cannot even imagine having to deal with the issues she dealt with." Overtly reported racial prejudice has become so rare that researchers now use indirect methods to measure it.

Being a minority in the United States today is much different from forty or fifty years ago. There is a growing minority middle class. In 1970, most blacks did not even have a high school diploma; now 90% do, and almost four times as many blacks are college educated. The percentage of college degrees awarded to Hispanics has almost tripled since 1980. These trends are likely to continue as college-educated minorities have their own children and pass on their ambitions and success.

These changes are all around us in popular media, from the black newscaster to the Mexican American actress. Like other trends, these changes were mostly in place by the time GenX and especially GenMe came along. From *The Jeffersons* ("Baby, movin' on up . . .") to *The Cosby Show* to *ER* to *Grey's Anatomy* to *Glee*, GenMe is accustomed to seeing diversity on TV. Today, lawyers, judges, and doctors on TV are just about every ethnicity. We do not find this unusual; most of us fail to notice it or comment on it.

Of course, racism still exists. Charles, 27, interviewed in *Emerging Adulthood*, recalls being called the n-word while at sports camp as a kid, and as a teenager, he got pulled over for "driving while black." Black and Hispanic job applicants still face an uphill battle against stereotyping and discrimination, and an enormous racial discrepancy remains in income and education. Sixty-one percent of black and 36% of Hispanic young adults say that it has been difficult for them to get the financial support they need to get a college education; in contrast, only 4% of whites and zero Asian Americans say it has been difficult. This is simple math, as black and Hispanic young people are more likely to come from lower-income families. There may be a burgeoning black middle class, but untold masses of minorities still live on next to nothing.

Most people admit to engaging in at least some racial stereotyping. The musical *Avenue Q* even has a matter-of-fact song about it: "Everyone's a Little Bit Racist" ("Ethnic jokes might be uncouth / But you laugh because they're based on truth"). Black comedian Dave Chappelle was equally straightforward—and hilarious—about race on his sketch show, which was wildly popular among college students in the mid-2000s. In one sketch, he hosted a mock game show called *I Know Black People*, with questions about the meaning of the term *badonkadonk* (hint: the same as "junk in her trunk") and why black people like menthol cigarettes (to which a white contestant admits, "I don't know," and Dave replies, "That is correct. Nobody knows"). Amid the goofiness is social commentary as well. When Dave asks how black people can "rise up and overcome," a white contestant says, "By getting out there and voting." Dave deadpans, "That is incorrect."

Nevertheless, much has changed. Most white people no longer work and live in places where they could expect not to interact with those of other races. Now workplaces, neighborhoods, and even many marriages are integrated. Eighty-seven percent of high school students in 2012 said they had a close friend of another race, up from 61% in the late 1970s. Twice as many say they "do things (like having a conversation, eating together, playing sports)" with those of other races "a lot" (47%, compared to 19% in the late 1970s). Only a third as many now live in a neighborhood that's exclusively one race (54% did in the late 1970s, versus only 18% in 2012). "All of my friends are a different race than I am," says Maria, 20. "It was never looked down upon to have friends that were not the same skin color as you. We are a generation more accepting of diversity."

Some of this is simple demographics: among Americans born

between 1977 and 1994, only 62% are white (compared to 75% of Baby Boomers and 85% of the World War II generation). GenMe is more comfortable with racial crossovers, in everything from dating to music. One of my students was a Filipino young man who lived, breathed, and ate hip-hop music; he proudly pointed out that one of the best hip-hop DJs is also Filipino. But, he says, "I am proud of my culture but not ethnocentric." He's not alone. More and more young whites and Asians enjoy rap music and watch black comedians. It's pretty much taken for granted that black people, their culture, and their music are cool. And so is Hispanic and Asian culture—it's a small sign of progress, surely, but who can get through the week without eating tacos, sushi, or Chinese takeout?

Many of the questions about race in the General Social Survey, first administered in 1972, are so outdated that most of them aren't even asked anymore. In 1972, 32% still favored laws that prevented people of different races from marrying one another. By the time the GSS stopped asking the question in 2002, only 3% agreed. Other questions ask if black and white children should go to the same school, a nonissue by 1985, when the question was dropped. Another item asks if one would vote for a black president—an unnecessary question after more than half the country did so in 2008 and 2012.

So have the changes in race relations over the last four decades had psychological effects? Back in the 1940s, psychologists Kenneth and Mamie Clark performed a famous experiment in which they gave black children the choice of playing with white dolls or black dolls. Most of the black children chose to play with the white dolls, leading the authors to conclude that the black children had low self-esteem. In its *Brown v. Board of Education* ruling against segregation, the Supreme Court mentioned these results as an example of the inferiority felt by black children.

So do blacks and other minorities have lower self-esteem than whites, and has this difference changed over the generations? To find out, Jennifer Crocker and I gathered data from 712 samples of 375,254 people of all races and ethnicities who filled out self-esteem questionnaires between the 1950s and the 1990s.

In the 1960s and early 1970s, black and white Americans scored about the same on measures of self-esteem. During the 1980s, however, black Americans' self-esteem increased until it was noticeably higher than whites'. By the 1990s, 58% of blacks, and 61% of black college students, displayed above-average self-esteem. This is surprising given the usual belief that ethnic minorities will have lower self-esteem; clearly, young black Americans feel good about themselves. In fact, blacks' self-esteem is higher than that of any other racial or ethnic group.

The change over the decades also tells an intriguing historical story: the civil rights movement and the general shift toward racial equality has had a striking effect on the self-esteem of minority youth. Black GenMe kids grew up hearing that Black Is Beautiful, seeing people who looked like them play doctors and lawyers on TV, and (particularly if they were middle-class) expecting to go to college—why shouldn't they feel good about themselves?

Some of the increase in blacks' self-esteem might be traced to school programs. Similar to the general self-esteem programs mentioned in chapter 2, many school districts have specific programs aimed at minority youth. Sondra, 20, participated in one of these programs when she was in the fifth grade. The school's small number of black children were brought together in a group, where they learned about their culture and were taught to take pride in their background. "We were really proud of who we were and where we came from," says Sondra. "The pride I received by being a part of this group has allowed me to know exactly who I am today and what I want to become in the future." These groups have become even more common in recent years.

A glance at any recent high school history textbook shows that this ethnic pride is fostered even in schools without specific programs. When the Boomers were growing up, history textbooks were basically the history of white men and discussed slavery for its political implications rather than for its effect on African Americans. Native Americans were portrayed as enemies. Now history texts are careful to emphasize the victimization of Africans and Native Americans and vividly describe their cultures. Ethnic minority youth see their history taught in school and come to understand more about their cultures and their origins.

This trend is not limited to black youth. In our comprehensive study, we found that Hispanic and Asian young people's self-esteem has also increased relative to whites'. Though both groups still score lower than whites on measures of self-esteem, this gap has narrowed over the last three decades. It will most likely continue to narrow as younger generations are increasingly indoctrinated into the American ideal of high self-esteem.

Many Asian and Hispanic children of immigrants walk a delicate line between their parents' communal culture and the individualistic ethos of the United States. On a segment of MTV's *My Life (Translated)*, Korean American reporter SuChin Pak talked about immigrant children's college experiences. When SuChin went off to Berkeley, her parents moved in next door to her dorm! "Like every good Korean daughter, I always did exactly what my parents told me to do," she says. SuChin then interviewed Sonia, a 19-year-old Mexican American struggling to study for her college classes because her parents expect her to cook, clean, and take care of her younger siblings. ("What have you ironed for me?" her father asks her.) Sonia thinks about dropping out of college, but decides to stay in school when her parents say they will support her and that they want her to "become somebody."

Many young Hispanics take pride in their ethnic identity and fully recognize that their generation has opportunities that their parents never dreamed of. Twenty-four-year-old Jose says that his mother attended school in Mexico only until the third grade. She worked as a maid and as a seamstress at a sweatshop after arriving in the United States when she was 13. When Jose finished high school, he says, he was "indifferent" about college, since he had already completed more schooling than anyone else in his family. Yet when his college acceptance letter came, "I read the first sentence and started to cry. I wanted to thank God for giving me so much. I told my mother this was just a start and that I would do everything possible to be the best man I could be." Laura, 22, grew up in a poor Hispanic family in Miami and got a scholarship to a prestigious private college in the Northeast. Though fitting in at the college was difficult, she was empowered by the experience. "Being from a different generation has given me the opportunity to be educated, to take opportunities and make great things out of them," she says. "I have come to see myself as a role model for future generations."

Some young people find that even experiences with ignorance or prejudice can heighten their ethnic pride. Rosa, 21, is Cuban American and grew up in Miami. When she moved to northern Florida for college, she was shocked when people came up to her and said things like "What are you? Are you Mexican?" She finally realized that many of these students, as she put it, "came from places where the closest thing to Spanish heritage was the Taco Bell on the corner." She says this helped her focus more on her identity. "I had never felt so Cuban in my whole life! It really became a huge part of how I saw myself, and I started to appreciate every part of my culture—the food, the music, and even the language."

These stories clearly show one of the upsides of individualism: young people who appreciate their culture and can take advantage of opportunities their parents never had. Although economic pressures still limit the goals of many minority youth, their race or ethnicity is no longer an automatic disqualification.

But is the upswing in minority kids' self-esteem an unmitigated good? As I argued in chapter 2, maybe not. It's certainly good for young people to take pride in their ethnic identity, no matter what their background; feeling comfortable in your own skin is obviously important. But like the general self-esteem programs, ethnic self-esteem programs often take things too far and focus on the wrong causes. Raising children's self-esteem is not going to solve the problems of poverty and crime. It doesn't do much good for a child to have high self-esteem if his grades are poor, he gets in trouble in class, and he has no concrete plan for the future. Ethnic differences are a prime example of the disconnect between self-esteem and achievement. For example, Asian American kids have the lowest self-esteem of all ethnic groups, but, on average, they achieve the most academically. Black youngsters have the highest self-esteem, yet lag behind in academic achievement. Because self-esteem does not cause school achievement, self-esteem programs are once again putting the cart before the horse. The time spent on self-esteem programs—for children of any background—is probably better spent on teaching academics and self-control.

CHANGES FOR WOMEN

One of the biggest sporting events of 1973 was the tennis match between Billie Jean King, then 29, and Bobby Riggs, 54. Hyped as the "Battle of the Sexes," the match inspired countless water-cooler bets. While today few would bet on the aging player, at that time many people believed that a woman could never beat a man in sports, no matter what his age or her skill. When King arrived on the court, Howard Cosell commented on her hairstyle, saying she could be a Hollywood actress if only her hair were longer. Not surprisingly, Cosell was virtually speechless when King won—and won easily.

Sexist attitudes and discrimination against women went far beyond sports. Before the late 1960s, medical schools systematically capped the enrollment of women at 5% of each class, regardless of how many talented women applied. When former Supreme Court justice Sandra Day O'Connor graduated near the top of her Stanford Law School class in 1952, no law firm would hire her—although one firm offered her a position as a secretary.

As late as the 1970s, there were no female news anchors, few female lawyers, and even fewer women scientists. The *New York Times* and other newspapers ran want ads under "Help Wanted: Male" and "Help Wanted: Female." In 1964, Virginia congressman Howard Smith, a staunch opponent of civil rights for blacks, added sex discrimination to the Civil Rights Act as a joke, in hopes of defeating the bill. In his speech, he quoted a sarcastic letter from a woman complaining about "sex discrimination" in the shortage of husbands, as the House of Representatives roared with laughter. The bill passed anyway, sex discrimination clause intact. I have always imagined Congressman Smith kicking himself well into the next decade.

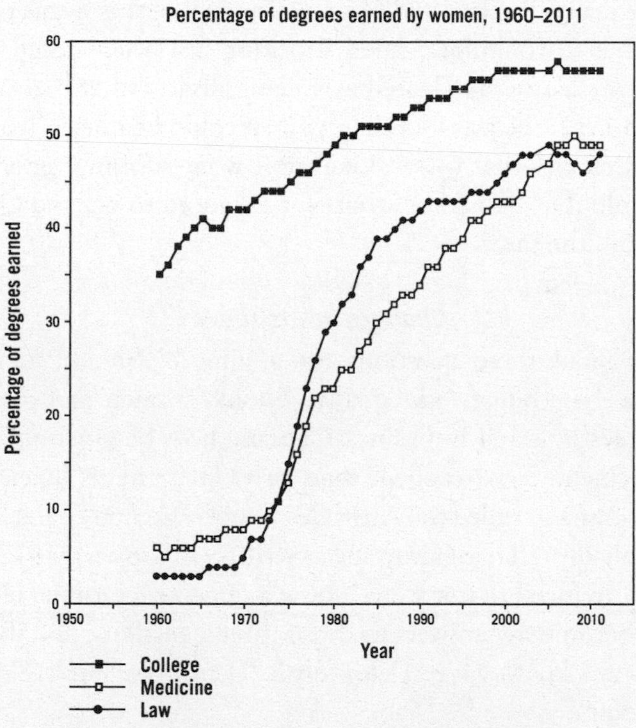

Women now earn the majority of college degrees, and almost half of all medical and law degrees.

If Smith were alive today, he would be flabbergasted by what he would see. Girls play soccer alongside boys. Women earn 57% of college degrees and almost half of degrees in law and medicine. Television news is filled with female reporters and anchors, sometimes reporting on the actions of the many women now in government leadership positions (including eighty-three in Congress, an all-time high). Most women in their 20s have never been married, and in 2005—for the first time in American history—more women (51%) lived without a spouse than with one. More than six times as many women had their first child after the age of 30 in 2012 compared to 1970. As of 2009, only 18% of married couples had the husband as the single breadwinner. Women are now the majority of accountants, financial managers, medical scientists, and pharmacists. All of this seems normal to us, but it would have been shocking just a few decades ago. When my mother graduated as valedictorian of her high school class in 1962, she was told that women could be nurses, teachers, or secretaries—that was it. Like most women of my generation, I was told that I could be whatever I wanted to be, and GenMe has heard the same.

Changes in Attitudes

Think about these questions for a minute: Should men and women share housework equally? Should women participate in the professions and in business? Should boys be given more encouragement to go to college than girls? These items appeared on a questionnaire called the Attitudes toward Women Scale. As you can probably tell right away, it was written in the early 1970s, and I was convinced that it would show a large generational change, partly because my answers to those three questions, and those of everyone I knew, were "Definitely," "Definitely," and "No! Are you kidding?"

So I spent the summer of 1995, when I was 23, gathering data on 71 samples of 19,101 college students who had filled out this questionnaire between 1970 and 1995. Though I was sure I'd find change in this scale, I wasn't certain what the pattern would look like—after all, weren't the 1980s a more conservative decade than the 1970s? In 1991, Susan Faludi had argued that a backlash against feminism occurred during the decade of Reagan and the Moral Majority. So would attitudes toward women slide backward during the 1980s?

Nope. Attitudes about women's roles continued to become more egalitarian throughout the 1980s and into the early 1990s. Although Faludi was right that the media in the 1980s were not profeminist, young people seemed to ignore this. The change over the three decades was also substantial. The average 1990s college woman had more feminist attitudes than 87% of her counterparts in the early 1970s, and the average 1990s college man had more feminist attitudes than 82% of early 1970s college men. What was once the province of hippies and radicals had become mainstream. At least the attitudes had, even if the labels hadn't. As Paula Kamen found in her 1991 book, *Feminist Fatale*, young women believed in feminist values but rejected the label *feminist* (prompting the frequent statement "I'm not a feminist, but . . . ," after which the young woman makes a strong statement about equality between the sexes).

So why was there a media obsession with tearing down feminism and unearthing day-care abuse scandals (almost all later proved to be untrue) during the 1980s? Probably because the country was reeling from the breakneck pace of cultural change. In 1984, for the first time, the majority of married women with children under six were in the workplace. At college graduation ceremonies in 1982, American women earned more undergraduate degrees than men for the first time in history.

Many GenX babies weren't even born when these changes got under way in the 1970s and 1980s. So, as always, GenX entered a world where things had already changed, and they soaked it up like little sponges. Even in my conservative Texas town, a favorite school film in the early 1980s was *Free to Be . . . You and Me*, an anthology of songs and stories designed to fight sexism (my personal favorites: "William Has a Doll" and the one where the prissy girl who always says "Ladies first" gets her way—she gets eaten by the tiger first!). We would sit entranced in the dark room as the puppet babies discussed which of them was a girl or a boy and the cheerful theme song began, about a place where the children are free and "every boy grows to be his own man . . . every girl grows to be her own woman."

GenMe didn't even need a film to tell them this stuff. Equality between the sexes is such a given that Anne, 16, says that in her neighborhood "being a feminist is considered almost nitpicky and trivial." Heather, 19, agrees, "Girls of my generation take everything for granted. We grew up with the understanding that girls were equal to guys. I think of it as something that should come naturally, not as a privilege."

Kristin Donnelly and I decided to find out if this was true—did attitudes toward women's roles continue to become more progressive since the 1990s, or has there instead been a backlash? The data show continued acceptance of broader roles for women in the transition from GenX to GenMe. Among high school students in 2012, 69% believed working mothers could establish just as warm a relationship with their children, up from 53% in the late 1970s and 63% in 1990–91. Only 20% thought a preschool child would suffer if his/her mother worked, down from 59% in the 1970s and 42% in the early 1990s. This might have occurred because twice as many of GenMe's own mothers worked for most of their childhoods (67% in 2012, up from 31% in the late 1970s).

Even the pronouns we see are different now. Using the Google Books database of 5 million books, my coauthors and I discovered a profound shift toward gender equality in language. In the early 1970s, books used 4.5 times as many male pronouns (he, him) as female pronouns (she, her). By 2008, this shrunk to 1.75 male pronouns for each female pronoun—not equality, but a lot closer than before.

Many young women recognize those who fought for women's rights—including their mothers. Erin, 20, says, "My mother was a housewife. She urged me to break the tradition of women sacrificing their identities and their opportunities to be a mother. Women are finally starting to emerge from their domestic quarantine, and I am proud to be a part of a new generation of women who won't stand for it any longer, and grateful to my forerunners who made it possible." Erin is not the only one unwilling to enter the "domestic quarantine." In 2012, only 1 out of 1,000 incoming college students chose "homemaker (full-time)" as their expected career. This suggests that either fewer and fewer women will stay home with their children, or more and more women—or men—will end up with a role they never expected to have.

These trends, like so many, have their roots in the movement toward individualism and the self. Many young women said their mothers explicitly told them to act as individuals. "My mother has always encouraged me to be independent and never depend on anyone but myself," wrote Melinda, 22. "She wants me to be able to stand on my own two feet and not depend on a man when I'm married." Elizabeth, 20, says that her mother "continually told me never to surrender my power as she did, to find a way to do right by my children, but to do right by myself also." Tiffany, 18, says that her mother was married and had a child by 19, a life Tiffany has no desire to replicate: "I want to be able to live my life and become a pediatrician. I don't want to depend on my husband or anyone else. I want to be able to show people, and myself, that I can achieve the goals I have set for myself."

The feminist message for women is inextricably linked to the individualist message, and whether girls heard the call of independence from their family or only from the outside culture, they listened. Gender equality is so taken for granted now that these trends are unlikely to reverse; girls growing up right now will become the most liberated generation of women in history—until their own daughters outstrip them.

Kristin's study did find one small sign of backlash. Slightly more 2010–12 students than 1990–91 students agreed that "it is usually best for everyone involved if the man is the achiever outside the family and the woman takes care of the home and family" and "the husband should make all of the important decisions in the family" (though agreement is still down since the late 1970s). The small decline in progressive attitudes toward wives' roles since the 1990s might be due to these students' views of marriage: with nearly half of babies born to unmarried mothers, young people may be more likely to see marriage as increasingly distant, traditional, and idealized. The idea that marriage leads to unequal gender roles might be one of the reasons why more couples live together instead of getting married.

Changes in Personality

Beliefs about women and their roles are very different from what they used to be. But does this mean that women are actually different now, with different personalities and different behaviors? Specifically, are GenX and GenMe women more likely to have personality traits that were once associated more with men? Could expectations have changed while women remained just as unassertive and passive as they were before?

As you might remember from the introduction, this was the question that drove my first study of generational differences. After noticing that college women in the early 1990s were scoring very differently from 1970s women, I decided to do a systematic study of the question. I gathered 103 samples of 28,920 college students on two questionnaires that measured stereotypically masculine and feminine traits. The "masculine" scale items included words such as *competitive*, *independent*, *never give up easily*, *self-reliant*, *forceful*, and *ambitious*. Sure enough, college women endorsed these traits at a higher rate with every passing year.

More than 50% of 1990s women scored as masculine on the scale, compared to only 20% of early 1970s women. The average 1990s college woman reported more masculine traits than 80% of Boomer college women in the early 1970s. The change was so large that by the early 1990s men's and women's scores on the scale of so-called masculine traits were indistinguishable. The generational change in personality had turned the very definition of the scale on its head: clearly these traits were no longer masculine, but simply human.

Perhaps because the masculine scale isn't so masculine anymore, these questionnaires were not used much in the 2000s and 2010s, so I wasn't able to update these statistics to more recent, GenMe years. But the nationally representative sample of 11 million college students was helpful, as it includes self-ratings on attributes with a lot of overlap with the masculine scale, such as leadership ability, drive to achieve, intellectual self-confidence, and creativity. They show an intriguing change: in some cases, women are now outscoring men in their self-ratings of once-masculine traits. In 1989, 72% of college men described themselves as above average in their drive to achieve, compared to 69% of college women. By 2012, 77% of college women said they had a high drive to achieve, compared to 75% of college men. College men used to rate themselves as much more creative than college women—58% of men versus 47% of women in 1993—but by 2012 they rated themselves about the same (54% versus 53%).

Much of this change is probably due to upbringing. GenMe girls have seen their mothers work outside the home more than any previous generation. Studies have found that girls with working mothers are more likely to embrace traditionally masculine traits such as ambition and independence. Seeing Mom go off to work provides a daily role model for girls, showing them that women have roles outside the home. Many GenMe women—and men—take it for granted that mothers will work at least part of the time.

It's now cool for girls to play sports . . . although this ad suggests you still need to worry about how you smell while doing it.

In addition, nearly ten times as many high school girls participate in interscholastic sports now than in 1972. Before the passage of Title IX, girls' athletics was almost a joke, with little funding and even less enthusiasm. Many girls today don't even realize that it was once unusual for females to play sports, since girls and boys now participate in sports at a nearly equal rate. It's likely that sports participation has affected girls' personalities, as research shows that girls who participate in sports are more likely to develop traits such as independence and competitiveness.

Many young women told me that their fathers encouraged them to play sports and didn't treat them differently from their brothers. "My father never drew a line between what girls should do and what boys should do," said Amanda, 25. "My sister and I played soccer and got filthy playing outside tending to goats and chickens and catching snakes." I also had a father who made few distinctions between the sexes. To this day I can throw a softball from third to first because my dad showed me how—no "throwing like a girl" for me. When my mother and I watched beauty pageants, my dad would walk through the room and mutter disapprovingly, "Meat market." I clearly saw that my dad cared a lot more about my ability to throw a ball than my ability to look good doing it—quite a change from the dads in the 1950s, many of whom would never have allowed a girl to play softball.

Women are increasingly invested in work and education as integral parts of their identities. Keith Campbell and I examined 446 studies of 312,940 individuals with data on the link between self-esteem and socioeconomic status, which includes job status, income, and education. For men, the correlation between self-esteem and socioeconomic status has decreased; men now show a weaker link between their self-esteem and their job status or education than previous generations did. For women, the opposite is true; the correlation between women's socioeconomic status and self-esteem has grown stronger with each generation. Women's self-esteem is now more strongly linked to their work and education than men's is. Work, income, and education, once relatively unimportant to a woman's identity, are now even more important to women than to men.

Yet when women get home, they often face a sink full of dirty dishes. How does that make young women feel? The title of the recent edited volume *The Bitch in the House* pretty much sums it up. In one of the essays, E. S. Maduro, 24, describes her feelings of anger at her live-in boyfriend when she comes home to a messy apartment: "Does it just not occur to him that I worked all day and might like to come home to a place where I don't immediately have to start cleaning in order to feel some sense of peace with where I am? I will cook and clean, and all the while think about how I am falling into the same trap of housework that my own mother fell into."

Her mother, however, saw things differently: "The fact that I did all the shopping and cooking and cleaning at home was just part of the territory; all the women I knew did this, and I never thought to question or resent it. You seem to feel in your essay that I have some anger about all I did, particularly the domestic roles that fell to me. But I do not now, and don't believe I ever did, feel angry about these roles and tasks."

But GenX and GenMe women do. I find the peacefulness in the mother's letter typical of her generation, and atypical of GenX and GenMe—we just have no tolerance for such blatant inequality. (To put it more succinctly, we don't put up with that shit.) GenMe women spend less time on housework than their mothers did, but expect to split things 50-50 with their male partners, and when this doesn't happen, watch out. Or we do the work to avoid the fight, since we've fought about it so many times before, but are still steaming inside.

The Generation Me Man

Where are the men in all of this? On the questions measuring attitudes toward women, men's opinions have shifted right along with women's, though they still espouse more conservative views than women (which might explain why conflict between the sexes has persisted). Men have also increased in assertiveness and stereotypically masculine traits just as women have, suggesting that both men and women have caught the train toward greater individualism. But have men taken on more stereotypically feminine traits, as women have embraced masculine traits? Maybe, but maybe not. College men's scores on measures of nurturance and caring from the 1970s to the 1990s show mixed results; men's scores on nurturance increased on one scale but not on another. Even on the scale that showed change, the trend was not nearly as strong as the shift toward more assertive and independent traits for women. In the large college survey, women used to rate themselves as much more cooperative—a "feminine" trait—than men (in 1990, 76% of women and 70% of men said they were above average). But by 2012, an equal percentage of men and women said they were above average in cooperativeness (69%). Another so-called feminine trait, understanding others, still has more women (69%) saying they are above average than men (63%).

So women have become more stereotypically masculine, but men show only a weak trend toward more stereotypically feminine nurturance. It does seem that young men are now more comfortable with the more appearance-based feminine things. Suddenly, just because you know how to dress well doesn't necessarily mean you're gay. But a man who has primary responsibility for his children is still rare.

However, today's married fathers are clearly more involved than those of previous generations. It's no longer considered strange for men to change diapers, but does that mean that men are actually changing the diapers? Well, sometimes—and definitely a lot more than the men of previous generations. Married fathers spent three times as much time interacting with their kids, and twice as much time on housework, in 2011 as they did in 1965. One problem: fewer dads are married, so the involvement of dads may not have changed that much after all on average. Those who are around are more involved, but fewer are around.

In addition, the emphasis on individualism means that work remains on its exalted throne. It's still uncommon for the man to be the one to stay home with the kids, even if he makes less money than his wife. A lot of men say they would find it isolating to be at home; others say they would lose prestige in their careers if they took too much time off. There's still a stigma against stay-at-home dads, though this is fading some with time. With more women earning college and graduate degrees, in more and more couples in the future the woman will earn more than the man. GenMe might well make stay-at-home dads cool.

Especially in the time before parenthood, young men are a fairly liberated bunch. Even those who are conservative in their politics don't usually expect their wives to always stay home or to do all of the housework. Although men don't usually think much about women's earning power, this may change as housing gets even more expensive. One friend of mine, an investment banker, told me that he thought New York men were looking for successful women who made a lot of money—having two good incomes was the only way to afford a decent apartment! In a mid-2000s poll, 79% of young men said they'd feel comfortable dating a woman who earned significantly more than they did.

Well, But: The Big Caveat

The arrival of a child can rock the most deeply held notions of sexual equality. As Susan Douglas and Meredith Michaels point out in *The Mommy Myth*, "A dad who knows the name of his kids' pediatrician and reads them stories at night is still regarded as a saint; a mother who doesn't is a sinner." GenMe dads are more involved than ever, which is fantastic; it's just that "more than ever" often still means "not much." In spite of the tremendous progress in diaper changing, bath giving, and baby cuddling among men, in the vast majority of cases it's still Mom who knows where Madison's shoes are and when Jacob takes his nap.

GenMe women are expected to lead a contradictory existence. They are told (and believe) that they can do anything, but once they become mothers, "anything" becomes "that you can do from home" or "that is strictly nine to five" (ha!). Even "anything that pays enough so you can afford a British nanny" isn't good enough—do you really want "someone else raising your children"? Writer Peggy Orenstein said that after going around the country lecturing on self-esteem, she realized, "There was this big gap in messages between what we were telling teenage girls and what we were telling women when they came to be around 30. For girls and teens, we say, 'You Can Do Anything,' and then for women, we turn around and say, 'You Can't Have it All.'" As a culture, we still carry an incredible amount of ambivalence toward working mothers that working fathers are still able to neatly sidestep. As Sheryl Sandberg pointed out in *Lean In*, these attitudes have persisted into the 2010s.

Obviously, working mothers are much more accepted now than in previous decades. But an incredible amount of resistance remains to day care and nannies, which are—like it or not—the logical outcome of women's fully participating in the working world. Many people still strongly believe that day care is harmful. At a recent party, I met a charming, incredibly bright 3-year-old who could rattle off the names of dinosaurs whose pronunciation stumped most of the adults in attendance. After the child left with her mother, one woman asked if the mother stayed home. She was surprised to learn that the child was in full-time day care—the implication being that a child who went to day care couldn't possibly be that smart.

In fact, children who attend day-care centers are actually smarter; a comprehensive study shows that they score higher on measures of cognitive development and academic achievement than children exclusively in their mother's care. This study was conducted by a government agency (the National Institute of Child Health and Human Development, part of the National Institutes of Health) and involved more than 1,000 children at ten locations around the country who were followed since 1991. The results are particularly strong for children who went to day care between the ages of 2 and 5, but even children who went to day care when they were younger than 2 showed a trend toward improved intellectual development. The results were the strongest for kids whose mothers had less education, but the trend toward day care's improving cognitive development remained even when mothers' education was controlled. None of the results showed lowered cognitive development from day care.

But you would never know this from watching the news; this study was not covered in any major media outlet that I could find. Instead, newspapers and television endlessly cover all of the bad stuff that can happen when mommies work. At the same time, standards for mothering have reached unrealistic heights. The popularity of attachment parenting—cosleeping, baby wearing, and breast-feeding for at least a year—comes, ironically, at a time when more and more women are working and thus less able to do these things. In *Perfect Madness*, Judith Warner criticizes the American standard of übermothering in which women's lives are completely consumed by their children's activities, leaving no time for anything else. Perhaps, she muses, this is what happens when women quit corporate jobs to stay home—they become just as competitive at home as they were in the boardroom. Douglas and Michaels label this new standard of intensive mothering "the New Momism." "It is no longer okay," they point out, "to let (or make) your kids walk to school, tell them to stop bugging you and go outside and play, or God forbid, serve them something like Tang . . . for breakfast."

It's enough to make one long for the days of yesteryear, when the goal of most mothers was to get the kids out of their hair so they could go play cards and gossip with their friends. Although these women were unquestionably good mothers as a group, that generation did not adhere to the belief that kids should be monitored—and preferably taught something—every minute, as society now believes. Several studies have found that despite more mothers being in the workforce, mothers in 2011 actually spent more time one-on-one with their kids than mothers did in 1965 and 1975, and they spent twice as much time teaching and playing with them. Given modern work schedules, this seems like an impossible time equation until you realize the differences in standards for motherhood between the two eras. Favorite phrase of Cold War–era mothers: "They're around here somewhere." These days, mothers are supposed to know exactly where their kids are every second—and be a teacher, a doctor, a chauffeur, and a developmental psychologist. Mothers are expected to be interacting with their kids every minute that the kids aren't watching Baby Einstein tapes.

If you have enough money and enough fame, all of this is easy, and the societal message is that it should be easy for you too. As Douglas and Michaels hilariously document in their chapter "Attack of the Celebrity Moms," women's magazines now devote endless pages to profiling the mothering of the rich and famous. We learn that Kirstie Alley pays for all of her houses with cash; that celebrity moms all say that having a baby is much more important than being famous; and that it's hard to be a working mother even when you have two nannies and a housekeeper (boo-hoo). The website theglow.com, which premiered in 2011, features profiles of rich and famous moms who do everything "effortlessly" amid their "enviable décor." One *People* magazine cover story titled "The Sexy New Moms" stated, "Postpartum depression isn't an option for such celebrity moms as Whitney Houston, Madonna, and supermodel Niki Taylor." Douglas and Michaels wryly comment, "Unlike you, being subjected to sleep deprivation and raging hormones was a choice for these women, and they just said no."

Even if we realize the ludicrous nature of these media portrayals, we are still left with a world in which women prepare for careers but find little support once they have children. Peggy Orenstein describes the modern world as "half-changed," where "old patterns and expectations have broken down, but new ideas seem fragmentary, unrealistic, and often contradictory." In *Midlife Crisis at 30*, Lia Macko and Kerry Rubin express "the echoing, pervasive anxiety" of young women living with "the persistent gap between What Has Changed in terms of women's progress and What Has Stayed the Same in terms of old-school corporate structures and rigid social conventions." GenMe mothers, many of whom work outside the home, can lay out every one of these contradictions. Men and women are equal; no, wait, kids are your responsibility as the woman. You need two incomes to survive; no, wait, learn to live on one income. You should retain the status and satisfaction of working; no, wait, it's more important to stay home. There's a reason I discussed many of these problems in the chapter on depression and anxiety. As Douglas and Michaels put it, "Both working mothers and stay-at-home mothers get to be failures."

Even if the work-versus-stay-home decision is crystal clear to you, the realities of both situations aren't always manageable. You might always have wanted to stay home, but then find that you can't make ends meet if you're not a two-income family. Even if finances aren't an issue, you might find yourself unprepared for life cooped up with young children every day (and let's face it—who is really prepared for that?). If you're fine with going back to work, you might find it difficult to construct a manageable work schedule, and even harder to find good child care (and perhaps impossible to find good child care that's affordable). As Orenstein puts it, young women have "a sneaking suspicion that the rhetoric of 'choices' is in part a con job, disguising impossible dilemmas as matters of personal preference."

Almost everyone I know has a difficult time with these issues. Amy, 32, is a high-ranking corporate executive. After her son was born, she asked her boss if she could take a few more months of unpaid leave after her twelve-week maternity leave was up, and if she could work part-time after she returned to work. Her boss said no on both counts; Amy would have to come back to work, and full-time. Amy decided to resign; for one thing, the day care near her office only takes children older than a year (which is surprisingly common). Fortunately, Amy is a valued employee, so her boss called back the next day and offered her six more weeks of unpaid maternity leave and a three-day-a-week schedule, but only until the end of the summer. Also fortunately, Amy's mother, a teacher, can watch the baby during that time. After that, Amy will have to find other child-care arrangements and go back to working the twelve-hour days that are standard in her profession. She has no idea what she will do. And this is someone with two advantages most people don't have—a high-ranking job and child care provided by a relative. Yet it's still a mess.

In *Perfect Madness*, Warner documents the new "problem that has no name": young families struggling to pay the mortgage and take care of their kids in a country with little support for parents. Warner was living in France when her children were born, a place featuring the mandatory paid maternity leave and low-cost preschools common in Europe (yes, Virginia, there are places where these things exist). French culture also saw nothing wrong in leaving kids with babysitters every once in a while so the adults could enjoy a night out. Warner was shocked to return to the United States, where so many parents felt cast adrift and worn down by doing everything themselves. It is no coincidence that Warner subtitled her book *Motherhood in the Age of Anxiety*. The contradictions and lack of good choices for women with children lie at the center of her attack. When you've always been taught that you have choices and then something goes wrong, she writes, "you tend . . . to assume you made the wrong choices—not to see that the 'choices' given you were wrong in the first place."

Warner argues that many of these problems can be traced to individualism and inertia: young women's belief that we should handle everything on our own, and our cynicism that trying to change government policies would just be "knocking their heads against the wall." These are, of course, two central aspects of the GenMe personality. Their inherent self-focus and lack of confidence in political action lead them to assume that no alternatives exist to either (a) staying home and giving up income and a career, or (b) working and scrambling to find and pay for expensive day care. Young authors Macko and Rubin found the same thing: "Our peers were all wrestling with the same issues, yet responding to them by turning their anxiety inward and focusing on their own lives instead of seeing the bigger picture—let alone lobbying for universal changes." Douglas and Michaels sum up the "prevailing common sense" of the last two decades as "only you, the individual mother, are responsible for your child's welfare: The buck stops with you, period, and you'd better be a superstar." So we're supposed to raise our kids without help from anyone, an unrealistic expectation in the best of times. But it's what we believe, so we soldier on. This is one of the more solvable problems faced by GenMe; more about that in the next chapter. Sometime in the next decade, the system will begin to break down: either more and more women will forgo having children, or government policies will change. Before that happens, there will be more and more tired, frustrated, and angry parents—particularly moms, but a growing number of dads too (because if mama ain't happy, nobody's happy).

But would we go back? Hell no. "I think women having more opportunities than previous generations is a good thing—a very good thing. I cannot think of a single reason why it could be bad," says Natalie, 21. Certainly, some GenMe women might desire to return to a simpler time when families could get by on one income and staying at home with one's child was the only accepted course. But more would rather not. GenMe women cannot begin to imagine what it was like to be told that only some professions were open to them. They cannot imagine making an absolute choice between having children and continuing to pursue a career. And they cannot imagine being told girls can't do something.

ATTITUDES TOWARD GAYS AND LESBIANS

On *Glee*, Burt Hummel is a guy's guy. He runs a car-repair shop in Ohio, and his idea of fashion is a flannel shirt. One day, his 16-year-old son, Kurt, has some news for him. "I don't want to lie anymore. I'm gay," he says. "I know," Burt says. "I've known since you were three. All you wanted for your birthday was a pair of sensible heels. If that's who you are, there's nothing I can do about it. And I love you just as much, okay?" Burt is clearly not a gay rights advocate ("I sat through that whole [movie] *Brokeback Mountain*. From what I gather, something went down in the tent"). But he loves his son, and if he's gay, so be it.

Describing the revolution in equality would not be complete without mentioning the enormous change in attitudes toward gays and lesbians. American society has, without question, grown more accepting of homosexuality recently, and nowhere is that more evident than among young people. When I requested stories on my website about "being open to differences among other people," everyone who responded wrote about tolerance for gays and lesbians. In less than two decades, those supporting gay and lesbian rights have become the majority: 50% of Americans supported same-sex marriage in 2013, up from 27% in 1996. This is clearly a generational sea change: In 2013, two-thirds (66%) of those born after 1981 supported same-sex marriage, compared to 35% of those born before 1945. As the Pew Center puts it, "Much of the shift in support of same-sex marriage is attributable to the arrival of a large cohort of young adults . . . who are far more open to gay rights than previous generations." The law followed public opinion when same-sex marriages were recognized at the federal level in 2013. This is what I predicted in the 2006 first edition of *Generation Me*, though I would not have guessed gay marriage would become legal just seven years later.

It's not just political attitudes, or attitudes about same-sex marriage, that have shifted. Americans are now much more likely to say they like gay and lesbian people—only 38% of Americans in the Pew survey viewed gays and lesbians favorably in 2003, which rose to 57% in 2013. Fewer believe that homosexuality is wrong—in the Gallup poll, 55% saw gay and lesbian relations as "morally wrong" in 2002, which declined to 38% in 2013. This shift in attitudes might be due to more gays and lesbians coming out. In 1985, only 24% of Americans said that a friend, relative, or coworker had personally told them they were gay or lesbian. By 2013, that number had more than tripled, to 75%. These are enormous cultural shifts.

Abby, 18, wrote, "I remember my mom telling me and my siblings that if we were gay she would disown us. My sister and I found this extremely funny. Even though we weren't gay we are all extremely accepting of gays. We love them." Elizabeth, 27, went to a conservative Catholic school growing up, but often babysat a lesbian couple's son. "I always thought this was so cool," she says. "I thought, 'Wow, I don't care if they are lesbians or not.'" When Megan, 15, was in middle school, her gay teacher brought his partner along on a school trip to Washington, DC. Her schoolmates' parents thought this was inappropriate and called the school. "But my friends and I never really understood what the problem was. I really don't see how bringing his partner along was any different than if he had brought his wife—which our parents would have had no trouble with, of course," Megan says. "People make homosexuality into such a big deal, but I just don't understand why anyone would care if two people want to be together. It's like race or gender—you can't control it, so why would anyone try to force someone to change?"

Despite the parents' protests, Megan's story illustrates change because she can tell it. Apparently, everyone knew the teacher was gay; it was just his partner's coming on the trip that they didn't like. Not that long ago, a gay teacher who was out of the closet would have been fired outright—no trip to Washington, DC, and no job at all. This happened to my favorite high school English teacher in 1989 in suburban Dallas. Despite being one of the best teachers in the school, the rumors caught up with him after two years and that was it; the school used some flimsy excuse not to renew his contract. They were in sync with the times: in a 1988 Gallup poll, 57% of Americans believed that "homosexual relations between consenting adults" shouldn't even be legal.

Don't forget—until 1989 there had never been a major TV character who was gay. Ellen didn't come out of the closet until 1997, and even then several major advertisers yanked their support after the episode aired and Ellen appeared on the cover of *Time* under the headline "Yep, I'm Gay." (As if people hadn't figured this out yet about a woman who regularly did her stand-up routine wearing men's shirts, suspenders, and tennis shoes.)

It's pretty amazing to realize that a gay television character was controversial as recently as 1997; when I went to look up this date, I was sure it was 1992 or 1993 instead. (Although the *Seinfeld* line "Not that there's anything wrong with that" beat the curve, premiering in 1993.) After that, things changed remarkably quickly. *Will & Grace* was an instant hit after its premiere in 1998, and a year later the teen show *Dawson's Creek* had a 16-year-old gay character. In 2000, *All My Children* introduced the first lesbian teen on daytime television, especially interesting since daytime TV skews toward an older demographic. Several young people in my online survey noted that the first time they thought about homosexuality was when they watched *Glee*. In 2012, the sitcom *The New Normal* featured a gay couple who became fathers when a surrogate carried their baby. And since 2003, Ellen DeGeneres has hosted a successful daytime talk show, where her sexual orientation is accepted but rarely acknowledged. It just is.

And we can't ever forget the stunning though now faded glory of *Queer Eye for the Straight Guy*, which premiered in 2003. An entire generation of kids grew up seeing straight men freely hug gay men, and gay men having all of the answers while the poor, slobby straight dude shaves wrong, wears hockey jerseys on dates, and breaks things in the kitchen. And let's not even talk about moisturizer. Main point: gay people are not only queer, and here, but they are very, very cool.

The General Social Survey, conducted since 1972, illustrates this enormous change. It asks if "a man who admits that he is homosexual" should "be allowed to teach in a college or university, or not?" In the 1970s, 64% of Americans born before 1930 said no, he should not be allowed to teach. Among those born in the 1940s—mostly Boomers—only 31% said no in the 1970s and 1980s. By the 2010s, only 13% of Americans born since 1980 said no. So over 50 birth years, firing a professor for being gay went from the opinion of a solid majority—2 out of 3—to a fringe minority of 1 out of 8. Now *that* is a generational difference.

Acceptance of gay and lesbian families has also risen. In just the three years between 2009 and 2012, support for gays and lesbians adopting children jumped from 54% to 61%. This may have occurred because solid social science research consistently finds that children raised by gay and lesbian parents do not differ in psychological adjustment or outcomes compared to the children of heterosexual parents.

Young people often comment to me that they have a casual attitude about homosexuality that their parents don't understand at all. Lauren, a 21-year-old from North Carolina, was describing to her parents how a male friend of hers liked interior decorating, but, she added, "He's not gay—he has a girlfriend." Her father was shocked that Lauren was so nonchalant about sexual orientation. Jake, 28, has a gay uncle, but Jake's father and his family refused to acknowledge his homosexuality. When Jake and his fiancée invited Jake's uncle and his partner to their wedding, his parents were angry. "I quickly seized the opportunity to finally address the issue," said Jake. "I explained to them that I have no problem with whatever sexuality a person chooses. I also told them it made me feel good that my 48-year-old uncle would take his first step toward coming out to the family at my wedding."

Some teens find their experiences at odds with their religious upbringing. For many, this means that they see gays as sinners and/or believe that gays can change to be straight. Others are shaped by the culture's tolerance very early on. Madison, 15, wrote, "I wasn't taught about homosexuality when I was younger, so when I was in the sixth grade I just assumed it was okay. People are people and our differences make the world an interesting place. Then I found out my parents were totally against it, but it was too late. I already thought it was all right. I still haven't told them what I believe, though."

GenMe also confronts these issues at much younger ages than previous generations did. "Kids are coming out a lot earlier than they would have ten or twenty years ago," says Virginia Merritt, a psychiatrist who works with gay teenagers. Nathan, 23, grew up in a small town in the Midwest. "Growing up, I always thought homosexuality was a bad thing. My parents would often use the phrase 'that's gay' to refer to something stupid that they didn't like." After learning more about homosexuality in college, he finally had the courage to come out to his family and friends.

Unfortunately, hate is not long past. In 2002, my University of Michigan graduate school friend Carla Grayson and her partner, Adrianne Neff, petitioned the University of Montana, where Carla was an assistant professor, to provide health-care benefits for Adrianne, who was staying home to care for the couple's 22-month-old son. Four days after a newspaper story reported on the lawsuit, Carla and Adrianne awoke in the early morning to the sound of the smoke detector going off. They ran to the front door to escape but were met by a wall of fire. Carla climbed out the window and Adrianne handed her the baby, finally escaping herself. The fire was ruled an arson, and police investigated it as a hate crime.

Although what happened next in no way made up for the crime, it was still notable. More than 700 townspeople turned out for a rally in support of the couple. A sign on the door of the

Missoula First United Methodist Church read OPEN HEARTS. OPEN MINDS. OPEN DOORS. But not surprisingly, Carla and Adrianne soon moved back to Michigan.

This story also illustrates how the change for gays has been slow in coming, and that although most straight people's attitudes are now much more tolerant, it's still difficult to be gay or lesbian in the United States. Coming out of the closet to parents is terrifying; though certainly many parents are more tolerant now, few other bits of news carry such a high risk of your parents never speaking to you again. But even in the decade since the first edition of *Generation Me* was published, change has come. No matter what your opinion on these issues, it's hard to deny that the tide of history flows toward equality.

8

Generation Me at Work

The young applicant seemed so promising on paper. When she arrived for the interview, however, she was holding a cat carrier—with the cat in it. She set the carrier on the interviewer's desk and periodically played with it during the interview.

She did not get the job.

Another job applicant took a call on his cell phone 15 minutes into the interview. A third brought his father with him. These are, apparently, not isolated examples. A 2013 *USA Today* story notes that such behavior is gaining notice across the country: "Human resource professionals say they've seen recent college grads text or take calls in interviews, dress inappropriately, use slang or overly casual language and exhibit other oddball behavior."

Some blame new technology for this apparent lack of social skills, but it goes deeper than that. Raised on "just be yourself," GenMe doesn't always process the need to change behavior depending on the situation. If it's good for them, they assume it's good for everyone else—even in an interview. Jonathan Singel, director of talent acquisition for Avery Dennison, favors this explanation. GenMe's parents, he observes, said, "You're perfect just the way you are" and "Do whatever you're comfortable doing." As you know from the previous chapters, his observation is consistent with the numerous studies showing GenMe's lower need for social approval and higher individualism.

That's not all bad. We have GenMe—and the individualism that gives them their name—to thank for casual Fridays (or casual every-days). Hierarchies are flatter, with bosses more likely to treat employees with respect and explain why they're doing what they're doing. Companies realize that time off and work-life balance make for more productive employees. The key is for all of the generations to find the strategies that accommodate GenMe's preferences—but that also preserve the bottom line. With Boomers rapidly retiring and GenMe set to be 40% of the workforce by 2020, the time to do this is now.

The first step is to get the right information on how the generations differ. You've already learned about the generational differences in personality and behavior, and some of those translate directly into the workplace. But what about attitudes toward work? What does GenMe want out of a job that's different from what Boomers or GenX'ers wanted when they were young?

Many popular press articles, consultants, and books on generations at work have tried to answer these questions. However, few are based on data comparing the generations—unfortunate given the emphasis on evidence-based management. Some describe the events each generation experienced and then guess how that will affect their attitudes toward work, rather than actually measuring attitudes. Other books interview managers who reflect on the changes they have witnessed in the workplace. That's problematic, too, as perceptions are easily warped by fading memory, aging, and flawed recall. Most people have an overly rosy memory of what they were like when they were young employees—I was *never* late! I *always* did exactly what my boss said! Other authors who interview young employees can tell managers what young employees want, but that tells us little about generational differences. Perhaps this is what young employees have always wanted, so recruiting and retaining strategies can stay just the same. Interviews are also notoriously subjective—how does the author decide which parts of the interview to highlight? Often that depends on what point the author is trying to make, which introduces bias right off the bat.

A more objective approach is to use standard questionnaires that measure work attitudes, which ask people to respond to standard questions and result in a numerical score. Researchers often use such questionnaires to survey a large group of workers at one time. This has the advantage of more objective measurement, but any one-time survey has a big downside: it's impossible to tell whether any differences are caused by age or by generation. For example, if more GenMe'ers than Boomers say they want a lot of time off, that could be because young people have always wanted time off, or because GenMe'ers like time off more than Boomers did when they were young. If it's just being young, GenMe will grow out of it just as every generation before them has grown out of some notions of its youth. If GenMe'ers preferences are due to their age and not to their generation, the same recruiting programs that worked for young employees 15 or 30 years ago will work now.

Given these issues with one-time studies, it's clearly best to study generational differences in work attitudes with an over-time study—one that has sampled people of the same age at different points in time. Until recently, only one or two studies had used data like this, and none with a large or nationally representative sample. Fortunately, the nationally representative Monitoring the Future Survey of high school students has measured work attitudes and desired job characteristics every year since 1976. That made it possible to trace work attitudes from Boomers to GenX'ers to GenMe'ers among those getting ready to enter the workforce. Because everyone was the same age, this dataset clearly shows the generational shifts in attitudes toward work without any concern that differences could be due to age. Along with my coauthors Stacy Campbell, Brian Hoffman, and

Chuck Lance, we published the results of this analysis in the *Journal of Management*.

The results of the study fall into four primary categories: leisure and work-life balance; helping and finding meaning; money and status; and high expectations and impatience. In some cases, the data confirm the perceptions of managers and journalists about what GenMe (also called Millennials) values at work. In other cases, the data suggest that common perceptions of GenMe are wrong. I also feature data from one-time studies when their results concur with the over-time data. However, always keep in mind that any differences in a one-time study could be due to age and experience instead. Each section includes concrete suggestions for managing this generation—or, if you're GenMe yourself, for finding a match between your expectations and the reality of the workplace.

LEISURE AND WORK-LIFE BALANCE

New York investment banks such as Goldman Sachs were known for working young employees hard. Analysts were hired straight out of college on two-year contracts, paid around $100,000 a year, and expected to work 100 hours a week.

Until now. In October 2013, Goldman Sachs began discouraging young analysts from working weekends. Instead of two-year contracts, they are permanent employees from the start. Why the change? Many young employees were leaving for private equity funds and start-ups, so the company's "junior banker task force" suggested ways to keep young employees from quitting.

Chegg, Inc., an online textbook-rental company, had a similar experience—many of its young employees left the company after a year or less. In their exit interviews, GenMe workers said they wanted to be more involved in projects, wanted more time off, and wanted to be able to work wherever they wanted.

The company moved quickly to change things, giving younger

workers more important roles in projects and instituting unlimited paid vacation. It worked: Turnover among GenMe employees fell by 50% a year for two years.

In our over-time analysis, the largest generational difference appeared in the importance of work and views of work-life balance. More in GenMe said they "worked to live," unlike the Boomers, who "lived to work." In 1976, 3 out of 4 (74%) high school senior Boomers said they expected work to be "a central part" of their lives, but by 2012 only 2 out of 3 (66%) felt that way. Under 1 in 4 (23%) Boomers agreed that "work is just making a living," but 1 out of 3 (32%) GenMe'ers thought so in 2012. GenMe is also more likely to say they wouldn't work if they had enough money (28% vs. 23% in 1976). In a small over-time study of adult workers, those in the 2000s (versus the 1970s) were significantly less likely to agree that "rich people should feel an obligation to work even if they do not need to" and "work should be one of the most important parts of a person's life." Catalina, 20, reflects, "My generation views work as if it does not matter. It is not taken as seriously as it should be."

More in GenMe said it was important to have a job with a lot of vacation time, that allowed them to work at an easy pace, and that left a lot of time for other things in their lives. Fifty-three percent of GenMe in 2012 agreed they were "willing to work overtime to do a good job," down from 60% in earlier years. In one study, college career counselors named "flexible schedules" and "want balance of life and work" among the top three characteristics GenMe wants out of a job. Bill George, a professor at Harvard Business School, says that his students "want an integrated life" and "are committed to having life the way they want it."

How you interpret this trend is a matter of perspective. Americans take much less vacation than most Europeans, who place more value on enjoying life. Perhaps GenMe is taking a page out of that book, wanting to focus on things other than work. Balanced workers may also be better workers. On the other hand, people have to earn a living—and recall that 82% of GenMe thinks it's important to "be very well-off financially." So how is GenMe going to achieve these riches while working fewer hours? That's unclear.

A study of Canadian young people by Harvey Krahn and Nancy Galambos suggests that this attitude may stem at least in part from increased entitlement. At age 25, 1996 high school graduates (compared to 1985 graduates) were more likely to agree with statements such as "if someone has worked hard in school, they are entitled to a good job" and "everyone has the right to the kind of job their education and training has prepared them for." This suggests that the generational differences in work attitudes persist into GenMe's mid-20s, the years when young adults settle into the workforce.

In my GenMe online survey, lack of work ethic was a nearly universal theme. "I think my generation is mainly focused on a job that is easy to do but pays very well," observes Ethan, 19. "More people want a job that gives them the most benefits with the least amount of work and responsibility necessary," says Ashley, 29. I'd seen this belief in my undergraduate classes for several years. When I asked the students to name five qualities of their generation, "lazy" almost always made the top five. This surprised me at first, as more in their generation go to college, which seems more ambitious than lazy. Yet several studies suggest that college students now study for fewer hours than students in previous eras, so perhaps it's not surprising that students recognize this deficit.

In addition, a decline in the work ethic appears in several over-time studies. In the over-time survey of high school seniors, 40% of 2012 GenMe students admitted that "not wanting to work hard" might prevent them from getting the job they want, compared to only 24% of Boomers in 1976. A study of adults in the General Social Survey found a decline in the number who would continue working after a financial windfall, from 77% in

1980 to 68% in 2006. "I think everybody in my generation wants important high-end jobs but are really lazy and would rather not put in the work to get there," says Kayla, 18. In a 2012 survey of 19-to-28-year-olds conducted by MTV, half of GenMe'ers said they would rather have no job than a job they hate.

Adult workers in the 2000s were less likely than those in the 1970s to agree that "a worker should do a decent job whether or not his supervisor is around." They were also less likely to agree that "a worker should feel a sense of pride in his work" or that working hard made them "feel more worthwhile and [like] a better person." Another study found that manual workers in 2006 were willing to lift or carry only 70% as much as workers tested prior to 1991. This is the logical outcome of our modern cultural system that emphasizes self over duty. In past eras, working hard at a job was (at least for men) the only way to be a respected member of society. Now it is often seen as boring and restrictive.

However, working yourself to death is no way to live, and no way to have a family. The idea of work-life balance began when fathers and mothers of young children wanted to work fewer hours. It's now reached down to young single people, who want to enjoy life in other ways. With US workers getting an average of only eight vacation days after a year on the job, they have a point. The United States is the only developed nation that doesn't mandate paid time off. Architect Ari Meisel, 30, uses a simple question to set his priorities: "Every decision I make, I calculate, how much time will it take away from time with my kids?"

In many cases, the key is flexibility, not necessarily fewer hours. GenMe'ers want to be able to work from home, at a coffee shop, and when they want. Some companies are beginning to realize this might not be a bad thing. Electronics retailer Best Buy instituted their "Result-Only Work Environment" program, recognizing that getting the work done is more important than putting in face time at the office. Tyler Shaw, one of the proponents of the plan, likes that his time is no longer wasted in so many meetings. "I do my best work when I am rested, when I eat breakfast and lunch, work out regularly, spend time with my family, and play video games occasionally to recharge," he says. "I just see so many people running ragged; they work hard, but too much and not at one hundred percent." In other words, the company gets Tyler's best work when he can balance it with the rest of his life.

Flexible hours are quickly becoming expected. In a recent PricewaterhouseCoopers survey, only 29% of GenMe said they expected to work regular office hours. The MTV survey found that 81% of GenMe thinks they should be allowed to make their own hours at work. The key to making flexibility effective is clear expectations and deadlines, especially at first. Some in GenMe may dream of getting paid to "do nothing" (as the cult movie *Office Space* promotes), but most want to work smarter, not harder—and might reward the company with better performance.

If you're GenMe yourself, how can you get the flexible work schedule you desire? First, don't expect it to happen right away. Most managers want to see you for at least a few months to make sure you're capable of working independently. If you're lucky enough to get a flexible schedule, put in your best work if you want to keep it. "Working at home" does not equal "answering a few e-mails between bouts of video games." A flexible schedule often means you're not wasting as much time in traffic or in meetings, but you have to be focused enough not to waste time on other temptations. Working at home can also be lonely—those water-cooler conversations may sometimes seem like a waste of time, but they can generate good ideas and often build trust among coworkers. Many employees find that coming into the office a few days a week while spending the rest at home (or at the coffee shop) is a good compromise.

WHY AM I HERE? HELPING OTHERS, FINDING MEANING, AND SEEKING PRAISE

The accounting firm Ernst & Young offers employees the opportunity to volunteer—on company time. One young employee spent three months volunteering in Buenos Aires, with the company paying for her travel expenses *and* her salary. "First-rate corporate volunteer programs help attract and retain . . . workers born after 1980," explained the *Wall Street Journal* article that documented the trend. "Millennials are saying, 'I don't want to park my values at the door,'" says Carol Cone, head of a Boston consulting firm. The book *The M-Factor* advises, "When recruiting Millennials, make sure your websites, print materials, and even the recruiters themselves emphasize your contributions to society."

The view that Millennials/GenMe'ers are uniquely interested in helping others, especially at work, is widespread. Books and articles describe them as "a generous generation" and an "empathic generation." Many point to the large number of young people involved in Teach For America, AmeriCorps, and organizations aiming to help the environment. One recent survey found that 79% of 13-to-25-year-olds say they want to work for a company that cares about how it affects or contributes to society.

However, that might also have been true of Boomers and GenX'ers when they were young. But this survey—and most others presented as proof that Millennials are altruistic meaning-seekers—don't have data from other generations. It is impossible to make a generational comparison with data from only one generation. Perhaps young workers in previous decades also sought meaning and wanted to help others.

That's exactly what the over-time data show. Boomers, GenX'ers, and GenMe'ers placed about the same importance on a job "directly helpful to others" (50% said that was "very important" in 1976, 48% in 1994, and 48% in 2012) or "worthwhile to society" (44% in 1976, 45% in 1994, and 47% in 2012).

A one-time study of US workers in 2010 came to a similar conclusion: when deciding which company to work for, GenMe did not value corporate social responsibility and business ethics any more than GenX and valued them a little less than Boomers. So these altruistic and "social cause" work values are generational universals, not differences. Thus, recruiting programs emphasizing paid volunteering or helping others may be attractive for today's young workers, but on average no more than they were (or are) for GenX'ers or Boomers.

Another common theory is that GenMe'ers/Millennials want jobs that are highly meaningful—jobs they are passionate about. That would certainly fit with GenMe's high expectations and individualistic focus. However, the over-time survey showed that GenMe is actually *less* likely to favor these intrinsic work values. An overwhelming 88% of Boomers in 1976 wanted an interesting job, but that sank to 79% of GenMe'ers in 2012. More than half (54%) of Boomers wanted a job where they could make friends, compared to only 39% of GenMe'ers in 2012. Perhaps because they see work as less central to their lives overall, fewer in GenMe see meaning at work as important.

Does that mean companies should not emphasize meaning and helping others? Of course not. Just don't expect it to work uniquely well for young employees. While GenMe'ers are significantly more attracted to work-life balance than young workers were in the past, they are not any more attracted to helping or meaning. Organizations will reach the widest segment of GenMe if paid volunteering is presented as a way to regain work-life balance, see the world, or "find yourself." These themes are closer to GenMe's unique outlook.

Emphasizing meaning should also be approached differently. As young workers, many Boomers were on a quest for meaning and purpose. GenMe sees things a little differently: work is meaningful if *they* feel meaningful. They don't want to see themselves as cogs in the wheel and don't want to do only what they've been told to do. They want to matter, to feel important, and to believe that they are having a personal impact. When they talk about wanting to help others, it's often put in individualistic terms: "*I* want to make a difference."

Drew Lichtenberger, a young manager at Northwestern Mutual, made some changes to their college student internship program a few years ago. Many interns found it difficult to see themselves as financial services providers—it didn't fit their identities. They were having a hard time transitioning from being college students to professionals. He helped them see that they could bring their individual identity and goals to the job. Lichtenberger asked interns, "What's your worth? What are your gifts? What do you want to do? You need to be finding that. You need to do that for yourself." Lichtenberger suggests having more personal conversations with employees. "Get him out of the office, sit down, have coffee with him, and just say, 'Tell me, how did you decide to become an attorney? How did you make that decision? Tell me about your mom. Tell me about your dad.' You just get to know them." When managers protest that this type of conversation isn't billable, or that they don't have time for it, Lichtenberger has a simple answer: "The companies that will be more successful are the ones that would do that."

The online shoe retailer Zappos has found a unique solution to helping their employees find personal meaning. Every year, they publish a book with their employees' thoughts about the company. Their office space also follows a GenMe principle: everyone's is the same, with no enclosed offices even for the senior executives. It's the idea that "everyone is special, so no one is special," that equality extends beyond race and gender to employee status as well.

GenMe grew up in an era of praise and grade inflation, which resulted in their highly positive self-views. They expect that praise to continue after they enter the workforce. In the 2012 MTV poll, 80% of GenMe'ers said they thought they deserved to be recognized more for their work, and 92% said their company was lucky to have them as an employee. And 76% of GenMe said they thought their boss could learn a lot from them, compared to only 50% of Boomers—despite Boomers' 30 additional years of work experience. Drawing from a one-time study of Canadian workers, Sean Lyons and his colleagues concluded, "Millennials appear to be seeking recognition, status, and autonomy in their work, and are less satisfied than other generations with their progress in meeting these goals thus far in their careers."

Helping GenMe workers feel valued is a three-step process. First, tell them why what they are doing is important. A common label for this group is Generation Y, but some say it should instead be spelled Generation Why? This generation wants to know the meaning behind what they are doing—not the philosophical, abstract meaning important to the Boomers, but what it means overall. If the task is important, then they will feel important doing it. For GenMe, there is no better motivator. If possible, tie the job or skill to their eventual career goals. If you can tell them how what they are doing will help them succeed in the future, they will listen.

I once presented my GenMe research to a group of officers in the US Coast Guard. After the talk, one young officer stood up and said, "I want the senior officers to hear the part about explaining why. I really want to know why I'm doing something. It's not because I'm whining—it's because it really motivates me." One of the senior officers commented, "Well, you know, this *is* the military. Sometimes we're going to say we need boats in the water, and we won't be able to tell you why." "I know," said the junior officer. "But most of the time, you can." And that's the good news: in most businesses, you do have at least a little time to let employees know why what they are doing is important—or at least its larger goal.

One way to meet this goal is to put GenMe's skills to good use.

GenMe does not remember a time when computers did not exist. They are digital natives—the rest of us just immigrated to this interconnected world. It makes sense to use their technological skills as much as possible. Their impatience might just help them find a faster way to do something.

Second, give praise when it's earned. Many Boomers say that when they were young workers, not getting yelled at was the only praise they received. If they weren't criticized, they knew they were doing a good job. Now young workers want feedback (including praise) for everything—and they want it now. This may sound like entitlement, but it can actually be a good thing for everyone. Why wait to tell Jared he did a good job on his presentation? And why wait to tell him how he can improve it?

In a video parodying generational workplace training seminars, a dim-witted GenMe employee admits he searched Google instead of relying on the company's specially commissioned market research. When his manager criticizes him, he says, "I quit. This job isn't what I thought it would be." Tongue in cheek, the narrator suggests instead that the manager should offer "overflowing amounts of praise," then shows her saying, "You're so smart," as she pats him on the head like a dog. Satire, yes, but in 2007 the *Wall Street Journal* noted that many companies were hiring "celebrations assistants" and "praise consultants" to hand out certificates and even throw confetti.

That's probably going too far. But the idea that no feedback is praise is also not a great system. The best place is somewhere in the middle: praise for work well done, as soon as possible, but with the same principle for criticism. One idea is the "praise sandwich," beginning with praise, mentioning places for improvement, and ending with praise. That works as long as the criticism is actually getting through. If not, no more sandwich, just meat. Another tip is to use *and* instead of *but*. Don't say, "You worked hard on this, *but* . . . ," as that cancels out the praise in the first part of the sentence. Instead, say, "You worked hard on this, *and* it would be even better if next time . . ."

Third and last, give feedback more frequently than the classic model of an annual review. To GenMe'ers, a year might as well be a century. If they don't like the job, they will have left before then. As formal reviews take up a lot of managers' time, the solution is probably not more frequent formal reviews. But informal feedback frequently is both expected and appreciated by GenMe. In universities, this has taken the form of four or more tests a semester rather than the traditional midterm and final. It means more grading, but students do better because they realize more quickly what they know and don't know—also a useful correction to their overconfidence.

If you're GenMe yourself, you might wonder how to get your boss or coworkers to give you more frequent feedback or explain more about what you're doing. The key is how you frame it. Tell them you want to know the why or want faster feedback because it will help you do a better job. Don't sound as if you're just fishing for praise or whining about "why, why, why" you have to do something. Let people know it will increase your motivation and drive, and they'll be more likely to provide the feedback you crave.

MONEY AND STATUS

"Millennials: All We Want for Christmas Is . . . Cash," read the FOX Business headline, reporting on a 2013 poll finding that 94% of 13-to-30-year-olds wanted cash instead of gifts. Further down the page was a link to another story: "Matt Damon's Miami Estate Is Just as Luxurious as You'd Expect." GenMe lives between a rock and a hard place: still searching for well-paying jobs in the wake of the recession, but with TV and websites portraying extreme wealth glittering just out of reach.

In the over-time survey, 58% of high school seniors in 2012 said it was "very important" to have a job where they could "earn a good deal of money," up from 47% in 1976. And recall that the importance of "being very well-off financially" reached an all-time high among college students in 2013, at 82%. In the study of Canadian 25-year-olds, the 1996 high school graduates were more likely than the 1985 graduates to value jobs that paid well and had a good chance for promotion. As you saw in chapter 4, some of this is practical: with high housing prices and staggering college debt, GenMe needs more just to stay afloat. Yet the wording of these questions—"a good deal of money," "very well-off"—also suggests a yearning for the trappings of wealth.

Given that fewer in GenMe say they are willing to work hard, these longings for higher earnings may also be overconfident. In one study, Tim Kasser and I found that the gap between materialism and work ethic grew larger as the generations transitioned to GenMe. More in GenMe (versus Boomers) were interested in owning expensive material goods such as a vacation home and a new car every two to three years, but fewer said they were willing to work hard. "Our generation wants the job that will make us the most money where we will have to do the least amount of work and have the most time off," explains Chris, 18. Such jobs are exceedingly rare. Most people who earn high salaries put in long hours. Unfortunately, that's not how young people see it, perhaps because they were raised on media portraying overnight success and instant fame.

Some have speculated that GenMe will earn their money by becoming a generation of entrepreneurs. This seems to fit the GenMe personality—do your own thing, be your own boss. Most will not at first realize how much hard work goes into founding a business, but perhaps they will learn along the way. However, it's not clear that GenMe actually is any more interested in entrepreneurship. In the over-time survey of entering college students, 41% said it was important to "become successful in a business of my own" in 2013, compared to 43% of Boomers in the 1960s. It's possible that the 2013 prospective entrepreneurs weren't in college, underestimating the number with this interest, but that's just as likely to have been true in the 1960s as well. Whether GenMe will go on to found more independent businesses than previous generations remains to be seen.

If you're a manager, you know that compensation is always a sensitive issue. You can only do so much to increase your employees' salaries. Just realize that with this generation's penchant for job-hopping, today's competition for talent is fierce. If an employee can get a better-paying job elsewhere, he's probably going to take it. If you can't offer more money, perhaps you can offer more time off or more flexible hours, two benefits important to this generation.

If you're GenMe yourself and want to get paid more, realize two things. First, your manager would rather you not quit—then she has to spend time and money training a new employee. On the other hand, she's not going to respond well to constant requests for raises. If you're considering leaving over pay issues, let her know that and lay out clear evidence of what you do for the company—but you only get once or twice for that gambit. After that, leaving might be the only way to significantly increase your salary. Then consider things other than money: Will this other job be worth making a little more? Research consistently finds that workers who are intrinsically motivated—say, by enjoying their work—are happier than those motivated by outside forces such as compensation.

HIGH EXPECTATIONS AND IMPATIENCE

"Where do you see yourself in five years?" the manager asks the young man interviewing for an entry-level position. "I'd like to be the CEO of the company," he replies. This is an extreme example, of course, but unheard of just a generation ago. A drawing accompanying the MTV survey on GenMe at work shows a "trapdoor" allowing employees to skip four levels while climbing the corporate ladder to CEO. The book *Grindhopping*, written by GenMe'er Laura Vanderkam, is subtitled *Build a Rewarding Career without Paying Your Dues*. Whether such trapdoors and grindhops actually exist for all but a minuscule few is another question.

Many managers find the overconfidence and impatience of GenMe breathtaking. They complain that young workers don't want to pay their dues, have unrealistic expectations for how quickly they will be promoted, and believe they will be the ones to break the curve. In one study, 40% of GenMe'ers believed they should be promoted every two years, no matter what their performance. In a recent survey of 23,000 Canadian university students, 69% expected to be promoted within the first 18 months in their first job. "People tell me I need to be more patient, that I will get rewarded in time," says Larissa Kravanja, a 25-year-old Merrill Lynch employee interviewed in *The Trophy Kids Grow Up*. "But at times, it's hard to be patient for the bigger reinforcement payoffs like bonuses and promotions." In the MTV survey, 75% of GenMe'ers believed they would be promoted faster than others. As you might remember from chapter 3, 68% of GenMe high school students expect to have a professional job by age 30—even though only about 20% actually will.

Overall, GenMe'ers have high expectations around jobs—true to their "never compromise" mind-set, they're looking for the job that has it all: fulfillment, flexibility, high pay, and everything else they want. "A lot of my friends are looking for the 'perfect job' and refuse to settle," says Scott, 29. "I think our generation all expects to be able to work in the corner office straightaway, just because that's what they see their parents doing," observes Emma, 16. In the MTV survey, 90% of GenMe'ers said they felt they deserved their dream job.

This dream job is often high in prestige and power. More than previous generations at the same age, GenMe longs for recognition and authority. In the over-time survey of high school students, 46% of GenMe in 2012 valued a job "that most people look up to and respect," compared to only 34% of 1976 students. Twenty-seven percent of those in 2012 thought it was important to have a job that "has high status and prestige," up from 20% in 1976. In 2007 among entering college students, 42% said it was important to one day have "administrative responsibility for the work of others"—in other words, be the boss—compared to only 26% of Boomers in the 1960s. In a 2012 survey, college career counselors believed that "opportunities for advancement" was second only to "flexible schedules" on GenMe's list of desired job attributes. But maybe not: High school students in 1976 and 2012 rated the importance of a job "with a good chance for advancement and promotion" about the same. Overall, though, the generational shift is toward a desire for more prestige, and more status. "I feel as though I am somebody and I should be able to take a high-end job such as lawyer/judge or even the CEO of a large business," says Kristin, 18.

In an over-time analysis of career preferences by Shawn Bubany and Jo-Ida Hansen, US college students in the 2000s (compared to those in the 1970s) were more attracted to "enterprising" careers—those that involve power and influencing others, such as manager, judge, or school principal. The change was particularly large for college women.

Many companies want to hire ambitious young employees—and they should. But managers also don't want to be stuck with employees who are overconfident and entitled. It's sometimes difficult to distinguish the two, especially in a brief job interview. Management professor Paul Harvey suggests asking job candidates, "Do you feel you are generally superior to your coworkers/classmates, and if so, why?" If the candidate says yes but struggles to explain why—or offers vague reasons—that might indicate entitlement.

In the spoof Millennials training video, a young worker does "what was asked of her—nothing more, nothing less. She expects a raise and a promotion," explains the narrator. The young woman hands her report to the manager and waits. "Thanks . . . ," says the manager, and pauses, remembering her "training." She then finishes, "Thanks, junior executive manager of data consulting!" The young employee smiles excitedly. "Is that better than assistant manager of junior accounts? Thank you! I'm going to go call my parents!"

Silly, yes, but a good idea is embedded here. Instead of having promotions and title changes every three to five years, some companies now add more levels that can be achieved in six months to a year. For a generation raised on "everyone gets a trophy" and instant gratification, more promotions at a faster pace is attractive. If the promotions are given for outstanding performance, not just showing up, having more steps on the ladder has no real downside, so it's a win-win.

Even in a company with faster promotions, however, it's unlikely that the new hire will be CEO in five years—and he or she needs to know that. Sometimes it's helpful for a young employee with a few years of experience to explain the usual career paths to new hires. Aiming high is good, but they also need to know that they will not start at the top.

For GenMe: I am not suggesting you become less ambitious, just more clear-eyed. Keep thinking about how to do things better, and keeping thinking about how you can get ahead. Just don't expect it to happen overnight. Tim Urban, whose piece on "Why Generation Y Yuppies Are Unhappy" went viral online, gives this advice: "Stop thinking you're special. The fact is, right now, you're not special. You're another completely inexperienced young person who doesn't have all that much to offer yet. You can become special by working really hard for a long time." I'd go a little less extreme—you *can* make a contribution in your job right now, and you can keep working toward your goals. But Urban is right that building a career takes time. For all but the lucky few, it does not happen overnight. And that's okay—especially if you like what you do, getting there can be the fun part.

AND THE UNKNOWN: TEAMWORK

When I give talks on generations at work, people often ask me about GenMe'ers attitude toward teamwork: "Aren't they better at working in teams because they did that in school?"

I went looking for data on teamwork—I wanted to know whether this generation truly did more group projects in school, and whether they wanted to work in teams more. I found virtually nothing. One of the few studies that looked at teamwork was a one-time study of adult employees that compared Boomers to those born in the 1970s and early 1980s (GenX and the first wave of GenMe). They found that GenX/GenMe was more likely to agree with statements such as "in the long run, the only person you can count on is yourself" and "if you want something done right, you have got to do it yourself." Thus, if anything, GenX/GenMe was *less* interested in teamwork. The authors concluded that the workplace needs new models around teamwork that emphasize the contribution of the individual—pretty consistent with the other findings on GenMe.

It's possible that the teamwork idea shifted with those born in the late 1980s and 1990s, but as far as I know, no data exists on teamwork among this group. The personality data showing more self-focus, less empathy, and more narcissism suggests that teamwork will not be high on their list. So why are young people so often seen hanging out with large groups of friends? Well, because they are young, and young people have always been more attracted to larger groups while socializing. It's an age effect, not a generational one. My view is that young employees may like feeling connected with many people—partially due to their online social networking use—but that they will become frustrated with working in teams if their individual effort is not recognized.

QUICK SUMMARY: THE SEVEN PRINCIPLES OF WORKING WITH GENME

1. Focus on results instead of BIC (butt in chair).
2. Offer flexible hours.
3. Explain to GenMe'ers why they're doing the project, why it's important, and why their role is important.
4. Don't invent new programs around helping others; those that worked before will work now.
5. Realize that compensation is more important to GenMe, who face high rents and student loan bills.
6. Give feedback more frequently.
7. Create more rungs on the ladder of career advancement, so promotions occur more often.

THE TAKE-HOME MESSAGE

When the Boomers began their careers, they entered a traditional corporate culture. Employees stayed at the same company, and often in the same job, for years. Your boss was "Mr. Jones," not "Dave," and when he asked you to do something, you did it and did not ask why. You may have waited years to get promoted. No one worked at home, and almost everyone kept the same nine-to-five schedule.

Things have, obviously, changed. Many businesses are finding that they can give GenMe'ers what they want—flexibility, less hierarchy, more context—and get better performance from their employees. As with most things, the key is in finding balance. Working at home isn't productive for every business or every employee. If asking why and calling bosses by their first names becomes disrespect, that's not a good outcome. Every manager and every business must find the practices that both satisfy this generation and make the company profitable.

I face a similar dilemma in my classroom. I primarily teach juniors or seniors in college, just before they start their first post-college jobs. For some students, their ideal class is one where they can get an A with little to no effort. But that's not the best for them in the long run: they likely won't learn the material, nor will they learn a work ethic. Others want special accommodations. "I have to take the final late so I can go to Vegas for my birthday," said one. I thought, "What is your boss going to say if you make the same request a year from now—'I have to miss the big presentation because I'm going to Vegas for my birthday.'" So I said no.

I have no problem giving the students what they want in other realms—those that enhance, rather than take away, from their learning. I tell them how the material applies to their lives, ask for their opinions and perspectives, use interactive materials, give four exams a semester instead of two, spell everything out carefully in the syllabus, and show short videos. They like these things, and they learn more. Everybody wins, and these same principles of engagement and frequent feedback can be applied to the workplace.

Fairness is also key. If I said "Sure" to the guy who wanted to put his out-of-town birthday extravaganza ahead of his education, he would feel as if he'd won. But the other students would lose—why should they have to take the final at the regular time when someone else gets special treatment and might hear answers from those who'd already taken it? Even birthday dude loses in the long run, when he tries this trick with his boss and makes a bad impression. It's the same at a company. Take the generational accommodations too far, and employees might get what they *want*, but not what they *need* for the long haul. What they need is a company that makes a profit and coworkers who don't resent them for being "special." The organizations that can find this balance between want and need will be the most successful in the coming years as Generation Me comes to dominate the workplace.

9

What Do We Do Now?

So here's how it looks: Generation Me has the highest self-esteem of any generation, but also the most depression. They are more free and equal, but also more cynical. They expect to follow their dreams, but are anxious about making that happen. In a recent poll, 2 out of 3 adults said that young people in the United States today face more challenges than opportunities.

GenMe faces a very different world from what they were led to expect as children. The messages of their youth were unflaggingly optimistic: You can be anything. Just be yourself. Always follow your dreams. To borrow Alan Greenspan's phrase, their upbringing was "irrationally exuberant." Irrational, because when they reach adulthood, they often find themselves lonely, rejected by graduate schools, stuck in a boring job, and/or unable to afford a house. Like the housing market of the mid-2000s, the bubble of high expectations bursts once GenMe hits adulthood. Older generations have also struggled during young adulthood, but GenMe has been led to expect bounty in a time of famine. In a 1980s Talking Heads song, a rich man wonders, "How did I get here?" and says, "This is not my beautiful house! . . . This is not my beautiful wife!" as if he is unsure how he obtained the riches around him. GenMe feels the opposite—they wonder instead, "Where is my beautiful house? Where is my beautiful wife?"

(And "Where is my fulfilling job and my shot at fame?") The gap between expectations and reality has widened to a yawning gulf of disappointment. That disappointment is the main source of the anger many in GenMe feel—why, they ask, did you tell us we were special when we can't even get an entry-level job to pay off our gargantuan student loans?

The good news is that GenMe turned around some of the more negative GenX trends. Although 16% of teens said they seriously considered suicide in 2011, this was down from a staggering 29% in 1991. In the high school survey, fewer 2010–12 students said they fought with their parents five or more times a month (37%), down from 46% in 1989–91 and 41% in 1976–78. Teen pregnancy decreased markedly, as did the crime rate. The last few years have also seen lower rates of fighting, cheating, and stealing among teens.

However, these encouraging trends may be due to the kids themselves rather than any systematic change in our culture. As the book *Freakonomics* demonstrated, much of the crime drop after the 1990s can be traced to a surprising source: the nationwide legalization of abortion in 1973. After this time, millions of unwanted children were simply not born. Those children—all of them unwelcome, and many of them poor—might have been the most likely to commit crimes as teenagers and young adults. They might also have been the most likely to get into fights, carry weapons, and drink alcohol. The teen girls among them might have been the most likely to become pregnant. But they didn't, because they didn't exist. So American culture probably can't take credit for the improvements that began in the early 1990s, when more teenagers than usual grew from babies who were planned and wanted.

THE DELICATE ART OF PREDICTING THE FUTURE

What can we expect from Generation Me in the future? With the youngest of this generation (those born in the late 1990s) still in high school, there's a lot of future to predict. As more GenMe'ers reach adulthood over the next few years, a full-scale collision will occur between their high expectations and the unfortunate realities of modern life. More and more young people in their 20s will be disappointed that they cannot pursue their chosen profession, that their job performance is criticized, and that they cannot afford to buy a house. This will lead to a lot of anxiety, depression, and complaining. Older generations will perceive this as whining, but they should realize that they created this monster by telling kids they could do anything they wanted—and that it really is more difficult to get by economically. More and more employers will notice that their young employees expect quick promotions and flexible schedules.

GenMe will continue the shift toward equality across races, men and women, and gays and lesbians. The country will become progressively more color-blind, which might reduce racism, but is also likely to reduce support for affirmative action programs. Race will become increasingly complex as it moves beyond the old issue of white versus black. Hispanics are already the largest minority group in the United States, and Asians, though a small percentage of the overall population, are a large presence at universities and in the professions. More and more young people are multiracial, with parents from different racial groups, making race issues even more difficult to define. Race will become less important as a defining characteristic as more children with multiple racial identities are born.

In the 2006 first edition of *Generation Me*, I wrote, "Because young people are much more tolerant of homosexuality than older people, gay marriage and other reforms might well become a reality in the next few decades." That did indeed happen, and it took only seven years—not decades. In the coming decade, gays will continue to move toward the mainstream of American life, and more will come out of the closet at younger ages as this identity becomes more accepted. Young people's tolerant attitudes toward homosexuality will stay with them as they age, so that in a few decades the majority of people in their 50s and 60s will be accepting of gays and lesbians. Transgender people will also become increasingly accepted and supported by society and their families.

Women will continue their pursuit of college degrees and their moves into the professions. This will be especially true in fields that deal with people rather than things (a preference that has a large sex difference). Because doctors, lawyers, and politicians all work with people, women will be the majority of young people in these professions within the next ten to twenty years. Engineering and physics, on the other hand, are likely to always remain majority male.

GenMe has a strong desire to have children: 74% of 2012 college freshmen named "raising a family" as an important life goal, compared to only 59% of Boomer college students in 1977. Whether young people will reach this goal is uncertain, given their career ambitions, the paucity of affordable child care, and the growing child-related costs of such things as housing and health care. In this area GenMe's ideals will again conflict with reality, leading to anger and dissatisfaction. More and more young people want to become parents, but more and more will find that they cannot have children and maintain a middle-class standard of living. Many who do have children will find themselves unprepared to be full-time caregivers (a role often necessitated by the high cost of child care). Given that only 1 in 1,000 incoming college students chose "full-time homemaker" as their probable career, many GenMe'ers, mostly women, will find themselves staying at home when they never expected to do so.

If the United States does not develop a better system of child care, more women will choose not to have children. If that is the case, the United States will experience the underpopulation problems already prevalent in Europe and Japan. The Social Security system will fall apart, and the economy will falter. The ideology of the population may also change, perhaps negating some of the equalizing trends I just predicted. If women in conservative religious groups have significantly more children than other women, the political leanings of the country will begin to shift. This may already be happening, although it does appear that young people as a group are liberal on many social issues such as gay rights and race relations.

And what will GenMe's children be like? It is difficult to tell right now if GenMe'ers are adopting the same child-rearing approach as their parents, but it appears that they are. As a result, the next generation may be even more self-focused. Over time, more and more parents might draw the line at children's bad behavior and begin using more discipline. Another trend that will shape today's and tomorrow's children is the decreasing standard of living for young families. As the economic squeeze of housing prices and child-care expenses intensifies, fewer children will get good-quality day care or have their own yard to play in. The next generation will have fewer siblings, as fewer families will be able to afford large houses, day care for multiple children, and several college tuition bills. Only children will become more common. The gulf between rich children and poor children will grow as economic pressures sort people more definitively into the haves and the have-nots.

In the following sections, I'll discuss what these trends mean at a practical level. Chapter 8 already addressed the implications for employers and executives, who are managing this generation right now and will be for years to come. Here, we'll start with how to sell to this still–often-misunderstood generation. I'll then move on to what comes next—things that all of us together, and parents and young people in particular, can do to change things for the better in the future, for this generation and the next.

FOR MARKETERS AND ENTREPRENEURS

Marketers and salespeople already know about—and use—the self-focus of Generation Me. This generation is, by definition, interested in products that satisfy their personal wants and help them express themselves as individuals. At the same time, this generation feels tremendous anxiety about succeeding in life. The market for products that help young people get into college or graduate school, polish their résumés, and do well in interviews will continue to grow. Young women in particular will respond to an advertising campaign that shows them how to dress professionally in a way that is still attractive. This balance is still difficult to strike, and more and more young women are anxious about their job or graduate-school interviews. They've gotten mixed messages from TV and movies about how to dress on such occasions, since these sources often show professional women showing lots of leg and cleavage (anything for ratings). Sisterly advice in this department will be welcomed.

Young people are also starving for good advice on career paths. Fifteen years ago, who had ever heard of a "life coach"? Companies like My Guidewire (myguidewire.com) ask if you are "unhappy with your job" or "wanting to shift from surviving to succeeding" and promise to help you "gain a competitive advantage" (for a monthly fee). Expect this market to expand as more and more young people find it difficult to navigate the transition from college to first job or find themselves dissatisfied with their first job (or second or third). With more college graduates emerging with business and psychology degrees, many young people will gladly pay someone to help them find a job that uses their skills.

The continuing rise in the age at first marriage and young people's long working hours both suggest that Internet dating services and "speed dating" will continue their rise in popularity. Services that attempt to match people on certain characteristics will do particularly well, as they save time by sifting through the pool of candidates. Products aimed at single people will also be good bets. Grocery items in smaller packages might do particularly well; people who live alone are sick of watching half a loaf of bread turn to mold and half the cheese learn to walk inside the fridge. The popularity of the two-serving bag of salad is a good illustration of a product whose time has come: it saves the busy person from taking apart heads of lettuce and provides the product in the right amount. It also makes a nice profit. Other products that can corner this market will do well.

With the move away from dating and toward hookups, the already huge market for appearance-enhancing products will continue to expand. Women—and increasingly men—will flock to the clothes and products that convey sexual appeal. The plastic surgery trend will continue as standards for appearance require unreachable perfection.

One sobering fact is that young people today have less money left over for luxuries, decreasing the market for some items and increasing it for others. Spiraling costs for housing, health care, and day care mean less discretionary income. The continued demand for child care and the increasing cost of day-care centers both suggest that home day cares will continue to be profitable, as will nanny services. There will also be an increasing demand for affordable preschools, as more and more research proves its benefits. The trend toward educational products for children will continue as parents realize that the competition for the best schools will only increase in the coming decades.

With the birth rate declining, more couples—and single people—will opt to have pets instead of children. "I'd rather have a dog over a kid," said Sara Foster, 30, in a 2014 *New York Post* article. "It's just less work, and honestly, I have more time to go out. You don't have to get a babysitter." Animals have befriended and helped humans since the caveman days, and research studies show many health benefits for pet owners. The new twist, though, is to bestow human privileges on pets and treat them like children. In a

2011 survey, 77% of pet owners said they bought their pets birthday gifts, and 58% referred to themselves as their pet's "mommy" or "daddy." Pets are a fast-growing market, with spending increasing every year, including for human luxuries such as purified water and nail polishing. Much of the advertising for these products uses the phrase "pet parent" instead of the now-outdated "pet owner." You can now buy a pet stroller. A company called Party Animals will plan your pet's party for you. On a recent airplane trip, the woman sitting in front of me brought on a full-size bulldog who sat, uncaged, in the seat next to her. She talked to the dog for most of the flight. On another occasion, I overheard a man say about his cat, "Oh, Mr. Mittens loves holidays." In future years, I predict an increasing movement to treat animals like humans, partially because they will replace children in some families. Pet products will continue to be a growing market segment.

Marketing and advertising should also pay close attention to changes in language use. Several studies using the Google Books database show language has become more self-focused and less communal. One of the biggest increases was in the use of *you* and other second-person pronouns. Individualistic words such as *unique* and *personalize* also increased, as did the use of female pronouns. If you want to market to this generation, you need to speak their language, and this huge database is one of the fastest ways to see what that language is.

WHERE DO WE GO FROM HERE?

Like most of GenX and GenMe, I am skeptical that simply calling for change will actually change anything. But three changes would make an enormous difference in the lives of Generation Me and the generations who follow. One will cost no money and might even save money; another may cost universities a small amount but will greatly benefit their students; and the last will vary in cost but in the long run might pay for itself.

Ditch the Self-Esteem Movement and the Unrealistic Aphorisms

It is not who you are underneath, but what you do that defines you.

—*Batman Begins*

The first change we must make is to abandon the obsession with self-esteem. Instead of creating well-adjusted, happy children, the self-esteem movement has created an army of little narcissists. Schools should eliminate self-esteem programs. It does not do any good for a child to hear that he or she is "special" or to "win" a trophy just for participating. Decades of research have shown that high self-esteem does not cause good grades or good behavior. So the programs are not doing any good. What's more, they may actually be harming some kids by making them too self-centered. Praise based on nothing teaches only an inflated ego. The purpose of school is for children to learn, not for them to feel good about themselves all the time.

Another facet of this movement says that teachers should not correct children's mistakes, lest this hurt their self-esteem. This is misguided: children learn by having their mistakes corrected, and their self-esteem is hurt when they later find out that they've been doing something wrong for years and aren't prepared. "We are in danger of producing individuals who are expert at knowing how they feel rather than educated individuals who know how to think," writes education professor Maureen Stout. Children will feel good about themselves—and rightly so—when they develop real skills and learn something. Children also need to learn how to deal with criticism, in preparation for the inevitable day when it is not delivered as gently as you—or they—would like. We are doing young people an enormous disservice by sending them into an increasingly competitive world thinking they will be praised for substandard work. It is too late to change this for adult GenMe'ers, who are now struggling to succeed in the workplace after having their self-esteem boosted throughout their childhoods. But schools can still make these changes for future generations.

Fortunately, most schools do still correct children's mistakes. However, the majority of schools consider it their mission to cultivate children's self-esteem, even though decades of research make clear that this is a waste of time. Some schools say instead that they aim to help each child cultivate his or her unique skills and abilities. This is fine as long as that still means that all kids learn math, and that kids still learn that people differ in their talents. There is nothing wrong with being good at some things and not others—that's life.

Many schools have stopped publishing the honor roll since kids who don't make the list might "feel bad." But feeling bad can be good; it can motivate hard work. The Japanese have known this for ages, which is why Japanese kids often say they're no good at something, work hard, and then blow American kids out of the water on international tests. We have to get away from the notion that negative self-feelings are to be avoided at all costs. There is no need to shelter kids from differences in abilities among people; they're going to encounter this in college or the workplace soon enough anyway. We have to be clear, especially with young children, that doing badly does not mean you should give up. It means you should work at it more.

Parenting magazines should stop insisting that a parent's most important duty is to raise a child who "likes herself." As any parent of a two-year-old can tell you, most kids like themselves just fine—and make the demands to prove it. Even as children grow older, most are confident and self-assured. A small percentage of kids might need extra encouragement, but a much larger percentage will believe you if you say they are the best kids in the world. Children do not need to be sheltered from failure. "We do not need to completely shield our children from pain, discomfort, and unhappiness," advises the sane book *The Over-Scheduled Child.*

"When life undoes all that hard work, as real life invariably must, our carefully 'shielded' children may not have developed the tools they need to cope with adversity." If children are always praised and always get what they want, they may find it difficult to overcome challenges as adults. "The risk of overindulgence is self-centeredness and self-absorption, and that's a mental health risk," says psychologist William Damon.

It's also time to do away with trophies for participation. Life requires more than just showing up. I like Ashley Merryman's advice in the *New York Times*: "If I were a [Little League] baseball coach, I would announce at the first meeting that there would only be three awards: Best Overall, Most Improved, and Best Sportsmanship. Then I'd hand the kids a list of things they'd have to do to earn one of those trophies. They would know from the get-go that excellence, improvement, character and persistence were valued." Merryman is right: we should reward performance, effort, and consideration for others, not mere participation. Why try hard and improve when you're going to get the trophy anyway? Nor is this good preparation for the rest of life. Many in GenMe are angry that they were so ill-prepared for the tough job market and today's harsh economic realities. We can prepare the next generation better by banishing the idea that simply participating is good enough.

Much of the "self-esteem movement" encourages narcissism, the belief that one is better and more important than anyone else. Narcissism is linked to aggression and poor relationships with others. Somehow we've developed the notion that it's not okay to have a few insecurities, but it is okay to think you're the greatest and everyone else should get out of your way. Instead, children should learn to have empathy and respect for others. Eventually, children will learn that the world does not revolve around them. As an added bonus, children who are sensitive to others' needs get along better with their peers and thus enjoy all of the benefits that come with good friendships. Children are naturally self-centered;

growing up is the process of learning how to empathize with other people.

Instead of children doing "All about Me" projects, or writing "commercials" advertising themselves, perhaps they could learn about another child in the class. What is her life like? What are her beliefs, and why does she have them? What has she learned from her experiences? Children would learn a lot more from this type of project and might also develop empathy.

Psychologist Roy Baumeister argues that parents and teachers should focus on teaching self-control instead of self-esteem. Children who learn how to persevere at a difficult task and delay rewards until a later time grow up to accomplish much more than children who do not have these skills. Children should be rewarded for good behavior, not indulged when they whine or get upset. Kids who learn to control their emotions and actions will reap the benefits for years to come. Their actions are more important than their feelings about themselves.

We also need to stop talking in unrealistic platitudes, and this goes for teachers, parents, and Hollywood screenwriters alike. We must stop telling children, "You can be anything you want to be" or "You should never give up on your dreams." Why? Because both of these statements are patently untrue. Not everyone is good at what he would like to do, and even if he is, the profession might be competitive and full of talented people. Adults cannot follow their dreams all the time, but must deal with the practical matters of getting a job that pays the bills. It's fine to tell kids to try to find a profession that they enjoy, but talk of "dreams" and being "anything you want" creates unrealistic expectations that are bound to disappoint. We're raising idealistic children who expect the world and can't even buy a condo, who believe that every job will be fulfilling and then can't even find a boring one. It's especially tempting to utter these aphorisms to smart and talented kids, but they especially need to realize that it will still take a lot of hard work and luck to make it—lots and lots of smart people don't get into the law school of their choice or get their dream job. Yes, your talent will open up more possibilities, but it doesn't mean that you will be able to do anything you want to do. No one is truly, objectively good at everything.

Not only do these phrases create unrealistic expectations, but they can also give kids the idea that the world is an ever-expanding, scarily large universe of possibilities. Author Chris Colin quotes his classmate Lesley Kato, who says, "I was told, growing up, that I could do whatever I wanted, and I fully believed I could. And therefore I had no idea what to do."

Instead, children should learn that growing up is a gradual process of learning what you're good at and what you're not. Then they have to figure out how to apply that to a career. Some talents aren't going to lead to a paying job, and others might. It's also useful to consider skills in relation to other people—what do you do better than most others? (Again, ignore the empty self-esteem proposition that you shouldn't "compare yourself to others"—everyone else will, so you might as well start now.)

These skills also need to be viewed through a realistic lens. Even the extremely skilled baseball player is unlikely to make it to the major leagues. The talented actor probably won't become a movie star. Few young people realize how difficult it is to get into med school or become a corporate executive. This doesn't mean that young people should be discouraged from pursuing these professions, but that they should be prepared for how difficult it might be.

Another aphorism that should be chucked is "You must love yourself before you love others." A mountain of research shows that people who have good relationships with other people are happier and less depressed—and have higher self-esteem. The idea that self-esteem rises fully formed and perfect from inside the individual is a complete myth. We develop our sense of ourselves primarily from interacting with others. There is nothing wrong with this. Not only that, but narcissists—people who really love themselves—are horrible relationship partners. Self-centered people are rarely fun to be around, and we all know this. So why do we keep telling people to love themselves first before others? Beats me. An aphorism that makes a lot more sense, to modernize John Donne, is "No one is an island."

Provide Better Career Counseling for Young People

The book *The Ambitious Generation* was subtitled *America's Teenagers, Motivated but Directionless*. That's because young people are usually not told how to achieve their goals. As the book documents, many parents focus on their kids' getting into the "best" college, not the college that is best for the young person and his or her career goals. In some fields, doing internships and developing contacts are key; in others, college grades count. Many teens are focused on a goal but have no idea how to achieve it; parents and counselors can help them take the practical steps toward reaching their goals. Many books and websites detail some of this "insider" knowledge.

Not every teen should be encouraged to go to college. Many high-paying and rewarding occupations do not require a college degree. Just to name a few—plumbers, auto mechanics, carpenters, and electricians make excellent money. Young people who enjoy mechanical things and have little interest in college should not be browbeaten into going. If they learn a skilled trade, they'll often be making more money than a college graduate of the same age. A cultural value shift is also in order. College-educated people should consciously reconsider their attitudes toward skilled trades and give them the respect they deserve. It should not be an embarrassment to be without a college degree if you're in a job that requires skills not taught in college.

Students who do go to college need more career direction. Most college students are ill-equipped to choose a profession and receive little guidance during their four years at school. As noted in the marketing section above, many companies have stepped in to fill the gap with job-search services. Placement offices at universities have a tough job, and students often need more help than they can provide.

One way to solve this is to start early by teaching students about the career paths in their field. About 10 years ago, our psychology department at San Diego State began requiring a one-credit class for psychology majors called Academic and Career Opportunities in Psychology. Many older faculty members were against requiring this course, as it does not teach psychology per se. My younger peers on the faculty thought it was a great idea, and so do I. I would go further: every college student should take a class like this in her major, preferably during sophomore year. Job placement offices at colleges can only spend so much time with any one student, and often students arrive there without any clear idea of what kind of job they would like. Career-path classes organized by major can give students the information they need to help decide on a profession. In the SDSU course, students learn about career opportunities and graduate schools and get a primer on job-search skills. Students also get help developing an educational plan that will help them reach their goals.

Ideally, these classes should feature guest appearances by alumni who can give students a view of what it's like to work in a specific profession and perhaps provide a useful networking contact. In general, alumni should have more opportunities to visit campus and give advice and mentoring to young people.

Create More Support for Working Parents

In the coming years, two of the greatest challenges for young people will be getting health care and child care. Both eat up increasingly large chunks of young families' incomes. The debate over nationalized health care is beyond the scope of this book.

Child care, on the other hand, is relatively simple: most mothers work, and their kids need care. Yet there is no nationalized system, and young families often have few choices; good care is expensive, and even mediocre care is hard to find and costly. Millions of people deal with this every day. American parents are going broke trying to pay the mortgage and the child-care bill. One out of four children lives below the poverty level in the United States today, and nearly 1 out of 2 lives in a family making less than double the poverty cutoff (about $47,000 a year for a family of four). Even the middle-class families making more than this struggle to pay for care for their children.

So why isn't anything being done about this? Why is the United States one of the few industrialized nations without mandatory paid maternity leave or state-sponsored day care? Why aren't the problems of young families—the expense of day care, the cost of housing, the lack of good choices—at the forefront of politicians' agendas, instead of Social Security and prescription drugs?

It's at least partially because young people have not put them there. Two of GenMe's most prominent characteristics are individualism and lack of political engagement. Confidence in government has reached an all-time low. Many don't vote, and many don't think political action will do any good. GenMe thinks everything is up to the individual, even though millions are experiencing the same problems at the same time. GenX and GenMe are so uncomfortable with group action that we have seemingly thrown in the towel for getting back any of our tax dollars. If older Americans faced a problem that made their checkbooks impossible to balance, they'd take political action and get results. In *Perfect Madness*, Judith Warner writes, "There is right now no widespread feeling of social responsibility—for children, for families, for anyone, really—and so [young parents] must take everything onto themselves. And because they can't, humanly, take everything onto themselves, they simply go nuts."

Ever since large numbers of mothers went to work in the 1970s, Americans have had their collective heads in the sand about day care. Our workplaces and much of the rest of our lives are still structured as if we all had wives at home. Yet couples in which the husband works and the wife doesn't are only 18% of young marrieds. Even that minority would benefit from many of the changes suggested to improve things for working parents, such as paid parental leave, paid sick leave, and state-sponsored preschool. It is as close to bulletproof as a political issue gets: a recent poll found that 60% of registered Republicans and 84% of registered Democrats supported a proposal to fund public preschool by raising the federal tax on tobacco. Another poll found that 74% of Americans support mandating paid sick leave, and 61% supported a requirement for paid maternity leave. Generation Me was the most likely to support these policies.

Imagine getting into your time machine and seeing this: Kids playing together at a day care completely free of cost to their parents, with children learning about colors and shapes and letters while their parents work. And when mom or dad swings by to pick up the kids, there is a hot meal waiting to take home. Unrealistic? No, because that time machine didn't zip you into the future; it transported you to the past. From 1943 to 1945, the US government ran child-care centers for women who worked in war-related industries, hot meals and all. Imagine what we could do now in the time of such newfangled devices as the copy machine, the ballpoint pen, and the microwave oven.

Actually we don't even need to imagine it; the US government already subsidizes day care for hundreds of thousands of children right now: the children of military personnel. Far from being sterile institutions, these day cares are, author Ann Crittenden reports, extremely well-run and stimulating for children. Government child care sounds scary to some, but the day care enjoyed by these military kids sounds more like heaven. If only we didn't have to join the army to get it.

With the economic squeeze of college loans and expensive housing, fewer in GenMe will be able to afford to have children. Those that do will have fewer. Within a few decades the United

States will end up like many countries in Europe, with the working population not large enough to support retirees. This is happening already: in 2011, the US birth rate hit an all-time low—again (it's been on the decline for a while). The total fertility rate was 1.9, below the so-called replacement rate of 2.1. This is likely to continue as everything associated with children is skyrocketing in price: houses with enough bedrooms and in good school districts, health care, child care, a college education. Even apart from that, making sure children are well taken care of and educated ensures better workers, better citizens, and better parents in the future. It's in the country's best interests to help families.

Here are some specific suggestions for how governments (local and national) can help working families.

1. *Create a nationwide system of paid parental leave*. When the Family and Medical Leave Act passed in 1993, conservatives predicted that it would hurt business. That didn't happen, and the next seven years were some of the best the economy ever had. The law, however, mandates only unpaid leave, a difficult proposition when paying the rent often requires two hefty incomes. Canada and many European countries provide paid parental leave for a year. The United States has nothing. Of 168 industrialized nations around the world, 163 guarantee paid leave for new mothers. Not only is the United States one of the five countries without paid parental leave, but we are also one of the few that does not mandate paid vacation for workers. As a result, a third of women workers in the United States get no paid vacation at all. For someone living paycheck to paycheck (i.e., most people), no paid leave often means going into considerable credit card debt to have a baby.

The tide may be turning, however. In the 2000s, California introduced a paid-leave system that pays 55% of your income for six weeks. It is not paid through taxes but through a small payroll deduction. It's a small step, but it's a step. A system of mandated paid parental leave nationwide would be an even better step.

2. *Create a system of public preschools for 3- and 4-year-olds.* This will benefit both GenMe parents and their children. Children who attend preschool are smarter and more academically prepared for school. The benefits are especially large for lower-income kids, but middle-class kids show significant gains as well. Children at this age are eager to learn; it is a unique opportunity to capture kids at their best and create children who will become confident readers and great math-problem solvers. Yet when not publicly funded, preschool is out of the reach of most lower-income families and a big strain on the already-taxed budgets of the middle class. Florida, Georgia, and Oklahoma introduced such programs in the last decade.

When I advocated for universal preschool in the first edition of *Generation Me*, it was still a fairly contentious issue. Now the idea is gaining widespread acceptance. President Obama mentioned it in his 2014 State of the Union address, and in February 2014, the *New York Times* described preschool as the rare issue with bipartisan support, a "favored cause for politicians and interest groups who ordinarily have trouble agreeing on the time of day." Republican governors in states such as Michigan and Alabama have raised spending for preschools.

Only about 17% of 4-year-olds were enrolled in state-funded preschools in 2001, which jumped to 28% in 2010 as states such as Florida, Oklahoma, and Georgia introduced state-sponsored preschool programs. States that wish to keep current workers productive and create better workers for the future should follow suit. The money that middle-class families save on preschool will probably go right back into the economy—most families with young children are so strapped for cash that they will probably have the money spent the minute their state funds the program. In addition, as Crittenden argues, the tax revenue generated by more women working might also offset a good portion of the cost of these types of programs, particularly if they are full-time. Even if preschools aren't funded, a national system for accrediting them would be extremely helpful to parents.

3. *Make child-care expenses tax-deductible*. If you haven't used the day-care tax credit yourself, you might think that the tax code already allows this deduction. But the amount of expenses allowed is pitifully small, barely enough to put a kid in day care for two months, not an entire year. The amount is capped at such a low figure that the average family gets back only a few hundred dollars. Another program available through some businesses allows parents to have an account to pay for child care that draws from pretax funds, but the limit on this account is also only a fraction of the amount needed to pay for full-time care (about $5,000 a year, when full-time care often costs over $12,000 a year, and sometimes more). This account can also be used only for day-care centers, and not for more informal arrangements such as many nannies or babysitters. It is also only available for some jobs.

Compare this with the incentive to buy a house: all mortgage interest is tax-deductible (even if your house is worth several million—and this is still deductible even under the alternative minimum tax). Yet few child-related expenses are tax-deductible. It is in the government's best interest for people to have children and for both parents to keep working, since working creates more income tax, as do child-care centers, as will the children themselves eventually (not to mention that their paychecks will be sorely needed to fund the Social Security system, assuming it doesn't collapse before then). Crittenden also details other changes to the tax code that would benefit working families, such as taxing the second earner's income at a lower rate. The authors of *The Two-Income Trap* write, "Any program that helps families save money is a program that helps keep the middle class secure."

4. *Change school hours*. At virtually no cost to themselves, local schools could save working parents thousands of dollars a year, improve student performance and behavior, cut the crime rate, and reduce the teenage pregnancy rate. How? By bringing school hours more in line with business hours. I'm not talking about after-school programs—just shifting the hours when kids are in school.

The vast majority of school-age children have mothers who work: 77% of married women and 83% of divorced and widowed women with children aged 6 to 17 now work. Parents of younger kids have little choice now but to pay for day care in the afternoon, since their children are released from school around 2:00 or 3:00 p.m. and most parents don't get off work until 5:00 or 6:00. After-school day care is expensive, often costing $500 a month or more. Once kids are older, they are usually left at home to fend for themselves in the afternoon. Teenagers and an empty house: great combination, right? Yet the early school day is the norm around the country, with many high schools starting at 7:30 a.m. and releasing at 2:30 p.m. Some even start at 7:00 a.m.!

If schools instead started at 9:00 a.m. and released at 4:30 or 5:00, a number of benefits would accrue. Day-care costs for the parents of young children would go down, often to zero, and teenagers would not have the entire afternoon to get into trouble. And they do get into trouble—a large percentage of teenage pregnancies occur between 3:00 and 5:00 p.m., as do a large percentage of teenage crimes. Other teens sit in front of the television, surf the Web unsupervised, or play video games for hours.

The early start time of many high schools also runs exactly counter to the ingrained tendencies of the average teenager. A biologically driven shift in circadian rhythms makes it next to impossible for adolescents to fall asleep early and wake early. This is not laziness; it is a well-documented biological tendency. (For a great description of this research, see *The Promise of Sleep* by renowned Stanford sleep expert William Dement.) In addition, teens are more impaired by sleep loss than adults are and need at least an hour more sleep than adults. For a school that starts at 7:30 a.m., this means getting up, at the latest, at 6:30 a.m. and thus going to bed at 9:30 p.m. (to get the nine hours of sleep teens need). What teenager goes to bed at 9:30 p.m.? Few, so most are simply tired all the time. Teens who begin school at 7:30 a.m. are simply not awake. School start times ask teenagers to come to school an hour earlier than most adult jobs begin, at an age when they need more sleep and have a difficult time falling asleep before 11:00 p.m. or midnight, if not later. Sleep deprivation can lead to anxiety, depression, drug use, car accidents, and aggression. As teenagers are already vulnerable to these dangers, it is important to do everything we can to help them get enough sleep.

Changing school start times can have amazing effects. When the Edina, Minnesota, school system shifted their start time to 8:30 a.m., academic performance improved and misbehavior went down. Teens were more awake and alert in classes and learned more, and everyone's mood improved.

Some parents might protest that they need to be at work early, and then what will they do with their kids? First, this is a minority of people—most businesses start at 8:00 or 9:00 (whereas few adults leave work at 2:30 or 3:00 in the afternoon). Also, most elementary schools already have a system of supervising kids in the cafeteria if they need to be dropped off early; many serve breakfast. Older teenagers can sleep later and get ready on their own in the morning. Even teens who wake earlier are much less likely to get into trouble in the morning than during the long stretches of parentless afternoons. Parents and coaches might also protest that a later day leaves less time for sports. But isn't it more important that kids are awake to learn and not spending entire afternoons unsupervised? Why compromise the education of everyone, and the dollars of many hardworking parents, for the convenience of sports programs? Sports practice can be held in the morning just as well, or after 4:30 p.m. if need be. It makes a lot more sense for a few athletes to get up early so that everyone can learn more, instead of the current system where everyone gets up early and many fall asleep in class. A later schedule might also require some older teens with jobs to adjust their hours, though these adjustments would probably be more positive than negative. Teens would be able to "close" at their retail or fast-food jobs at 9:00 or 10:00 p.m. and still get enough sleep before the next school day.

Later school start times make sense for so many reasons, and the research on teen sleep has been around for more than 20 years now. School boards and administrators should take action on this issue as soon as possible. It would cost so little, and benefit so many.

FOR PARENTS

Many personal solutions exist for the dilemmas faced by Generation Me. If you are a parent, you might be wondering how you can help your children avoid some of the pitfalls of being young today. First, recognize that you will not be able to completely isolate children from the influences of their generation. Your children will be heavily influenced by their peers, the media, and the broader social environment. You can, however, counteract some of the more negative influences by reinforcing positive traits.

• *Junk the self-esteem emphasis and teach self-control and good behavior.* Self-esteem has limited benefit, whereas self-control is linked to success in life. You can teach your children self-control early on: even toddlers notice the consequences of their actions. If a child cries and cries for a piece of candy at the grocery store and you give it to her, you have just taught her that crying is an effective way to get what she wants. The next time she wants something, she will cry and whine because that worked last time. Instead, give the child treats for good behavior. Many parents cave in to a crying child because it feels easier, or because they can't stand to deprive a child of something she wants. However, you're depriving her of a lot more if you give in. Rewarding the child who asks nicely teaches social skills as well as self-control. Resist the urge to give children everything they want and teach them the importance of working toward important goals. Many excellent books are available on the gentle, firm discipline that teaches self-control (Ruth Peters's book *It's Never Too Soon to Discipline* comes to mind). Discipline doesn't always mean punishment; it usually means not rewarding bad behavior, and praising good behavior.

When I wrote this advice in the first edition of *Generation Me*, I did not yet have children. I now have three. Yet my viewpoint remains more or less the same. I now know just how hard it is to listen to your child cry, but I have also seen the great results of loving and consistent discipline (my family relies mostly on time-outs plus prizes for good behavior). No, my kids aren't perfect, but they behave much better when they know the rules and the consequences for breaking them. One of the most effective techniques is to say "Stop doing that or . . ." followed by a consequence (time-out, taking the toy away, and so on). If she keeps doing it, the key is to follow through with the consequence—every time, and immediately. Time-out also has to be done correctly, with no interaction, to work. Time-out works because you are taking away something the child wants (to participate in the family and interact with you). If you talk to a child while he's in time-out, even about the offense, it defeats the purpose. The general rule of thumb is one minute in time-out per year of age. It's a short time, but effective. It's tempting to want our children to be happy all of the time, but what would make them the happiest? Probably eating candy for dinner, not brushing their teeth, watching TV all day, and staying up late. Not exactly a recipe for health and happiness in the long run.

Teaching discipline and self-control is also important for children to get along with each other—and with you. Children are naturally selfish when they are young; for millennia, the role of parents and teachers was to tell them that the world does not revolve around them. Now we tell them it does. It's better to teach them consideration for others. This is yet another thing that might not make them happy in the short term—sharing does not come naturally to preschoolers. (I recall my daughter Kate's statement when she was 2 years old: "*Everything* is mine.") Many parents have emphasized self-esteem because they think it will help children succeed in school and build healthy relationships. It probably won't. But social skills and empathy for others will—and, as an added bonus, it's the right thing to do.

Self-control and hard work are also essential. Amy Chua's 2011 book, *Battle Hymn of the Tiger Mother*, was both controversial and bestselling because it exposed the secret fear of every non-Asian parent: we're doing it wrong, and that's why the Asian kids have been valedictorian every year. I don't agree with all of Chua's views, but I do agree with her basic point that perseverance, delay of gratification, and hard work are more important than "believing" in yourself. No matter what your ethnicity or cultural background, we'd all do well to move the focus from self-esteem to hard work. The book *Willpower*, by Roy Baumeister and John Tierney, is a great place to read about the research on the science of self-control and its many benefits.

Basically, the lesson is to not rest on your laurels. Everyone, no matter how smart or accomplished, can always learn something new. If you're completely self-confident and know exactly what you're doing, chances are you're a few seconds away from being bored. If you don't feel a little overwhelmed or confused, you're not learning anything. Being continually challenged is much more conducive to success than believing you already know it all.

The bottom line: Yes, you want your children to be happy. But sometimes they have to be unhappy in the short term to be happy in the long term. As parents, our job is to give our children what they need, not just what they want.

• *Leave behind the obsession with specialness and uniqueness*. In June 2012, Wellesley High School teacher David McCullough made national headlines when the theme of his commencement speech was "you're not special." "Contrary to what your soccer trophy suggests, your glowing seventh-grade report card, despite every assurance of a certain corpulent purple dinosaur . . . you're nothing special," he said. "We have of late . . . come to love accolades more than genuine achievement. . . . We're happy to compromise standards, or ignore reality," if that's the way to have something to brag about, he said. Instead, he noted, "The fulfilling life . . . is an achievement, not something that will fall into your lap. . . . Climb the mountain not to plant your flag, but to embrace the challenge. . . . The sweetest joys of life, then, come only with the recognition that you're not special."

I'm with McCullough. We are doing kids a tremendous disservice when we lead them to believe that just because they are special to us (their parents), the rest of the world will treat them this way. The best preparation they can receive is not narcissism or even self-esteem, but your love and support—and your message to them that hard work and perseverance are more important to success than self-belief. The last part of McCullough's speech is especially poignant—in essence, what he's saying is to focus on intrinsic goals (affiliation, community, and self-understanding) rather than the extrinsic goals of money, fame, and image. That also agrees with the psychological research on the topic. In short: Do it to live, not to put it on Facebook. Do it to help someone else, not so you can brag about it.

Some parents have asked me, shocked, "You mean I shouldn't tell my son he's special? Should I instead say, 'You're not special'?" No. Just say, "I love you." It's what you mean anyway, and it's a much better message, emphasizing connection to others instead of superiority.

Others have asked if we should instead emphasize uniqueness. After all, although not everyone is special, everyone is unique.

That's the point behind school programs such as "All about Me" that ask students to discover how they are different from each other, or another called "I'm Thumbody," which points out that everyone has a unique fingerprint. The problem: virtually every war in human history began when one group decided another group was different from them. Why don't we instead emphasize what we all have in common as human beings? That's much more likely to help children develop a sense of empathy for others. Emphasize to your children that everyone has feelings, everyone feels pain, and everyone gets hungry. Being able to take someone else's perspective is an extremely useful skill for relationships—both personal relationships and work relationships. It's the foundation of most of society. Yet when we focus so much on specialness and uniqueness, we leave behind the message that we have a lot in common too.

• *Do not automatically side with your child.* Imagine that your neighbor knocks on your door one day to tell you that your child has been skateboarding outside her house, an activity that is not allowed in your neighborhood. How would you respond? Some parents would immediately defend their child, saying it could not have been their son or that he was just trying to have some fun. While it's instinctual to protect your children, this reaction teaches your child that he is not responsible for his actions. It would be a better lesson to ask your child not to skateboard because it is against the rules and disturbed your neighbor. Some social rules are worth following, and this is not a war of us against them.

The same principle applies when a child says she flunked a test because the teacher was unfair. Defending your child by going after the teacher lets your child know that she can blame others for her problems. Children who believe that grades are just up to the teacher usually underperform in school because they don't see the point in studying. A child may also learn that Mom and Dad will always solve her problems, a lesson that will backfire later in life.

If fewer parents complained to teachers, teachers would also have more time and energy left over for what they do best: teaching, not arguing with parents. Choose your battles carefully when dealing with your child's teacher—or with college professors and administrators. Over the past few years, I have heard story after story from college staff of parents who call when their (adult) child fails a class or fights with a roommate. When I've asked student-affairs deans about the biggest change they've witnessed during their careers, the universal answer is "the involvement of the parents." Parental involvement in education can be a great thing, especially at younger ages, but by the time your no-longer-child is in college, he needs to learn to stand on his own. If a student has a problem with his roommate, the student, not his mother, should work it out.

- *Limit exposure to violence*. In her book *"Mommy, I'm Scared"* Joanne Cantor explains that many children become extremely frightened after watching violent or scary television programs or movies. Most parents limit young children's exposure to these programs, but school-age children can also be seriously affected by them. Even the evening news can make many children anxious. Cantor found that many college students still feel afraid when remembering scary movies or TV shows they watched as children or adolescents. As TV and the movies become more violent, children need to be protected from these harmful influences more and more.

Violent TV, movies, music, and video games can also cause aggressive behavior. A huge amount of research finds that kids exposed to violent media act aggressively in real life. The scientific research in this area is definitive. Many people I mention this research to (including my own husband) say things like "But I played violent video games and I'm not aggressive." Maybe, but that's not the way science works—it relies on average effects across hundreds of people, not individual stories. If you heard that eating apples made kids more aggressive on average, you would never let your child eat apples. We defend violent movies, TV, and video games because we enjoy them ourselves, but that doesn't make them any less harmful.

• *Don't use words like "spoiled."* Yes, young people often focus on their own needs. But guess who taught them to do this? You. Even if you didn't, the entire culture has fed GenMe this message since they were born. Many older people dismiss the concerns of young people, particularly those in their 20s, as "whining." But it is the natural result of high expectations meeting reality. Many older people also forget just how confusing and overwhelming it can be to "have your whole life ahead of you"—that sounds good, but it's also scary. The anxiety and depression that result from this confusing time need to be taken seriously. When young people are told that they have no reason to be depressed, this just makes them feel more depressed and alone.

FOR YOUNG PEOPLE

If you're young yourself, you might be wondering how you can sidestep some of the more negative trends of GenMe. Some of my suggestions may seem intuitive, but others might surprise you.

• *Limit your exposure to certain kinds of TV.* Shows such as *Keeping Up with the Kardashians*, the *Real Housewives*, and *Rich Kids of Beverly Hills* detail the extravagant homes and cars of wealthy celebrities. They're tremendously entertaining, but they can also be depressing. You see all of the things that you'll probably never have (and maybe didn't even know you wanted). Avoid overexposing yourself to the lifestyles of the lucky few and look around you in real life—likely plenty of people have less money than you.

• *Avoid overthinking.* In *Women Who Think Too Much*, Susan Nolen-Hoeksema reports that young people—particularly young women—are more likely to brood over their problems than older people. It's a common cycle: you begin by mulling over a problem and before long you've spent half an hour turning it over and over in your head. Nolen-Hoeksema called this overthinking, and research has linked it to an elevated risk of depression. Talking it over with a friend is a far better solution. You're still considering your problems, but sharing them with someone else unburdens you enough to stop overthinking. People who seek support from others are consistently more mentally healthy than those who don't.

• *Value social relationships*. Keeping up a friendship takes work—work and time many people feel they don't have in their busy lives. But one day you'll look up and wonder where all of your friends went. You will be much happier if you make the extra effort needed to see friends and family. E-mail, Facebook, and the phone are great, but person-to-person contact is better. It might go against your generational mind-set, but try to make those little social gestures that came so naturally to previous generations: welcoming a new neighbor, having friends over for dinner, joining a club. And if you're single, don't neglect dating. Yes, it sucks sometimes, but all it takes is one.

You are going to hear a lot of people tell you that being alone is great, because of the old self-esteem mantra. *Conquering Your Quarterlife Crisis* has a section called "Why Is It So Hard to Live Alone?" One of the "mentors" in the book, Raquel Aviva, 32, offers as her lesson, "You don't always have to count on others. Work on counting on yourself."

Later in the book, Michael Coviello, 25, said, "I wish I had known at twenty-one that true happiness and strength come from inside our hearts and not through others." After the first edition of *Generation Me* was published, Michael wrote to me to tell me his perspective had changed. Now 35, Michael says, "My relationships with family and friends were always important to me, but [back then] I didn't think you needed them to find your identity. . . . [But now I realize that] much of your identity includes the people closest to you. If you want to get to know someone more personally, one way is to know that person's inner circle. I think having good relationships is the biggest achievement in life, and that's the ultimate way to be remembered. Being around family and friends reminds me of how fortunate I am to have them in my life and that I have earned something authentic."

Michael is right. People who have good relationships with others—partners, family, friends—are happier and less depressed than other people. Few people are happy living an isolated life. If you hate living alone, you are one among many. Instead of telling yourself that you ought to be happy with this arrangement, spend your time dating, seeing family, and laughing with friends. Not only will this help you feel better, but eventually these social activities will help you find someone to live your life with, and you won't live alone anymore. And if not, you'll still have a great group of friends.

• *Realize that narcissism and positive self-views are unlikely to help you succeed.* When I present the Generation Me research to undergraduates, most don't disagree that their generation thinks highly of themselves. But, they invariably say, "We have to be this way because the world is so competitive now." I agree that things are competitive, but positive self-views will not necessarily help you compete. Self-esteem does not cause success, and narcissism leads to failure, especially in the long run. When people have vehemently disagreed with the conclusions of *Generation Me*, this is almost always the misunderstanding at the center of the argument: many simply cannot believe that "believe in yourself and anything is possible" is untrue. Like a fish that doesn't realize it's in water, GenMe finds it difficult to fathom that self-belief is not the number one cause of success in life.

Some of the confusion lies in the terms we use. Many talk about self-confidence, but that's not a term used in research psychology. Instead, research separates self-esteem—thinking highly of yourself—from self-efficacy, the belief that one's actions have an impact. Being confident enough to try something (self-efficacy) is important for success. Thinking you're fantastic (self-esteem) is not. That also means that someone encouraging you to do something (self-efficacy) is a good idea, but someone saying you're the best ever (self-esteem, maybe narcissism) is not.

Recall that Asian Americans have the lowest self-esteem but the best academic performance. The lesson there is not that low self-esteem leads to success—it's that hard work and self-control, heavily emphasized in Asian culture, do. Those behaviors are much more likely to help you succeed than simple self-belief. Yes, have the confidence (high self-efficacy) to try something new. But if you don't succeed and feel bad about yourself (low self-esteem), that's not necessarily a bad thing. Keep trying, keep working at it, and you will get better.

- *Combat depression naturally*. A few simple, natural things can fight depression. I have already mentioned the first two: socializing and avoiding overthinking. You are also less likely to feel depressed if you (1) get enough sleep, (2) expose yourself to sunlight for at least an hour a day, (3) exercise regularly, and (4) eat a diet rich in omega-3 fatty acids (found primarily in fish, especially salmon, halibut, herring, white tuna, and trout; fish oil supplements are another source). University of Kansas professor Steve Ilardi, author of the excellent book *The Depression Cure*, has shown that these steps improve mood as much as prescription medication; he calls the therapy "therapeutic lifestyle change." Research has already shown that the individual elements (e.g., light exposure, omega-3 acids) can reduce depression. Ilardi's therapy often works for people whose depression has not responded to medication. "I'm not antimedication," he says. "It's just that for a lot of people [drugs] don't work—and if they do work, it's short-term. Relapse is a huge issue. So, if you can achieve superior results long-term without medication, the advantage seems pretty clear." The other great benefit of such strategies: you can employ them even if you're not depressed and perhaps avoid becoming depressed in the first place.

• *Cultivate realistic expectations*. Have realistic goals rather than believing that you should "follow your dreams" no matter what. It's fine to aim high, but talk to your parents and teachers about your goals and the timeline you have in mind. You will not be CEO of your company in five years. It might be difficult to get into graduate school. If you move to LA to become an actor, you will be lucky to make enough money so you don't have to wait tables, much less become a movie star. Only a few people become rich or famous with little effort. For most people, it takes hard work just to get a decent job and keep it. Does that mean you should be satisfied with that and not want anything better? Of course not, but realize that moving up might not happen overnight.

• *Be cautious about multitasking*. Many people these days are trying to do two (or three) things at once: drive and talk on their cell phone; talk with someone in person and send a text to someone else; study while listening to music and keeping Instagram open on their computer. The inherent problem: The human brain is not capable of multitasking. It cannot do more than one thing at a time. So if you're trying to do two things at once, it's necessary to switch your attention back and forth. This takes time and effort and generally is not the most efficient way to do things. It's possible that GenMe has learned to switch attention a little faster than older generations, but true multitasking is not possible for any generation of humans.

For at least some time each day, turn off your cell phone and restrain yourself from checking Facebook or e-mail. Learn to concentrate on one thing—reading a book, writing a paper or report, doing a math problem—for a sustained time. I know it seems important that you be the first to respond to a friend's post or return your boyfriend's text right away, but people used to get by just fine without being in touch with each other every second during the day. They may also have gotten more done and talked to the people around them more. Some journalists have written about their experiences of "unplugging" for weeks at a time and reported they ended up feeling happier and more relaxed. You don't have to take it this far—just set aside an hour or two to do one thing and work up from there. Many jobs require this kind of sustained attention, not to mention that texting all day is not the way to get on your boss's good side.

- *Get involved in your neighborhood and community*. The fulfillment that GenMe seeks might be found in helping other people. It's one of the best ways to find deeper meaning in life and build those true relationships that are otherwise so hard to find.

Many young people are taking this advice. A few chapters ago I mentioned Drew Lichtenberger, who is now working on a book titled *The Twenties BeatDown*. Like many young people, Drew had a great job in business but then realized it wasn't fulfilling. He went back to working at his alma mater, Virginia Tech, helping prepare college students for their transition into the professional world. He says he is "passionate about developing people." One of his main messages is that volunteering and helping others is one of the best ways to be fulfilled and gain meaning. He leads a high school youth group and encourages other young people to get involved in volunteer work as well. Someone once told him, "The only way that you'll ever feel good about yourself is by helping other people," and he passes this advice on to young people who are looking for meaning and fulfillment. "Individualism and serving yourself are dead ends," Drew says. "Service to others and leaving a lasting legacy is really at the core of the deepest human needs. Strong relationships and community keep us true to who we are and help us see what our lives are meant to be."

This is the upside of young people's taking time during their 20s to find out what they want to do. Many young people volunteer and end up finding a career from their experience. For instance, my cousin Sarah Kilibarda volunteered for Catholic Charities for two years after she graduated from college, helping immigrants with their legal paperwork. She then went to law school and now works as an immigration lawyer. Even if you don't find a career from volunteering, you will more than likely develop valuable skills and make some great friends. Just as important, many people discover that helping others gives them the meaning missing from the emptiness of pure self-focus.

The Great Recession of the late 2000s has led to a greater focus on others. Communalism has not returned to the levels of the 1960s and 1970s, but it's improved. High school students in 2008–10 were more likely than those in 2004–6 to donate to an international relief fund, to say they thought about social problems, and to take steps to save energy and help the environment. The importance of "helping others in difficulty" reached an all-time high among college students in 2013 (72%, up from 70% in 1966 and 62% in 2000). Preliminary data suggests the rise in narcissistic personality traits continued until at least 2009, but may have receded some since then. As psychologist Patricia Greenfield has theorized, economic deprivation leads people to think of others. The Great Recession was a natural social experiment, showing the effects of an economic disruption on culture, and thus on individuals.

At the same time, the percentage of students who thought they were above average in agentic traits such as drive to achieve remained high, and the importance of "being very well-off financially" was also at an all-time high. Among both high school students and adults, trust in others and large institutions have reached all-time lows. So positive self-views are as high as ever, and civic engagement remains mired in cynicism even as the value placed on caring for others is on the upswing. This is an unusual moment in generational history, characterized by both transcendent individualism and a newly surging communalism. The next few years may provide another natural experiment as the economy recovers and (presumably) surges again. Will the renewed interest in helping others continue, or will it again recede? Only time will tell.

Generation Me came of age at a unique time in American history. They were raised to believe in themselves, and to have a wildly optimistic outlook. Yet they are entering adulthood at a time when just getting by is increasingly difficult. Many will weather this collision of youthful expectation and harsh adult reality by becoming anxious or depressed; others feel angry that the optimistic mantras of their childhood have not prepared them for the real world. Most have avoided much interest in larger issues and more serious commitments such as religion, political activism, or social causes, instead choosing to focus on themselves and their circle of friends and family. Others are finding that caring for others brings the meaning and fulfillment they could not find alone.

If you are a young person, I hope you realize you are not alone. If you are older, I hope you have gained the understanding that today's young people were raised differently from you, and that growing up today is not easy. In the coming years, perhaps we will all realize that we can't make it solely on our own. GenMe'ers need realistic expectations, careful career guidance, and support when they become parents. In return, they will gladly lend their energy and ambition toward having a personal impact and making a difference.

Appendix

Further Details about the Scientific Studies in This Book

If you've turned here, you're probably curious about the psychological terms and search methods I've used. Here I'll address a few topics that often raise questions. If you'd like the real nitty-gritty on the statistics and methods of the studies, I recommend finding my (and others') scientific-journal articles through Google Scholar, the Web of Science, PsycInfo, or another database. Many of these are listed in the notes section.

Personality traits and attitudes. What exactly are traits? Basically, they are the internal attributes of people that cause their behavior. Traits summarize the way someone behaves across most situations. For example, someone who expresses her opinions and speaks up when she feels wronged would be high in the trait of assertiveness. Most questionnaires ask fairly specific questions; one measure of assertiveness asks, "If a friend unfairly criticizes you, do you express your resentment there and then?"

So if a questionnaire wanted to measure the trait of "silliness," it might ask about a number of different silly behaviors, such as making funny faces, asserting amusingly absurd statements, and playacting unconsciousness. We learn to group behaviors this way early. If you do all of the things I just listed, for example, you will eventually hear from your child, "Mommy, you're silly!" So when you read that a trait (such as anxiety or assertiveness) has changed, remember that this seemingly abstract concept is based on these more specific questions about actions in real life. Traits are about behavior.

I also mention attitudes, such as attitudes toward working women, support for same-sex marriage, or confidence in large institutions. In the psychological sense, an attitude is a favorable or unfavorable opinion of a group or a group's actions. If you have a strong attitude and express it, you have "attitude" in the more colloquial sense. Here, though, I will focus mostly on attitudes toward the roles of certain groups. For example, attitudes toward the roles of women have changed quite a bit. Like the questionnaires on traits, attitude questionnaires also ask specific questions (e.g., Do you agree or disagree that "Sons in a family should be given more encouragement to go to college than daughters"?). Attitudes are about beliefs, often deeply held beliefs.

The content of the questionnaires used in the studies. As you've seen, some of the generational data comes from people's responses to questionnaires. These questionnaires usually consist of a number of statements that people are asked to agree or disagree with. Sometimes they can answer only yes or no, and other times they give their response on a scale, say from 1 to 5. A few questionnaires (such as the Narcissistic Personality Inventory) use what's called forced choice, meaning you have to choose which statement out of two you agree with the most. The statements tend to ask about specific behaviors, feelings, or opinions. It's fairly difficult to know what these specifics are, though, if you just hear the name of a scale. To give you a better idea of what the questionnaires are actually measuring, sometimes I quote at least a few items from the questionnaires I studied when I describe the results. It helps, for example, to know that one of the items on a scale measuring narcissism is "If I ruled the world, it would be a better place." This shows that the questionnaire isn't just talking about physical vanity. When my students fill out the narcissism questionnaire in class, someone will inevitably raise his hand right away, announce that he scored high on narcissism, say, "I think that . . . ," and go on and on about himself and his ideas. It increases my confidence in personality questionnaires every time.

Changes in college populations. Especially in this updated edition, many of the studies are based on high school samples. But other studies are based on college students. But haven't those samples changed a lot recently? Surprisingly, the answer is no. A large yearly study found that the median income of college students' parents, when adjusted for inflation, did not change between 1965 and 2013. College students come from middle-class and upper-middle-class families, and this has not changed much over time. There has not been a large influx of working-class students, partially because yearly tuition increases have kept four-year colleges out of reach for many. Changes in racial composition are also small, with minority-student enrollment increasing only a few percentage points in the last forty years. College enrollment for black students actually declined during the 1980s. Most college-student samples remain mostly white, just as they were in earlier eras. However, large changes have occurred in gender composition: 36% of college students were women in 1958, compared to 58% in 2012. To correct for this, I analyzed the data within gender; for example, I looked at the changes in women's anxiety scores over time, and men's anxiety scores over time. In most cases, the results were similar. College samples do have more Latinos and Asian Americans than they once did. Interestingly, these two groups tend to score lower on positive self-views, so if changes in ethnic composition caused the differences, self-esteem and narcissism would have gone down over the generations instead of up.

In many of these studies, I also looked at samples of schoolchildren. Children of elementary school and middle school age are almost always enrolled in school, and their samples have not changed much in composition (compared to the small changes in college populations). The new studies also draw from a large sample of high school students. These samples are also more diverse and thus better represent the country as a whole, and the high school sample is nationally representative, meaning it exactly reflects the composition of high school students across the country. When I compared the results for children and high school and college students, they usually showed exactly the same pattern. This gave me further confidence that the changes were not an artifact of shifts in college-student samples. It also showed that children were not immune to these larger social changes—the generational shifts appeared in samples of children as young as 9. Kids are absorbing the ways of their society, and they are doing it at an early age.

Willingness to admit to problems. Perhaps the changes in the questionnaires happen because people now have fewer qualms admitting to problems. However, this is unlikely to account for much of the change. First, I collected data on a scale measuring socially desirable responding—how much people change their questionnaire answers in order to look good in the eyes of others. When I matched that to data on other questionnaires, they weren't correlated over time. So changes in traits happened independent of people's comfort with admitting to things. Also, the questionnaires across all of these studies were given on paper and not in interviews, and they're anonymous—respondents don't put their names on them. The questionnaires also ask about specific symptoms ("Some unimportant thought runs through my mind and bothers me") rather than asking point-blank something like "Are you anxious and depressed?" The responses to all of the symptoms are added up to form the score, so the respondent only admits to small parts of a problem at a time. Finally, the changes described in this book are diverse. Some of them are in "good" traits (such as self-esteem), but others are in "bad" traits (such as anxiety), and some (such as who controls your fate, or narcissism) have questions worded with no obvious "good" or "bad" answer. If people were more comfortable admitting to bad things, we'd expect to see change only in traits that are considered undesirable, but the changes show up in all kinds of characteristics.

The ecological fallacy. Some of the studies in this book use a method I call cross-temporal meta-analysis (CTMA), which gathers the average scores of samples over time. But, some have asked, doesn't this overestimate the change, as means differ less from each other than individual scores? (This is sometimes called the ecological fallacy, or alerting correlations.) It does not—starting with the first CTMA, I computed the effect size using the individual standard deviation (SD), not the SD of the means. Thus the effect sizes of these studies are not overestimates—they rely on the same measure of variance that studies with individual data do. Some critics still try to claim that CTMAs commit the ecological fallacy, but they do not, and have not from the very first one published in 1997. It is puzzling that some still make this patently false claim.

The effects of specific events (such as 9/11/01 and the Great Recession of the late 2000s). In many studies, I have to estimate the year data were collected based on the date of publication, since most researchers don't report the exact year in their articles. Statistically speaking, this means, if anything, that changes are stronger than I've found (as the imprecise year introduces more uncertainty). Even if I could pinpoint the exact year, though, I'm guessing that the change would still be slow and steady. Specific events don't have as much influence as the social climate they create over a period of years. Social change does not happen overnight, particularly in traits and attitudes—characteristics of people that tend to be fairly stable. In fact, I've found in several studies that the change in traits lags about ten years behind statistics such as divorce rate, age at marriage, or crime rate. This suggests that we absorb the environment that surrounds us when we are about 10 years old. Morris Massey, who traveled the country lecturing about generational differences in the 1970s and '80s, calls this "Where were you when you were 10?" and my data support this idea. The environment we experience as children stays with us our whole lives.

In other cases, it was possible to see how multiyear changes such as the recession of 2007–9 impacted young people. My coauthors and I have published one paper on that topic and are working on several others. The recession provided a cultural reality check that has increased young people's concern for others and caring about social issues. In the coming years, it will be fascinating to see if it has also reduced narcissism—and, if so, whether narcissism will come back once the economy does.

Age differences versus generation differences. You might also wonder why all of the library work and huge database trolling was necessary. Why not give these personality questionnaires right now to a big sample of people of different ages? Shouldn't that tell us how generations differ? If we did that, though, we wouldn't know if age or generation was causing the difference. First, I'll show you some examples of differences that are clearly one or the other. Let's say we find that people in their 20s have more energy than people in their 40s. Does this mean that the generation of people in their 20s is more energetic than those in their 40s and always will be?

Probably not; every generation finds that their energy level decreases as they age. This is clearly a difference due to age and not to generation. In contrast, consider your skill with Internet message boards, ATM machines, and programming your DVR. If you're a little older, these might not be your strong suit. (My parents, for example, still don't use ATMs—they go to the bank.

I just don't get it.) This is clearly a difference based on generation and not age, because people who are young now will not suddenly forget their current technology skills when they are older.

But in a one-time sample of people of different ages (called a cross-sectional study), it's impossible to tell if differences are due to age or generation. If a study finds, for example, that people in their 20s are more anxious than people in their 40s, this could be due to aging (maybe people become less anxious as they get older) or to generation (maybe the younger generation will always be more anxious than the older generation). The method I use gets around this problem by looking at samples of people of the same age collected at different points in time. Each of these data sources is a snapshot in time of what each generation was like when young, either children or young adults in college. Because age is held constant, generation and time are clearly the forces at work. Of course, it's possible that people of all ages showed these same changes; if so, that would be a time-period effect rather than a generational effect, and I can't rule that out. But anyone who has observed people knows that young people are more susceptible to change. For example, older people don't use computers as proficiently because they didn't learn how when they were young. Social change hits the young first, and I wanted to see how that happened from the 1950s to the present.

Without a time machine, I couldn't get these data myself. Since so many psychological scales have been used over and over, though, the library became my time machine. Those old journals and dissertations were my looking glass to the past, showing me how things used to be and how they are now. Since the last edition, I've also trolled through the enormous datafiles of over-time surveys such as the Monitoring the Future, the American Freshman, and the General Social. Amid screen after screen of numbers, the picture of social change slowly emerged.

Acknowledgments

As a child, I loved to read so much that I would often stay up past my bedtime to finish a book. My practical Midwestern parents, however, had the radical idea that I should get enough sleep. I tried to finish a book in the bathroom once but was promptly busted. After that, I learned to leave on the aquarium light, which was just bright enough to read by but not bright enough to shine under the door and alert the parental units to my stolen reading time. I would lie at the foot of my bed, late into the night, turning the magic pages in the dim light.

Twenty-five years later, I have read the acknowledgments sections of so many books that I can recite the typical one from memory ("It is fiction that it takes only one person to write a book . . . to my agent extraordinaire . . . to my 546 closest friends [Aaron, Adam, Alice, Amanda . . . (insert 540 names here) . . . Zachary, and Zelda] . . . and finally, to my spouse for cooking all the meals for the last year/raising several children by himself while I slaved away at this godforsaken project/reading the whole book/typing the whole book/writing the whole book"). After writing a book myself, I have suddenly realized why acknowledgment sections all sound the same: you're a massive pain in the ass when you're working on a book, and a little ink is small consolation for all of the people who had to put up with it. I was no different, so my acknowledgments will probably sound no different.

I was a pain partially because writing this book was the most fun I've had at work in years, and enthusiasm, although infectious, can get annoying. Everyone, please forgive me. It's just that any project in which I can quote *Us Weekly* and academic research on the same page is a damn good time.

I owe my first, large sums of gratitude to those who made writing this book even more fun than it was already. Brooke Wells wrote her amazingly thorough master's thesis on changes in sexuality over time, providing the data for chapter 6 and enabling me to spend several enjoyable weeks writing about sex. How can I not be grateful for that? Brittany Gentile and Joshua Foster provided much-needed updates to data, and Kristin Donnelly, Elise Freeman, Joshua Grubbs, Julie Exline, and Nathan Carter put in crucial work on new projects. W. Keith Campbell, my colleague, coauthor, and friend, has sharpened my thinking on just about everything for fifteen years now, including several parts of this book. I'm not sure I would have made it through the jungle of academia without Keith's hatchet of wry irony to clear the way. Next conference, let's skip the symposia and go talk and eat doughnuts again. I learned more that way anyway.

I am also profoundly grateful to the hundreds of young people who opened their lives to me by contributing stories for the book. A large thanks in particular to those who volunteered their time by submitting material through the www.generationme.org and www.jeantwenge.com websites. Your honesty, insight, and eloquence made this book immeasurably stronger. Your stories and opinions brought your generation to life.

My agent, Jill Kneerim, is the reason I got to write this book in the first place. I am amazed, and truly grateful, at how she was able to guide me so encouragingly toward a book proposal that bore no resemblance to my first pathetic attempts. I can only hope to someday develop even an ounce of Jill's ability to pleasantly guide someone into doing her best. My editor, Leslie Meredith, has been equally delightful. Writing your first book can be terrifying, but all of that melted away once I saw Leslie's enthusiasm for my first few chapters. ;-) Long live the deadline emoticon! 8-] The brilliant Brettne Bloom came up with the title and thus deserves a huge high five.

I have been blessed with truly outstanding academic mentors: Roy Baumeister, Jennifer Crocker, Susan Nolen-Hoeksema, Randy Larsen, Abby Stewart, Dianne Tice, and David Winter all helped guide some aspect of this project. Susan showed me the research on changes in depression and generally gave fantastic advice. Her passing in 2012, much too early, saddened all of us in the field, but especially those who had the pleasure of knowing her personally. David guided me through the uncharted territory of lagged analyses and obscure personality measures, gently shaping my overenthusiastic grad-student ideas into a more conventional psychology dissertation. We also had quite a good time just chewing the fat. Roy was the best postdoctoral adviser I could have asked for, and a good friend. His pioneering research on the downsides of self-esteem also strengthened the book considerably. And in the beginning, when I was only 15, Melissa McMillan-Cunningham and Patrick McCann both told me I would someday write a book. We all thought it would be a book of poetry, but I hope this is just as good.

Charles Im and Liqing Zhang spent hours upon hours in the library collecting some of the data I use here, and they deserve ample praise and gratitude. Your hard work made these projects possible. Mark Reid photocopied numerous articles on changes in depression and provided inspiration through his excellent writing. A true man of many talents, he also designed the www.generationme.org website, where I collected stories from young people around the nation. Andrew Chapman designed my newer websites (jeantwenge.com and igenconsulting.com) and is a Web-design genius if you ask me.

The library staff at so many locations have been surprisingly tolerant of the mess one of my projects can create: my thanks to the libraries of the University of Iowa, Eastern Michigan University, Case Western Reserve University, Carnegie Mellon University, the University of Wisconsin, San Diego State University, the Library of Congress, and especially the University of Michigan, particularly the Interlibrary Loan Department. You are saints. The U is also the host of the Monitoring the Future survey that I draw from so often; here's to keeping this national treasure going.

Other academic colleagues have provided excellent ideas, inspiration, and friendship. Jeff Bryson, Kate Catanese, Niels Christensen, Natalie Ciarocco, Thierry Devos, Nathan DeWall, Amanda Diekman, Julie Exline, Craig Foster, Linda Gallo, Christine Harris, Benita Jackson, Markus Kemmelmeier, Laura King, Elizabeth Klonoff, Sander Koole, Joseph Lewis, Deborah Megivern, Kathi Miner-Rubino, Claire Murphy, Radmila Prislin, Scott Roesch, Brandon Schmeichel, Tom Scott, Kathleen Vohs, May Yeh, and Alyssa Zucker, thank you for listening to me blather on about this research for years. I am particularly grateful to those of you who told your classes about the www.generationme.org website. I will always remember Mark Leary, whom I got to know later in another line of research, saying kind words about this work—before breakfast, no less—at an APA conference. Alice Eagly was one of the first to cite my work on changes for women and has lent me her expertise as if I were one of her own students. Daniel Cervone, personality psychologist extraordinaire, engineered my first major presentation of this work to the field. I am continually grateful for how Dan saw the promise in this research and was able to articulate its importance even better than I could. Lynne Baker-Ward and James Kalat were also kind enough to encourage me and to believe in the importance of birth-cohort work within psychology. The SDSU press office, particularly Jason Foster, Aaron Hoskins, and Jennifer Zwiebel (now at NYU), Gina Jacobs, and Beth Downing Chee, have done excellent work to publicize these studies and impress my relatives by getting me on TV.

And to my U of C posse, what can I say except, you rule! Stacey Amodio, Anne Becker Gruettner, Ken Bloom, Lawrence

Charap, Rocky Dhir, Sonia Orfield, and Adam Shah, your loyalty and love are unsurpassed. Lawrence and Shasta Charap deserve special mention for their warm hospitality during several Library of Congress sojourns; Ken Bloom also helped with library searches several times. Kim and Brian Chapeau, George Ekeren-Moening, Sarah and Dan Kilabarda, Jane Moening, Brian and Roxanne Moening, Sarah Moening and Rodney Haug, Bud and Pat Moening, and Marilyn, Ray, and Anna Swenson have belied the phrase that you can't choose your relatives—I'd choose you guys every time. Ron Louden and Alice Zellmer and Susie and Jud Wilson have also been the best in-laws I could have ever chosen. Thanks to Brandelyn Jarrett, our nanny and friend, for making so many days good ones for me and our young charges.

I have read enough acknowledgments sections to know that you save the best for last. My brother Dan has grown from my childhood playmate to my steadfast friend and confidant, as well as being the father of my daughter's (and thus my) favorite person in the world. Kendel, thanks again for planning the perfect New York visit. My parents, Steve and JoAnn Twenge, instilled in me the love of reading and the highest respect for education and also put their money where their mouth was by subsidizing my time at the University of Chicago. They also provided a window on past decades, always willing to help me understand how things have changed and why. I've lost count of the ideas in these projects that had their genesis in one of our conversations.

To Kate, Elizabeth, and Julia, I love you. Thanks for your smiles and hugs that make it all worthwhile. Finally, to my husband, Craig, for tolerating my hours of (over)work and (over)stress, but mostly for making me the luckiest woman in the world.

Notes

Preface

PAGE

xi *Young people are told to "pull yourself up"*: Tiffany Vang, "Reflections of an Annoyed Millennial (or Entitled Brat, Narcissist, Etc.)," *Twin Cities Daily Planet*, December 16, 2013.

xi *"We are said to be entitled"*: Matt Bors, "The Generation We Love to Dump On," cnn.com, July 9, 2013.

xii *finally published a cover article on Millennials*: Joel Stein, "The Me Me Me Generation," *Time*, May 20, 2013.

xii *One video featured a group*: Stephen Parkhurst, "Millennials: We Suck and We're Sorry," September 18, 2013, https://www.youtube.com/watch?v=M4IjTUxZORE.

xiv *Some, such as Elspeth Reeve in* Atlantic Wire: Elspeth Reeve, "Every Every Every Generation Has Been the Me Me Me Generation," *Atlantic Wire*, May 9, 2013.

Introduction

PAGE

2 *Reflecting on her role*: Joan Ryan, "The Millennial Generation," *San Francisco Chronicle*, December 13, 1998.

3 *head of the Roper Youth Report*: Don Tapscott, *Growing Up Digital* (New York: McGraw-Hill, 1998), 94.

7 *Marketing studies, for example, find*: J. Walker Smith and Ann Clurman, *Rocking the Ages: The Yankelovich Report on Generational Marketing* (New York: HarperCollins, 1997).

11 *As early as June 2000,* Time: Daniel Okrent, "Twilight of the Boomers," *Time*, June 12, 2000.

11 *Morris Massey, for years a popular speaker*: Morris Massey, *The People Puzzle* (Reston, VA: Prentice-Hall, 1979), 21.

13 *Ellen DeGeneres said that the most important*: *Ellen*, CBS, January 27, 2005.

13 *Dan Atkins, 17, says*: Tapscott, *Growing Up Digital*, 94.

13 *Here's Mario, a recent college graduate*: Alexandra Robbins and Abby Wilner, *Quarterlife Crisis* (New York: Tarcher/Putnam, 2001), 42.

15 *In his popular syndicated column*: Cecil Adams, *The Straight Dope* (Chicago: Chicago Review Press, 1984), 14.

16 *I begin by searching computer databases*: For example, see J. M. Twenge,

S. Konrath, J. D. Foster, W. K. Campbell, and B. J. Bushman, "Egos Inflating over Time: A Cross-Temporal Meta-analysis of the Narcissistic Personality Inventory," *Journal of Personality* 76 (2008): 875–901; J. M. Twenge, "The Age of Anxiety? Birth Cohort Change in Anxiety and Neuroticism, 1952–1993," *Journal of Personality and Social Psychology* 79 (2000): 1007–21; or J. M. Twenge, "Changes in Masculine and Feminine Traits over Time: A Meta-analysis," *Sex Roles* 36 (1997): 305–25.

1. You Don't Need Their Approval: The Decline of Social Rules

PAGE

24 *The phrase* my needs: Google Books database of American English, https://books.google.com/ngrams.

24 *Young people today are only half as likely:* From the 1972–2012 General Social Survey, National Opinion Research Center, University of Chicago, http://www3.norc.org/GSS+Website/Download/.

24 *Filmmaker Kevin Smith:* Margot Hornblower, "Great Xpectations," *Time*, June 9, 1997.

27 *But when researchers tried:* S. Perrin and C. Spencer, "The Asch Effect—a Child of Its Time," *Bulletin of the British Psychological Society* 33 (1980): 405–6. A similar thing happened in 2009 when a psychologist tried to replicate the Milgram study: J. M. Burger, "Replicating Milgram: Would People Still Obey Today?" *American Psychologist* 64 (2009): 1–11; and J. M. Twenge, "Change over Time in Obedience: The Jury's Still Out, but It Might Be Decreasing," *American Psychologist* 64 (2009): 28–31.

28 *In 1924, a group of sociologists:* Anne Remley, "From Obedience to Independence," *Psychology Today*, October 1988.

28 *In* Growing Up Digital, *an 11-year-old girl says:* Don Tapscott, *Growing Up Digital* (New York: McGraw-Hill, 1998), 195.

29 *Sure enough, the parents of* GenMe'ers*:* J. M. Twenge, E. M. Abebe, and W. K. Campbell, "Fitting In or Standing Out: Trends in American Parents' Choices for Children's Names, 1880–2007," *Social Psychological and Personality Science* 1 (2010): 19–25.

29 *The boys' names that increased the most:* Social Security Administration, "Change in Popularity from 2011 to 2012," http://www.ssa.gov/OACT/babynames/rankchange.html; and "King, Messiah, Major Fastest-Growing Baby Names," Associated Press, May 10, 2013.

31 *only 2% of GenMe has served:* http://www.pewsocialtrends.org/files/2010/10/millennials-confident-connected-open-to-change.pdf.

31 *Polls of 16-to-24-year-olds conducted:* For example: http://jamrs.defense.gov/Portals/20/Documents/Youth_Poll_20.pdf.

31 *2 out of 3 (67%) said they "definitely won't":* See http://www.monitoringthefuture.org/ or http://www.icpsr.umich.edu/icpsrweb/NAHDAP/series/35/studies. Monitoring the Future datafiles compiled and analyzed by the author.

31 *recent analysis of data:* J. M. Twenge, W. K. Campbell, and N. T. Carter, "Declines in Trust in Others and Confidence in Institutions among American Adults and Late Adolescents, 1972–2012 (unpublished manuscript, 2014).

32 *"Society has gotten increasingly callous":* Sonja Steptoe, "Minding Their Manners," *Time*, June 7, 2004.

32 *the story of a company founder:* Claire Raines, *Beyond Generation X: A Practical Guide for Managers* (Menlo Park, CA: Crisp Publications, 1997), 40.
32 *A recent article related numerous stories:* P. Davidson, "Managers to Millennials: Job Interview No Time to Text," *USA Today*, April 29, 2013, http://www.usatoday.com/story/money/business/2013/04/28/college-grads-job-interviews/2113505/.
32 *Jaime Fall, vice president:* Ibid.
32 *"Life has gotten more casual":* Ibid.
32 *Business professor John Trinkaus finds:* J. Trinkaus, "Compliance with a School Zone Speed Limit: Another Look," *Perceptual and Motor Skills* 87 (1998): 673–74.
32 *fewer observe the item limit:* J. Trinkaus, "Compliance with the Item Limit of the Food Supermarket Express Checkout Lane: Another Look," *Psychological Reports* 91 (2002): 1057–58.
32 *More people cut across parking lots:* J. Trinkaus, "Cutting Corners: An Informal Look," *Perceptual and Motor Skills* 79 (1994): 1089–90.
33 *In 1979, 29% of people failed:* J. Trinkaus, "Stop Sign Compliance: A Final Look," *Perceptual and Motor Skills* 85 (1997): 217–18.
33 *number of people who paid the suggested fee:* J. Trinkaus, "Honesty When Lighting Votive Candles in Church: An Informal Look," *Psychological Reports* 94 (2004): 1435–36.
33 *A 2008 study found that 95%:* Joan Oleck, "Most High School Students Admit to Cheating," *School Library Journal*, March 10, 2008.
33 *34% of high school students admitted to cheating:* U. Bronfenbrenner et al. *The State of Americans: This Generation and the Next* (New York: Free Press, 1996), 4.
33 *which rose to 61% in 1992:* Josephson Institute Center for Youth Ethics, "2012 Report Card on the Ethics of American Youth"; M. Josephson, "The Hole in the Moral Ozone: Ethical Values, Attitudes, and Behaviors in American Schools," ESTD, 1992, issue 19–20.
33 *a 2002 survey found that 80%:* J. D. Heyman, "Psssst . . . What's the Answer?" *People*, January 24, 2005.
33 *a 2012 study of 25,000 high school students:* Josephson Institute Center, "2012 Report Card."
33 *McCabe has found this attitude:* D. L. McCabe, "Are Business Schools to Blame?," *Harvard Business Review* 87, no. 6 (2009): 107.
35 *Education professor Maureen Stout tells:* Maureen Stout, *The Feel-Good Curriculum* (Cambridge, MA: Perseus Books, 2000), 93.
35 *they seemed uncomfortable:* Peter Sacks, *Generation X Goes to College* (Chicago: Open Court Press, 1996), 84.
36 *In a recent survey of college faculty, 61%:* C. Lampman, A. Phelps, S. Bancroft, and M. Beneke, "Contrapower Harassment in Academia: A Survey of Faculty Experience with Student Incivility, Bullying, and Sexual Attention," *Sex Roles* 60 (2009): 331–46.
36 *In her first class, she always announced:* Sacks, *Generation X Goes to College*, 89.
37 *As a famous* New Yorker *cartoon:* Peter Steiner, *New Yorker*, June 5, 1993, 61.
37 *"Parents are no longer eager":* Debra Pickett, and Janet Rausa Fuller, "Teens Shifting Balance of Power," *Chicago Sun-Times*, April 27, 2003.

37 *Chicago-area parent Richard Shields:* Debra Pickett, "One Reason Roles Are Changing: Dad's Desire to Be Son's Friend," *Chicago Sun-Times*, April 27, 2003.

38 A Chicago Sun-Times *article interviewed:* Pickett and Fuller, "Teens Shifting Balance of Power."

38 *One family's two daughters convinced:* Debra Pickett, "Girls Decided When Family Needed a Second Car," *Chicago Sun-Times*, April 27, 2003.

38 *In 1957, 80% of people said:* Susan Mitchell, *The Official Guide to the Generations* (Ithaca, NY: New Strategist Publications, 1995), 92.

38 *in 2012, 41% of babies: Statistical Abstract of the United States*, 2012, http://www.cdc.gov/nchs/fastats/unmarry.htm; http://cnsnews.com/news/article/terence-p-jeffrey/cdc-us-fertility-rate-hits-record-low-2nd-straight-year-407-babies; and J. A. Martin, B. E. Hamilton, M. J. K. Osterman, S. C. Curtin, and T. J. Mathews, "Births: Final Data for 2012," *National Vital Statistics Reports* 62, no. 9 (December 30, 2013), http://www.cdc.gov/nchs/data/nvsr/nvsr62/nvsr62_09.pdf.

39 *39% of cohabitating couples break up*: "Knot Yet: The Benefits and Costs of Delayed Marriage in America," National Campaign to Prevent Teen and Unplanned Pregnancy, National Marriage Project, University of Virginia. For example, see Ezra Klein, "Nine Facts about Marriage and Childbirth in the United States, WashingtonPost.com, *Wonkblog*, March 25, 2013, http://www.washingtonpost.com/blogs/wonkblog/wp/2013/03/25/nine-facts-about-marriage-and-childbirth-in-the-united-states/.

39 *accounting for more than 1 in 7: Statistical Abstract of the United States*, 2012.

39 *the last antimiscegenation law*: http://en.wikipedia.org/wiki/Miscegenation.

39 *Almost half of Asian women:* Michael Lind, "The Beige and the Black," *New York Times Magazine*, August 16, 1998.

39 *In 2012, 86% of Americans:* Pew Research Center for the People and the Press, "Section 8: Values about Immigration and Race," June 4, 2012, http://www.people-press.org/2012/06/04/section-8-values-about-immigration-and-race/.

40 *only 10% of white young people*: Jeffrey Jensen Arnett, *Emerging Adulthood* (New York: Oxford University Press, 2004), 84.

40 *In the mid-1960s,* Brides *magazine:* Carol McD. Wallace, *All Dressed in White* (New York: Penguin, 2004), 213.

42 *Wedding gown designer Reem Acra:* Ibid., 265.

42 *In* Millennials Rising, *Neil Howe and William Strauss predicted:* Neil Howe and William Strauss, *Millennials Rising* (New York: Vintage, 2000), 234–37.

42 *my coauthors and I examined six:* J. M. Twenge, J. J. Exline, J. B. Grubbs, and R. Sastry, "Generational Differences in American Adolescents' Religious Orientation, 1966–2013," *Journal of Research on Adolescence* (forthcoming).

42 *These massive datasets, with respondents aged 13 to 98:* J. M. Twenge, J. J. Exline, J. B. Grubbs, and N. T. Carter, "Birth Cohort, Time Period, and Age Differences in Religious Affiliation, Religious Belief, and Religious Entitlement" (unpublished manuscript, 2014).

43 *In* Soul Searching, *his extensive survey of teens:* C. Smith and M. L. Denton, *Soul Searching: The Religious and Spiritual Lives of American Teenagers* (Oxford: Oxford University Press, 2005).

43 *In 2012, 30% of Americans:* Kosmin et al., *American Nones.*
43 *Among high school seniors, most of whom:* Twenge et al., "Generational Differences in American Adolescents' Religious Orientation, 1966–2013."
44 *"Starting in middle school we got":* http://www.npr.org/2013/01/15/169342349/more-young-people-are-moving-away-from-religion-but-why.
44 *in 2013, Pope Francis said:* http://www.uscatholic.org/blog/201309/are-abortion-and-gay-marriage-only-issues-catholics-not-according-pope-francis-27843.
45 *The percentage of college students who:* Twenge et al., "Generational Differences in American Adolescents' Religious Orientation, 1966–2013."
45 *Christian Smith labels:* Smith and Denton, *Soul Searching.*
46 *In* Emerging Adulthood, *Jeffrey Arnett:* Arnett, *Emerging Adulthood*, 172.
46 *Many don't adhere to:* Ibid.
46 *in a 2013 poll:* http://www.nytimes.com/2013/03/06/us/poll-shows-disconnect-between-us-catholics-and-church.html.
46 *Interviewed in* Emerging Adulthood, *Dana:* Arnett, *Emerging Adulthood*, 172–74.
47 *Rick Warren, author:* Rick Warren, "Learn to Love Yourself!," *Ladies' Home Journal*, March 2005.
47 *Groups such as the Elks:* Robert Putnam, *Bowling Alone* (New York: Simon & Schuster, 2000).
47 *In 1976, 36% of high school seniors:* J. M. Twenge, W. K. Campbell, and E. C. Freeman,. "Generational Differences in Young Adults' Life Goals, Concern for Others, and Civic Orientation, 1966–2009," *Journal of Personality and Social Psychology* 102 (2012): 1045–62.
47 *In 1976, 46% of high school students:* Twenge, Campbell, and Carter, "Declines in trust."
49 *In a mid-2000s survey of men, 62%:* Michele Orecklin, "Stress and the Superdad," *Time*, August 23, 2004.
49 *In an episode of the teen show: Dawson's Creek*, Episode 510: "Appetite for Destruction" airdate December 19, 2001.
51 *"When I'm alone, I do masturbate a lot":* Maureen O'Connor, "James Franco Is a Chronic Masturbator," Gawker.com, September 7, 2010.
51 *"We have sex like Kenyan marathon runners":* "Olivia Wilde: Jason Sudeikis and I Have 'Sex Like Kenyan Marathon Runners,'" *US Weekly*, October 9, 2012.
51 A *survey by babycenter.com:* http://www.babycenter.com/0_birth-in-america-survey-1-000-women-tell-it-like-it-is_10338347.bc#articlesection7.
51 *A recent survey found that 28%:* J. R. Temple, J. A. Paul, P. vanden Burg, V. D. Le, A. McElhany, and B. W. Temple, "Teen Sexting and Its Association with Sexual Behaviors," *Archives of Pediatric and Adolescent Medicine* 166 (2012): 828–33.
51 *In one episode of the teen soap: The* O.C., episode "The Distance," airdate November 4, 2004.
53 *When psychologist Bella DePaulo:* B. DePaulo, "People Posting Vile, Hateful Comments: What's That About?," *Psychology Today* blog, December 29, 2009, http://www.psychologytoday.com/blog/living-single/200912/people-posting-vile-hateful-comments-what-s-about.
54 *The Google Books database proves the point:* Google Books Ngram Viewer, American English corpus.

54 *In December 2013, the movie* The Wolf of Wall Street: F. Wickman, "Is *Wolf of Wall Street* Really the Sweariest Movie of All Time? A *Slate* Investigation," Slate.com, January 7, 2014, http://www.slate.com/blogs/browbeat/2014/01/07/wolf_of_wall_street_sets_f_word_record_we_counted_every_last_f_bomb_in_the.html.

55 *The scale measures a person's need:* D. P. Crowne and D. Marlowe, *The Approval Motive* (New York: Wiley, 1964), 39.

55 *follow "conventional, even stereotyped":* Ibid., 85.

55 *My student Charles Im and I:* J. M. Twenge and C. Im, "Changes in the Need for Social Approval, 1958–2001," *Journal of Research in Personality* 41 (2007): 171–89.

55 *Similar results appeared on two other measures:* J. M. Twenge, B. Gentile, C. N. DeWall, D. S. Ma, K. Lacefield, and D. R. Schurtz, "Birth Cohort Increases in Psychopathology among Young Americans, 1938–2007: A Cross-Temporal Meta-analysis of the MMPI," *Clinical Psychology Review* 30 (2010): 145–54.

55 *Children ages 9 to 12 showed:* Twenge and Im, "Changes in the Need for Social Approval," 171–89.

56 *Take the line yippie radical:* Jerry Rubin, *Growing (Up) at Thirty-Seven* (New York: Lippincott, 1976), 117.

2. An Army of One: *Me*

PAGE

58 O Magazine *published "Why Women Have Low Self-Esteem":* Aimee Lee Ball, "Why Women Have Low Self-Esteem: Women and the Negativity Receptor," *O Magazine*, August 2008, http://www.oprah.com/omagazine/Why-Women-Have-Low-Self-Esteem-How-to-Feel-More-Confident.

58 *while* Parenting *offered:* Yanick Rice Lamb, "Proud to Be Me!," *Parenting*, April 2005.

58 *October 2011 saw the premier issue*: http://www.byoumagazine.com/.

58 *the American Academy of Pediatrics guide:* Steven Shelov, ed., *Caring for Your Baby and Young Child: Birth to Age 5* (New York: Bantam, 1998).

60 *In a 1976* New York *magazine article:* Tom Wolfe, "The Me Decade and the Third Great Awakening," *New York*, August 23, 1976.

60 *When asked what's next in her life:* "Pop Quiz: Kim Basinger," *People*, September 27, 2004.

61 *In answer to the same question:* Jeanne Marie Laskas, "Sarah's New Day," *Ladies' Home Journal*, June 2004.

61 *Gillon describes Boomers:* Steve Gillon, *Boomer Nation* (New York: Free Press 2004), 263.

61 *Even food becomes:* David Brooks, *Bobos in Paradise* (New York: Simon & Schuster, 2000), 58.

61 *In 1967, a whopping 86%:* J. M. Twenge, W. K. Campbell, and E. C. Freeman, "Generational Differences in Young Adults' Life Goals, Concern for Others, and Civic Orientation, 1966–2009," *Journal of Personality and Social Psychology* 102 (2012): 1045–62.J.

62 *"Instead of seeking":* Jerry Rubin, *Growing (Up) at Thirty-Seven* (New York: Lippincott, 1976), 175.

62 *Aleta St. James, a 57-year-old woman:* Jonathan Schienberg, "New Age Mystic to Become Mom at 57," cnn.com. November 9, 2004.

64 *In* Conquering Your Quarterlife Crisis*:* Alexandra Robbins, *Conquering Your Quarterlife Crisis* (New York: Perigee, 2004), 51–52.

64 *Even a brief frolic through the Google Books database:* Google Books Ngram Viewer, American English corpus; J. M. Twenge, W. K. Campbell, and B. Gentile, "Increases in Individualistic Words and Phrases in American Books, 1960–2008," *PLoS ONE* 7 (2012): e40181.

65 *Dr. Phil, the ultimate in plainspoken: Today*, NBC, December 27, 2004.

66 *Psychologist Martin Seligman says:* M. E. P. Seligman, "Boomer Blues," *Psychology Today*, October 1988, 50–53.

67 *In 2013, the* Oxford English Dictionary's*:* T. Barrineau, "'Selfie' Named Word of the Year for 2013: We Like Taking Pictures of Ourselves, and It Shows," *USA Today*, December 5, 2013, http://www.usatoday.com/story/life/people/2013/11/18/selfie-named-word-of-the-year-2013/3634727/.

67 *Even the pronouns we use have changed:* J. M. Twenge, W. K. Campbell, and B. Gentile, "Changes in Pronoun Use in American Books and the Rise of Individualism, 1960–2008," *Journal of Cross-Cultural Psychology* 44 (2013): 406–15.

67 *In an initial study, W. Keith Campbell and I examined:* J. M. Twenge and W. K. Campbell, "Age and Birth Cohort Differences in Self-Esteem: A Cross-Temporal Meta-analysis," *Personality and Social Psychology Review* 5 (2001): 321–44.

68 *For her master's thesis with me, Brittany Gentile:* B. Gentile, J. M. Twenge, and W. K. Campbell, "Birth Cohort Differences in Self-Esteem, 1988–2008: A Cross-Temporal Meta-analysis," *Review of General Psychology* 14 (2010): 261–68.

68 *GenMe high school students anticipate:* J. M. Twenge and W. K. Campbell, "Increases in Positive Self-Views among High School Students: Birth Cohort Changes in Anticipated Performance, Self-Satisfaction, Self-Liking, and Self-Competence," *Psychological Science* 19 (2008): 1082–86; and updates from the Monitoring the Future datafiles.

68 *When asked to compare themselves:* J. M. Twenge, W. K. Campbell, and B. Gentile, "Generational Increases in Agentic Self-Evaluations among American College Students, 1966–2009," *Self and Identity* 11 (2012): 409–27; and updates from the American Freshman Survey reports.

69 *We examined the responses:* Twenge and Campbell, "Age and Birth Cohort Differences in Self-Esteem."

69 *In a later analysis of the self-esteem scores:* Gentile, Twenge, and Campbell, "Birth Cohort Differences in Self-Esteem, 1988–2008."

70 *Research on programs to boost:* Twenge and Campbell, "Age and Birth Cohort Differences in Self-Esteem.".

70 *Journal articles on self-esteem:* John Hewitt, *The Myth of Self-Esteem* (New York: St. Martin's Press, 1998), 51.

71 *One children's book:* Diane Loomans, *The Lovables in the Kingdom of Self-Esteem* (New York: H. J. Kramer, 1991).

72 *One program is called:* Maureen Stout, *The Feel-Good Curriculum* (Cambridge, MA: Perseus Books, 2000), 131.

72 *Another program, called "Pumsy in Pursuit of Excellence":* "Teaching Self-Image Stirs Furor," *New York Times*, October 13, 1993.

72 *The Magic Circle exercise:* http://www.globalideasbank.org/site/bank/idea.php?ideaId=573; and M. L. Summerlin, V. L. Hammett,; and M. L. Payne, "The Effect of Magic Circle Participation on a Child's Self-Concept," *School Counselor* 31 (1983): 49–52.
72 *One Austin, Texas, father:* William Swann, *Self-Traps: The Elusive Quest for Higher Self-Esteem* (New York: W. H. Freeman, 1996), 4.
74 *When self-esteem programs:* Hewitt, *Myth of Self-Esteem*, 84–85.
74 *In one program, teachers:* Lauren Murphy Payne and Claudia Rolhing, *A Leader's Guide to Just Because I Am: A Child's Book of Affirmation* (Minneapolis: Free Spirit Publishing, 1994); and Hewitt, *Myth of Self-Esteem.*
75 *children are asked to finish:* Hewitt, *Myth of Self-Esteem*, 79.
75 *A sign on the wall:* Rita Kramer, *Ed School Follies: The Miseducation of America's Teachers* (New York: Free Press, 1991), 33.
75 *Perhaps as a result, 60% of teachers:* C. G. Scott, "Student Self-Esteem and the School System: Perceptions and Implications," *Journal of Educational Research* 89 (1996): 292–97.
75 *A veteran second-grade teacher:* Nancy Gibbs, "Parents Behaving Badly," *Time*, February 21, 2005.
75 *For example, the popular Christian:* Max Lucado, *You Are Special* (Wheaton, IL: Crossway Books, 1997).
76 *In an article in* Ladies' Home Journal, *Christian author:* Rick Warren, "Learn to Love Yourself!," *Ladies' Home Journal*, March 2005.
76 *Children in some schools:* Lynn Sherr, "Me, Myself and I—the Growing Self-Esteem Movement," *20/20*, ABC, March 11, 1994.
76 *Other students pen:* Ibid.
76 *The children's museum in Laramie:* Sherr. "Me, Myself and I.".
77 *In a CBS News poll:* CBS News, *The Class of 2000* (New York: Simon & Schuster, 2001), ebook, 64.
78 *The 1997 premier episode: Daria*, episode "Esteemsters," MTV, March 3, 1997.
78 *Hewitt, who teaches:* Hewitt, *Myth of Self-Esteem*, 1–3.
79 *In 2002, the Girl Scout Council:* www.girlscouts.org/program/program_opportunities/leadership/uniquelyme.asp.
79 *In 1999, a carefully researched:* K. C. Kling et al., "Gender Differences in Self-Esteem: A Meta-analysis," *Psychological Bulletin* 125 (1999): 470–500.
80 *"We may create":* www.news.wisc.edu/wire/i072899/selfesteem.html.
80 *When Keith Campbell and I did:* Twenge and Campbell, "Age and Birth Cohort Differences in Self-Esteem."
81 *One popular method tells:* Sandra Wilde, "A Proposal for a New Spelling Curriculum," *Elementary School Journal* 90 (1989): 275–89.
81 *Teacher-education courses emphasize:* Kramer, *Ed School Follies*, 116.
81 *A British teacher proposed:* "Teachers Say No One Should 'Fail,'" BBC News, July 20, 2005. See news.bbc.co.uk/1/hi/education/4697461.stm.
81 *Only 19% of high school graduates boasted:* Twenge and Campbell, "Increases in Positive Self-Views"; Twenge, Campbell, and Gentile, "Generational Increases in Agentic Self-Evaluations"; and updates from the Monitoring the Future datafiles and American Freshman Survey datafiles.
81 *"Each year we think":* Steve Giegerich, "College Freshmen Have Worst Study

Habits in Years but Less Likely to Drink, Study Finds," Associated Press, January 27, 2003, www.detnews.com/2003/schools/0301/27/schools-70002.htm.

81 *"Teachers want to raise"*: Carol Innerst, "Wordsmiths on Wane among US Students," *Washington Times*, August 25, 1994.

83 *As education professor Maureen Stout notes*: Stout, *Feel-Good Curriculum*, 3–4.

83 *in 2013, 38% of college freshmen*: American Freshman Survey datafiles.

84 *research shows that when people*: T. F. Heatherton and K. D. Vohs, "Interpersonal Evaluations Following Threats to Self: Role of Self-Esteem," *Journal of Personality and Social Psychology* 78 (2000): 725–36.

85 *Lippman quotes an e-mail*: S. Lippman, R. E. Bulanda, and T. C. Wagenaar, "Student Entitlement: Issues and Strategies for Confronting Entitlement in the Classroom and Beyond," *College Teaching* 57, no. 4 (2009): 197–204.

85 *in a 2008 survey, 66%*: E. Greenburger, J. Lessard, C. Chen, and S. P. Farruggia, "Self-Entitled College Students: Contributions of Personality, Parenting, and Motivational Factors," *Journal of Youth and Adolescence* 37 (2008): 1193–1204.

85 *Students "look and act like"*: Hewitt, *Myth of Self-Esteem*, 84.

86 A USA Today *article concluded*: Cindy Perman, "Are Millennials Really the 'Me' Generation?," *USA Today*, August 24, 2013, http://www.usatoday.com/story/money/business/2013/08/24/millenials-time-magazine-generation-y/2678441/.

86 *There is a small correlation*: R. F. Baumeister et al., "Does High Self-Esteem Cause Better Performance, Interpersonal Success, Happiness, or Healthier Lifestyles?," *Psychological Science in the Public Interest* 4 (2003): 1–44; and M. V. Covington, "Self-Esteem and Failure in School," in *The Social Importance of Self-Esteem*, *ed.* A. M. Mecca, N. J. Smelser, and J. Vasconcellos (Berkeley: University of California Press, 1989), 79.

86 *Which ethnic group in the United States*: J. M. Twenge and J. Crocker , "Race and Self-Esteem: Meta-analyses Comparing Whites, Blacks, Hispanics, Asians, and American Indians and Comment on Gray-Little and Hafdahl (2000)," *Psychological Bulletin* 128 (2002): 371–408.

87 *Narcissists are not any more successful*: For a review, see J. M. Twenge and W. K. Campbell, *The Narcissism Epidemic: Living in the Age of Entitlement* (New York: Atria Books, 2009).

87 *Several comprehensive reviews*: Ibid.

87 *Even the book sponsored*: N. J. Smelser, "Self-Esteem and Social Problems," in *Social Importance of Self-Esteem*, *ed.* Mecca, Smelser, and Vasconcellos.

87 *However, Kyung Hee Kim of the College of William*: K. H. Kim, "The Creativity Crisis: The Decrease in Creative Thinking Scores on the Torrance Tests of Creative Thinking," *Creativity Research Journal* 23 (2011): 285–95.

88 *Psychologist Martin Seligman has criticized*: Martin Seligman, *The Optimistic Child* (New York: Harper Perennial, 1996).

88 *"It is very questionable"*: Roy Baumeister,. "The Lowdown on High Self-Esteem: Thinking You're Hot Stuff Isn't the Promised Cure-All," *Los Angeles Times*, January 25, 2005.

88 *"What the self-esteem movement"*: Stout, *Feel-Good Curriculum*, 263.

89 *As psychologist Jennifer Crocker documents*: J. Crocker and L. E. Park, "The Costly Pursuit of Self-Esteem," *Psychological Bulletin* 130 (2004): 392–414.

89 *Don Forsyth and his colleagues decided:* D. R. Forsyth, N. K. Lawrence, J. L. Burnette, and R. F. Baumeister, "Attempting to Improve the Academic Performance of Struggling College Students by Bolstering Their Self-Esteem: An Intervention That Backfired," *Journal of Social and Clinical Psychology* 26 (2007): 447–59.

90 *When Asian students find out:* S. J. Heine et al.. "Divergent Consequences of Success and Failure in Japan and North America: An Investigation of Self-Improving Motivations and Malleable Selves," *Journal of Personality and Social Psychology* 81 (2001): 599–615.

91 *"There is no self-esteem movement":* Robert Shaw, *The Epidemic* (New York: Regan Books, 2003), 152.

92 *are so focused on themselves:* W. Keith Campbell, *When You Love a Man Who Loves Himself* (Chicago: Source Books, 2005). *For a review, see* Twenge and Campbell, *Narcissism Epidemic.*

92 *Narcissists are also more likely:* V. S. Helgeson and H. L. Fritz, "Unmitigated Agency and Unmitigated Communion: Distinctions from Agency and Communion," *Journal of Research in Personality* 33 (1999): 131–58.

92 *In the early 1950s, only 12% of teens:* C. R. Newsom et al., "Changes in Adolescent Response Patterns on the MMPI/MMPI-A across Four Decades," *Journal of Personality Assessment* 81 (2003): 74–84.

92 *Narcissistic personality is usually measured with:* M. Tamborski and R. P. Brown, "The Measurement of Trait Narcissism in Social-Personality Research," in *The Handbook of Narcissism and Narcissistic Personality Disorder*, ed. W. K. Campbell and J. D. Miller (New York: Wiley, 2011).

93 *My coauthors and I analyzed the responses:* J. M. Twenge and J. D. Foster, "Birth Cohort Increases in Narcissistic Personality Traits among American College Students, 1982–2009," *Social Psychological and Personality Science* 1 (2010): 99–106; and J. M. Twenge, S. Konrath, J. D. Foster, W. K. Campbell, and B. J. Bushman, "Egos Inflating over Time: A Cross-Temporal Meta-analysis of the Narcissistic Personality Inventory," *Journal of Personality* 76 (2008): 875–901.

93 *samples of 4,152 students from:* Twenge and Foster, "Birth Cohort Increases."

93 *and among students from Frostburg State University:* K. D. Stewart and P. C. Bernhardt, "Comparing Millennials to Pre-1987 Students and with One Another," *North American Journal of Psychology* 12 (2010): 579–602.

93 *A 2009 study found that Americans:* F. S. Stinson et al., "Prevalence, Correlates, Disability, and Comorbidity of DSM-IV Narcissistic Personality Disorder: Results from the Wave 2 National Epidemiologic Survey on Alcohol and Related Conditions," *Journal of Clinical Psychiatry* 69 (2008): 1033–45.

93 *a set of other researchers reported:* K. H. Trzesniewski, M. B. Donnellan, and R. W. Robins, "Do Today's Young People Really Think They Are So Extraordinary? An Examination of Secular Changes in Narcissism and Self-Enhancement," *Psychological Science* 19 (2008): 181–88.

94 *The yearly increase among these students:* J. M. Twenge and J. D. Foster, "Mapping the Scale of the Narcissism Epidemic: Increases in Narcissism 2002–2007 within Ethnic Groups," *Journal of Research in Personality* 42 (2008): 1619–22.

94 *Another paper by different authors:* B. W. Roberts, G. Edmonds, and E.

Grijalva, "It Is Developmental Me, Not Generation Me: Developmental Changes Are More Important Than Generational Changes in Narcissism," *Perspectives on Psychological Science* 5 (2010): 97–102.

94 *Josh and I published this analysis:* Twenge and Foster, "Birth Cohort Increases in Narcissistic Personality Traits."

94 *some—such as Elspeth Reeve in* Atlantic Wire *in May 2013:* Elspeth Reeve, "Every Every Every Generation Has Been the Me Me Me Generation," *Atlantic Wire*, May 9, 2013, http://www.thewire.com/national/2013/05/me-generation-time/65054/.

94 *Between 1976 and 2012, high school students:* Twenge, Campbell, and Freeman, "Generational Differences."

95 *In 2013, 82% of college students:* Ibid.; and updates based on the American Freshman datafiles.

95 *In the late 1970s, 22% of high school students:* Ibid.

96 *Nathan and his graduate student Richard Pond:* C. N. DeWall, R. S. Pond, W. K. Campbell, and J. M. Twenge, Tuning In to Psychological Change: Linguistic Markers of Psychological Traits and Emotions over Time in Popular US Song Lyrics," *Psychology of Aesthetics, Creativity, and the Arts* 5 (2011): *200–207*; and J. Tierney, "A Generation's Vanity, Heard through Lyrics," *New York Times*, April 25, 2011.

96 *Kanye West's 2013 declaration:* R. J. Cubarribia, "Kanye West: 'I'm the Number One Living and Breathing Rock Star.'" *Rolling Stone*, June 24, 2013.

97 *Lilian Katz, a professor:* Stout, *Feel-Good Curriculum*, 178.

97 *A scale that measures entitlement:* W. K. Campbell et al., "Psychological Entitlement: Interpersonal Consequences and Validation of a Self-Report Measure," *Journal of Personality Assessment* 83 (2004): 29–45.

98 *An Associated Press article printed:* Martha Irvine, "Young Labeled 'Entitlement Generation,'" AP, June 26, 2005, biz.yahoo.com/ap/050626/the_entitlement_gen eration.html2.v3. Also reprinted in many newspapers.

99 *Eric Harris, one of the Columbine:* Nancy Gibbs and Timothy Roche, "The Columbine Tapes," *Time*, December 20, 1999.

99 *Singer Lorde casually mentioned:* Julie Gerstein, "Teenage Fandom in the Age of Twitter: An Analysis of the Alarming Phenomenon," *StyleCaster*, December 23, 2013.

99 *High narcissism usually means:* Twenge, Campbell, and Freeman. "Generational Differences."

100 *"We are a socially conscious generation that cares":* Jenna Gourdreu, "Are Millennials 'Deluded Narcissists'?," *Forbes*, January 15, 2013, http://www.forbes.com/sites/jennagoudreau/2013/01/15/are-millennials-deluded-narcissists/.

100 *GenMe'ers were* less *concerned:* Twenge, Campbell, and Freeman, "Generational Differences in Life Goals."

100 *However, community service was increasingly:* M. Planty, R. Bozick, and M. Regnier, "Helping Because You Have to or Helping Because You Want to? Sustaining Participation in Service Work from Adolescence through Young Adulthood," *Youth & Society*, 38 (2006): 177–202.

101 *The closest we can get is to compare:* Twenge, Campbell, and Freeman, "Generational Differences in Life Goals."

101 *Psychologists Pelin and Selin Kesebir found:* P. Kesebir and S. Kesebir, "The Cultural Salience of Moral Character and Virtue Declined in Twentieth Century America," *Journal of Positive Psychology* 7 (2012): 471–80.

101 *UCLA psychologist Patricia Greenfield found:* P. M. Greenfield, "The Changing Psychology of Culture from 1800 through 2000," *Psychological Science* 24 (2013): 1722–31.

101 *Among the 18-to-23-year-olds interviewed:* C. Smith, K. Christoffersen, H. Davison, and P. S. Herzog, *Lost in Transition: The Dark Side of Emerging Adulthood* (New York: Oxford University Press. 2011).

102 *The good news is that 72%:* Twenge, Campbell, and Freeman, "Generational Differences in Life Goals"; and updates from American Freshman datafiles.

102 *high school students expressed more concern:* Park, Twenge, and Greenfield, "Great Recession."

102 *Sara Konrath and her colleagues used:* S. H. Konrath, E. H. O'Brien, C. Hsing, "Changes in Dispositional Empathy in American College Students over Time: A Meta-analysis," *Personality and Social Psychology Review* 15 (2011): 180–98.

102 *Lori Malahy and her colleagues examined:* L. W. Malahy, M. A. Rubinlicht, and C. R. Kaiser, "Justifying Inequality: A Cross-Temporal Investigation of US Income Disparities and Just-World Beliefs from 1973 to 2006," *Social Justice Research* 22 (2009): 369–83.

103 *Dharun Ravi thought it would be fun:* Collected from various accounts of the incident, including Christina Boyle, "Dharun Ravi Texted Apology to Rutgers Roommate Tyler Clementi Night of His Suicide," *New York Daily News*, March 8, 2012, http://www.nydailynews.com/new-york/dharun-ravi-texted-apology-rutgers-roommate-tyler-clementi-night-suicide-article-1.1035376.

104 *At least five studies have found:* For example, L. E. Buffardi and W. K. Campbell, "Narcissism and Social Networking Web Sites." *Personality and Social Psychology Bulletin* 34 (2008): 1303–14; C. J. Carpenter, "Narcissism on Facebook: Self-Promotional and Anti-social Behavior," *Personality and Individual Differences* 52, no. 4 (2012): 482, doi:10.1016/j.paid.2011.11.011; and B. Gentile, J. M. Twenge, E. C. Freeman, and W. K. Campbell, "The Effect of Social Networking Websites on Positive Self-Views: An Experimental Investigation," *Computers in Human Behavior* 28 (2012): 1929–33.

104 *Larry Rosen and his colleagues found:* L. D. Rosen, K. Whaling, S. Rab, L. M. Carrier, and N. A. Cheever, "Is Facebook Creating 'iDisorders'? The Link between Clinical Symptoms of Psychiatric Disorders and Technology Use, Attitudes and Anxiety," *Computers in Human Behavior* 29 (2013): 1243–54.

104 *My colleagues and I designed:* Gentile, Twenge, Freeman, and Campbell, "Effect of Social Networking Websites."

105 *I reviewed the research literature:* J. M. Twenge, "Does Online Social Media Lead to Social Connection or Social Disconnection?," *Journal of College and Character* 14 (2013): 11–20.

105 *For example, one study had students ask:* M. A. Stefanone, K. H. Kwon, and D. Lackaff, "Exploring the Relationship between Perceptions of Social Capital and Enacted Support Online," *Journal of Computer-Mediated Communication* 17 (2012): 451–66.

106 *Another study examined whether:* N. Park, K. F. Kee, and S. Valenzuela, "Being Immersed in Social Networking Environment: Facebook Groups, Uses and Gratifications, and Social Outcomes," *Cyberpsychology and Behavior* 12 (2009): 729–33.

106 A *third study, conducted:* J. Vitak, P. Zube, A. Smock, C. T. Carr, N. Ellison, and C. Lampe, "It's Complicated: Facebook Users' Political Participation in the 2008 Election," *Cyberpsychology, Behavior, and Social Networking* 14 (2011): 107–14.

3. You Can Be Anything You Want to Be

PAGE

107 *"proving," as Luke Epplin observes:* Luke Epplin, "You Can Do *Anything*: Must Every Kids' Movie Reinforce the Cult of Self-Esteem?," *Atlantic*, August 13, 2013.

107 *Chris Colin notes that his classmates:* Chris Colin, *What Really Happened to the Class of '93* (New York: Broadway Books, 2004), 51.

108 *Alexandra Robbins and:* Alexandra Robbins and Abby Wilner, *Quarterlife Crisis: The Unique Challenges of Life in Your Twenties* (New York: Putnam, 2001), 109.

108 *Lia Macko, the coauthor:* Lia Macko and Kerry Rubin, *Mildlife Crisis at 30: How the Stakes Have Changed for a New Generation—and What to Do About It* (New York: Plume Penguin, 2004), v, 16.

108 *As Epplin observes of the kids' movie characters:* Epplin, "You Can Do *Anything.*"

109 *In 2012, 58% of high school students:* J. Reynolds, M. Stewart, R. MacDonald, and L. Sischo, "Have Adolescents Become Too Ambitious? High School Seniors' Educational and Occupational Plans, 1976 to 2000," *Social Problems* 53 (2006): 186–206; and updated with Monitoring the Future datafiles.

110 *In* The Ambitious Generation, *sociologists:* Barbara Schneider and David Stevenson, *The Ambitious Generation: America's Teenagers, Motivated but Directionless* (New Haven: Yale University Press, 1999).

110 *In 2012, 3 out of 4 American college freshmen:* American Freshman Survey datafiles.

110 *the number of PhDs granted each year: Statistical Abstract of the United States*, 2012 and earlier years. Available online at www.census.gov/prod/www/abs/statab.html.

110 A Chronicle of Higher Education *study found:* http://collegecompletion.chronicle.com/.

111 *In a 2011 survey, 16-to-18-year-olds:* "2011 Teens & Money Survey," Charles Schwab, http://www.aboutschwab.com/images/press/teensmoneyfactsheet.pdf.

111 *Fifty-seven percent of high school seniors:* J. M. Twenge and T. Kasser, "Generational Changes in Materialism and Work Centrality, 1976–2007: Associations with Temporal Changes in Societal Insecurity and Materialistic Role-Modeling," *Personality and Social Psychology Bulletin* 39 (2013): 883–97; and Monitoring the Future datafiles.

111 *In the 2011 survey, 59% believed:* "2011 Teens & Money Survey," Charles Schwab.

112 *One young employee told:* Claire Raines and Jim Hunt, *The Xers and the Boomers* (Menlo Park, CA: Crisp Publications, 2000), 25.
114 *Emily, 22, says that if:* Robbins and Wilner, *Quarterlife Crisis*, 83.
114 *Quarterlife Crisis does discuss:* Ibid., 76.
115 *Jeffrey Arnett, author:* Ibid.
116 *"In the past, people got married":* Lev Grossman, "Grow Up? Not So Fast," *Time*, January 24, 2005.
116 GenMe *marries later: Statistical Abstract of the United States*, 2004 and earlier years, www.census.gov/prod/www/abs/statab.html.
116 *Only 20% of today's adults ages 18 to 29:* Paul Taylor, *The Next America: Boomers, Millennials, and the Looming Generational Showdown* (New York: Public Affairs, 2014).
116 *"I want to get married":* Grossman, "Grow Up?"
116 *A recent study found:* W. Bleidorn, T. Klimstra, J. Denissen, P. Rentfrow, J. Potter, and S. Gosling, "Personality Maturation around the World—a Cross-Cultural Examination of Social Investment Theory (unpublished manuscript, 2013).
117 *Arnett describes Albert:* Jeffrey Jensen Arnett, *Emerging Adulthood* (New York: Oxford University Press, 2004), 158.
117 *Adrianne, 16, dreamed:* Bob Meadows, "This Teen Wanted to Be Popular. Did That Lead to Her Murder?," *People*, February 14, 2005.
118 *"My big goal is to have":* Bill Hewitt, "Wearing Out Their Bodies?," *People*, June 13, 2005.
118 *Former Hollywood producer Elisabeth Robinson:* Elisabeth Robinson, *The True and Outstanding Adventures of the Hunt Sisters* (New York: Back Bay Books, 2004), 19.
119 *Cowell chided him: American Idol*, FOX, January 27, 2004.
119 *In a later interview with* Star *magazine:* Jennifer Birn, Joyce Hogan, and Maggie Kim, "Introducing William Hung: Untrained, Uncensored, Unstoppable!," *Star*, March 1, 2004; and www.williamhung.net/wst_page16.html.
120 *TV critic James Poniewozik noted:* James Poniewozik, "Simon Cowell: Picking Our Winners," *Time*, April 26, 2004.
120 *"It's mind-boggling how":* Molly Lopez, "Chatter: False Idols," *People*, February 14, 2005.
121 *In a 2007 survey, 51%: Sharon Jayson, "The Goal: Wealth and Fame," USA Today, January 10, 2007.*
121 *Use of the phrase* want to be famous: Google Books database, American English corpus.
121 *When musician Nellie McKay was 19:* "'I'm Going to Be Famous': Nellie McKay Makes Bid for Stardom," cnn.com, April 13, 2004.
122 *"Ten years after leaving high school":* Colin, *What Really Happened*, 55.
123 *as author Carol Wallace points out:* Carol McD. Wallace, *All Dressed in White* (New York: Penguin 2004), 278.
123 *One bride said, "Finally":* Ibid., 280.
123 *As part of my dissertation:* J. M. Twenge, "Birth Cohort Changes in Extraversion: A Cross-Temporal Meta-analysis, 1966–1993," *Personality and Individual Differences* 30 (2001): 735–48.
123 *My former student Brittany Gentile found:* B. Gentile, "Birth Cohort Changes in the Big Five Personality Traits, 1985–2012" (unpublished manuscript, 2013).

126 *The popular school program:* Charles J. Sykes, *Dumbing Down Our Kids* (New York: St. Martin's Press, 1995), 42.
126 *The growing primacy:* J. M. Twenge, "Changes in Masculine and Feminine Traits over Time: A Meta-analysis," *Sex Roles* 36 (1997): 305–25; and J. M. Twenge, "Changes in Women's Assertiveness in Response to Status and Roles: A Cross-Temporal Meta-analysis, 1931–1993," *Journal of Personality and Social Psychology* 81 (2001): 133–45.
126 *In the study of college students' beliefs:* J. M. Twenge, W. K. Campbell, and B. Gentile, "Generational Increases in Agentic Self-Evaluations among American College Students, 1966–2009," *Self and Identity* 11 (2012), 409–27.
127 *Yet, as* The Mommy Myth: Susan Douglas and Meredith Michaels, *The Mommy Myth* (New York: Free Press, 2004), 306–7.
127 *Douglas and Michaels refer:* Ibid.
127 Culture Shock! USA, *a guidebook:* Esther Wanning, *Culture Shock! USA* (London: Kuperard, 1995), 70.
128 *One mother says she treated:* Anne Remley, "From Obedience to Independence," *Psychology Today*, October 1988, 56–59.
128 *Psychologist Bonnie Zucker, interviewed:* Thomas Fields-Meyer, "Kids Out of Control," *People*, December 20, 2004.
128 *Another mother didn't make:* Ruben Naverrette, "Parents Can't Buy Their Children's Respect," *Dallas Morning News*, November 28, 2004.
128 *Writer Martin Booe recently:* Martin Booe, "Generation Me-Me-Me," *Jackson Free Press*, October 21, 2004.
128 *educational psychologist Michele Borba:* Ibid.
128 *Douglas and Michaels argue:* Douglas and Michaels, *Mommy Myth*, 307–8.
129 *Paula Peterson's two kids:* Fields-Meyer, "Kids Out of Control."
131 *We gain self-esteem:* A. Aron, M. Paris, and E. N. Aron, "Falling in Love: Prospective Studies of Self-Concept Change," *Journal of Personality and Social Psychology* 69 (1995): 1102–12; and M. R. Leary et al., "Self-Esteem as an Interpersonal Monitor: The Sociometer Hypothesis," *Journal of Personality and Social Psychology* 68 (1995): 518–30.
131 *Study after study shows:* David Myers, *The Pursuit of Happiness* (New York: Morrow, 1992).
131 *Research by Sandra Murray:* S. L. Murray et al., "Through the Looking Glass Darkly? When Self-Doubts Turn into Relationship Insecurities," *Journal of Personality and Social Psychology* 75 (1998): 1459–80.
132 *narcissists—people who really love themselves:* W. Keith Campbell, *When You Love a Man Who Loves Himself* (Chicago: Sourcebooks, 2005); and W. K. Campbell, "Narcissism and Romantic Attraction," *Journal of Personality and Social Psychology* 77 (1999): 1254–70.
132 *They think they are better:* W. K. Campbell, E. A. Rudich, and C. Sedikides, "Narcissism, Self-Esteem, and the Positivity of Self-Views: Two Portraits of Self-Love," *Personality and Social Psychology Bulletin* 28 (2002): 358–68.
132 *"If I were to name the top ten":* W. Keith Campbell, interview, December 28, 2004.
133 *In a cross-temporal meta-analysis:* S. H. Konrath, W. J. Chopik, C. K. Hsing, and E. O'Brien, "Changes in Adult Attachment Styles in American College Students over Time: A Meta-analysis," *Personality and Social Psychology Review* (2014), DOI: 10.1177/1088868314530516.

133 *One young woman, interviewed in the book* Flux: Peggy Orenstein, *Flux: Women on Sex, Work, Love, Kids, and Life in a Half-Changed World* (New York: Doubleday 2000), 73.
133 *In an analysis of data from 47,692 respondents:* J. M. Twenge, W. K. Campbell, and C. A. Foster, "Parenthood and Marital Satisfaction: A Meta-analytic Review," *Journal of Marriage and the Family* 65 (2003): 574–83.
134 *When* People *magazine interviewed:* "Facing Off over Plastic Surgery," *People*, October 18, 2004.
136 *Thirty-eight percent of* GenMe: Taylor, *The Next America*.
136 *In a survey of 766 college students:* J. Greif, W. Hewitt, and M. L. Armstrong, "Tattooing and Body Piercing," *Clinical Nursing Research* 8 (1999): 368–85.
137 *In 1967, when the Boomers:* J. M. Twenge, W. K. Campbell, and E. C. Freeman. "Generational Differences in Young Adults' Life Goals, Concern for Others, and Civic Orientation, 1966–2009," *Journal of Personality and Social Psychology* 102 (2012): 1045–62; and updates from the American Freshman database.
137 *high school students are now more likely:* Twenge and Kasser, "Generational Changes in Materialism."
138 *College kids spend $50 billion a year:* Ashley Lutz, "The Average College Student Is Spending a Record $907 on Dorm Décor," *Business Insider*, September 4, 2012, http://www.businessinsider.com/average-spending-on-dorm-decor-skyrockets-2012-9.
138 *"She's a very good girl":* Nancy Jeffrey, "Proms Gone Wild!," *People*, May 30, 2005.
138 *A recent survey found that the average:* Erik Ortiz, "Prom Gets Pricier for Average US Family Spending More Than $1,000 for the Night," *New York Daily News*, May 4, 2012.
138 *In his survey of 18-to-23-year-olds:* C. Smith, K. Christoffersen, H. Davison, and P. S. Herzog. *Lost in Transition: The Dark Side of Emerging Adulthood* (New York: Oxford University Press, 2011).
139 *A Sears ad for girls' clothing:* John de Graaf, David Wann, and Thomas H. Naylor, *Affluenza* (San Francisco: Berrett-Koehler, 2002), 55.
139 *A young woman in Smith's survey put it this way:* Smith et al., *Lost in Transition*.
140 *"I want to do things that conform":* "Notebook," *Time*, June 6, 2005.
140 *The coffee choices at Starbucks:* S. Waldman, "The Tyranny of Choice: Why the Consumer Revolution Is Ruining Your Life," *New Republic*, January 27, 1992.
140 *"Shopping, like everything else":* David Brooks, *Bobos in Paradise* (New York: Simon & Schuster, 2000), 101.
141 *"Years ago, cell phones":* Ken Belson, "I Want to Be Alone. Please Call Me," *New York Times*, June 27, 2004.

4. The Age of Anxiety (and Depression, and Loneliness): Generation Stressed

PAGE

143 *Only 1% to 2% of Americans born:* R. C. Kessler, P. Berglund, O. Demler, R. Jin, K. R. Merikangas, and E. E. Walters, "Lifetime Prevalence and Age-

of-Onset Distributions of *DSM-IV* Disorders in the National Comorbidity Survey Replication," *Archives of General Psychiatry* 62 (2005): 593–602; L. N. Robins, et al., "Lifetime Prevalence of Specific Psychiatric Disorders in Three Sites," *Archives of General Psychiatry* 41 (1984): 949–58; G. L. Klerman and M. M. Weissman, "Increasing Rates of Depression," *Journal of the American Medical Association* 261, no. 15 (1989): 2229–35; P. M. Lewinsohn et al., "Age-Cohort Changes in Lifetime Occurrence of Depression and Other Mental Disorders," *Journal of Abnormal Psychology* 102, no. 1 (1993): 110–20; P. J. Wickramaratne et al., "Age, Period, and Cohort Effects on the Risk of Major Depression: Results from Five United States Communities," *Journal of Clinical Epidemiology* 42, no. 4 (1989): 333–43; and R. C. Kessler et al., "Lifetime and 12-Month Prevalence of *DSM-III-R* Psychiatric Disorders in the United States: Results from the National Comorbidity Study," *Archives of General Psychiatry* 51 (1994): 8–19.

143 *In past generations, suicide:* Klerman and Weissman, "Increasing Rates of Depression"; and Jane M. Murphy, "The Stirling County Study: Then and Now," *International Review of Psychiatry* 6 (1994): 329–48.

143 *One out of 10 Americans took:* L. A. Pratt, D. J. Brody, and Q. Gu, "Antidepressant Use in Persons Aged 12 and Over: United States, 2005–2008," *National Center for Health Statistics Data Brief* 76 (October 2011).

143 *At the Kansas State University:* Sherry A. Benton et al., "Changes in Counseling Center Client Problems Across 13 Years," *Professional Psychology: Research and Practice* 34 (2003): 66–72. For a nontechnical review, see Sue Shellenbarger, "Workers Struggle with Kids' Depression," *Wall Street Journal*, April 22, 2003.

144 *A 2010 study found:* J. C. Guthman, L. Locin, and D. D. Konstas, "Increase in Severity of Mental Illness among Clinical College Students: A 12-Year Comparison" (paper presented at the annual meeting of the American Psychological Association, San Diego, August 2010).

145 *In a nationwide survey of teens:* "Centers for Disease Control Youth Risk Behavior Survey," http://www.cdc.gov/HealthyYouth/yrbs/index.htm.

145 *As part of my doctoral dissertation:* J. M. Twenge, "The Age of Anxiety? Birth Cohort Change in Anxiety and Neuroticism, 1952–1993," *Journal of Personality and Social Psychology* 79 (2000): 1007–21.

145 *I analyzed data from 63,706 college students:* J. M. Twenge, B. Gentile, C. N. DeWall, D. S. Ma, K. Lacefield, and D. R. Schurtz, "Birth Cohort Increases in Psychopathology among Young Americans, 1938–2007: A Cross-Temporal Meta-analysis of the MMPI," *Clinical Psychology Review* 30 (2010): 145–54.

146 *Thirty percent of college freshmen reported:* J. M. Twenge, "Time Period and Birth Cohort Differences in Depressive Symptoms in the US, 1982–2012," *Social Indicators Research* (forthcoming).

146 *teen suicides are down 22%: Statistical Abstract of the United States*, 2012 and earlier volumes. For data on suicidal ideation declining, see the Youth Risk Behavior Survey.

146 *self-reports of anxiety and depression have leveled off:* For a review, see J. M. Twenge, "Generational Differences in Mental Health: Are Children and Adolescents Suffering More, or Less?," *American Journal of Orthopsychiatry* 81 (2011): 469–72.

146 *More high school students in 2012:* Twenge, "Time Period and Birth Cohort Differences in Depressive Symptoms."
146 *Drawing from the nationwide:* C. M. Herbst, "'Paradoxical' Decline? Another Look at the Relative Reduction in Female Happiness," *Journal of Economic Psychology* 32 (2011): 773–88.
147 *Someone commits suicide:* www.suicidememorialwall.com.
147 *While the suicide rate for middle-aged people: Statistical Abstract of the United States*, 2004 and earlier years, http://www.census.gov/prod/www/abs/statab.html.
148 *In 2011, 16% of high school students:* Centers for Disease Control, "Youth Risk Behavior Surveillance System," http://apps.nccd.cdc.gov/yrbss.
148 *Years of bullying led:* Kristin Hussey and John Leland, "After Boy's Suicide, Questions about Missed Signs," *New York Times*, August 30, 2013, http://www.nytimes.com/2013/08/31/nyregion/after-boys-suicide-questions-about-missed-signs.html?_r=0.
148 *After a dispute over a boy:* Lizette Alvarez, "Girl's Suicide Points to Rise in Apps Used by Cyberbullies," *New York Times*, September 13, 2013, http://www.nytimes.com/2013/09/14/us/suicide-of-girl-after-bullying-raises-worries-on-web-sites.html?pagewanted=all.
149 *In a well-publicized 2009 report:* B. Stevenson and J. Wolfers. "The Paradox of Declining Female Happiness," *American Economic Journal: Economic Policy* 1 (2009), 190–225.
149 *Chris Herbst analyzed:* Herbst, "'Paradoxical' Decline?"
150 *More than four times as many:* Gregg Easterbrook, *The Progress Paradox* (New York: Random House, 2003), 180.
150 *One study found that in 1985:* M. McPherson, L. Smith-Lovin, and M. E. Brashears, "Social Isolation in America: Changes in Core Discussion Networks over Two Decades," *American Sociological Review* 71 (2006): 353–75.
150 *"There is a kind of famine":* Robert E. Lane, *The Loss of Happiness in Market Democracies* (New Haven, CT: Yale University Press, 2000), 9.
151 *One 26-year-old participant called it:* "Group Hug," *People*, September 27, 2004.
151 *In* Prozac Nation, *her memoir:* Elizabeth Wurtzel, *Prozac Nation: Young and Depressed in America* (New York: Riverhead Books, 1994), 33.
151 *This has a clear link:* P. R. Amato and B. Keith, "Parental Divorce and the Well-Being of Children: A Meta-analysis," *Psychological Bulletin* 110 (1991): 26–46.
151 *the four characters on* Sex and the City: *Sex and the City*, episode "Unoriginal Sin," HBO, airdate July 28, 2002.
153 *Laurie, interviewed:* Jeffrey Jensen Arnett, *Emerging Adulthood* (New York: Oxford University Press, 2004), 110–11.
153 *Another couple described in the book:* Ibid., 106.
154 *As Jake puts it, "I could be thirty-five":* Ibid., 105.
154 *Thousands more young men than women: Statistical Abstract of the United States*, 2004 and earlier years, http://www.census.gov/prod/www/abs/statab.html.
154 *In 1950, only 9%:* http://www.pbs.org/newshour/bb/social_issues-jan-june12-goingsolo_03-27/. See also Eric Klinenberg, *Going Solo: The Extraordinary Rise and Surprising Appeal of Going Alone* (New York: Penguin, 2013).

154 *A recent in-depth study found that Chicago:* Peter Gorner, "U. of C. Sex Study Sees Love, Loneliness," *Chicago Tribune*, January 9, 2004.
155 *Author Chris Colin summed it up:* Chris Colin, *What Really Happened to the Class of '93* (New York: Broadway Books, 2004), xiv.
155 *"A decade after high school":* Ibid., 60.
155 *Seventy-five percent of women aged 25 to 35:* "The Next Generation: Today's Professionals, Tomorrow's Leaders," (New York: Catalyst, 2001), http://www.catalystwomen.org.
155 *In* The Costs of Living, *Barry Schwartz describes:* Barry Schwartz, *Costs of Living* (New York: Norton, 1994), 18.
156 *A mountain of scientific evidence links:* D. R. Williams, D. T. Takeuchi, and R. K. Adair, "Marital Status and Psychiatric Disorders among Blacks and Whites," *Journal of Health and Social Behavior* 33 (1992): 140–57; Lee Robins and Darrel Reiger, *Psychiatric Disorders in America* (New York: Free Press, 1991); R. F. Baumeister and M. R. Leary, "The Need to Belong: Desire for Interpersonal Attachments as a Fundamental Human Motivation," *Psychological Bulletin* 117 (1995): 497–529; and David Myers, *The American Paradox* (New Haven, CT: Yale University Press, 2000), chap. 3.
157 *Harvard rejects between 25%:* Marisa Meltzer, "The Swarm of the Super-Applicants," *New York*, October 24, 2007, http://nymag.com/news/features/24398/; and http://thechoice.blogs.nytimes.com/2013/03/28/ivy-league-college-admission-rates-2013/.
158 *Two million high school students:* http://research.collegeboard.org/programs/ap/data/archived/2012.
158 Time *magazine interviewed Marielle Woods:* Sonja Steptoe, "Ready, Set, Relax!," *Time*, October 27, 2003.
158 *Medical schools and law schools, especially:* http://www.statisticbrain.com/medical-school-acceptance-rate-statistics/; http://www.usnews.com/education/best-graduate-schools/the-short-list-grad-school/articles/2013/04/30/10-most-selective-medical-schools; http://law-school.findthebest.com/; and http://poetsandquants.com/2011/04/22/the-50-most-selective-mba-programs-in-the-u-s/.
159 *"When I graduated from college":* Alexandra Robbins and Abby Wilner, *Quarterlife Crisis* (New York: Tarcher/Putnam, 2001), 173.
161 *between 1984 and 2011, the wealth:* Taylor, *The Next America*.
161 *"You need a college degree":* Lev Grossman, "Grow Up? Not So Fast," *Time*, January 24, 2005.
162 *That's exactly the change:* E. Saez, "Striking It Richer: The Evolution of Top Incomes in the United States" (updated with 2012 preliminary estimates), University of California at Berkeley, September 3, 2013.
162 *The median wage of American men:* Joe McKendrick, "Men's Incomes Have Declined 28% since 1968: Study," *Smart Planet*, September 12, 2012, http://www.smartplanet.com/blog/business-brains/mens-incomes-have-declined-28-since-1968-study/.
162 *In 2010, 40% of all American families:* Taylor, *The Next America*.
162 *$44,750 at the average private university:* https://www.collegedata.com/cs/content/content_payarticle_tmpl.jhtml?articleId=10064.
162 *Student loan debt has doubled:* Adolfo Flores, "Student Loan Debt Nearly Doubles in Last Five Years, Report Says," *Los Angeles Times*, June 18, 2013.

163 *In 1960, only 12%:* Peter Coy, "Harvard Study Finds: The Rent Is Way Too High," *Bloomberg Businessweek*, December 9, 2013.

163 *This is a relative bargain:* Katy Steinmetz, "San Francisco's 1 Percent: Tech Wealth's Displacement Effect," *Time*, February 1, 2014, http://www.npr.org/2013/12/03/247531636/as-rent-soars-longtime-san-francisco-tenants-fight-to-stay; http://www.huffingtonpost.com/2013/07/09/new-york-city-rent_n_3568278.html; http://www.apartmenttherapy.com/what-does-it-really-cost-to-live-in-chicago-apartment-therapys-cost-of-living-report-chicago-2013-193139; and http://la.curbed.com/archives/2013/09/average_rent_in_los_angeles_county_has_jumped_to_1435.php.

163 *Former mayor Art Agnos says:* http://www.npr.org/2013/12/03/247531636/as-rent-soars-longtime-san-francisco-tenants-fight-to-stay.

166 *In* Nickel and Dimed, *Barbara Ehrenreich reports:* Barbara Ehrenreich, *Nickel and Dimed: On (Not) Getting By in America* (New York: Metropolitan Books, 2001), 199.

166 A *stunning 1 out of 3:* Ronald D. White, "Law School Grad Learns How to Pay Off a Heavy Debt," *Los Angeles Times*, September 20, 2013.

166 *"I graduated from college with honors":* *Time*, February 14, 2005.

166 *"When my parents were my age":* Emily Alpert and Ricardo Lopez, "Leaving Nest Isn't Easy for Millennials," *Los Angeles Times*, August 2, 2013.

166 *The* LA Times *profiled Andrew Post:* White, "Law School Grad Learns."

167 *The cost varies from state to state:* Child Care Aware, "Parents and the High Cost of Child Care," 2012 report, https://www.naccrra.org/costofcare.

169 *In* The Baby Book*'s 2003 edition:* William Sears and Martha Sears, *The Baby Book* (New York: Little, Brown, 2003), 413.

171 A *2010 survey raised the bar:* "26% of Teens Expected to Become Famous by Age 25," Barna Group Youth Poll, May 10, 2010, https://www.barna.org/barna-update/article/16-teensnext-gen/366-teenagers-want-successful-careers-and-global-travel-expect-to-delay-marriage-a-parenting.

172 Quarterlife Crisis *concludes that twentysomethings:* Robbins and Wilner, *Quarterlife Crisis*, 109.

172 *Tim Urban recently published an article:* "Wait but Why, Why Generation Y Yuppies Are Unhappy," *Huffington Post*, September 15, 2013, http://www.huffingtonpost.com/wait-but-why/generation-y-unhappy_b_3930620.html

173 A *Kaiser Family Foundation study found:* V. Rideout, U. G. Foehr, and D. F. Roberts, "Generation M2: Media in the Lives of 8-to-18-Year Olds," Kaiser Family Foundation study, January 2010, http://kff.org/other/event/generation-m2-media-in-the-lives-of/; and http://kaiserfamilyfoundation.files.wordpress.com/2013/04/8010.pdf

173 *Writer Cathi Hanauer sums this up:* Cathi Hanauer. ed., *The Bitch in the House* (New York: Harper Collins Perennial, 2002), xv.

174 *In* Quarterlife Crisis, *Joanna says:* Robbins and Wilner, *Quarterlife Crisis*, 93.

174 *In her book on eating disorders:* Joan Jacobs Brumberg, *Fasting Girls* (New York: New American Library, 1989), 267.

174 As Midlife Crisis at 30 *puts it:* Lia Macko and Kerry Rubin, *Midlife Crisis at 30: How the Stakes Have Changed for a New Generation—and What to Do about It* (New York: Plume Penguin, 2004), 59.

175 *Sure enough, research shows:* L. J. Shrum, J. E. Burroughs, and A. Rindfleisch, "Television's Cultivation of Material Values," *Journal of Consumer Research*,

2005; and L. J. Shrum, J. E. Burroughs, and A. Rindfleisch, "A Process Model of Consumer Cultivation: The Role of Television Is a Function of the Type of Judgment," in *The Psychology of Entertainment Media: Blurring the Lines between Entertainment and Persuasion, ed.* L. J. Shrum (Mahwah, NJ: Lawrence Erlbaum Associates, 2004), 177–91.

176 *Because fewer of us ride buses:* James Fallows, "The Invisible Poor," *New York Times Magazine*, March 19, 2000.

176 *People whose primary motivations:* T. Kasser and R. Ryan, "A Dark Side of the American Dream," *Journal of Personality and Social Psychology* 65 (1993): 410–22.

176 *Psychologist Ed Diener got many:* E. Diener, J. Horowitz, and R. A. Emmons, "Happiness of the Very Wealthy," *Social Indicators* 16 (1985): 263–74.

176 *People who win the lottery:* P. Brickman, D. Coates, and R. Janoff-Bulman, "Lottery Winners and Accident Victims: Is Happiness Relative?," *Journal of Personality and Social Psychology* 36 (1978): 917–27.

176 *In a Gallup poll, 94%:* David Popenoe and Barbara Defoe Whitehead, *The State of Our Unions: The Social Health of Marriage in America, 2001* (New Brunswick, NJ: National Marriage Project, 2001).

176 *Norval Glenn, an expert:* Lisa Bereson, "The State of the Union: A Special Report," *Ladies' Home Journal*, March 2003.

176 *The authors of* Midlife Crisis at 30 *call:* Macko and Rubin, *Midlife Crisis at 30*, 89–90.

177 *"It's as if some idiot":* M. E. P. Seligman, "Boomer Blues," *Psychology Today*, October 1988, 50–53.

177 *people who watch many hours:* D. Romer, K. H. Jamieson, and S. Aday, "Television News and the Cultivation of Fear of Crime," *Journal of Communication* 53 (2003): 88–104.

178 *"His biggest fear, he told me":* "Utah Scout Feeling 'Good' after Ordeal," cnn.com, June 23, 2005.

5. Yeah, Right: The Belief That There's No Point in Trying

PAGE

183 *Liqing Zhang, Charles Im, and I found 97 studies:* J. M. Twenge, L. Zhang, and C. Im, "It's Beyond My Control: A Cross-Temporal Meta-analysis of Increasing Externality in Locus of Control, 1960–2002," *Personality and Social Psychology Review* 8 (2004): 308–19.

184 *cynical statements such as:* S. J. Pharr, R. D. Putnam, and R. J. Dalton, "A Quarter-Century of Declining Confidence," *Journal of Democracy* 11 (2000): 5–25.

184 *More recently, a Pew survey of adults:* Pew Research Center for the People & the Press, "Section 3: Values about Economic Inequality and Individual Opportunity," June 4, 2012, http://www.people-press.org/2012/06/04/section-3-values-about-economic-inequality-and-individual-opportunity/.

184 *As it turned out, kids were:* Twenge, Zhang, and Im, "It's Beyond My Control."

186 *Out of 30 items measuring:* J. M. Twenge, W. K. Campbell, and E. C. Freeman, "Generational Differences in Young Adults' Life Goals, Concern for Others, and Civic Orientation, 1966–2009," *Journal of Personality and Social Psychology* 102 (2012): 1045–62.

186 *In later analyses, we found:* Park, Twenge, and Greenfield, "The Great Recession."

187 *Another study comparing generations:* R. Rasch and B. Kowske, "Will Millennials Save the World through Work? International Generational Differences in the Relative Importance of Corporate Social Responsibility and Business Ethics to Turnover Intentions," in *Managing the New Workforce: International Perspectives on the Millennial Generation*, ed. S. T. Lyons, E. S. Ng, and L. Schweitzer (Northampton, MA: Edward Elgar, 2012).

188 *GenMe'ers were significantly* less: Twenge, Campbell, and Freeman, "Generational Differences."

189 *In 1992, 90% of American adults:* Pew Research Center for the People & the Press, "Partisan Polarization Surges in Bush, Obama Years," 2012, http://www.people-press.org/2012/06/04/partisan-polarization-surges-in-bush-obama-years/.

189 *Between 2000 and 2013, twice:* http://www.gallup.com/poll/1615/environment.aspx.

190 *In the high school survey, confidence:* J. M. Twenge, W. K. Campbell, and N. T. Carter, "Declines in Trust in Others and Confidence in Institutions among American Adults and Late Adolescents, 1972–2012" (unpublished manuscript, 2014).

190 *Less than 20% of young people:* David T. Z. Mindich, *Tuned Out: Why Americans Under 40 Don't Follow the News* (New York: Oxford University Press, 2005).

190 *Only 32% of people aged 18 to 24:* Ibid.

191 *found that 60% of American:* Ibid.

191 *In another poll, high school seniors:* CBS News, *The Class of 2000* (New York: Simon & Schuster, 2001), ebook, 126.

192 *As author Neil Postman notes:* Neil Postman, *The Disappearance of Childhood* (New York: Vintage, 1994), 95.

194 *"when they encounter teachers":* Maureen Stout, *The Feel-Good Curriculum* (Cambridge, MA: Perseus Books, 2000), 263.

196 *"Kids see people like Bill Gates":* Peter Sacks, *Generation X Goes to College* (Chicago: Open Court Press, 1996), 169.

196 *Susan Peterson, who teaches:* Amazon.com, "You Think Gen X Is Bad? Watch Out for Gen Y," review of *Generation X Goes to College, by Sacks*, posted April 11, 2003.

197 *"the impulse to flee":* Charles Sykes, *A Nation of Victims: The Decay of the American Character.*(New York: St. Martin's Press, 1992), 15.

197 The Myth of Laziness *author Mel Levine:* Mel Levine, *The Myth of Laziness* (New York: Simon & Schuster, 2003).

197 *As Sykes puts it:* Sykes, *Nation of Victims*, 144.

198 *In 1940, about 20,000 civil lawsuits:* Theodore Caplow, Louis Hicks, and Ben J. Wattenberg, *The First Measured Century* (Washington, DC: AEI Press, 2001), 198.

198 *by 2012, this had increased more than tenfold:* http://www.uscourts.gov/Statistics/JudicialBusiness/2012.aspx.

198 *One young man sued:* "Former Law Student Stages Hunger Strike," *Chronicle of Higher Education*, January 23, 1998.

198 *Chris Colin was heartened:* Colin, *What Really Happened*, 258.
199 *"Kids today have extremely":* Sacks, *Generation X Goes to College*, 59.
199 *Another student asked if:* Ibid., 16.
199 *Sacks reports with irony:* Ibid., 20.
199 *"Students who receive a C, D, or F":* Daniel Kazez, "A Is for Anybody," *Newsweek*, August 8, 1994, 10.
199 *In his book* I'm the Teacher: Patrick Allitt, *I'm the Teacher, You're the Student* (Philadelphia: University of Pennsylvania Press, 2005), 211.
199 *After Sacks pointed out:* Sacks, *Generation X Goes to College*, 122.
200 *In her book* Not Much Just Chillin'*:* Linda Perlstein, *Not Much Just Chillin': The Hidden Lives of Middle Schoolers* (New York: Ballantine, 2003), 183.
200 Time *magazine ran a cover story:* Nancy Gibbs, "What Teachers Hate About Parents," *Time*, February 21, 2005.
200 *Scott McLeod, the headmaster:* Michael Lewis, "Coach Fitz's Management Theory," *New York Times Magazine*, March 28, 2004.
202 *People who believe that outside forces:* V. A. Benassi, P. D. Sweeney, and C. L. Dufour, "Is There a Relation between Locus of Control Orientation and Depression?," *Journal of Abnormal Psychology* 97 (1988): 357–67; S. E. Hahn, "The Effects of Locus of Control on Daily Exposure, Coping and Reactivity to Work Interpersonal Stressors: A Diary Study," *Personality and Individual Differences* 29 (2000): 729–48; J. Mirowsky and C. E. Ross, "Control or Defense? Depression and the Sense of Control over Good and Bad Outcomes," *Journal of Health and Social Behavior* 31 (1990): 71–86; and M. P. Naditch, M. Gargan, and L. Michael, "Denial, Anxiety, Locus of Control, and the Discrepancy between Aspirations and Achievements as Components of Depression," *Journal of Abnormal Psychology* 84 (1975): 1–9.
202 *anxious:* D. G. Kilpatrick, W. R. Dubin, and D. B. Marcotte, "Personality, Stress of the Medication Education Process, and Changes in Affective Mood State," *Psychological Reports* 34 (1974): 1215–23; and G. Morelli, H. Krotinger, and S. Moore, "Neuroticism and Levenson's Locus of Control Scale," *Psychological Reports* 44 (1979): 153–54.
202 *cope poorly with stress:* N. Krause and S. Stryker, "Stress and Well-Being: The Buffering Role of Locus of Control Beliefs," *Social Science and Medicine*, 18 (1984): 783–90; and I. N. Sandler and B. Lakey, "Locus of Control as a Stress Moderator: The Role of Control Perception and Social Support," *American Journal of Community Psychology* 10 (1982): 65–80.
202 *externals have weakened:* S. A. Karabenick and T. K. Srull, "Effects of Personality and Situational Variation in Locus of Control on Cheating: Determinants of the 'Congruence Effect,'" *Journal of Personality* 46 (1978): 72–95; and W. Mischel, R. Zeiss, and A. Zeiss, "An Internal-External Control Test for Young Children," *Journal of Personality and Social Psychology* 29 (1974): 265–78.
202 *externals consistently achieve less:* E. Cappella and R. S. Weinstein, "Turning Around Reading Achievement: Predictors of High School Students' Academic Resilience," *Journal of Educational Psychology* 93 (2001): 758–71; M. J. Findley and H. M. Cooper, "Locus of Control and Academic Achievement: A Literature Review," *Journal of Personality and Social Psychology* 44 (1983): 419–27; and A. D. Kalechstein and S. Nowicki, "A Meta-analytic Exam-

ination of the Relationship between Control Expectancies and Academic Achievement: An 11-Yr Follow-Up to Findley and Cooper," *Genetic, Social, and General Psychology Monographs* 123 (1997): 27–56.

202 *A definitive report concluded:* J. S. Coleman et al., *Equality of Educational Opportunity: Report from the Office of Education* (Washington, DC: US Government Printing Office, 1966).

202 *"Our society has":* Julian Rotter, "External Control and Internal Control," *Psychology Today*, June 1971, 59.

6. Sex: Generation Prude Meets Generation Crude

PAGE

204 *In Valerie Frankel's novel:* Valerie Frankel, *The Not-So-Perfect Man* (New York: Avon Trade, 2004).

204 The Hookup Handbook *notes that hookups:* Andrea Lavinthal and Jessica Rozler, *The Hookup Handbook* (New York: Simon Spotlight Entertainment, 2005), 2–3.

205 *A recent article in the* Atlantic: Hanna Rosin, "Boys on the Side," *Atlantic*, September 2012, http://www.theatlantic.com/magazine/archive/2012/09/boys-on-the-side/309062/.

205 *"I think you can compare friends":* "The 411: Teens & Sex," NBC, January 26, 2005.

205 *80% of people age 18 to 29:* Pew Research on Social and Demographic Trends, "Barely Half of US Adults Are Married—a Record Low," December 14, 2011, http://www.pewsocialtrends.org/2011/12/14/barely-half-of-u-s-adults-are-married-a-record-low/.

207 *For her master's thesis with me, Brooke Wells:* B. E. Wells and J. M. Twenge, "Changes in Young People's Sexual Behavior and Attitudes, 1943–1999: A Cross-Temporal Meta-analysis," *Review of General Psychology* 9 (2005): 249–61.

207 *in 1970, the average woman: Statistical Abstract of the United States*, 2012 and earlier years, http://www.census.gov/prod/www/abs/statab.html.

207 *An Oregon high school sophomore:* CBS News. *The Class of 2000* (New York: Simon & Schuster, 2001), ebook, 14–15.

208 *In a 2013 Gallup poll, twice as many:* Joy Wilke and Lydia Saad, "Older Americans' Moral Attitudes Changing," Gallup Poll Report, June 3, 2013.

208 *The General Social Survey (GSS) asks:* General Social Survey, analysis performed for this book.

209 *As recently as 2004:* Ibid.

210 *Author Paula Kamen studied:* Paula Kamen, *Her Way: Young Women Remake the Sexual Revolution* (New York: New York University Press, 2000), 225.

210 *A whopping 88%:* Lawrence K. Altman, "Study Finds That Teenage Virginity Pledges Are Rarely Kept," *New York Times*, March 10, 2004.

210 *participants in abstinence programs:* American Psychological Association press release, "Based on the Research, Comprehensive Sex Education Is More Effective at Stopping the Spread of HIV Infection, Says APA Committee," February 23, 2005, http://www.apa.org/releases/sexeducation.html or http://www.apa.org/releases/sexed_resolution.pdf.

211 *numerous newspaper stories:* Laura Sessions Stepp, "Unsettling New Fad

Alarms Parents: Middle School Oral Sex," *Washington Post*, July 8, 1999; Anne Jarrell, "The Face of Teenage Sex Grows Younger," *New York Times*, April 3, 2000; and Barbara Cooke, "When Is Sex Not Sex?," *Chicago Tribune*, March 4, 2001.

211 *Many kids say that oral sex:* Benoit Denizet-Lewis, "Friends, Friends with Benefits, and the Benefits of the Local Mall," *New York Times Magazine*, May 30, 2004.

211 *In a mid-2000s NBC special:* "The 411," NBC.

211 *In the late 1960s, only 42%:* Kamen, *Her Way*.

211 *In a 2010 study conducted:* http://www.nationalsexstudy.indiana.edu/.

212 *in the Indiana University 2010 survey:* Ibid.

212 *In Alfred Kinsey's studies:* Kamen, *Her Way*, 76.

213 *In 2010, members:* Angelica Bonus, "Fraternity Pledges' Chant Raises Concerns at Yale," cnn.com, October 18, 2010, http://www.cnn.com/2010/US/10/18/connecticut.yale.frat.chant/.

213 *"When I was in porn":* Ariel Levy, *Female Chauvinist Pigs* (New York: Atria Books, 2005).

214 *In her 2013 book,* Masterminds and Wingmen*:* Rosalind Wiseman, "What Boys Want," *Time*, December 2, 2013.

214 *In a 2013 Gallup poll, half:* Wilke and Saad, "Older Americans' Moral Attitudes Changing."

214 *Three times as many women:* "Cosmetic Surgery National Data Bank: Statistics 2012," American Society for Aesthetic Plastic Surgery, http://www.surgery.org/sites/default/files/ASAPS-2012-Stats.pdf.

216 *in the* New York Times Magazine *article:* Denizet-Lewis, "Friends, Friends with Benefits."

216 *In an NBC/*People *poll, almost half:* Michelle Tauber, Thomas Fields-Meyer, and Kyle Smith, "Young Teens and Sex," *People*, January 31, 2005.

216 *A survey conducted between 2005:* Kate Taylor, "Sex on Campus: She Can Play That Game, Too," *New York Times*, July 12, 2013.

216 *Sociologist Elizabeth Armstrong observes:* Rosin, "Boys on the Side."

217 *Young authors Andrea Lavinthal:* Lavinthal and Rozler, *Hookup Handbook*, 4.

217 *Features of the hookup:* Ibid., 182.

217 *One woman says she knew:* Ibid., 221.

217 *As* The Hookup Handbook *puts it:* Ibid., 10.

218 *As* The Hookup Handbook *notes:* Ibid., 232.

218 *Monica, 16, said: Today*, NBC, January 27, 2005.

219 *This is art imitating life:* Ibid.

219 *A study of almost 2,000 teens found:* "Study Links TV to Teen Sexual Activity," cnn.com, September 7, 2004; and R. L. Collins, "Sex on Television and Its Impact on American Youth: Background and Results from the RAND Television and Adolescent Sexuality Study," *Child and Adolescent Psychiatric Clinics of North America*, 14 (2005): 371–85.

219 *young black women who watch:* G. M. Wingood et al., "A Prospective Study of Exposure to Rap Music Videos and African American Female Adolescents' Health," *American Journal of Public Health* 93 (2003): 437–39.

219 *Thirteen-year-old Maya, interviewed:* Tauber, Fields-Meyer, and Smith, "Young Teens and Sex."

220 *Pediatrician Meg Meeker calls it: Today*, NBC.

220 *Linda Perlstein, the author:* Linda Perlstein, *Not Much Just Chillin': The Hidden Lives of Middle Schoolers* (New York: Ballantine Books, 2003), 87.
220 *sexual terms and talk are:* Marnie Huner, "The Secret Lives of Middle Schoolers," cnn.com, November 19, 2003.
220 *In the* New York Times Magazine *article on hooking up:* Denizet-Lewis, "Friends, Friends with Benefits."
220 *A Kaiser Family Foundation study found that 70%:* Richard Jerome, "The Cyberporn Generation," *People*, April 26, 2004.
221 *"It's a big ego boost":* Wiseman, "What Boys Want."
221 *the rate of syphilis cases doubled:* "Sexually Transmitted Disease Surveillance 2012," Centers for Disease Control, Division of STD Prevention, January 2014, http://www.cdc.gov/std/stats12/Surv2012.pdf.
221 *one young man said he found out:* Jeffrey Jensen Arnett, *Emerging Adulthood* (New York: Oxford University Press, 2004), 92.
221 *One study examined the sexual geography:* Claudia Wallis, "A Snapshot of Teen Sex," *Time*, February 7, 2005. I calculated the 61% figure myself from the figure in the article.
222 *A Kaiser Family Foundation study found that 75%:* Melissa Alexander, "Television Programs Lack Safe Sex Message," *Daily Aztec* (San Diego State University student newspaper), March 7, 2005.
222 *When watching TV, says college freshman Joyce Bryn:* Ibid.
222 *11,295 people died of HIV: Statistical Abstract of the United States*, 2012 and earlier years, http://www.census.gov/prod/www/abs/statab.html.
223 *Births to teens aged 15 to 19:* Ibid.
224 *From 2006 to 2010, 48% of women:* Karen Kaplan, "More Americans Are Living Together before Marriage, Study Finds," *Los Angeles Times*, April 4, 2013.
224 *In a 2001 poll, 62%:* David Popenoe and Barbara Defoe Whitehead, "The State of Our Unions: The Social Health of Marriage in America, 2001" (New Brunswick, NJ: National Marriage Project).
224 *Author Linda Perlstein saw a girl's website:* Perlstein, *Not Much Just Chillin'*.
225 *The authors of* Midlife Crisis at 30 *relate:* Lia Macko and Kerry Rubin, *Midlife Crisis at 30: How the Stakes Have Changed for a New Generation—and What to Do about It* (New York: Plume Penguin, 2004), 92.
225 *As of 2010, 77% of US married couples:* Kaplan, "More Americans Are Living Together."

7. The Equality Revolution: Minorities, Women, and Gays and Lesbians

PAGE
227 *Reflecting on the events:* "From the Front Lines of Freedom," *People*, March 7, 2005.
228 *In 1970, just 5%: Statistical Abstract of the United States*, 2012 and earlier years, http://www.census.gov/prod/www/abs/ statab.html.
230 *In 1970, most blacks did not:* Ibid.
230 *Charles, 27, interviewed:* Jeffrey Jensen Arnett, *Emerging Adulthood* (New York: Oxford University Press, 2004), 129.
230 *Sixty-one percent of black:* Ibid.
231 *Eighty-seven percent of high school students:* Monitoring the Future Survey of high school seniors. Analyses performed for this book.

231 *among Americans born:* New Strategist Editors. *Generation X: Americans Born 1965 to 1976*, 4th ed. (Ithaca, NY: New Strategist Publications, 2004), 221.
232 *In 1972, 32% still favored:* General Social Survey. Analyses performed for this book.
232 *Back in the 1940s, psychologists:* David Myers, *Social Psychology*, 4th ed. (New York: McGraw-Hill, 1993), 378; and Richard Severo, "Kenneth Clark, Who Fought Segregation, Dies," *New York Times*, May 2, 2005.
232 *Jennifer Crocker and I gathered data:* J. M. Twenge and J. Crocker, "Race and Self-Esteem: Meta-analyses Comparing Whites, Blacks, Hispanics, Asians, and American Indians," *Psychological Bulletin* 128 (2002): 371–408.
236 *For example, Asian American kids:* Ibid.
238 *Women earn 57% of college degrees: Statistical Abstract of the United States*, 2004 and earlier years, http://www.census.gov/prod/www/abs/statab.html.
238 *Most women in their 20s:* Susan Mitchell, *American Generations*, 4th ed. (Ithaca, NY: New Strategist Publications, 2003), 334.
238 *in 2005—for the first time:* Sam Roberts, "51% of Women Are Now Living without Spouse," *New York Times*, January 16, 2007.
238 *More than six times as many women:* CBSNews.com, August 7, 2012, http://www.cbsnews.com/media/common-myths-about-having-a-child-later-in-life/.
238 *As of 2009, only 18% of married couples:* New Strategist Editors, *Generation X*, 144.
239 *Attitudes about women's roles continued:* J. M. Twenge, "Attitudes toward Women, 1970–1995: A Meta-analysis," *Psychology of Women Quarterly* 21 (1997): 35–51.
239 *In 1984, for the first time: Statistical Abstract of the United States*, 2004 and earlier years, http://www.census.gov/prod/www/abs/statab.html.
240 *Among high school students in 2012:* K. Donnelly, J. M. Twenge, and N. T. Carter, "Change over Time in Americans' Attitudes towards Women's Work and Family Roles, 1976–2012" (unpublished manuscript, 2014).
240 *In the early 1970s, books used:* J. M. Twenge, W. K. Campbell, and B. Gentile, "Male and Female Pronoun Use in US Books Reflects Women's Status, 1900–2008," *Sex Roles* 67 (2012): 488–93.
241 *In 2012, only 1 out of 1,000:* American Freshman Study.
242 *Slightly more 2010–12 students:* Donnelly, Twenge, and Carter, "Change over Time in Americans' Attitudes Toward Women's Work and Family Roles."
242 *I gathered 103 samples:* J. M. Twenge, "Changes in Masculine and Feminine Traits over Time: A Meta-analysis," *Sex Roles* 36 (1997): 305–25.
243 *In 1989, 72% of college men:* American Freshman Study.
243 *Studies have found that girls with working mothers:* R. O. Hansson, M. E. Chemovetz, and W. H. Jones, "Maternal Employment and Androgyny," *Psychology of Women Quarterly* 2 (1977): 76–78.
244 *In addition, nearly ten times:* "Women's Sports Foundation, Title IX: What Is It?," womenssportsfoundation.org, http://www.womenssportsfoundation.org/en/home/advocate/title-ix-and-issues/what-is-title-ix/title-ix-myths-and-facts; and A. Guttman, *Women's Sports: A History* (New York: Columbia University Press, 1991).
244 *It's likely that sports participation:* J. E. Butcher, "Adolescent Girls' Sex Role Development: Relationship with Sports Participation, Self-Esteem, and Age at Menarche," *Sex Roles* 20 (1989): 575–93.

245 *Keith Campbell and I examined 446 studies:* J. M. Twenge and W. K. Campbell, "Self-Esteem and Socioeconomic Status: A Meta-analytic Review," *Personality and Social Psychology Review* 6 (2002): 59–71.
246 *In one of the essays, E. S. Maduro:* E. S. Maduro, "Excuse Me While I Explode: My Mother, Myself, My Anger," *The Bitch in the House, ed.* C. Hanauer (New York: HarperCollins, 2002), 8.
246 *Her mother, however, saw:* Hanauer, *Bitch in the House*, 281–82.
247 *women used to rate themselves:* American Freshman Survey.
247 *Married fathers spent three times:* Tara Parker-Pope, "Surprisingly, Family Time Has Grown," *New York Times*, April 5, 2010; and Kim Parker and Wendy Wang, "Modern Parenthood," Pew Research on Social & Demographic Trends, March 14, 2013, http://www.pewsocialtrends.org/2013/03/14/modern-parenthood-roles-of-moms-and-dads-converge-as-they-balance-work-and-family/.
248 *In a mid-2000s poll, 79% of young men:* Michelle Orecklin, "Stress and the Superdad," *Time*, August 23, 2004.
248 *As Susan Douglas and Meredith Michaels point out:* Susan Douglas and Meredith Michaels, *The Mommy Myth* (New York: Free Press, 2004), 8.
249 *Writer Peggy Orenstein said:* Lia Macko and Kerry Rubin, *Midlife Crisis at 30: How the Stakes Have Changed for a New Generation—and What to Do about It* (New York: Plume Penguin, 2004), 241.
249 *children who attend day-care centers:* National Institute of Child Health and Human Development Early Child Care Research Network and G. J. Duncan, "Modeling the Impacts of Child Care Quality on Children's Preschool Cognitive Development," *Child Development* 74 (2003): 1454–75; and P. Schuetze, A. Lewis, and D. DiMartino, "Relation between Time Spent in Daycare and Exploratory Behaviors in 9-Month-Old Infants," *Infant Behavior and Development* 22 (1999): 267–76.
250 *Douglas and Michaels label:* Douglas and Michaels, *Mommy Myth*, 5.
250 *Several studies have found that despite:* L. C. Sayer, S. M. Bianchi, and J. P. Robinson, "Are Parents Investing Less in Children? Trends in Mothers' and Fathers' Time with Children," *American Journal of Sociology* 110 (2004): 1–43.
251 *One* People *magazine cover story:* Douglas and Michaels, *Mommy Myth*, 122.
251 *Peggy Orenstein describes the modern world:* Peggy Orenstein, *Flux: Women on Sex, Work, Love, Kids, and Life in a Half-Changed World* (New York: Doubleday, 2000), 2.
252 *In* Midlife Crisis at 30, *Lia Macko and Kerry Rubin express:* Macko and Rubin, *Midlife Crisis at 30*, 3.
252 *As Douglas and Michaels put it, "Both":* Douglas and Michaels, *Mommy Myth*, 12.
252 *As Orenstein puts it, young women have:* Orenstein, *Flux*, 18.
253 *When you've always been taught:* Judith Warner, *Perfect Madness* (New York: Riverhead Books, 2005), 9.
253 *Warner argues that many:* Ibid.
254 *Young authors Macko and Rubin found the same thing:* Macko and Rubin, *Midlife Crisis at 30*, 25.
254 *Douglas and Michaels sum up:* Douglas and Michaels, *Mommy Myth*, 7.

255 *In less than two decades, those supporting:* http://features.pewforum.org/same-sex-marriage-attitudes/.
258 *It asks if "a man who admits":* J. M. Twenge, N. T. Carter, and W. K. Campbell, "Changes in Tolerance for Controversial Beliefs and Lifestyles in the US, 1972–2012" (unpublished manuscript, 2014).
259 *"Kids are coming out":* Ibid., 117.
259 *In 2002, my University of Michigan graduate school friend:* Betsy Cohen, "Community of Support: Hundreds Rally behind Family That Lost Home in Fire Friday Morning," *Missoulian*, February 10, 2002.

8. Generation Me at Work

PAGE
261 *When she arrived for the interview:* P. Davidson, "Managers to Millennials: Job Interview No Time to Text," *USA Today*, April 29, 2013, http://www.usatoday.com/story/money/business/2013/04/28/college-grads-job-interviews/2113505/.
261 *"Human resource professionals say":* Ibid.
261 *Jonathan Singel, director of talent acquisition:* Ibid.
262 *GenMe set to be 40%:* L. Kwoh, "More Firms Bow to Generation Y's Demands," *Wall Street Journal*, August 22, 2012.
264 *we published the results of this analysis:* J. M. Twenge, S. M. Campbell, B. R. Hoffman, and C. E. Lance, "Generational Differences in Work Values: Leisure and Extrinsic Values Increasing, Social and Intrinsic Values Decreasing," *Journal of Management* 36 (2010): 1117–42.
264 *In October 2013, Goldman Sachs:* M. J. Moore, "Goldman Pushes Junior Investment Bankers to Take Weekends Off," *Bloomberg Personal Finance*, October 28, 2013.
264 *Chegg, Inc., an online textbook-rental company:* Kwoh, "More Firms Bow."
265 *In 1976, 3 out of 4:* Twenge, Campbell, Hoffman, and Lance, "Generational Differences."
265 *More in GenMe said it was important:* Twenge, Campbell, Hoffman, and Lance, "Generational Differences in Work Values."
265 *In one study, college career counselors named:* L. M. Hite and K. S. McDonald, "Career Counseling for Millennials: Practictioner's Perspectives," in *Managing the New Workforce: International Perspectives on the Millennial Generation*, ed. S. T. Lyons, E. S. Ng, and L. Schweitzer (Northampton, MA: Edward Elgar, 2012).
265 *Bill George, a professor:* E. Kampinsky, "Millennial Males Seek Work-Life Balance Too," *Daily Beast*, September 2, 2013.
266 *A study of Canadian young people:* H. J. Krahn and N. L. Galambos, "Work Values and Beliefs of 'Generation X' and 'Generation Y,'" *Journal of Youth Studies*, 2013.
266 *40% of 2012 GenMe students:* J. M. Twenge and T. Kasser, "Generational Changes in Materialism and Work Centrality, 1976–2007: Associations with Temporal Changes in Societal Insecurity and Materialistic Role-Modeling," *Personality and Social Psychology Bulletin* 39 (2013): 883–97.
266 *A study of adults in the General Social Survey:* S. Highhouse, M. J. Zickar, and M. Yankelevich, "Would You Work if You Won the Lottery? Tracking

Changes in the American Work Ethic," *Journal of Applied Psychology* 95 (2010), 349–57.

267 *Adult workers in the 2000s:* K. W. Smola and C. D. Sutton, "Generational Differences: Revisiting Generational Work Values for the New Millennium," *Journal of Organizational Behavior* 23 (2002): 363–82.

267 *Another study found that manual workers:* V. M. Ciriello, P. G. Dempsey, R. V. Maikala, and N. V. O'Brien, "Secular Changes in Psychophysically Determined Maximum Acceptable Weights and Forces over 20 Years for Male Industrial Workers," *Ergonomics* 51 (2008): 593–601.

267 *With US workers getting an average of only eight:* H. Maass, "America's War on Vacation: By the Numbers," *The Week*, May 28, 2013.

267 *Architect Ari Meisel, 30:* Kampinsky, "Millennial Males Seek Work-Life Balance."

267 *Electronics retailer Best Buy instituted:* R. Alsop, *The Trophy Kids Grow Up: How the Millennial Generation Is Shaking Up the Workplace* (San Francisco, CA: Jossey-Bass, 2008).

268 *In a recent PricewaterhouseCoopers survey:* PricewaterhouseCoopers, "Millennials at Work: Reshaping the Workplace."

268 *The MTV survey found that 81%:* A. Hillhouse, "Consumer Insights: MTV's 'No Collar' Workers," October 4, 2012.

269 *"First-rate corporate volunteer programs":* S. E. Needleman, "The Latest Office Perk: Getting Paid to Volunteer: More Companies Subsidize Donations of Time and Talent; Bait for Millennial Generation," *Wall Street Journal*, April 29, 2008.

269 *The book* The M-Factor *advises:* L. C. Lancaster and D. Stillman, *The M-Factor: How the Millennial Generation Is Rocking the Workplace* (New York: Harper Business, 2010).

269 *Boomers, GenX'ers, and GenMe'ers placed:* Twenge, Campbell, Hoffman, and Lance, "Generational Differences in Work Values."

270 *A one-time study of US workers:* R. Rasch and B. Kowske, "Will Millennials Save the World through Work? International Generational Differences in the Relative Importance of Corporate Social Responsibility and Business Ethics to Turnover Intentions," in *Managing the New Workforce: International Perspectives on the Millennial Generation*, ed. S. T. Lyons, E. S. Ng, and L. Schweitzer (Northampton, MA: Edward Elgar, 2012).

271 *In the 2012 MTV poll, 80%:* Ibid.

272 *"Millennials appear to be seeking recognition":* S. T. Lyons, E. S. Ng, and L. Schweitzer, "Generational Career Shift: Millennials and the Changing Nature of Careers in Canada," in *Managing the New Workforce: International Perspectives on the Millennial Generation*, ed. S. T. Lyons, E. S. Ng, and L. Schweitzer (Northampton, MA: Edward Elgar, 2012), 79–80.

274 *"Millennials: All We Want for Christmas Is . . . Cash":* K. Rogers, "Millennials: All We Want for Christmas Is . . . Cash," FOX Business, November 27, 2013.

274 *In the over-time survey, 58%:* Twenge, Campbell, Hoffman, and Lance, "Generational Differences in Work Values."

275 *In the study of Canadian 25-year-olds:* Krahn and Galambos, "Work Values and Beliefs."

275 *Tim Kasser and I found that the gap:* Twenge and Kasser, "Generational Changes in Materialism."
275 *In the over-time survey of entering college students:* J. M. Twenge, W. K. Campbell, and E. C. Freeman, "Generational Differences in Young Adults' Life Goals, Concern for Others, and Civic Orientation, 1966–2009," *Journal of Personality and Social Psychology* 102 (2012): 1045–62.
276 A *drawing accompanying the MTV survey:* Hillhouse, "Consumer Insights,"
277 *In one study, 40%:* J. Stein, "The Me Me Me Generation," *Time*, May 20, 2013.
277 *In a recent survey of 23,000 Canadian:* E. S. W. Ng, L. Schweitzer, and S. T. Lyons, "New Generation, Great Expectations: A Field Study of the Millennial Generation," *Journal of Business and Psychology* 25 (2010): 281–92.
277 *In the MTV survey, 75%:* Ibid.
277 *In the MTV survey, 90%:* Hillhouse, "Consumer Insights."
277 *In the over-time survey of high school students, 46%:* Twenge, Campbell, Hoffman, and Lance, "Generational Differences."
278 *among entering college students, 42%:* Twenge, Campbell, and Freeman, "Generational Differences in Young Adults' Life Goals."
278 *College career counselors believed:* Hite and McDonald, "Career Counseling for Millennials."
278 *In an over-time analysis of career preferences:* S. T. Bubany and J. C. Hansen, "Birth Cohort Change in the Vocational Interests of Female and Male College Students," *Journal of Vocational Behavior* 78 (2011): 59–67.
278 *Management professor Paul Harvey:* Tim Urban, "Why Generation Y Yuppies Are Unhappy," *Huffington Post*, September 15, 2013.
280 *One of the few studies that looked:* D. Sirias, H. B. Kapr, and T. Brotherton, "Comparing the Levels of Individualism/Collectivism between Baby Boomers and Generation X," *Management Research News* 30 (2007): 749–61.

9. What Do We Do Now?

PAGE
283 *In a recent poll, 2 out of 3 adults:* Ronald Brownstein, "The American Dream—under Threat," *National Journal*, September 19, 2013.
284 *Although 16% of teens said:* Centers for Disease Control, "Youth Risk Behavior Surveillance System," http;//apps.nccd.cdc.gov/yrbss.
286 *74% of 2012 college freshmen:* American Freshman Survey.
289 *"I'd rather have a dog":* Antonio Antenucci and David K. Li, "More Young Women Choosing Dogs over Motherhood," *New York Post*, April 10, 2014.
289 *In a 2011 survey, 77% of pet owners:* Sharon L. Peters, "Are Americans Crazy for Treating Our Pets Like Kids?," *USA Today*, December 20, 2011.
291 *"We are in danger of producing":* Maureen Stout, *The Feel-Good Curriculum* (Cambridge, MA: Perseus Books, 2000), 119.
292 *"We do not need to completely shield":* Alvin Rosenfeld and Nicole Wise, *The Over-Scheduled Child* (New York: St. Martin's Press, 2000), 56.
293 *"The risk of overindulgence":* Peg Tyre, Julie Scelfo, and Barbara Kantrowitz, "Just Say No: Why Parents Must Set Limits for Kids Who Want It All," *Newsweek*, September 13, 2004.

294 *Psychologist Roy Baumeister argues:* R. Baumeister and J. Tierney, *Willpower* (New York: Penguin Press, 2011).

295 *Author Chris Colin quotes his classmate:* Chris Colin, *What Really Happened to the Class of '93* (New York: Broadway Books, 2004), 56.

298 *In* Perfect Madness, *Judith Warner writes:* Judith Warner, *Perfect Madness* (New York: Riverhead Books, 2005), 277.

299 *a recent poll found that 60%:* Richard Perez-Pena and Motoko Rich, "Preschool Push Moving Ahead in Many States," *New York Times*, February 3, 2014.

299 *Another poll found that 74%:* Emily Swanson and Dave Jamieson, "Paid Sick Leave Supported by Most Americans, Poll Finds," *Huffington Post*, June 20, 2013, http://www.huffingtonpost.com/2013/06/20/paid-sick-leave-poll_n_3471789.html.

300 *in 2011, the US birth rate: Statistical Abstract of the United States*, 2004 and earlier years, http://www.census.gov/prod/www/abs/statab.html.

300 *Of 168 industrialized nations:* John de Graaf, *Take Back Your Time* (San Francisco: Berrett-Koehler, 2003).

301 *Only about 17% of 4-year-olds:* "State-Financed Preschool Access in the U.S.," *New York Times*, February 13, 2013.

302 *The authors of* The Two-Income Trap *write:* Elizabeth Warren and Amelia Warren Tyagi, *The Two-Income Trap* (New York: Basic Books, 2003).

303 *77% of married women: Statistical Abstract of the United States*, 2012, http://www.census.gov/prod/www/abs/statab.html.

303 *A biologically driven shift:* William C. Dement, *The Promise of Sleep* (New York: Delacorte Press, 1999).

304 *When the Edina, Minnesota, school system:* Ibid.

310 *A huge amount of research:* C. A. Anderson et al., "Violent Video Game Effects on Aggression, Empathy, and Prosocial Behavior in Eastern and Western Countries: A Meta-analytic Review," *Psychological Bulletin* 136 (2010): 151–73.

312 *Raquel Aviva, 32, offers:* Alexandra Robbins, *Conquering Your Quarterlife Crisis* (New York: Perigee, 2004), 130.

312 *Michael Coviello, 25, said:* Ibid., 206

314 *You are also less likely to feel:* Dave Ranney, "KU Study Exploring Treatment for Depression without Drugs," *Lawrence Journal-World*, June 1, 2005, http://www2.ljworld.com/news/2005/jun/01/depression/?ku_news; and Steve Ilardi, interview, December 16, 2004.

314 *University of Kansas professor Steve Ilardi:* Stephen Ilardi, *The Depression Cure* (New York: De Capo, 2010).

Index

About the Author

Jean M. Twenge, PhD, is a professor of psychology at San Diego State University and the author of more than 100 scientific-journal articles and book chapters and the books *The Impatient Woman's Guide to Getting Pregnant* and *The Narcissism Epidemic* (with W. Keith Campbell). Accounts of her research have appeared in the *New York Times*, *USA Today*, the *Wall Street Journal*, *Time*, and *Newsweek*, and she has appeared on the *Today* show, *Good Morning America*, *CBS This Morning*, and *Dateline* NBC. She received a BA and an MA from the University of Chicago in 1993 and a PhD in personality psychology from the University of Michigan, Ann Arbor, in 1998. After living in Texas, Chicago, Michigan, Minnesota (twice), and Cleveland, she is happy to be settled with her husband and three daughters in beautiful San Diego, California. When not slaving over a hot computer writing something, she can usually be found swimming, reading, sitting in the sun, or reading and sitting in the sun—though usually not swimming while reading and sitting in the sun.